War Ga

1095

War Games

RICHARD HARDING DAVIS
AND THE NEW IMPERIALISM
JOHN SEELYE

University of Massachusetts Press

Copyright © 2003 by
University of Massachusetts Press
All rights reserved
Printed in the United States of America
LC 2002003312
ISBN 1-55849-372-7 (cloth); 386-7 (paper)
Designed by Richard Hendel
Set in ITC Charter and The Serif Black
Printed and bound by Thomson-Shore, Inc.

Library of Congress Cataloging-in-Publication Data
Seelye, John D.
War games : Richard Harding Davis and the new imperialism /
John Seelye
p. cm.
Includes bibliographical references and index.
ISBN 1-55849-372-7 (cloth : alk. paper)—ISBN 1-55849-386-7
(pbk : alk. paper)
1. Davis, Richard Harding, 1864–1916—Views on
imperialism.   2. Imperialism—Government policy—United
States—History—19th century.   3. Public opinion—United
States—History—19th century.   4. Imperialism—Public
opinion—History—19th century.   5. United States—Foreign
relations.   6. Imperialism in literature.   I. Title.
PS1523 .S44 2003
070'.92—dc21   2002003312

British Library Cataloguing in Publication data are available.

On title page: Frederic Remington's *Charge of the Rough
Riders at San Juan Hill,* 1898. (Oil on canvas. Courtesy Frederic
Remington Art Museum, Ogdensburg, New York.)

FOR ED FUSSELL

Or, 'Tis Forty Years Since

It's not for the sake of a ribboned coat,

Or the selfish hope of a season's fame,

But his Captain's hand on his shoulder smote—

"Play up! play up! and play the game!'

SIR HENRY JOHN NEWBOLT

There is plenty of time to win this game,

and to thrash the Spaniards too.

SIR FRANCIS DRAKE

CONTENTS

ILLUSTRATIONS

Sometimes people call me an idealist.
Well, that is the way I know I am an American.
America is the only idealistic nation in the world.
WOODROW WILSON

PREFACE

Let me begin this book by stating as briefly as possible what I hope to accomplish in the chapters that follow, a several-fold purpose that emerged during the early stages of composition. First, there is my original motive, which is to examine the writings of Richard Harding Davis so as to understand better the reasons for the popular impetus in the United States to support the Cuban insurgency against the Spanish colonial presence. Second, and closely related to the first motive, is a demonstration of the extent to which Davis's attitude toward the emergence of the United States as a world power reflects that revised notion of empire defined by Walter LaFeber in his highly influential book on the "new" imperialism.

Third, I mount a case that Davis is an undeservedly neglected author, most especially in his travel writings, which were journalistically motivated but retain a freshness and a vividness that have allowed them to survive the contemporary circumstances of their composition. Moreover, they lead naturally into his subsequent work as a war correspondent, the fame of which long endured. Thanks to the 1992 biography by Arthur Lubow, to which I am indebted throughout, there is no need to stress the complex interlock between Davis the man and his writings, but his popularity as a writer was due in large part to his personality, which therefore is a subject that cannot be ignored and to which I will attend here.

Because of this multipurposed errand and because of my personal inclination, I have with a few exceptions given what follows a chronological order, running through Davis's life and writings in sequence rather than reorganizing them by subject headings, this last being the usual academic practice, reducing the whole to an abstract sum of parts chosen to support a thesis. As with most writers, there is both a topical flow and a complex undercurrent in Davis's work, especially during the first decade of his career, and both are best captured by studying his writings as they were written and published.

As a journalist consciously engaged in seeking out material that would

have a wide appeal, Davis followed the changing direction of national interests, with a consequent inconsistency in his own point of view. This lack
of consistency may have ultimately stemmed from Davis's personal qualities, an intellectual superficiality and a lack of ideological conviction, as
well as a tendency to react impulsively to a given situation that is typical of
reporters even today. Whatever its source, this characteristic makes any
simplistic reduction of his work based on a reading of a single volume,
whether journalism or fiction, both misleading and unjust.

Moreover, and perhaps most important, to render an account of the often
contradictory messages that Davis was communicating to his readers is to
suggest the confusion of the citizenry of the United States during the last
decade of the nineteenth century regarding their nation's emerging role in
the international arena. This national perplex has been variously explained,
often with a stress on the economic turmoil experienced during the opening years of the decade, but most authorities agree that it was given a violent resolution with the outbreak of war in 1898. The U.S. intervention in
the Cuban insurrection was a conflict that Richard Harding Davis is uniformly given credit for having interpreted to his readers in ways that confirmed their belief that the Spanish-American War was both warranted in
purpose and noble in execution.

What is left to demonstrate is the extent to which his writings over the
years preceding the invasion of Cuba can be read as a prelude to that high-
minded attitude, as well as a canvass of other issues indirectly related to
it. These include the closing of the frontier and the resulting inclination of
celebrants of the western spirit (as they saw it) to fix their gaze on the
Caribbean, with a consequent stretching of the Monroe Doctrine to fit new
occasions. The foremost champion of U.S. expansionism in the early 1890s
was Captain Alfred Thayer Mahan, who called for an enlarged navy to protect national commerce, but in Davis's case, as in that of such politicians
as William McKinley, revised notions of imperialism were less a matter
of master strategy than a series of cumulative responses to changing
circumstances.

I do not cite Walter LaFeber's thesis in *The New Empire* in the pages that
follow with the intention of establishing an argument that would give definitive hence delimiting purpose and meaning to Davis's reporting. When
in my subtitle I promise a discussion of Davis and the new imperialism, the
man *and* the ideology should be seen as separate if related entities. LaFeber
recommends himself chiefly because he does his best to demonstrate the extent to which persons in power tend to drift rather than sail before the

steady wind of conviction toward the conclusions that finally seemed obvious to them, and that was also characteristic of Davis's progress toward the
war in Cuba.

President McKinley, much more than Captain Mahan, is central to
LaFeber's advancing argument, and McKinley was a not a geopolitical theo-
rist but a politician who tended to point the way in which popular winds
listed. Davis resembles McKinley in that particular, but where McKinley
was pragmatic to the core, Davis was at heart a romantic, impulsively chivalric, and it is only by abstracting elements from their contexts that he
can be clearly aligned with the dominant geopolitics of his age. Indeed,
it is the very fuzziness of his thinking, his writing from the heart not the
head, that is among Davis's attractive characteristics. Moreover, it is this
wavering viewpoint that aligns him with his American readership, whose
own certainty regarding the inevitability of war with Spain cohered in perfect synchronization with Davis's hardening attitude toward the situation
in Cuba.

The war in Cuba was for Davis a high point in a journalistic career that
seemed to lead from the start in that direction, not inevitably perhaps but
suggesting the kind of pattern we associate with fate. Most of the many recent books on the Spanish-American War mention or quote extensively
from the reports Davis sent back to Hearst's *Journal* and other newspapers
and magazines. He is always included among the most important of the
"Yellow Kids" who fed the public appetite for news stories that cast the
Spanish as cruel foreign oppressors and the insurrectionists as heroic
native-born champions of liberty. He was there at the start of tabloid journalism and will forever be associated with the development of sensational
news reporting.

But when one takes a larger view, opening up to include Davis's reporting
throughout the decade that ended with the war in Cuba—or, more properly, with the Boer War, which he also covered—then a somewhat bigger
picture emerges. Following his early career as a newspaper reporter, much
of Davis's journalistic work, chiefly accounts of his travels abroad, was sent
as stories to *Harper's Weekly,* a venerable paper in magazine format that
while filled with illustrations was hardly a tabloid. Still, as a reporter, Davis
sought out material that was novel, that would capture the public's attention thereby, and from the start he was fortunate in finding likely subjects,
having as a fledgling reporter made his way to the site of the Johnstown Flood soon after that disaster struck. He was also an enthusiast for college sports, which he occasionally covered for *Harper's,* another bid for a

popular readership. Davis was, in short, much more than a war correspondent, but it was his stories filed from Cuba that made him famous in his day.

By personal inclination Davis was without ideology—that is, he did not select material in order to enforce a thesis. That was Hearst's role, and it is to Davis's credit that his service for Hearst was of brief duration and despite its lucrativeness was ended by his own choice. As an American male of the late nineteenth century, he was influenced by the dominant ideals and prejudices of the day, but unlike the expansionists who figure largely in *The New Empire,* Davis was not an ideologue, viewing the world as through the bright prospect provided by the long-promised Isthmian canal.

Theodore Roosevelt was such a one, and though he was hardly an armchair soldier and shared with Davis a love of the active life (including sports), there remain critical differences between the impulses that brought both men into the Spanish-American War. If we can say of Roosevelt that he was in Cuba to prove something about himself and about the virtues of grace under fire, we can say of Davis that he was there to prove nothing save his abilities as a war correspondent. He was in Cuba to report back to his readers as accurately as he could what he was seeing, albeit as a patriot he sought to relate as favorable a picture of the American soldier as possible. When he celebrated Roosevelt's heroism it was because in Davis's mind the young colonel of volunteers was as fine an American officer as one could find in Cuba.

But, once again, if we take those steps backward necessary to open the frame, putting Davis's experience in Cuba in perspective with his earlier journalistic career, we find that from the beginning, as reflected in his work as a travel writer and an author of short stories and novels, he was in sympathy with the ideals that Roosevelt and his cronies sought to implement as public policy. And yet Davis was never a member of that Washington coterie, nor do his writings reveal any conscious awareness of the debates and arguments gathered together by LaFeber. During the critical period of mounting pressure for U.S. intervention in Cuba, Davis was traveling about Europe and the Near East, recording his impressions of old empires, not crusading for new. Only in 1897, relatively late in the game, did he travel to Cuba in the service of Hearst's effort to raise circulation by promoting war, sending back detailed reports on the atrocities being committed under Spanish rule.

This fact of distance is matched in importance by Davis's popularity as a reporter, for his journalistic and travel writings express attitudes that can be regarded as very much in the spirit of his times, whether cruising the

British-controlled Mediterranean, tramping through unstable Central American republics, or assessing the troubling situation in Cuba. Young men are not inspired to volunteer for a war in foreign parts because it will open up opportunities for commercial exchange, the moving spirit behind the new imperialism. Something must appeal to their altruism, and Davis in reporting on the horrific conditions in Cuba made that appeal.

Again, this does not mean that Davis used his reporting to mount a coherent thesis. Rather, it means that from his reporting we can glean a gathering of consistent thought, equivalent to that argument which LaFeber shakes out of the confusion of the 1890s, but with significant variations that are Davis's own. Through the often contradictory statements that were Davis's reflections regarding what he was witnessing as he roved about the world seeking journalistic material there runs a vector that took him necessarily to Cuba.

It is a progress as certain (if not so direct) as Roosevelt's, whose self-conscious Anglo-Saxonism, his obsessive love of physical combat, carried him from the boxing ring at Harvard to his celebrated charge up San Juan Hill. Again, it was Davis's account of that charge that brought Roosevelt his sudden fame as a hero of the war, for Roosevelt the heroic Rough Rider was in part a creation of Richard Harding Davis, in that he fulfilled what had for so long been Davis's notion of ideal male—which is to say, chivalric—behavior. Their coming together in Cuba was in all ways a literary event, and it is toward that concurrence that this book is intended to move.

War Games

History is a study of the mistakes of dead white men.
ANONYMOUS

INTRODUCTION (A POSITIONING PAPER)

: I :

Beginning with the publication of Walter Millis's *Martial Spirit: A Study of Our War with Spain* in 1931, there has never been a significant pause in the production of revisionist scholarship dealing with the Spanish-American War. During the epoch of the cold war, which certified the United States as a powerful international presence, there was a burgeoning of historical studies that regarded the War of 1898 as signifying the emergence of this country as an imperial power, for better or, more often than not, for worse: Most of the books and essays concentrated on the problematics of the Philippine campaign, which illustrated the evils of American imperialism, as well as its consequent failures.

Perhaps the most influential of these revisionist studies is Walter LaFeber's *New Empire: An Interpretation of American Expansion, 1860–1898,* first published in 1963 and reissued with a new introduction in 1998 in recognition of the extent to which LaFeber had revised the accepted historical interpretation of the causes of the Spanish-American War. It is LaFeber's thesis that the war with Spain was a logical if not inevitable (a word that the author self-consciously avoids) conclusion to nearly fifty years of U.S. commercial policy that moved inexorably (if not inevitably) toward a policy of international expansion. By the time Frederick Jackson Turner announced the closing of the frontier, in 1893, American geopoliticians had already begun looking toward distant, transoceanic horizons for territories in which the energies of the westward movement could continue, in terms of both economic opportunity and the spread of democratic institutions.

These expansionists were not seeking to establish "colonies" in the traditional sense of that word, whether by conquering or annexing already well populated places. They regarded any such action as being contrary to U.S. principles and policies. Instead, they sought to create a "new" imperialism by gaining control of commercial exchange with the kinds of countries we now identify with what is called the "third world"—that is, countries with relatively large populations and relatively few industrial centers. One such American champion of this new imperialism cited the "younger Pitt," who sought to "annex trade" rather than impose Great Britain's control over hitherto independent nations.

Commercial expansionists in the United States were at first chiefly interested in controlling trade with Latin American countries and exploiting raw materials there, but before the decade was out, they were looking eagerly at China, then under the threat of partition by foreign powers. A key text in these regards was Captain Alfred Thayer Mahan's *Influence of Sea Power upon History, 1660–1783*, first published in 1890, an influential book that was followed by a series of essays by Mahan supporting his essential thesis. It was his belief, based on the record of history, that if the United States wished to be a player in the emerging game of international trade, then it should develop a fleet of battleships and look toward establishing naval bases in the Caribbean. The situation was critical, given the predictable shift of trade routes that would follow the long-anticipated opening of what was by then called the Nicaraguan Canal. Captain Mahan subsequently expanded his purview and became a champion of the annexation of Hawaii and the Philippines as way stations for U.S. warships in anticipation of increasing trade in the transpacific zone, chiefly with China. Influential on the emerging new imperialists who are the subject of LaFeber's book, Mahan looms large in that massive and magisterial text.

If there is an omission from LaFeber's study, it is a concluding emphasis on the coterie of men surrounding Henry Adams who emerged during the mid-1890s as the chief proponents of the United States becoming a player in the imperial game. Not that LaFeber ignores the role played by Adams, Henry Cabot Lodge, and Theodore Roosevelt, all of whom were influenced by Mahan's geopolitical theory and worked closely with the captain in promoting war with Spain. LaFeber tends, however, to regard them as continuing the arguments of earlier commercial expansionists when there were strategic differences between the early and subsequent champions of new empire. One difference was that neither Adams nor his friends had served in the Civil War, an omission that seems to have had a marked effect on Lodge and his crony Roosevelt.

Lodge, the older of the two and in many ways Roosevelt's mentor (much he was Henry Adams's disciple at the start of his own career), was a boy during the Civil War and never forgot having watched young men marching off to risk their lives to preserve the Union. As a young congressman, Lodge may have been said to have waged the victory that followed, for he was a ferocious champion of a hard-line policy toward the South during the period of Reconstruction. Later in his career, as a senior senator, he spoke out in favor of restricting immigration lest our national institutions be diluted and corrupted by foreign influences, including the ideological. He was quite simply a retrograde Federalist with a puritanical turn of mind. By contrast, Roosevelt, whose mother was from the South and whose father was a New Yorker of Dutch ancestry who championed the preservation of the Union, had a more complex, even problematic, cultural background, which was reflected in both his personal and his political life.

Senator Lodge, unlike his protégé, has had little posthumous fame. We chiefly remember him not for his imperialist notions but for having led the Senate's defeat of Wilson's League of Nations and, more recently, for having been cuckolded by his friend, the statesman and sometime writer of fiction and poetry John Hay. Roosevelt, however, has attained mythic status, in part derived from his self-willed transition from a sickly boy to a man identified with great physical energy and prowess. This transformation was the result of a youthful course of rigorous self-improvement that contributed to his lifelong love of organized sports, chiefly football, that paramilitary American game.

Beyond this quasi-mythic dimension, Roosevelt's public career was from the start that of an earnest, hardworking reformer, efforts identified with his restructuring of the Civil Service and his subsequent appointment as police commissioner in New York City, but the man himself was inseparable from his sojourn in the Dakotas, where he was for a time a rancher and big-game hunter. These activities certainly encouraged Roosevelt's outspoken celebration of what he saw as "manly" characteristics, being heroic in conventional terms and, as he declared, brought to perfection by strenuous competition, whether on the field of sport or of war.

Both Lodge and Roosevelt were frequent celebrants of what they conceived as the Anglo-Saxon spirit, defined as single-mindedly enterprising in action, achieving territorial expansion through the ferocious exercise of arms. It was Roosevelt, however, not Lodge, who was truly a war lover, expressing an enthusiasm for combat that distinguished him as well from President William McKinley. Thanks to Lodge's influence, Roosevelt served as assistant secretary of the navy under McKinley, who in the eyes of the younger man was much too slow to sing of arms and the man. It was Roosevelt who, taking advantage of Secretary John Davis Long's momentary absence from the Navy Department, cabled Commodore George Dewey on station in Hong Kong, advising him to prepare the American fleet for

engagement with the Spanish forces at Manila, even though war had not yet
been declared.

McKinley, like a number of the senior statesmen and politicians cited by
LaFeber, had served in the Civil War and because of that experience was not
a war lover. He was, as we have learned from Margaret Leech's influential
biography, a skillful politician and a much more strongly centered human
being than many of his contemporaries (including Roosevelt) recognized.
He sought to gain economic advantage for the United States in what he
hoped would be an independent Cuba by peaceful, diplomatic means. His
administration continued to negotiate with Spain until armed intervention
in Cuba became politically unavoidable.

McKinley declared war when the sinking of the *Maine* was officially determined to be the result of a hostile, presumably Spanish, act, though it
was the pressure put on the president by jingoistic politicians and war-
hungry publishers that forced his hand. Still, as LaFeber suggests, McKinley
was not entirely unwilling to have his hand forced. Moreover, his was finally
the hand that did the writing on the wall, defending his decision as godsent
and proposing that victory in the war on Spain would carry "the blessings of
the flag" to benighted, long-suffering Cuba and even bring a new dawn to
that perpetual midnight in the garden of the Philippines.

Roosevelt showed his own hand as soon as war was officially declared by
resigning his Navy Department post and volunteering for service in the
Cuban campaign. For TR, it was one more opportunity to prove his manhood to himself and to whoever was worried over the matter. That is, for
Roosevelt there was an agenda in the war separate from expanding the
sphere of U.S. commercial influence, nor would his subsequent career prove
the episode of the Rough Riders an exception.

A rifle fell as naturally into Roosevelt's hand as did a Colt revolver into the
hands of those cowboys whose myth Roosevelt and his associates, Owen
Wister and Frederic Remington, were largely responsible for having promoted. Roosevelt's first book, on his western experiences, was essentially a
handbook on hunting, and his history of the "winning" of the West is an extended illustration of the game theory, emphasizing the violent (Teutonic)
tactics used in relentlessly pushing back the line that was the frontier.

LaFeber is not much interested in these psychohistorical matters, but his
omission, if it can be called that, has been amply rectified by Richard Slotkin
in a trilogy that traces the violent, testosterone-driven aspects of American
imperialism from the acts of Captain John Smith in Virginia to those of Captain James Medina in Vietnam. Roosevelt plays a central role in the third of

the series, ranked with Buffalo Bill and John Wayne as mythic avatars of violent imperialism. Thus, in *Gunfighter Nation* the Spanish-American War is seen chiefly, because of the active presence of Theodore Roosevelt, as a symbolic extension of the westering process. Notably, Slotkin gives Frederick Jackson Turner considerable room but ignores Alfred Thayer Mahan, and though *The New Empire* appears in Slotkin's bibliography, LaFeber does not receive significant mention in the text. Thus the rationale for extending the war to the Philippines is in large part explained by Roosevelt's blustery *Strenuous Life* (1899), which poses continuing peace as a threat to national manhood and war as a necessary corrective.

: II :

Slotkin's psychosexual reading of the Spanish-American War is in line with the revisionist interpretation of Amy Kaplan, a literary scholar who in two influential essays has emphasized the male-dominated and racist ethos that gave a gendered and bigoted cast to the war in Cuba. Kaplan's argument accords special attention to the contemporary vogue for romantic fiction with its stress on masculine displays of military prowess. Kristin Hoganson, a historian, has followed Kaplan up with a book-length analysis of the gendered political rhetoric that encouraged the United States to intervene in Cuba. Both scholars acknowledge an indebtedness to *The New Empire,* but their interpretation of the Cuban war and its extension to the Philippines is much more in harmony with Slotkin's argument than with LaFeber's.

Hoganson demonstrates that after the sinking of the *Maine* the propaganda for war with Spain involved what jingoes evoked as the national "honor," in effect an extension of Kaplan's thesis about American manhood and the war. What follows here is likewise in synchronization with Kaplan's work, especially her much cited essay "Romancing the Empire" (1990). This is an extended discussion of popular American novels that she regards as key to understanding the imperial impulse, with considerable emphasis on Richard Harding Davis's best-selling *Soldiers of Fortune* (1897). Slotkin, by contrast, makes only a passing mention of Davis—as one of a number of correspondents covering the war in Cuba—and pays no attention to the sequence of romances cited by Kaplan.

Kaplan's thesis about the connection between popular romance and the Spanish-American War is not in itself original. In *On Native Grounds* (1942), Alfred Kazin noted of American literature at the end of the nineteenth century that "traditional romanticism, which from the eighties on had flourished in prosperity and yielded dolefully to realism in periods of crisis and panic, was to attain unparalleled confidence in the expansive years after the Spanish-American War" (13). At a later point, Kazin drew a contrast between the "subterranean world" of "terrorism and uncertainty" in the 1890s, which *McTeague, Maggie,* and *Sister Carrie* reflected, and what was happening in literature "on the surface, in a world busy digesting industrialism and the fruits of the Spanish-American War" (53).

There, "it was the era of Richard Harding Davis and the Gibson Girl, of the rage for Stevenson and historical confectionary like George Barr McCutcheon's *Graustark* and Charles Major's *When Knighthood Was in Flower*" (53). And Kazin's argument was picked up in 1944 by Grant C. Knight, who in tracing the genealogy of the "Graustark novel," equated with the "Pastry Period" in American literature, noted that "the triumphant state of mind induced by our military victory over Spain" served to sponsor "the bourgeoning of historical romance in the years between the invasion of Cuba and Theodore Roosevelt's battle with the trusts" ("'Pastry' Period" 6).

Neither of these texts is cited by Kaplan, yet the unanimity of Kazin and Knight certainly modifies her point that "historical romances" were "overlooked by later critics in their characterization of the period as the 'Age of Realism.'" Moreover, their joint chronological emphasis should also be noted: Rather than simply regarding the invasion by the United States of Cuba and the Philippines as analogous to the plots of contemporary literary romances—Kaplan's stress—both Kazin and Knight emphasize that the romance revival followed the war, a result of the national euphoria aroused by the American victory. *Graustark* was published well after the war in Cuba had ended, and Major's novel, published in 1898, could hardly have had much influence on the popular enthusiasm for intervention in Cuba, which had been building since 1896. This puts a special onus on *Soldiers of Fortune,* published in 1897, giving Richard Harding Davis singular credit—or blame—for "romancing" the Spanish-American War.

Kaplan sees the romantic impulse of the American 1890s as having been rooted in an anachronistic notion of chivalry, an evolution that seems undeniable. Thus Theodore Roosevelt's friend Owen Wister (in an essay cited by Kaplan) traced the origins of the cowboy (hence, implicitly, the Rough Rider) back to the knight-errant. Kaplan is here in concurrence with Slotkin, who while virtually ignoring the chivalric context regards Roosevelt and Wister as having established a nostalgic, romantic frame for the cowboy and the cavalryman, even while with future expansionist adventures in mind they celebrated the Anglo-Saxon continuity with its emphasis on warfare and genocide. But Slotkin fails to add *Soldiers of Fortune* to his cultural formula, the hero of which is a westerner and a former cowboy who carries Roosevelt's favorite qualities of courage and initiative into Central America.

Where Kaplan enlists *Soldiers of Fortune* as an extended and influential example of gendered fiction expressing the chivalric (hence expansionist) impulse, I intend to study the entire body of Davis's work produced during the decade preceding the outbreak of war, a sequence that gives added meaning and heft to his novel. Moreover, where Slotkin ignores Davis's relevance to the ideological continuity which began with the proximity of the Chicago World's Fair and Buffalo Bill's Wild West Show and which ended with the explosion of expansive energies that was given human shape by TR's participation in the Spanish-American War, I hope to demonstrate that in his reporting and his fiction, Davis provided an alternative yet parallel track to that laid down by Roosevelt.

Reporting in *Harper's Weekly* on his two visits to the fair, Davis immediately thereafter took a train for the Far West, sending back to *Harper's* accounts of his travels through Texas, Colorado, and Oklahoma that were gathered in his first published travel book, *The West from a Car Window* (1892). And while his account of what he found was often humorously dismissive, in contrast to the heroic burden of writings by Roosevelt and Wister, it marked a starting point for Davis that, while taking a different route—traveling to England, to the Middle East, and finally to Central America—would end with the novel that Kaplan regards as integral to the impulse that resulted in the invasion of Cuba and the Philippines.

Along the way, Davis expressed opinions that are occasionally in harmony with those much more formal doctrines being framed at the same time by LaFeber's new imperialists. In *Soldiers of Fortune*, he would return to the whole matter of the West, yet by a route that gave it a shape and a meaning quite distinct from that provincial, chauvinistic frame imposed by Roosevelt and the champions of a new West, "new" only in the sense that it was revised so as to promote the very myth that Davis at the start was not so much debunking as discounting.

Kaplan wires Davis to Slotkin's thesis by emphasizing the elements of *Soldiers of Fortune* that echo a number of Roosevelt's favorite themes, most especially the ideal of American manhood. The Kaplan-Slotkin contingency is much stronger in her discussion of Wister's *Virginian*, which in Kaplan's view validates the new imperialism by evoking the old, which in return rejuvenates the cowboy myth, contributing to the idea of the new West. For

whatever reason, Kaplan overlooks the cowboy origins of Davis's hero, preferring to stress his history as a mercenary soldier and civil engineer,
whereas in Davis's mind a great deal of meaning resides in his hero's divided
biography.

A proper accounting of the complexities of *Soldiers of Fortune* requires
the understanding that Davis was operating outside the Roosevelt-Adams
axis, was following a track of his own. It is a track that has pretty much disappeared because it did not make the deep groove in our popular culture
like that left by the western myth. John F. Kennedy could arouse public enthusiasm for his programs by identifying them with a new frontier, while
flashing a toothy smile reminiscent of Teddy Roosevelt's and in other, not always publicized ways reinvoking the ideals of the strenuous life.

Ronald Reagan, both a movie and real-life cowboy, as Slotkin demonstrates, was a virtual reincarnation of the western myth set in motion by TR.
And we can add to that western amalgam the man who is now president of
the United States, whose origins are eastern and elitist but who promotes
himself as a Texas oilman and rancher. We are told that the chief executive
bears on his backside a brand, the Delta "D," not associated with cattle
roundups but with Ivy League fraternity initiation rituals, a mark that he is
understandably earnest about keeping shrouded in mystery.

Likewise, President John F. Kennedy self-consciously set aside his silk
topper during his inauguration as an unwelcome symbol, a hat that over the
intervening years had become identified with cartoon capitalists. By contrast, Richard Harding Davis, in his own time a figure as popular as any
writer before him or afterward, both contributed to and derived power from
a myth that drew its strength from an element of cosmopolitanism, complete with top hat and tails, which he favorably associated with the lives of
moneyed and privileged people.

For Davis, the costume was that of a hero who is not only a representative
of high society but also a man who could move with ease through dangerous environs, whether the slums of New York City or the jungles of Central
America. The alternative costume—and Davis was fond of dressing the
part—consisted of the jodhpurs, open-necked shirt, and riding boots or
puttees, which with a wide-brimmed felt hat or pith helmet made up the
traditional dress of the civil engineer, the explorer, the war correspondent,
and the soldier of fortune.

Aside from matters of sartorial style, the hero of *Soldiers of Fortune*
demonstrated a high-minded enterprise that was never exercised in the

" I wonder if I would like to be Dictator of Olancho. "

Robert Edeson in the stage version of Soldiers of Fortune, *written by Davis's friend Augustus Thomas. Edeson is dressed in what would become the standard costume for heroes of adventure of the period, associated with Davis himself. The line about becoming dictator is not in the novel itself. From the Play-Goer's Edition.*

service of self but rather was patriotically and idealistically enlisted in that dual errand that LaFeber identifies as the new imperialism, carrying U.S. capitalism into Central American countries and importing "civilized" order along with it. In Kaplan's view, Davis's romance, like others of its genre, "enacts the American fantasy of global conquest without colonial annexation," the precise formula of LaFeber's new imperialism ("Romancing the Empire" 680). Once again, *Soldiers of Fortune* must be given the priority in this regard, predating the declaration of war with Spain by a year and *Graustark* by five, nor did it spring unaided from the author's imagination.

As Kaplan states, Davis's story followed the outlines of Anthony Hope's *Prisoner of Zenda* (1894), which established the genre of contemporary (as opposed to historical) romance, but *Soldiers of Fortune* was also thoroughly grounded in the author's previous experience as a reporter and travel writer. Especially important was the arduous trip Davis took through Honduras and Nicaragua in 1895, recorded in *Three Gringos in Venezuela and Central America* (1896), a journey that was the ultimate end of a trajectory begun when Davis went west in 1892. In turn, the Central American tour was followed in 1896 by Davis's visit to Cuba in the service of Hearst's *Journal,* resulting in stories that served as propaganda for the conflict that followed, from which Davis emerged as the famous war correspondent so much admired by his contemporaries.

From this perspective, *Soldiers of Fortune* can be seen as a penultimate but hardly a unique expression of the author's romantic impetus, which, while verging strategically from the western myth engendered and encouraged by Roosevelt, merged at a critical moment with the geopolitical imperialism that was the statesman's main agenda, and in such a way as to accelerate Roosevelt's political career. Moreover, Davis and Roosevelt, though traveling separate routes, not only were together in Cuba but also for quite different reasons carried the western mythos into the Caribbean, the one for idealistic and the other for ideological ends.

Davis anticipated the Spanish-American War by a year in *Soldiers of Fortune,* but it was in his reporting that he both argued for American interference in Central America and Cuba and rendered popular journalistic accounts of the battles that followed, especially the charge at San Juan, the fame of which (and that of the colonel in charge) was largely the result of Davis's work. With Kaplan, we can read *Soldiers of Fortune* as a text promoting the ideals of the new imperialism, yet the best-selling novel is best seen as an intense, even mythic expression of attitudes already expressed in the author's equally popular nonfiction writing.

: III :

My interest, therefore, is less with Davis's fiction than with his journalism, to which his literary contemporaries likewise tended to give precedence, preferring it to his novels and stories. In his reportorial and travel writing, Davis avoids the simplistic formulas that a modern reader finds so annoying in his fiction and instead renders an honest appraisal of events, albeit an honesty that is shaped by contemporary contexts, hence its added interest to us today. His style, which tends toward the facile and mannered in his fiction, is in his journalistic writings a model of conciseness and clarity, given interest by a pervading irony, the sort of thing prized in his younger contemporary Stephen Crane.

Davis's fiction often mingles humorous with sentimental elements associated with courtship and marriage, a traditional aspect of literary romance that is missing from his travel writings, which are not only decidedly male in gender but also spiked with wit, a manner clearly reminiscent of Mark Twain's. As a reporter, moreover, Davis had a lively eye for those events that enlighten, journalistic equivalents of epiphanies, and a talent for anecdotes that in the classic formula both instruct and amuse, a characteristic shared with both Crane and Twain. But where Crane's travel writings, reporting, and fiction present a stylistically seamless whole, dictated by the canons of literary realism, Davis (like Twain) is primarily a realist in his nonfiction work and a romantic in his novels and stories. I say "primarily," for all his work evidences a certain idealism, which is closely allied to the romance genre.

Thus despite my emphasis, Davis's fiction will not be ignored. For one thing, in terms of theme and materials, there is a constant interplay between his travel writing and his romances. For another, that discontinuity needs to be accounted for, indeed can be shown as essential to the prevailing discourse of the day, which was given to evoking romantic tropes to dress out the realpolitik of Mahan, Lodge, and Roosevelt with appropriate costumes. The approximate cowboy outfits provided the Rough Riders may have been designed with practical considerations in mind, but they certainly helped Roosevelt make his point. Even the gendered argument laid bare in the studies of Kaplan and Hoganson was part and parcel of a carefully couched rhetoric intended to appeal to those ideals celebrated in Davis's fiction.

And yet, while Davis was indirectly supporting political discourse by means of his romances, he used his travel and reportorial writings to debunk contemporary myths, including those which licensed the imperial excesses of his day. These two sides of Davis's character can be seen in a list of short stories he defined as "great." Drawn up relatively late in his short life, as he was urging the United States to enter World War I, they include Bret Harte's "Luck of Roaring Camp" and Joseph Conrad's *Heart of Darkness,* Robert Louis Stevenson's "Lodging for the Night" and O. Henry's "Municipal Report." Notably, all four stories share in common an interest in persons who operate outside, even beyond, the law, a romantic theme that likewise dominates Davis's fiction, but the four are otherwise characterized by stylistic and thematic differences, which are also reflected in his work.

If as a romantic author he was consciously working in the Stevenson tradition, with an emphasis on adventure and physical action, as a writer of short fiction he can be seen as providing a bridge between Bret Harte's sentimental, mining-frontier realism and O. Henry's updated, urban version. Davis's list also included Kipling's "Man Who Would be King," like Conrad's novella a mordant anti-imperialist parable, the title of which Davis would adapt for a parable of his own, "The Reporter Who Made Himself King." Purportedly a story for boys, the tale is also a satire on the contemporary tendency to stretch the original meaning of Manifest Destiny to include islands in the far western Pacific. Published in 1891, it demonstrates Davis's early awareness of and his complex attitude toward the events chronicled in LaFeber's study of the rise of the new imperialism.

Most important, Davis's literary preferences were clearly for the works of his romantic contemporaries, not the popular writers with whom he has been compared, especially Anthony Hope Hawkins and George Barr Mc-Cutcheon, but those who gave a darker dimension to settings and actions that were exotic and daring yet tragic withal. These stories avoid the triumphant finales that characterize the popular romances of the day discussed by Amy Kaplan, in which heroes are conventionally heroic, winning both the day and the heroine.

Davis certainly wrote those kinds of optimistic parables, of which *Soldiers of Fortune* is typical, but he was capable also of grittier stories, closer to Kipling than to Stevenson. His journalism, once again, is often literally photographic in its realism, for a camera was his constant companion in the field. Moreover, if we take some account of his last Central American novel, *Captain Macklin* (1902), we find elements much closer to the Conradian model, expressing doubts about the neo-imperial mission central to *Soldiers of Fortune.* Contemporary with both *Graustark* and *The Virginian,* it is an antiromance left out of Kaplan's revisionist essay.

What unifies all Davis's work is an underlying idealism, the altruism that is in harmony both with the romantic impulse and with the desire to convey often unpleasant truths about contemporary conditions in the world. Davis's friends and contemporaries testified to his deep sense of decency, and though many who knew him were offended by what they took to be snobbery, the apparent dichotomy may have a common root in the man's very high standard of comportment, whether in clubrooms or in matters of state, on the playing field or on the battlefield. It is in Davis's accounts of the Cuban insurrection and the American involvement in what became an all-out war that we can find these impulses in perfect coordination, an idealistic unity that holds together both his popular romance, *Soldiers of Fortune,* and his journalistic writings about the war in Cuba.

From here, as we look back through seventy years of revisionist accounts of that war, which act to thicken and cloud, not clarify, the lens, it is difficult to regard it as susceptible to a romantic reading. Yet if we can ignore the intervening interpretations, that conflict, despite its international setting and implications, can be read as a sequel to the Civil War in terms of its idealistic basis at the start of hostilities. *Soldiers of Fortune* was published in the same year that Augustus Saint-Gaudens's *Shaw Memorial* was completed, a perfect expression of militant idealism sculpted in bronze and yet another link between the sanctified mood that engendered the Civil War and the equivalent zeal for supporting the insurrection in Cuba almost forty years later.

We may from our advantaged perspective share Walter LaFeber's view of the war as a giant step toward the new imperialism associated with Theodore Roosevelt's expansive geopolitics, but this does not discount the courage displayed by the young colonel, who, as we might say, put his own body on the advancing line of empire. Likewise, Richard Harding Davis may have been confused in his goals and an unwitting accomplice to the ambitious expansionism of Roosevelt and his cohort, but his conflicted impulses were intrinsic to the values of his culture, which makes Davis's writing still of interest to us today.

LaFeber's concern, as he states early on, was with those intellectuals who "speak not only for themselves but for the guiding forces of their society. Discovering such men at crucial junctures in history, if such a discovery can be made, is of importance and value. These figures uncover the premises, reveal the approaches, provide the details and often coherently arrange the ideas which are implicit in the dominant thought of their time and society" (62). Though Richard Harding Davis was no Alfred Thayer Mahan, his value to us is similar to that of LaFeber's geopoliticians, perhaps even more so,

given his celebrity not only as a journalist but also as a writer who seemed
to his readers the virtual incarnation of his subject matter.

LaFeber admits that it is impossible to determine the extent to which the
writings of such geopoliticians as Captain Mahan influenced those American policymakers responsible for creating the new empire. He thereby
evinces the kind of careful skepticism that does not pester latter-day revisionist historians. Likewise, the effect of Davis's opinions on his readership
can never be accurately gauged, but much as Mahan and company were
influential thinkers, able to appeal to elites because of their emphasis on
power and profits, so Davis was a popular writer, and we may, I think, make
certain assumptions about the nature of literary popularity. It results from
a synchronization of a writer's themes with the common pulse of an age
and therefore is a matter not of convincing a mass audience of a new and
startling truth but of asserting in familiar terms widely held values, novel
perhaps in subject matter but confirmatory, not confrontational, in effect.

For LaFeber, the age in which Davis became a popular writer was motivated chiefly by commercial considerations, and surely we can all agree
with Frederick Jackson Turner's notion, cited by LaFeber, that politics is
economics in motion. Yet in far different ways the careers of Davis and Roosevelt tell us that if the business of America is business, there are many different ways of conducting business affairs. The pursuit of property was
essential to Jefferson's notion of self-evident truths, but he chose to use the
word "happiness," thereby acknowledging that there is a transcendent element in human endeavor which shuns crass commercialism in preference to
acting in the name of high ideals.

"It is the object only of war that makes it honourable," wrote a champion
of militant idealism, "and if there was ever a *just* war since the world began,
it is this in which America is now engaged." The writer could have been
McKinley or Roosevelt, William Randolph Hearst or Henry Cabot Lodge,
but it was Thomas Paine, who later praised the virtues of "doing justice, loving mercy, and endeavoring to make our fellow-creatures happy," words
written in 1793 but equally applicable to the situation in America in 1898—
or 1998, for all that.

Who in remembering Hearst's attempts to encourage the U.S. invasion of
Cuba could not recognize the implication of the televised stories of atroci-
ties in Kosovo, with the concomitant if implicit argument that the United
States should maintain an armed presence there? If the Spanish-American
War lacked much by way of centennial commemoration, surely that echo
should serve in its stead. For ever and again Cuba becomes the Philippines,

a place in which the blessings of the flag become a curse, where the best and clearest intentions mire down in a morass of complex and conflicting problems, of which the Balkans are forever the essence. As Davis himself remarked, through the narrator-hero of *Captain Macklin,* "The Balkans are always with us and [are] always threatening" (44). In 1902, this may be accounted prophecy, but then Davis was something of a prophet in much that he wrote during the preceding decade, the period under discussion in the chapters that follow.

Note: While this book was in press, I was asked by my publisher to review a prospectus for a book by Professor Brady Harrison, titled "Against Empire: Walker, Roosevelt, and the Imperial Self in American Literature." The prospectus, and I assume the book manuscript itself, discusses Davis's *Soldiers of Fortune* and *Captain Macklin,* novels that reveal the influence of the famous filibuster William Walker. Although I am able only to infer from the prospectus Harrison's elaborated argument in the book, I take it that he is chiefly interested in Walker as a hero celebrated by a number of American writers, starting with Bret Harte. My anticipation and differing opinions in *War Games* of Walker, Roosevelt, and points I assume Harrison will make in his book should not, of course, discount the potential value of his study. I look forward to publication of Harrison's work and to ongoing dialogue about this important period in the development of the modern American self and self-projection in the world.

For when the One Great Scorer comes to write against your name,
He marks—not that you won or lost—but how you played the game.
GRANTLAND RICE

1 : THE GAME AND THE NATION

: I :

In this chapter I provide a brief portrait of Richard Harding Davis (RHD), derived from what we know about the facts of his life and from the glorified image that was sustained by his friends and admirers during the heyday of his reputation, which it did not long outlive. As we shall see, that image was essential to his reputation and reception as a writer, if only because he was regarded as the subject of much that he wrote, and it is an image that stresses the buoyant physical energy of the man as well as his decency and generosity.

They were qualities that explain the esteem in which Davis's work was held during his relatively brief life and for a decade or so longer. Indeed, the interlock between the man and his work testified to by his contemporaries suggests the importance to his audience of the idea of Davis himself, the iconic force we today sum up as "celebrity," which like so much popular literature is ephemeral. But then, as Davis's most recent biographer has insisted, if we wish to recapture the mood and motion of an era, "the ephemeral becomes essential" (Lubow 1).

It is my belief that Davis's journalism has, unlike the writer himself, out-lived its immediate occasion, or rather makes that occasion as vividly present as it did the day it was written. It was Thomas Beer who, in the closing chapter of *The Mauve Decade,* observed that Davis's nonfiction writing would have a "second value" in that it records so vividly the "greatness and parades" of the 1890s, so that "they remain, glitteringly stored in his swift, smooth sketches and long reports" (249). This sparkling record is something more than a sequence of events graphically described, however, and is a product of the age that regarded Davis's writings so highly. Therefore I should also like to discuss the cultural context out of which RHD as a writer emerged, accounting for the values that sustained his writing, especially his journalism, which is admittedly difficult to cut cleanly from his fiction, as his contemporaries attested.

In 1927, more than a decade after the death of Richard Harding Davis, the following tribute was written by a younger contemporary, the editor and writer Roger Burlingame:

> Every one has worshipped a hero once; I think most Americans who were young at the beginning of the century worshipped Davis. He loomed important to us, not simply because we liked his stories, but because we all knew so much about him. The Spanish War was still vivid as a very large affair and Davis was an exciting and romantic figure in it. In my mind he and that war were inseparable. I suppose, on thinking it over, maturely, the war might have been fought without him, but it always seemed to me as if they must have held the battles until he got there and then said, "All right, here's Davis; shoot!" And, too, I doubt if, without him, it would have lived long in the public mind. (v)

Surely, by 1927, the Spanish-American War, if it still lived in the public mind, followed as it had been by the Great War, was no longer regarded as a "very large affair" but rather as a small and unfortunate episode in our history. It was soon to be chronicled by Walter Millis as a comic opera, with "Mr. Richard Harding Davis . . . reporting our imperial glories in a prose style that sounded almost like Kipling" (361). Born in 1899, Millis was in his mid-teens when Davis died and was therefore immune to the spell the man had cast on his contemporaries.

Certainly Davis's posthumous celebrants were writers who like Burlingame had vivid recollections of the man himself, and if he is now forgotten as a writer it is in part because he is no longer remembered as a living, vibrant, energetic presence. The man who emerges from Burlingame's description is wrapped in a myth, inseparable from the emergence of the United States as a great world power and thereby epical in outlines. For Millis, on the other hand, "Mr. Richard Harding Davis" was merely a reporter who wrote for the *Journal* of "Mr. William Randolph Hearst."

Ironically, when Davis is remembered today, as by Amy Kaplan, it is less for his reporting than for his "masculine adventure tales" such as *Soldiers of Fortune.* Eric Sundquist likewise associates *Soldiers* with "Theodore Roosevelt's celebration of Anglo-Saxon virtues in *The Winning of the West* . . . and *The Strenuous Life,*" that is, as blatant propaganda for imperial adventures, expressing "the nationalist pride evoked by the Spanish-American War" (*Columbia Literary History* 517). But Davis's contemporaries tended to neglect his fiction for his reportorial work, if in a more admiring vein than Millis's: "He was," testified his fellow war correspondent John Fox Jr., "the first reporter of his time—perhaps of all time. Out of any incident or situation he could pick the most details that would interest the most people and put them in a way that was pleasing to the most people" (*R.H.D.* 66).

In his contribution to *R.H.D.: Appreciations of Richard Harding Davis,* a memorial collection of essays from which Fox's testimony is taken, E. L. Burlingame, Roger's father and the founding editor of *Scribner's,* in which many of Davis's early short stories were published, was unsure "whether Davis could or would have written a novel of the higher rank." But he did not hesitate to speak "with extravagance" of RHD's reporting: He was "quite the best of all contemporary correspondents and reporters; and his rivals in the past could be easily numbered" (37).

In the opinion of Finley Peter Dunne, Davis was "the most readable of war correspondents. He went to all the wars of his youth and middle age filled with visions of glorious action. Where other correspondents saw and reported evil-smelling camps, ghastly wounds, unthinkable suffering, blunders, good luck and bad luck . . . Davis saw and reported it first of all as a romance, and then filled in the story with human details, so that the reader came away with an impression that all these heroic deeds were performed by people just like the reader himself, which was exactly the truth" (*R.H.D.* 75).

By means of Mr. Dooley's hilarious accounts of the Spanish-American War, Dunne had poked fun at Davis for having in effect served as Colonel Roosevelt's personal press agent, and there is a sly subtext detectable in his eulogy as well, in which he suggests that as a correspondent Davis viewed the war through rose-colored binoculars. He also observed that Davis as an author was overshadowed by his personal fame, by "the man himself—the generous, romantic, sensitive individual whose character and characteristics made him a conspicuous figure everywhere he went—and he went everywhere" (71).

Like RHD's other eulogists, Dunne observed that to know Davis was to know his books: "He translated himself literally, and no expurgation was needed to make the translation suitable for the most innocent eyes. He was the identical chivalrous young American or Englishman who strides through his pages in battalions to romantic death or romantic marriage" (72). For Dunne, the work is all of a piece, and in the reportorial and travel writings the common element is Dick Davis himself, much as his fictive heroes borrow from his highly theatrical self-fashioning.

Beyond this personal equation, Dunne acknowledged that the events which made up the substance of Davis's fiction were "improbable," but Davis "had the faculty of giving the appearance of the truth to situations that in human experience could hardly exist" (74). Thus the romantic element in Davis's fiction was backed by "so many accurate details of description . . . that it leaves as definite an impression of realism as any of Mr. Howells's purposely realistic stories" (73–74). But unlike the realists—or, more to the point, the naturalists who were Davis's contemporaries—RHD was gifted with "a most enviable pair of eyes, which reported to him only what was pleasant and encouraging."

> A man is blessed or cursed by what his eyes see. To some people the world of men is a confused and undecipherable puzzle. To Mr. Davis it was a simple and pleasant pattern—good and bad, honest and dishonest, kind and cruel, with the good, the honest, and the kind rewarded; the bad, the dishonest, and the cruel punished; where the heroes are modest, the brave generous, the women lovely, the bus-drivers humorous; where the Prodigal returns to dine in a borrowed dinner-jacket at Delmonico's with his father, and where always the Young Man marries the Girl. And this is the world as much as Balzac's is the world, if it is the world as you see it. (76)

"In his writing," noted a fellow war correspondent, John T. McCutcheon, here speaking of Davis's fiction, "he was the interpreter of chivalrous, well-bred youth, and his heroes were young, clean-thinking college men, heroic big-game hunters, war correspondents, and idealized men about town, who always did the noble thing, disdaining the unworthy in act or motive. He seemed to me he was modelling his own life, perhaps unconsciously, after the favored types which his imagination had created for his stories. In a certain sense he was living a life of make-believe, wherein he was the hero of the story, and in which he was bound by his ideals always to act as he would have the hero of his story act" (98–99).

It was all, finally, the stuff of romance, which meant in the 1890s a celebration of virtues associated with the chivalric tradition, of which Davis seemed to be a living avatar, clad not in gleaming armor but casting an equivalent glory about him wherever he went. Among the many posthumous tributes gathered in *R.H.D.*, and perhaps the one most frequently quoted, is a passage by Booth Tarkington. Five years Davis's junior, Tarkington testified to the awe with which young men of his generation regarded the great adventurer:

To the college boy of the early nineties Richard Harding Davis was the "beau ideal of *jeunesse dorée*," a sophisticated heart of gold. He was of that college boy's own age, but already an editor—already publishing books! His stalwart good looks were as familiar to us as were those of our own football captain; we knew his face as we knew the face of the President of the United States, but we infinitely preferred Davis's. When the Waldorf was wondrously completed, and we cut an exam . . . for an excursion to see the world at lunch in its new magnificence, and Richard Harding Davis came into the Palm Room—then, oh, then our day was radiant! That was the top of our fortune: we could never have hoped for so much. Of all the great people of every continent, this was the one we most desired to see. (*R.H.D.* 25)

Booth Tarkington would early on establish himself as a writer of historical romances with *Monsieur Beaucaire* (1900), before shifting to a much more realistic chronicling of life in his native Indiana. It was a shift in coordination with the preferences of the age that soon extinguished that brief romantic efflorescence at century's end, which was associated by a number of critics with the euphoria following the Spanish-American War. Roger Burlingame, younger than Davis by a quarter century, may have celebrated RHD's drawing power from his association with that war, but Burlingame also shared his generation's "strong bias toward realistic fiction." Yet as late as 1927 he could recall the impact on him of Davis's near mythic presence in terms echoing Tarkington's:

He walked right out of his stories. He was big, sunburned, adventurous, and made you believe everything. Looking at him, the wildest of his tales became probable. . . . On the street, in the office [of *Scribner's Magazine*] where I worked, into which he often came, wherever he was, in the muftiest of clothes, for me he was always surrounded by soldiers, spies, naked savages, and tropical vegetation; always on the edge of some terrific and complex adventure from which he would emerge intact and smiling. I could not believe it when he died. That was the only incredible thing he ever did. He was the very essence, the flow, the motion of life. (v)

It is difficult not to think here of Edgar Rice Burrough's Tarzan, Lord Greystoke, created in 1912, at the height of Davis's fame, a hero equally at home in the jungles of equatorial Africa and in a clubroom in London or New York City and, though English by birthright, a creation of American

Anglophilia. For it is Tarzan's certified blue blood that gives the Lord of the Jungle both his raw courage and his ability to exchange a loincloth for a tuxedo.

That heritage is no longer an important part of the Tarzan story, which has been transmuted through the many films starring Johnny Weismuller and his successors, who speak in a primitivistic pidgin English, whereas Burrough's hero has not only mastered his mother tongue but speaks impeccable French as well. The aristocratic heritage of the original was not only essential to the age, it was also integral to the makeup of Richard Harding Davis and the myth he engendered. Indeed, elitism was so basic to both that it guaranteed a relatively rapid obsolescence, being not relevant to the American culture that emerged after the First World War, as the transmogrification of Tarzan suggests.

That RHD sought acceptance by the elites, and in his public persona as well as his fictional projections created an ideal image of himself, cannot be denied. But if we are to believe the testimony of his friends and contemporaries, what Davis made of himself was an admirable blend of characteristics perfectly suited to his age but doomed to quick obsolescence as times and tastes changed. In the twelve posthumous tributes printed in *R.H.D.* by his contemporaries, Davis is again and again praised as a man and a writer who was "clean," one of the honorifics favored by Teddy Roosevelt (who is included among the twelve). This means that the subject of sex is never openly discussed in his writings, and it would be difficult to think of another Victorianism that has less resonance for today's readers than "clean." Davis's fellow writers, Crane, Norris, and Dreiser, were, by contrast, not "clean," and theirs are the books we still read. But if in Victorian parlance cleanliness was next to godliness, then Davis was surely (as another tribute suggested) a man divinely favored.

Where, in the Sophoclean view, those whom God would destroy he first makes mad, in both the Quran and Calvinism God prospers those who keep clean. If Davis's prose was free of sexual matters, he was notorious as a reporter in the field for a portable rubber bathtub he carried with him so that he could bathe (always in cold water) before dressing for dinner. We can make too much of this fetish, but though it may suggest a fastidiousness approaching the pathological, it is indicative as well of something essential to his writing, which was not only the result of painstaking revision for clarity and simplicity but also intolerant of impurities in personal conduct. Frank Norris's *McTeague* is a great work of literature but is a novel that Dick Davis would not or perhaps could not have written.

And yet for a critical period his self-created personality was a very effective instrument registering the nation's emerging sense of itself as a national power, which was hardly limited to the commercial aspects of the new imperialism. Indeed, during the twenty years bracketed by its involvement in two wars, the United States seems to have been largely identified with the selfsame idealism that Davis's contemporaries associated with both the writer and his fictional projections. As Theodore Roosevelt brusquely testified, "He was as good an American as ever lived and his heart flamed against cruelty and injustice. His writings form a text-book of Americanism which all our people would do well to read at the present time" (*R.H.D.* 56). As such, he may be accounted a mediator, at once expressing and informing the culture he represented, if briefly, so well.

: II :

Few studies of American culture in the last decade of the nineteenth century fail to render an account of Richard Harding Davis, starting with Thomas Beer's *Mauve Decade* in 1926, already quoted. Thus Van Wyck Brooks could in 1952 declare of the 1890s that they "were the times of Richard Harding Davis, a young man who was so dramatic in such a special way that he became the symbol of 'a young man's epoch' . . . one of those magnetic types, often otherwise second-rate, who establish patterns of living for others of their kind, and the notion of the novelist as war-correspondent which prevailed so long in American writing began in the early nineties undoubtedly with him" (103).

In support of his argument, Brooks quotes both Sinclair Lewis's *Dodsworth* and H. L. Mencken's *Newspaper Days*—"The hero of our dreams was Richard Harding Davis"—adding further testimony to that of Booth Tarkington and suggesting the impact Davis had on both blithely romantic and grimly realist sensibilities: "There was something of Davis too in Jack London and Stephen Crane" as well as in Frank Norris, who when he "went to Africa . . . was emulating Davis" (103–4). The difference between realistic and romantic fiction may seem relatively easy to define, but when it came to the creation of self, the most cynical of naturalistic writers tended to emulate the model established by Davis.

Grant Knight, in a 1951 study devoted primarily to the dominance of realism in America in the 1890s, credits Richard Harding Davis and Charles Dana Gibson as having jointly created "ideals for the 1890 public," Davis "through his reputation as an energetic, chivalrous journalist with a handsome, square-jawed face which his friend delighted to use for his illustrations" (*Critical Period* 22). Larzer Ziff, writing only fifteen years after Brooks and Knight, observed that through his writings "Davis made an immense contribution to the fantasy of the natural superiority of the American" (180).

Like Brooks, Ziff testified to Davis's personal fame at a time when "the master of life was he who had experienced stark problems of survival in a ravening wilderness and who could stride into the Waldorf, his weather-beaten face proclaiming his experience, and use the correct fork while reluctantly permitting the young ladies to draw from him the story of his most recent adventure" (173–74). Ziff here echoes the testimony of Tarkington (RHD, as Finley Peter Dunne suggests, preferred Delmonico's cuisine) and admits that Davis's "adventurous achievements were proof against all the reservations the cynic could produce" that Davis thereby gave the rising generation of writers "its hero." At a time when "to be in it was everything," "Dick Davis was in it, and, from Crane to Hemingway, they wanted in too, in great part as a result of the attraction he exerted" (179).

Paradoxically, behind the RHD myth that was to a large extent self-created, derived as his contemporaries attest from the news stories and travel writing in which the reporter always played a central role, the "reality" of the man was an approximate fable, starting with his dual birthright. He was born in 1864 to parents who provided an appropriate heritage for a son known as both a reporter and a writer of fiction. Richard Harding's father was L. Clarke Davis, editor of the *Philadelphia Public Ledger,* and his mother was the well-known novelist Rebecca Harding Davis, southern in heritage and upbringing but brought to early prominence on the strength of her grimly realistic story "Life in the Iron Mills" (1861).

Moreover, the environment in which young Davis was raised was by all accounts centered by the theater, in terms of both plays and actors who were family friends. These influences have been credited with instilling in the boy a love of the stage as well as a tendency toward self-dramatization, sartorial preferences bordering on costume, and the use of theatrical devices in his reporting and fiction. In Davis's life and in his writing there was no clear line between fact and fantasy but rather a conglomerate effect, in which the two merged with synergetic results.

The myth was, as Tarkington and Burlingame testify, promoted from the start by an attractive appearance, Davis being a tall, well-built, handsome youth, with a love of team sports. Not gifted academically, the boy attended private academies before entering the recently founded Lehigh University, then primarily an engineering school, on the strength of family connections.

He remained for three years, where he played football and wrote for and edited college periodicals, activities that would all prove prophetic. Davis also studied (and played cricket) at Johns Hopkins for another year before giving up college for newspaper work.

Not widely liked by schoolmates or journalistic colleagues because of his rigid manner and inflexible adherence to what he thought was proper comportment, Davis was nonetheless always surrounded by a coterie of men who were devoted to him. He was popular with women, being so physically attractive that he provided the model for the "Gibson man," the artist being a close personal friend. Raised in an Anglophiliac community, with its social and athletic clubs and a thoroughly Victorian sense of morality, Davis was stiffly formal among strangers and preferred dining alone to associating with persons he considered his social or intellectual inferiors. He was, in sum, a snob, who bore his virtue like a shield and was therefore something of a prig.

And yet as a writer he had what can only be called a common touch, for much of what he wrote, especially early in his career, was popular and reached out intentionally to a very broad (albeit middle-class) audience. He was also, his contemporaries testified, extremely lucky in whatever he did, for as Gouverneur Morris noted in a posthumous tribute, RHD was a man loved by the gods. His reporting always seemed to place him in those locations which would earn great public attention, from the Johnstown Flood in 1889 to Brussels at the moment the German army invaded Belgium, a quarter of a century later.

These journalistic junctures also involved considerable risk to his life, yet he survived until succumbing to a heart attack at home, brought on by a fondness for rich food and the physical strain of preparing himself, at fifty-two, for participation in the last war that he reported. It was a death that warranted a posthumous association with Peter Pan, for it guaranteed he would never grow old. It was, moreover, a suitable death for a writer who had enjoyed his greatest fame as a young man, his early success lifting him to the managing editorship of *Harper's Weekly* by his midtwenties, in 1890.

Unlike the Emersonian idealist George W. Curtis, who was the general editor of *Harper's* from 1863 until his death nearly thirty years later and who used the popular weekly to promote social reforms, RHD did not rest easy or remain long in his editor's chair. Nor did he interest himself in reform beyond the makeup and contents of what had become an elderly gentleman among magazines, thanks in part to Curtis's long tenancy. Although he was responsible for revisions in layout and for journalistic emphases designed to appeal to younger readers—including coverage of college sports—Davis spent much of his short stay at *Harper's* traveling about the world on self-assignment, sending in the pieces that made him the model for so many rising young talents in the 1890s. Wrote Gouverneur Morris in 1917, anticipating Beer by a decade, "With the written word or the spoken word he was the greatest recorder and reporter of things that he had seen of any man, perhaps, that ever lived. The history of the last thirty years, its manners and customs and its leading events and inventions, cannot be written truthfully without reference to the records he has left, to his special articles and to his letters" (*R.H.D.* 5).

The Harper cousins, however, had a narrow view and thought less about Davis's contributions to history than about his frequent escapes from his editorial chores. Nor was Davis happy with the restrictions imposed on his freedom to travel by those chores, and by mutual accord he left the post after three years. RHD had written short fiction from the start of his public career, and while continuing to file news stories with magazines and newspapers as a foreign correspondent, he became the author of superficial, romantic novels popular in their day but now regarded as past canonical redemption. Mencken, notably, while praising RHD's newspaper work, would dismiss his romances as "cheesy," fit only for "servant-girl" readers (*Prejudices: Second Series* 23; quoted in Langford, *Alias O. Henry* xiv).

Davis's younger brother and admiring companion, Charles, was willing to acknowledge that even in RHD's prime there were differences of opinion "among the critics and the public as to Richard's fiction" (*Adventures* 124). But Charles felt it was "safe to say that as a reporter his work of nearly thirty years stood at least as high as that of any of his contemporaries or perhaps as that of the reporters of all time." Forever despairing that nothing new was to be found in the world, Davis, as his brother testified, was always able to lend vividness and freshness to hackneyed subjects: "It hasn't been done," RHD declared to an editor, "until *I* do it," a typical display of egotism that does not discredit his claim to superiority as a reporter.

In the movie *Foreign Correspondent,* the first film directed in America by Alfred Hitchcock and released in 1939, Richard Harding Davis is called "one of our greatest war correspondents forty years ago," a testimony to his enduring fame as a journalist. Ironically, however, Davis's lasting reputation as a reporter has influenced the opinion of most literary historians, who, if not resorting to Mencken's extreme opinion, have concurred with the article written for the *Dictionary of American Biography* by Fred L. Pattee in 1930. Pattee noted that although he was "the most widely known reporter of his generation . . . in all his fiction Davis was essentially a journalist, quick to sense the demands of the larger public and working in the fashions of the hour. . . . [A]lways vivid in his descriptive passages, often picturesque, and easily readable, he dealt mainly with the surface of life, and . . . even his best work will not long endure."

In a display of that collusion essential to the compiling of literary hand-books, we find Pattee's judgment repeated in unsubtle variations down through the years. In 1941 James D. Hart, in a relatively long entry in the *Oxford Companion to American Literature,* called Davis "the leading reporter of his time," whose journalism was "vivid and picturesque . . . always dram-atizing the bare facts of his stories." Hart thought that Davis's short fiction demonstrated "adept craftsmanship" but was "considered journalistic, with more stress on effect and form than on substance," defining his novels like-wise as "vivid but superficial." So also the opinion of Stanley Kunitz and Howard Haycraft in 1942, who in *Twentieth Century Authors* maintained that all of Davis's writing was essentially "journalism." Moreover, his work having been tied to the contemporary moment, he "is deservedly forgot-ten now."

This by then conventional evaluation of Davis was echoed seven years later by William Rose Benét, in his *Reader's Encyclopedia:* "His news stories were vivid and dramatic," opined Benét, whereas "his fiction is considered to be journalistic, slick, and superficial." And yet Benét, who having been born in 1886 was old enough to have remembered RHD in his prime, is quoted by Kunitz and Haycraft as having enthused that "Dick Davis was just about the best story he ever wrote!" As Benét testified, and as his friends and professional colleagues had maintained thirty years earlier, Richard Hard-ing Davis and his work were inseparable.

According to the elder Burlingham, RHD's fiction not only expressed "the indomitable youthfulness and health of spirit . . . that we associate with Davis himself," but "it had helped to clear the air and to give a new proof of the vitality of certain ideals" of which the author was an exemplar (*R.H.D.* 36). As Kunitz and Haycraft put it, less kindly, Davis was given to inserting "a moral pill below the sugar-coating" of his romances, and while they con-curred with his contemporaries that "Davis fitted his own time perfectly," it was in the service of dismissing his relevance for modern readers. Yet that perfect fit is the key to Davis's importance, and now, having considered how he was viewed by his (and our) contemporaries, I want to take his measure as a celebrant of what he construed to be the praiseworthy aspects of his age, of which he was such a representative part.

: III :

Davis's deeply chivalric nature, which gave a militant edge to virtue, was intrinsic to the 1890s and, like so much we can identify with the upper levels of society in that time, was absorbed from the aristocratic ethos of Great Britain, to the manner of which Davis was admittedly sedulous, but which has little popular resonance today. Yet, once again, things were different at the start of the twentieth century, when Great Britain was the empire to emulate. Mark Girouard has demonstrated the extent to which the chivalric ideal gripped Victorian society in England, not only in literature and art but in sports as well, and despite the often uneasy relationship between the United States and what had been the mother country, that cultural saturation definably had its influence here.

A teenager in the 1890s, when RHD's reputation was on the rise, the critic Henry Seidel Canby recalls in his memoir that complex and turbulent decade in terms which establish the literary milieu that was so receptive to Davis's writings. Canby provides an informal syllabus in which Tennyson and Longfellow headed the list of poets, Scott and Dickens the fiction, while side by side on the library shelf sat the "two volumes of Grant's Memoirs, and two of Henry M. Stanley" (*American Memoir* 93). From this acculturation, Canby claims, came the prevailing romanticism of the age, sentimental idealism from which was abstracted an arbitrary set of values, essentially an updated version of chivalry:

> The ideal relationships with one's sister, one's mother, one's family, one's sweetheart, were all determined by sentiment. So was affection for the home. So was one's attitude toward the poor or weak. So was every loyalty which young men of the period manifested loudly toward the alma mater that often educated them very badly. There was very little sentiment in what we were told to do by the preachers. That was right and wrong, sealed by punishment. The social code we really lived by was not an "ought" code, but a code of honor—what an honorable man should feel toward his friend, his wife, his duty;—and I find what we thought and felt and proposed to do far more exactly rendered in *David Copperfield* and implied in *The Antiquary* than in the Bible or the prayerbook. We all of us knew so well from our romantic reading how we should feel about such matters that I doubt if there was a single family in upperclass Wilmington capable of analysing themselves realistically. (97)

If, Canby recounts, "Mark Twain thought that the Civil War was caused by the false sense of chivalry engendered by the passionate reading of Scott in the South" (an opinion advanced in *Life on the Mississippi*), so, as Canby admits, Scott and his legion of imitators "were such real determinants of inner life for readers brought up in the eighties and nineties that no one will ever understand the America of that day without reading and pondering upon not only *Ivanhoe* but also *To Have and To Hold* and *Richard Carvel* and *Monsieur Beaucaire* and *Under the Red Robe*" (95). As the romanticism of the 1830s and 1840s hurried Americans into the Civil War, so the equivalent literature of the 1890s explains the Cuban crusade and what followed:

> The Spanish War, with its rather sordid imperialism, wrapped in guff about poor Cuba, the gallant onslaughts of the muckrakers upon the money-bags, the cult of Theodore Roosevelt, the glamorous expansiveness of the opening twentieth century, captains of industry, octopus trusts, the still young nation putting on greatness, up and on to the moral romance of our entry into the Great War—how much all this owes to the shot of romance in our veins and the virus of sentiment cannot be said definitely, but much I am sure. Certainly in our town, where the past and the future seemed to become romantic together at that turn of the century, I cannot separate in my own memory the bands and cheering of 'ninety-eight, Hobson, Dewey, and manifest destiny in an expectant world, from the extravagant romanticism of the shallow, unphilosophical unpsychological novels we had all been reading. (101)

Amy Kaplan quotes this last passage in support of her thesis that the Spanish-American War was the overripe fruit of too much reading of bad romances, a notion recalling the equivalent eighteenth-century animadversions against exposing innocent maidens to the seductive call of three-decker versions of the same overwrought genre. Canby, like most critics of his generation, preferred Stephen Crane's work to that produced by the romance revival. But he overlooks the fact that Crane and other young authors carrying forward to greater grittiness the realism espoused by William Dean Howells—like Frank Norris and Jack London—all ferocious champions of the New Naturalism, were drawn to the Cuban and other wars then breaking out around the world where they served as newspaper correspondents.

In heeding this impulse, the naturalist writers were obeying the same call to which Richard Harding Davis responded, yet Canby makes no mention of Davis, a strange omission given his re-creation of an age in terms so suggestive of RHD's work and personal character. Davis is described by Eric Sundquist as a perfect exemplification and anticipation of what Theodore Roosevelt called the "strenuous life," which was an American version of "muscular Christianity" in that it retained the emphasis on physical fitness coupled with sterling virtue but pretty much left the organized church out of the picture (*Columbia Literary History* 517). To this generational mix we need to add Joseph Conrad, whose *Heart of Darkness* was admired by Davis. The story begins with a description of Roman legionnaires rowing up the Thames into darkest Britain, a prolegomenon to the story of Kurtz, but also an image relevant to Davis's journalistic quest into tropic zones.

Conrad's frame was ironic, a viewpoint shared by Davis in some of his fiction, but in his travel writing RHD tended to present a positive image of his country, as the benevolent harbinger of civilization, bringing the blessings of law and order—and commerce—into purportedly benighted regions. This was the logical extension of the original Puritan errand into the wilderness, after all, and served President McKinley as the rationale for yielding to the demand that he declare war on Spanish Cuba, even though the negotiated peace that he preferred was still possible. At a critical moment in his own career, in his penultimate travel book in 1908, Davis testified to the ineptness and cruelty of the Belgian presence in Africa, but unlike Conrad he was not seeking to expose the essential folly of imperial adventures.

The problem, as RHD saw it, was not imperialism but the specifics of administration: what the Congo needed was a legion of young Kurtzes, which is to say a bright band of brothers modeled after Henry M. Stanley, whose narrative of his African adventures sat next to Grant's memoirs in the Canby family library in Wilmington and an account of which was published by *Harper's Weekly* during the first year of Davis's editorship. Famous for finding Livingstone and rescuing Emin Pasha, Stanley also brought steamboats and a railroad—hence civilization—to the Dark Continent (an epithet of his own coinage). A reporter himself, Stanley was the progenitor of a new breed of journalists who created the events they covered, of which Davis by 1900 had emerged as preeminent.

Canby merely mentions Stanley's account of his African adventures in passing, but they surely appealed to the upsurging romantic spirit in the United States, much as the outlines of the explorer's life could be seen by the 1890s as exemplifying that typical American rise from anonymous poverty to fame and fortune. In 1899, at the height of his fame as a correspondent, Davis visited Stanley at his new estate in England, Furze Hill, and later wrote to the great explorer's widow that he would "never forget one late afternoon when Stanley, in the gathering darkness, told us the story of Gordon," the tragic hero of Khartoum (Stanley 508). The recalled circumstances provide a parallel to the opening pages of Conrad's parable of

colonialism, also begun as twilight descended into a pervading gloom forever equated by Victorian England (and McKinley's America) with "hea-
then" countries.

With that characteristic American chauvinism, so rampant in the 1890s
and so repugnant to Canby in 1934, Davis thought in terms of his country's
exceptionalism, expressing in manifold if mostly implicit ways that the
United States was peculiarly blessed in all its endeavors. Manifest Destiny
was extended now beyond the borders of the continent, inspiring a revival
of the Monroe Doctrine, carrying the nation's influence past the waters'
edge into remote places of the Western world. Nothing but good could be
the result, in contrast to the imperial presence of nations from the Old
World, which like Leopold's Belgium brought corruption and horrid brutal-
ity with it. Only Great Britain provided a model of enlightened imperialism,
as well as supplying the bard of empire, Rudyard Kipling, who was popular
in the United States and influential on American writers associated with the
1890s.

Kipling's books were not on the Canby library shelves in Wilmington, as
he had not "written [them] in time for us" (Canby 66). But in the third and
last volume of his autobiography, Canby recalled as a young teacher, circa
1905, having discussed the works of Kipling "with the agreeable feeling that
I was introducing my classes to the literature of the future," an opinion
widely shared at the time in spite (as well as because) of Kipling's celebration of empire, both British and American (*American Memoir* 415). After all,
the poet's famous imperial paean, "The White Man's Burden," was subtitled
"The United States and the Philippine Islands." It was this later conflict
which soured so many Americans regarding the "sordid imperialism" that
Canby associated in his memoirs with the Cuban war—but apparently not
with Kipling.

Kipling's poems and stories first began to appear during Davis's apprentice years, and he regarded them with admiration mixed with envy: "I have
been reading Rudyard Kipling's short stories," he wrote his mother in 1890,
"and I think it is disgusting that a boy like that should write such stories. He
hasn't left himself anything to do when he gets old" (*Adventures* 52). The
"boy" in question was only a year younger than Davis, but Kipling served notice that if RHD wished to write short fiction, he had better get cracking. It
was an impetus perhaps accelerated when an enthusiastic article on Kipling
by Andrew Lang appeared in *Harper's Weekly* in late August of that same
year, singling out the stories in *Soldiers Three* for special praise: "Every sol-

dier should inspire himself with their gay daring and masterful adventure"
(34: 688).

A number of American literary critics and political jingoes, including
Theodore Roosevelt, sought to find an "American Kipling" following the
sudden appearance of the United States as a rival of British Empire, and
RHD was among the candidates, identified as such by an English reviewer
as early as 1891. The influence of Kipling on Davis is as problematic as it is
undeniable, but surely there was no American writer more eager for the
United States to get into "the great game" than was he, an eagerness
matched by persons in high political place, including Roosevelt, who were
the chief movers behind the entry of our country into the race for imperial
ascendancy.

Along with Robert Louis Stevenson, Kipling provided RHD a model for
a new kind of romantic fiction: from Stevenson he took the constant stress
on physical action, often violent, but where Stevenson wrote historical romances in the vein of Scott, Davis like Kipling chose the modern scene. By
setting his stories in India, Kipling provided the requisite romantic element
of exoticism, presumably inspiring Davis's use of Central American and
other tropical settings. Kipling also added a large measure of often shocking
realism, an element missing entirely from Stevenson's romances and from
Davis's as well. And yet without the example of Kipling's "masterful adventures" before him, Davis likely would not have written Soldiers of Fortune in
the form in which it appeared, with its undeniable fix on the contemporary
moment and a hero who is an idealization of the modern American man.

Whatever the Kipling connection, RHD's romantic idealism resulted in a
version of the imperial game in which young officers and other male elites,
not enlisted men from the working classes, played the decisive parts, an
emphasis derived from the romances of Scott, Cooper, and Stevenson.
Moreover, though Kipling could stoop to the maudlin, he was seldom sentimental in his effects, while Davis was often so; indeed it was his mixture of
sentimentality and derring-do that made him so popular a writer in an
America whose tastemakers were often offended by Kipling's coarseness
and full-throated bravado.

What Davis added to the mix of the new romanticism was primarily his
own very proper person, inextricable for his contemporaries from his created heroes. The emphasis of the tributes in R.H.D. on the subjective element may in part be attributed to Davis's uniqueness among the romantic
writers of his day in serving as the model for a number of his fictional

heroes, role-playing derived from his experiences as a correspondent. The dramatist Augustus Thomas testified that Davis could have figured in his most popular novel, *Soldiers of Fortune,* as any of several heroic characters, who served as virtual mouthpieces through whom the author himself was talking (*R.H.D.* 44). "Some critics," wrote Gouverneur Morris, "maintain that the heroes and heroines of his books are impossibly pure and innocent young people," yet Davis "never called upon his characters for any trait of virtue, or renunciation or self-mastery of which his own life could not furnish examples" (17).

E. L. Burlingame wrote that "one of the most attractive and inspiring things about Richard Harding Davis was the simple, almost matter-of-course way in which he put into practice his views of life—in which he acted, and in fact was, what he believed. . . . He had certain simple, clean, manly convictions as to how a man should act" and was able to project into his fiction "all the qualities that we associate with Davis himself" (35–36). Here again Davis established a model for the young naturalists who would eventually eclipse him, especially Jack London, whose fictional heroes were muscular autobiographical projections magnified by a Nietzschean lens.

According to the testimony of a friend who had first met RHD when he visited Oxford in 1892, the American reporter expressed "a wonderful spirit of adventure, an unprejudiced view of life, an almost Quixotic feeling for romance, a disdain of sordid or materialistic motives" (Davis, *Adventures* 83–84). It was a complex yet ingenuous impulse that not only characterized his fictional heroes but also carried Davis through a long journalistic career in which he was forever the adversary of those "legions" that trod on "the prostrate bodies of a small people," as his Oxford friend testified, whether the victims were Africans under Belgian rule or Belgians tramped by the invading armies of the kaiser.

Obeying the romantic idealism so well defined by Canby, RHD was forever drawn to the underdog, to an oppressed and nobly primitive people: When soon after the Cuban conflict he traveled to South Africa to cover the Boer War, his characteristic Anglophilia slipped away, and he found himself favoring the descendants of Dutch settlers in their struggle to throw off the British invaders of the Transvaal. He was clearly charmed by the simple ruggedness of the Dutch farmers, who with their bearded, patriarchal faces and simple faith in themselves and their religion were closer to the American frontier past than were the regimented ranks of the invading army.

Davis abandoned his characteristic Anglophilia and portrayed the commanding officers of the British forces as dilatory bunglers, criticism that cost him his English friends and admirers, much to his hurt bewilderment. After all, his championing of the Boers and their cause was of a piece with what he assumed was the party of virtue, an opinion widely shared in the United States, where the American occupation of the Philippines likewise had a number of well-known opponents, including Mark Twain and Richard Harding Davis, as well as his famous mother, Rebecca.

After 1908, RHD turned away from journalism and profitably devoted himself to popular fiction and drama, the earnings from which he spent as they came in, maintaining not only an extravagant lifestyle but his own version of Furze Hill, Crossroads Farm, the country estate built for his bride, Cecil Clark, an accomplished painter and portraitist. They were married in 1897, on the eve of the war in Cuba, and she was yet another aspect of his life that merged with (or emerged from) his fiction.

For Cecil was the sort of athletic and self-determined young woman found in his stories and novels, including *Soldiers of Fortune,* and she accompanied her husband when he traveled to South Africa to cover the Boer War. But though a steadfast companion, Cecil (today accounted a lesbian) was unwilling to consummate the union, an arrangement that involved separate sleeping quarters. As F. Scott Fitzgerald would discover, fiction and the realities of family life should not be confused, and the union was soon in trouble.

Yet Davis's sexual abstinence during his marriage to Cecil, whatever the reason for it, further demonstrates his radical, even impossible, idealism, being an extreme version of the chasteness described in Canby's recollections of life in the 1890s. For proper young people of the day, love was kept separate from sexuality, a dichotomy that Canby admits was a "double standard": "Beauty we estimated much more highly than today, and perhaps, as some believe, the girls were more beautiful, which is credible since seductiveness or any strong sex impulse is a disturbing factor in the absolute [i.e., Platonic] definition of beauty. Comradeship we ranked high, and good spirits, and character, though if a girl were pretty enough she could dazzle us out of such sensible perceptions of the truth about women. But sex, naked and unashamed, with no purpose but its own gratification, was kept in its place, which was not friendship, not even the state of falling in love" (81).

Davis's first marriage finally came apart in 1910, the same year that Rebecca Harding Davis died, thereby removing the most influential woman in his life. Divorced in 1912, Davis married again soon after, this time to a vivacious actress stage-named Bessie (for Elizabeth) McCoy, famous as the "Yama-Yama girl," who was decidedly not modeled after his boyish fictional heroines. It was, however, a union that testified to his lifelong devotion to the theater and validated Canby's notion that even in the 1890s a sufficiently pretty woman could jar a young man loose from his platonic commitment to a chaste companionship. Bessie soon gave birth to a child named Hope, a name resonant with newfound optimism but not lacking in irony. For Hope was the name of the athletic, boyish heroine in *Soldiers of Fortune,* modeled after Cecil Clark.

In 1914, at the start of World War I, RHD resumed his career as a war correspondent with much of his old power. In his accounts sent back from Belgium and France, he was in effect writing propaganda against the Germans with the intention of drawing the United States into the conflict. Davis died two years later, suffering a fatal heart attack that resulted from his over-exertion as an amateur soldier in "preparedness" exercises sponsored by pro-war activists. Along with Theodore Roosevelt, he was involved as much with the war in Europe as with the Cuban conflict, and had he lived Davis might well have earned a second fame, but it is with the Spanish-American War that he is now chiefly associated.

: IV :

Assessing the effect of a popular author on his readership is a dubious enterprise, but the phenomenon of best-sellers does suggest some sort of synergism at work, an arrangement by which the writer expresses the common thoughts and desires of the day. Here again Canby bears witness, if Wilmington was that symbolic zone he describes, set between the sere morality of New England's sphere of influence and the passionate chivalry of the South. Surely Hearst and Pulitzer were able to evoke a unanimity of response because they were sounding common chords, and if American manhood was the theme, no popular writer in the years before 1898 did more to swell the anthem than RHD.

Of course, there were other voices in the chorus as well, chronicled by Walter LaFeber, but geopoliticians inspired by Captain Mahan addressed themselves exclusively to elites. It is Davis's fiction and reportorial writing of the 1890s that give us some sense of the readiness of Americans for imperialistic adventurers. In place of dry geopolitical theory, Davis promoted a popular myth central to which is the adventurer, the soldier of fortune, in Davis's hands an updated version of the knight-errant, performing gallant and chivalric deeds for hire.

Given the contemporary prevalence of this ideal, the extent of which has been demonstrated by Mark Girouard, we cannot credit RHD with much originality. Yet it was he who gave what had largely been a British myth a distinctly American profile, which if it resembled his own handsome outline had by 1898 merged with Theodore Roosevelt's muscular silhouette. Davis's contemporaries acknowledged that his account of the attack on San Juan Hill assisted in promoting TR's reputation as a courageous avatar of the virtues later celebrated in *The Strenuous Life* (1900), a book that drew for material and impetus on the Spanish-American War and provides a companion text to *Soldiers of Fortune*.

Nor does the process stop with the war in Cuba. Whatever our evaluation of RHD's worth as a writer of fiction, we must acknowledge that he created an enduring archetype seldom credited to his invention. Under the influence of Stevenson, his fellow romancer during an age of rampant realism, with his acknowledged admiration for Bret Harte and a detectable debt to Kipling, Davis produced a new kind of American hero, an adventurer who came out of the West and translated the frontier spirit to foreign and exotic places. Like Roosevelt, this hero combined romantic idealism with wilderness know-how, but unlike Roosevelt, he was firmly associated with the practical aspects of technology, civil engineering in specific.

The Davis hero also evinced the kind of initiative and courage that was celebrated in Elbert Hubbard's *Message to Garcia* (1899), a popular and much circulated essay inspired by an incident in the Spanish-American War, the moral of which was in keeping with the strenuous idealism of Davis's *Soldiers of Fortune*. And, by way of Davis also, we can see Owen Wister's long-enduring cowboy emerging, for most of the short stories worked into the narrative of *The Virginian* postdate Davis's early reporting and adventure fiction. Equally important, the courtship that transformed Wister's realistic tales of cowboy life into a sentimental romance and ensured the novel's popularity was in harmony with, if not inspired by, Davis's example.

But though Robert Clay in *Soldiers of Fortune* has ridden the range in his youth and shares with Wister's Virginian the rugged good looks and fearlessness that win him a bride, as a hero he is identified with America's expansionist future, not the country's disappearing past. We know that Theodore Roosevelt participated in the creation of Wister's idealized cowboy, but despite his own association with, as he called it, "ranch life and the hunting trail," Roosevelt can in no way be confused with his friend's western hero.

On the other hand, whether because of coincidence or purpose, Roosevelt bears a remarkable resemblance to Robert Clay, a likeness that in large part explains the prominence he plays in Davis's account of the war in Cuba.

It was as if the myth was already prepared in which the young colonel would serve as a hero, not this time as a rancher and hunter but as an athletic champion of America's presence and purpose in the Caribbean. Wister used the romance form to elevate the cowboy into mythic stature; Davis used the genre to transform the imperial errand into a new crusade.

2 : NOT A LITTLE GIVEN TO ROMANCE

: I :

Though the eulogizing essays published in 1917 as *R.H.D.* were written as mortuary pieces, necessarily stressing the author's personal virtues, they agree that what was admirable about the author were the definitive characteristics of his writing as well. This unanimity of evaluation is borne out by the testimony elsewhere of Anthony Hope Hawkins, the British writer of popular romances who spent time with Davis when on a visit to America in 1903, cementing a friendship that was kept up by the two men thereafter on both sides of the Atlantic:

> He was not a great novelist, either in breadth of scene or in depth of penetration, but both his books of adventure and his stories of New York life—especially the Van Bibber series—are written with wonderful vividness and zest; his evident enjoyment in writing them infects the reader; and his keen eye for a scene and scent for an atmosphere enabled him to catch and express by his pen the spirit of the New York of his day much as Dana Gibson was doing by his pencil. And whatever may be, yesterday or today, his rank as a novelist, Dick Davis was unquestionably a great reporter. He could, so to say, impale on the reader's mind the vision of a place or the scenes of a war as a collector of butterflies impales a specimen on his board; and he hunted wars all over the world as other men hunt specimens; he hated to miss one. . . . Dick drew [on] his amazing pictorial power that never let you forget that armies were not merely machines, not merely corps, divisions or battalions, but also human beings, individuals, each with his qualities, his foibles, and his sufferings. He was a being very human himself—very full of life, courage, and high spirits, always a child (sometimes a petulant one) in some ways—he had, for example, an odd penchant for collecting obscure "Orders" from not too reputable Potentates and Presidents—but always a delightful

companion, always appreciating and enjoying, in love with life, with his
work, and with his friends. (227–28)

I quote from Hawkins's tribute at length not only because it seems a fair evaluation of Davis's strengths and weaknesses but also because, like so many
other testimonials by those who knew him, it puts an emphasis on RHD's career as a journalist in the field.

Though Davis, as Hawkins implies, was careful to promote his celebrity
to the point of boyish delight in honors received, as an author he was su-
premely unselfconscious. In contrast to his much admired Stevenson, who
began his own career as an essayist and belletrist, not a reporter, Davis
wrote nothing about the craft of fiction, perhaps because he thought of his
work as commercial and formulaic—which it certainly was—rather than as
original and innovative. Nor did he write explicitly about his aims as a reporter and travel writer, but fortunately, early in his career, he set down an
equivalent manifesto in a profile of his friend and colleague the correspondent Stephen Bonsal, which appeared in *Harper's Weekly* in 1892. That was
the year in which RHD himself began the travels that would provide the substance of several books during the remainder of the decade, and Bonsal, defined by Davis in the title of his article as "a newspaperman's man," would
serve as both inspiration and model for his own subsequent career. As we
might expect from the testimonials of his friends and professional associates, it is idealistic and romantic to the extreme.

"The correspondent," wrote Davis "is the modern knight-errant," who
"wanders around the face of the globe with a mission, fighting windmills
occasionally, sometimes dragons; and his loyalty to his paper as praiseworthy as was the knight's loyalty to his lady" (36: 856). The chivalric figure
is certainly self-defining, glorifying his profession as well as instilling it with
a missionary zeal, but it is followed by an argument that is in synchronization with Davis's yearning for celebrity and status: "Young men of other professions," he wrote, "are limited to that profession . . . but the correspondent knows all the kings of the Cannibal Islands and the pretenders to the
thrones of Europe. . . . He sits down with the Mahdi before Khartoom, and
rises [*sic:* rides?] on a jaunting-car with Parnell. He watches the downfall of
Balmaceda at Santiago, and the uprising of the Messiah at Wounded-Knee.
That is better than knowing whether or no Lackawanna is rising two or
three points, or whether one should or should not keep the reins in the hand
when one dismounts from the Aquidneck coach."

Yet for all his knocking about the savage places of the world, the correspondent, like Bonsal, is a perfect gentleman who never forgets "the usages of good society" and who is at once an "indolent member" of the Calumet Club and a man who has "a transatlantic cable attached to some part of his nervous system." It is Bonsal's easy adaptability, his perfect cosmopolitanism, that makes him "so interesting," and is the secret also of his success, "that and the fact that he is a Southerner, and is as impetuous and quick-tempered as he is quick-witted, and as chivalrous as Southern boys are, and as gentle. The very first assignment he received on entering the newspaper business was to go and ask a woman why her husband wanted to get a divorce. Bonsal tossed the paper back at the city editor, and explained that that was not the sort of work he meant to do."

It is not difficult here to see the outlines of Davis's own subsequent clean-lined profile emerging, for he too kept his head (and nose) above the yellow muck of so much journalism of his day, evincing an aristocratic reticence that went with knowing how boots were properly varnished. He may not have been willing, like Bonsal, to pass months at a time "in kneeless riding-breeches and a money-belt" for costume, being something of a fashion plate in unlikely places, but in this idiosyncrasy he was the essence of fastidiousness.

On the other hand, in his praise of Bonsal, RHD is perhaps unwittingly laying out the limitations of journalism as a profession even as he lauds its most notable representative, for many of the events and persons with which he associates Bonsal have long since, like the famous correspondent himself, been forgotten. The great reporter of today is all too often relegated to-morrow to the same dusty archives where newspapers are stored, giving a certain ironic resonance to Davis's phrase "newspaperman's man." But if personal notoriety is ephemeral, it is at the time a heady mix, being of celebrity the essence, in effect what passes for an aristocracy in a democratic society.

For Davis as for Bonsal, the foreign correspondent reaps his reward not so much from the salary he is paid (meager, according to Davis) but from the fame that comes from a constant flirting with danger and even death in distant places, the substance (as with their great predecessor Henry Stanley) of their writings. Moreover, an intimacy with the arbiters of power in this world brings respect from those fellow clubmen the correspondent has left at home in New York and to whom he returns at the end of his travels. Bonsal borrows fame from those with whom he associates as a correspondent; his own celebrity is validated by the association.

"To us who have only seen royalty drive by on parade," writes Davis, "it is interesting to hear Bonsal testify to such a one's not knowing a good cigar when it is offered him, and his conversation has in consequence a certain interest which that of young men in other professions does not possess. A man who has played billiards with Gambetta, and who has been given a three hours' audience by the Pope, must necessarily be an attractive companion." These last two words put an emphasis on sociability, suggesting that the celebrity Bonsal has gathered to himself by association may be borrowed by those who gather around him upon his return from his travels.

Davis goes on to note that Bonsal as a newspaperman is something more than a reporter in quest of exciting and novel material; he is a correspondent who always takes the part of "the people with whom his work associates him," becoming "a partisan" of any cause he is covering. But it is this deep involvement in his material—another quality borrowed from Stanley—that makes "whatever he writes interesting," the last being the key word in RHD's account both of Bonsal's conversation and of his written work. And if being an interesting and attractive companion was what Davis himself sought from his own career as a foreign correspondent, then clearly, as the testimony of the Burlingames, Tarkington, and Thomas Beer suggests, that is what he received, the romantic aura resulting from his association with both cannibals and kings, as well as the storied and dangerous places of a world far removed from the clubrooms and hotels of New York.

Ironically, however, he was no Bonsal. Davis was fated, as Beer's tribute attests, to view more parades than he took part in, and although he sought out and interviewed the great personages of his day, his was seldom the dangerous path taken by his friend and fellow correspondent. Until his Cuban adventure, where he found himself competing with Bonsal for copy, Davis was seldom more than a glorified tourist, viewing the world "from a car window," as the title of his first book of travels put it, and he often lamented that when he arrived at the scene of what he hoped would be exciting and novel events, they had already passed from the stage.

But what Davis excelled at—and what his contemporaries recognized in his work—was giving a new dimension through his writing to materials already well worn through previous use, and by that talent making the familiar novel, hence "interesting." If newsworthy events were over by the time he arrived, he would enlarge on what had been left behind, being a writer whose nature, as it were, adored a vacuum, as available space to fill. Like those knights-errant whom he regarded as his predecessors, Davis wrought virtue out of a search forever doomed to failure. So on his last trip into exotic places, he set off up the Congo along the track of Conrad's Marlow but never did find his Kurtz, yet Davis managed to convince the reader that the trip was nonetheless worthwhile.

He was, that is to say, a writer who made what he wrote interesting because he transformed his material through the power of his style into something different from what it had been before. In his travels he repeatedly encountered what other travelers had found, yet he was able to convince his readers that what he was describing was worth reading about. And it is this power, which is to be distinguished from the momentary fame that comes from association with mere event, that recommends Davis to us and makes him valuable in ways transcending the glory he enjoyed in his own day, which began to fade the day Dick Davis died.

"Romance was never dead," wrote an admiring contemporary, "while Davis was still alive," and certainly by 1916, the year of his death, the genre had been buried in critical oblivion (Davis, *Adventures* 84). But in Robert Louis Stevenson's heyday and for at least a decade thereafter, the romance was in full flower, and as a genre, wrote an American literary critic in 1898, it fit the idealist like "a garment" (Burton 75). We would be hard put to find a better metaphor in discussing Davis as a reporter as well as a writer of fiction, for as the admiring portrait of Bonsal suggests, his view of the reporter's calling was irradiated with romance, which it was the correspondent's job to transfer to the scene through which he was passing, thereby making it of interest to his readers.

: II :

The question yet remaining is whether Davis's journalistic writing remains of interest to us, and in what follows I attempt to make the case that it is, that his work is still of value not only because of his mastery of the language but also because the purposes in which he enlisted that verbal facility are relevant to modern concerns. In Davis's case, moreover, we may reverse Buffon's adage and declare that the man himself was style, a self-consciousness regarding manners and dress that likewise was reflected in his writings.

I think it is useful to begin here with a brief discussion of an essay Davis wrote in 1890, early in his career and at the start of his association with *Harper's Weekly*. Like so much of RHD's apprentice writing, it was not reprinted in his collected works, but it is in my opinion an accomplished exercise, a virtual tour de force. It certainly differs from much of Davis's work during his apprentice years, which was written for newspapers and though vividly graphic is relatively bald and ungraceful in execution.

Arthur Lubow explains that Davis was inspired to write this piece, which he defined as a "prose poem," by translations from the French symbolists and that it is singular among his early works. An experiment in style, it was a demonstration by Davis of his range of descriptive powers and proved to be an important transition piece, a bridge from his early, purely reportorial work to the travel writings and subsequent wartime journalism that brought him fame. But it can also be seen as belonging to that genre we now call feature writing, being much more personal in tone and more intensely descriptive than news reporting, emphasizing what was called "local color."

Most important, the essay displays in short form the stylistic qualities of Davis's writing which attracted contemporary readers and which I feel still recommend him to us today. A period piece, undeniably, it nonetheless demonstrates those human sympathies, displayed against a detailed scenic backdrop, that represent the best aspect of the sentimentalism so characteristic of the age, underwritten by a pervasive idealism yet photographic in realistic detail. The sentimental is a quality not much found in Davis's subsequent journalistic writing and will be channeled chiefly into his fiction, so that this early essay is a rare integration of those qualities of realism and romanticism that would subsequently part company in his writings, and as such it provides a key to the implicit wholeness of his work.

Titled "A Summer Night on the Battery," the essay begins by defining the ancient waterfront of lower Manhattan as "a sort of physical protest which the city of New York makes against itself. It is the one place where the New Yorker can put the city behind him, can turn his back on its close hot streets, its blazing shop fronts, and his tenement or his second floor back" (34: 594). Where other city parks are surrounded by great buildings, with windows that take away any feeling of privacy, reminders of the continued sprawl of Manhattan northward, the Battery puts all vestiges of the metropolis behind it and has benches placed "with their backs to the town, with nothing between them and the broad, free river but the rows of stone posts and the iron chains that swing between them. And here the Battery says to the city proper, 'So far shall you go and no further.'"

As Davis must have known, the Battery took its name from the site of old Dutch fortifications, designed to defend the city from invaders, but now, as he points out, it protects the residents of southernmost Manhattan from the city. More recently, as Davis notes, it provided a "fashionable promenade" in the days "before the mob knocked the leaden crowns off the iron railing which still encircles Bowling Green. . . . But as the town grew and fashion moved north with it, the Battery was left to the unfashionables, and to-day the Four Hundred know it only as the place where emigrants loiter before they become policemen, or begin cutting each other with poniards in Mulberry Street." The humor of this remark may offend modern readers, but ethnic slurs were common to contemporary periodicals, reflecting the tensions of a democracy expressed likewise in the allusions to the removal by the post-Revolutionary "mob" of decorative crowns traceable to New York's colonial past.

More to the point, however, is Davis's allusion to the Four Hundred, an epithet that in 1890 was of recent coinage. It is credited by the *Dictionary of American Biography* to Ward McAllister, the social arbiter of Manhattan, who on a specific occasion in 1892 limited to that number those persons in New York City who were considered to be members of "society," but was apparently in circulation somewhat earlier. McAllister spent nine months of the year in Newport and much of the winter in Savannah, giving validity to Davis's remark that "when the Four Hundred want to protest against the city, they have only to leave it," whereas "the longshoreman, and the young clerk, and the girl bachelor, and the family who live in two rooms, into one of which the sun beats all day," must find escape in the Battery: "It is their roof garden, their rocks at Bar Harbor, their surf at Narragansett, and their annual transatlantic voyage. They flock there these warm nights as soon as supper is finished, for the Battery's visitors dine in the middle of the day, and if you go there you will leave them behind you when you move homeward at midnight."

This is followed by a long descriptive paragraph, reminiscent of the opening chapter of *Moby-Dick,* but with quite a different meaning, describing as it does not a lonely crowd yearning for the open sea but people who desire merely to escape the stifling heat of the city in August: "A long crescent-shaped row of them, all with their backs to the city and with their faces to the open river."

> Some of them sit there and read in the wavering light from the electric lamps, and others have friends to talk with, or their wives, or the girls they are thinking would make good wives. Family groups composed of papa, and mamma, and the baby go there every night, and drink in the free salty air from the bay, and rest their eyes from the bricks and cobblestones with the sight of the green grass and the heavily leaved trees, even though they do look strangely theatrical and artificial in the electric light; and the young girls who chaperon each other, and young men who follow them and throw them into convulsive giggles by humorous remarks of a

gallant and complimentary nature. It is a very lively promenade indeed, for with all the life and motion of the visitors there is added all the life and noise from the river, the signalling of the steam-whistles, and the hilarious shouts and splashes of the boys in the free bathing-houses anchored close to the stone embankment. But you will find that the greater part of the visitors are alone—emigrants lately landed, who have come across the street from the licensed emigrants' boarding-house; longshoremen pacing carefully through the crowd with a sleeping or ailing baby in their arms; girls who have been running about a store all day, or girls whose backs ache through standing for ten hours in front of a loom.

In his lifetime Richard Harding Davis was notoriously a snob who yearned for membership in the highest levels of New York society and when he could spent his own summers at the shore. But here he displays at least a journalistic sympathy with those New Yorkers whom O. Henry, a decade later, would call the "Four Million," a calculated response to McAllister's delimiting statistic. There is in the distinction made here by Davis and later by O. Henry a social awareness of class differences, not shaded by any ideology beyond a democratic antagonism toward those persons privileged by wealth to distance themselves from the harsher realities of life in the swarming city.

Stephen Crane would bring a sharper edge to that distinction, a radicalism not shared by Davis, although in his descriptions of the Hudson we find characteristics that would become trademarks of Crane's style, identified with the Impressionists of France but perhaps closer in Davis's case to Whistler's Nocturnes set along the Thames:

The river stretches across to New Jersey like a rough black mirror, until it reaches the shore that frames it with a darker edge of black, in which the lights of many colors and of varying brilliancy shine steadily, or sparkle and sputter like hundreds of great candles.

The cold blue electric lights on the Jersey shore show the wharves and the big lettering of the signs on the sheds as clearly as though it were day; green, red, and yellow lights shine like jewels on the yard-arms of the ships lying at anchor; square open fireplaces of light stand where a ferryboat landing makes a break in the dark line of the shore; and, above all, and in the foreground of all, is the pure strong flame that lights the pedestal and the great bronze figure holding it aloft, and welcoming and warning the voyager that he is entering into a land of liberty.

More of this follows, vividly descriptive prose characteristic of Davis's best journalistic writing, but I stop here with his account of Bartholdi's great statue, dedicated only five years earlier, and because of Emma Lazarus's poem immediately transformed from its original intention, as *Liberty Enlightening the World,* to a figure whose upraised torch lights the way for immigrants to the new land of promise. In that phrase that can easily slip by unnoticed, "welcoming and warning the voyager that he is entering into a land of liberty," we have a precise demonstration of the kinds of irony of which Davis was capable. For in his account of the multitudes swarming to the Battery in search of relief from the crowded conditions that they are forced to endure, we have a subtle dramatization of the price to be paid by those who seek to improve their fortunes by coming to America.

Davis goes on to observe of "the drama" provided by "the people who come and go on the promenade" that "the most interesting of all, perhaps, are those who walk or stand alone. There are so many of them in New York." With enforced solitude comes loneliness, a situation that permits the kind of sentimentalism for which Davis may be faulted but which also serves to draw the reader's sympathy toward the persons being described, not in the service of any social reform but merely to establish a common bond of humanity. It is the sort of thing for which O. Henry, once again, has been celebrated without acknowledging Davis's priority:

> Young people who seem to have no one to speak to, no one who cares to know them after working hours, and whom you will see standing in rows along the iron chains, looking out at the river, and each with his own thoughts, and each seeing something the others cannot see. There was an emigrant there the other night in sabots, and with metal buttons on his waistcoat, who stood like a statue, looking out beyond the river, as if he could look further to the sea beyond, or further yet to the land he came from on the other side of the sea; and a young girl, well-gloved, well-booted, such a girl bachelor as teaches in the public schools, with an air of gentle breeding, of having known something and of wanting something better than the Battery's crowd, who did not sit on the bench, but on the brink of the stone embankment, leaning her head wearily against one of the stone posts, with her back turned to the passing crowd. A longshoreman, sun-tanned, unshaven, and with his blue blouse open at the throat, dozed, tired out with his day's work, on the other side of it; but she did not seem to know that he was there, or that any one else was near her. She had her face turned to the river, and what she saw there, and

what comfort it gave here, no one could tell by looking at her face, except that now and then she raised her handkerchief to her eyes, and then crushed and twisted it in her hands.

Stephen Crane's Maggie she obviously is not, but Davis's weeping girl most certainly anticipates O. Henry's sad and lonely heroines buried in those "second floor backs" mentioned by Davis in his opening paragraph. His style likewise differs from Crane's starkly realistic manner or O. Henry's often slangy and city wise-guy pose, and because of the immediate models before him, it has a rhetorical rhythm, poetic in resonance, as if meant to be read aloud, and is rather theatrical in this aspect. More concentrated here than in his subsequent travel writings, this quality will nonetheless survive as a defining characteristic of Davis's descriptive passages.

Davis's theatricality is also revealed in such flourishes as the repetition of "above all, and in the foreground of all," in his description of the Statue of Liberty, as well as in an earlier reference to the river as "a great drop-curtain for a background to the crowd" gathered along the Battery. But it is for his purposes an effective manner, reaching out toward this readers with a direct appeal to their emotions: "These are the sort of people to whom the Battery and the salt air that wings across it and the green trees over it is real, and to whom it is a relief. Its lights and its mysterious shadows gliding up and across the river, and its situation on the very stepping-off place of New York city, make it always new and foreign, and in consequence restful to them, and perhaps of interest even to you."

"Make it always new and foreign" is the clue to Davis's notion of his role as a journalist, keying this tour de force of description to his underlying romantic impulse, on the one hand, and to the reporter's quest for novelty, on the other. "Make It New" was the slogan of a superlative American master of style of the last century, himself indebted to the French symbolists, which is not to measure Davis on the same scale as Ezra Pound. Pound sought to give new life to the English language and to poetry itself by searching for forms and stylistic constructs that would regenerate meaning. Davis merely sought to throw a new light on familiar subjects, to bring into prominence the exotic aspects of what were to his readers familiar scenes and subjects. In the quest for the "new and foreign," he left New York for many faraway places but for the most part was frustrated in his search. Yet ever and again he made it new, made it—to borrow his favorite word regarding the journalistic necessity—"interesting." In so doing, he made what he saw his own, aligning it with his romantic perspective while never neglecting to point out what paradoxes and irony the scene before him yielded.

: III :

In the chapters that follow I will be following RHD's travels far afield in search of subjects new, but I end this discussion of his journalistic abilities and interests with Davis's visits as the editor of *Harper's Weekly* to the Columbian World's Fair in Chicago in 1892 and 1893. If some mention of RHD is necessary to any account of American popular culture in the 1890s, so is some mention of the fair. The exposition was seen at the time as an epochal celebration not only of the progress that had taken place on the North American continent over the five hundred years since Columbus's arrival but also of the material advances made in the United States during the thirty years following the end of the Civil War. Recently, it has been regarded as an overweening expression of nascent American imperialism, which as a commemoration of Columbus's voyage to the New World could also be read as presaging the death of the Spanish empire.

During the first two years of Davis's editorship of *Harper's Weekly,* which began early in 1891, stories about the coming attractions of the fair were a regular feature, often written by the staff journalist, Julian Ralph. These were accompanied with full-page illustrations taken from the designs for the sumptuous and grandiose buildings of Beaux Arts design that were to spring up like Aladdin's palace on the shores of Lake Michigan. Ralph's articles for *Harper's* about the construction and organization of the exposition were later gathered into a book in time for the official opening of the fair. In them he expressed the amazement and awe the exhibits were intended to evoke in visitors who wandered through what was obviously intended to be more a celebration of the future than the past.

From our present perspective, perhaps the most famous visitor to the fair was Henry Adams, who in his *Education* declared that the "Exposition itself defied philosophy" (339). But then, after lingering in the shadow of Richard Hunt's Beaux Arts dome, in emulation of Edward Gibbon seating himself in the ruins of the Capitol in Rome, Adams felt moved to prophecy, if darkly. He declared that Chicago was here asking "for the first time the question whether the American people knew where they were driving," and if one were to attempt to provide an answer to that question, "one must start" with the fair in Chicago, which "was the first expression of American thought as a unity" (343; cf. Trachtenberg, *Incorporation* 219).

Davis was not inspired by the exposition to any such cosmic thoughts. Before the official opening of the fair in May 1893, he, along with many other prominent persons, was sent a list of thirty-three questions by the American Press Association. All had a common theme: what the United States would be like a hundred years hence in 1993, and the responses were published in newspapers across the country so as to stir up interest in the great event. They predictably ranged from the utopian to the utilitarian and were generally optimistic concerning the 1990s, with frequent mention of the blessings that science—often citing the example of Thomas Alva Edison—would shower on the country over the next hundred years. By contrast, the young managing editor of *Harper's Weekly* politely declined to answer any of the questions: "They are," Davis explained, "too solemn" (Walter 101).

After all, RHD was no "futurist." He was a journalist and therefore interested professionally in contemporary events only. His response to the questionnaire also reflects the bumptiousness of a youth early raised to prominence, and much of what he had to say about the fair in his *Harper's* pieces is likewise facetious. Davis did, however, express admiration for its appearance and design, and the fair, as it were, admired him in return: just back from a trip to England when he traveled to Chicago for the dedication ceremonies in October 1892, Davis was not unhappy to be mistaken several times for the Prince of Wales.

Though displeased by the accommodations with which he was provided, located far from the fair and lacking a bathroom, Davis declared himself enraptured by "the wonderful beauty and magnitude of the World's Fair buildings. . . . [W]hen I saw them around the lagoon, in front of the main entrance, I wanted to be left entirely alone with them, as one wants to be left alone in front of a beautiful landscape or a great picture" (*Harper's Weekly* 36: 1038). As his account of the scenic backdrop of the Battery suggests, Davis had a strong aesthetic impulse, which carries through all his travel writings.

New York had hoped to host the fair, but its efforts were undercut when covert efforts to manipulate the decision were revealed. Like Julian Ralph, Davis was forced to admit that Chicago had succeeded where so many New Yorkers had thought (even hoped) the western city would fail: Ralph unavoidably stressed the sheer magnitude of the exposition, being "of unparalleled magnificence and interest and more nearly universal in character than any that has ever been held" (v). Wrote Davis, "If we doubted Chicago's taste in the past, and if the country was slow and is slow in believing she has shown it so wonderfully in these buildings" (*Harper's Weekly* 36: 1038). He insisted that the fair must be seen in all its glorious reality to be believed: "The day the stranger from the outside world visits Chicago and sees these buildings and lakes and pleasure-grounds merging into one another and forming one great picture, he becomes at once an advance agent and a herald for this World's Fair, and he is proud of his country and of her artists, and of Chicago and her men of business, who have shown that they are men of taste as well."

He hoped, Davis wrote in *Harper's,* to return to the Fair "when there are no dedication exercises to interfere with the broad sweep of her hospitality." But having spent the intervening months traveling about the world itself, RHD had to put off that return trip for almost a year, until October 1893, when the fair was about to close. His second article repeated his earlier emphasis, that the fair had to be seen to be appreciated, and Davis once again went into raptures over the architecture of the White City, declaring that the one thing that should not be missed "is the illumination of the Court of Honor at night" (*Harper's Weekly* 37: 1002).

Clearly, it was the aesthetic spectacle provided by the fair that most moved Davis. He virtually ignored the displays of industrial arts, the sort of thing that inspired exuberant enthusiasm in other accounts of the Columbian Exposition, and failed to praise Chicago's answer to the Eiffel Tower, the much ballyhooed Ferris Wheel. "If the fair has taught us nothing else," Davis concluded, "it has taught us to take our pleasure in beautiful places," and he predicted, quite correctly, that the influence of the fair would be demonstrated "in the architecture of every new State or Federal building, and in the artistic value of every statue that asks for a pedestal in a public park."

Equally important in Davis's view was the organization that had gone into making sure that the component parts of the complicated mechanism that was the exposition ran on time and in an orderly manner: "Things move so smoothly in the White City that one hardly appreciates how much is owing to those who help to make them move smoothly, and who are known by their works." If Chicago had indeed "arrived," it was thanks to the "executive part" of the fair, that invisible but pervasive dimension now called "infrastructure."

Where Henry Adams was abstract in his conclusions about the meaning of the fair, Davis in 1893 was specific and gave Adams's notion of "unity" a pragmatic dimension. For if the fair had a lesson for Americans, it was in the way Chicago went about creating it, not keeping "the designing and the entire work of the building up of the fair to her own people" but bringing the "best men in their several lines of work" not only from every state in the Union but also from many parts of the Old World: "This is her triumph, and this is where she showed herself as big and generous and unafraid as her citizens have always claimed to be." What had been earlier thought of as "the Chicago Fair" is now called "the World's Fair, and the people of Boston and New York tell you how proud 'we' should be, and how well 'our' fair compares with others" (1002).

Like Adams, Davis saw the fair in terms of an expansive democracy, a centripetal gathering together of artisans and artifacts that when the power was finally turned on had a centrifugal implication, all those foreign exhibits gathering representatives of established and emerging nations together under the aegis of the American flag. Davis's preference for the purity of the fair's architecture was an expression of his aesthetic idealism, but the frozen parade of neoclassical facades that was the White City had a subtext for those who, like Adams, could read as they sat contemplating the spectacle.

There is in Davis's concluding celebration of the effort in Chicago a latent imperialism, a sense that what was accomplished on the shores of Lake Michigan was an event of cosmic significance. The year 1893 was also when Frederick Jackson Turner read his famous obsequy for the American frontier before the annual meeting of the American Historical Society, held at the Columbian Exposition, and asked aloud what would happen to all those pioneer energies, so dramatically and variously displayed at the fair, now that the safety valve had been shut off.

It would prove to be a leading question, given added point by the structure erected on the fairgrounds by the Boone and Crockett Club of New York, a replicated log cabin, icon of the old frontier, to say nothing of the presence nearby of Buffalo Bill's Wild West Show. For in choosing to lend a neoclassical decor to the exposition, the architects were consciously evoking the old Roman example, an intense Palladianism that was the proper style for a newly emerging empire. Alan Trachtenberg confirms this connection, noting that "the imperial implications of that Roman dream would soon materialize in more brutal forms, in the Cuban and Philippine invasions of 1898, in McKinley's 'Open Door' to incorporation beyond these shores" (*Incorporation* 230).

The implication of the White City was of a piece with those battleships that were authorized by Congress in 1890. In that year, Captain Alfred Thayer Mahan, the emerging champion of naval preparedness, anticipated Turner's question by suggesting the direction in which American energies should be expanded, positing that the completion of the long-planned and often-delayed Nicaraguan Canal would necessitate a national presence in the Caribbean, unless ascendancy in that western Mediterranean was to be conceded to England. During the years of Davis's editorship, *Harper's Weekly* reported regularly on the growth of the new navy and published a graphic demonstration of America's naval inferiority in the number given for September 12, 1891. It showed the relative size of the navies of the Western world, Great Britain pictured as a giant sailor in arms towering over the rest, the smallest being a veritable midget in uniform—identified as the United States.

Harper's also devoted a page on April 4, 1891, to "The Government's Exhibit at the Columbian Exposition," emphasizing by means of an illustration the display planned by the Navy Department, "a structure resembling in every detail a 10,000 ton battle ship, like the *Indiana,* the *Massachusetts,* or the *Oregon,* now building" (35: 240). Described in *Harper's* as "an object-lesson," this exhibit was surely, in Henry Adams's term, "educational," as was the news that the anniversary replicas of Columbus's tiny fleet of caravels were being towed from Spain to America with an escort of U.S. warships.

But perhaps the most significant lesson of all was conveyed by a large painting exhibited at the fair by the American artist Walter L. Dean, titled *Peace.* As reported in *Harper's Weekly* in March 1893, the six-by-nine-foot canvas represented "the White Squadron at anchor in Boston Harbor," the "flag-ship *Chicago*" in the foreground with "the cruisers *Newark, Atlanta, Yorktown,* and *Boston*" providing the backdrop, and "the historic yacht *America* . . . running up the harbor between the *Chicago* and the *Atlanta.*" The painting was reproduced in the magazine in a full-page illustration, and the title was explained in the accompanying article by the observation that the artist, "in common with a great many other people, believes that one of the most effective ways of maintaining peace is to be prepared for war" (37: 286).

Further if implicit commentary on Dean's painting was provided the following month, in the short article "The Hawaiian Situation," which had resulted from the recent forced deposition by American planters and missionaries of Princess Kaiulani and the establishment of a provisional government that looked to the United States for direction and annexation. While arguing that despite the troublesome situation on the island, with threats of violence against Americans, there was at present no necessity for annexation, the article coupled a picture of Princess Kaiulani with one of

the USS *Boston,* one of two "modern steel vessels carrying heavy ord-
nance . . . at anchor in the harbor of Honolulu." As things turned out, law
and order were restored—or enforced—by a party of armed sailors sent
ashore from the warship, and the picture of the *Boston* not only replicates
Dean's painting but also provides assurances of the "peace" of his title: "If
there is danger to be feared from the populace, there is plenty of force at
hand for the protection of the whites and other foreigners" (299).

As editor of *Harper's,* Davis was surely aware of these stories, and his article "Last Days of the Fair" shares the page with a story about "the armored
cruiser, *New York,* now lying at the Brooklyn Navy-yard," advertised as "'the
most aggressive war-ship ever put into commission'" and described as
"white and clean" on the outside and inside a display of orderly "perfection," in effect a miniature in steel of the exposition. That is, from Chicago's
White City and Walter Dean's White Squadron in 1893 to Theodore Roosevelt's White House in 1901 and his White Fleet in 1908 would prove to be a
very short reach. And for Richard Harding Davis the architectonics of the
fair were an overwhelming vision of orderly perfection, the sort of thing associated with the imperial impulse: "If Chicago wants to do so," Davis observed, "she can . . . rear a Rock of Gibraltar" (36: 1038).

The stories published in *Harper's Weekly* that coupled the World's Fair
with the flexing of the nation's new military muscle were synchronized with
the thinking of a number of powerful men. They believed that the continental shores of the United States no longer represented limits but were
more correctly thought of as flexible borders opening to an expanding
sphere of influence. Prominent among them was Henry Adams, for whom
the fair was prognostic of a new national direction, much as the Spanish-
American War would later give him "for the first time in his life . . . a sense
of possible purpose working itself out in history" (*Education* 363).

Adams in 1896 would provide Senator Don Cameron a position paper on
the U.S. interest in the ongoing insurrection in Cuba, in effect a legal brief
for American intervention that was not only in harmony with the expansionist dream of his disciple and friend Henry Cabot Lodge but also, to
Adams's way of thinking, a logical (perhaps inevitable) extension of his
grandfather's argument set forth in what became known as the Monroe
Doctrine. Now, at long last, Adams reflected in his *Education,* "he could see
that the family work of a hundred and fifty years fell at once into the grand
perspective of true empire building" (363–64).

Again, these were not the kinds of thoughts RHD entertained about the
fair or about the Spanish-American War. And yet that both he and Adams

were visitors to the Columbian Exposition and that in 1896 Davis was in his own way preparing the United States for war with Spain are elements in a transcendent synchronicity. These elements are as important as Davis's keeping company with Colonel Roosevelt in Cuba, for despite their different points of view, Adams and Davis were both heading in the same direction. In 1898 Adams found that the war, like the fair, was an educating experience, for "it taught something exceedingly serious, if not ultimate, could one trust the lesson." And Richard Harding Davis, for his own part and for his own ends, played an important role in conveying to Americans the lessons of that war, though his conclusions were a matter of particulars and lacked Adams's "grand perspective."

But it was Davis's war, not Adams's, that Americans thought they were fighting, and for reasons that Davis had articulated for the citizens of the United States, from whom the friend and mentor of Henry Cabot Lodge had maintained a lifelong distance. Adams, with an egregious display of false modesty, claimed to have contributed nothing to the last and greatest culmination of the ancestral work, the conquest of Cuba, and took ironic consolation from his version of the Miltonic homily: "He too serves a certain purpose who only stands and cheers" (364). It was Adams's friend and Lodge's protégé Theodore Roosevelt who became famous for having fought in the war, but Roosevelt's fame was largely the work of Richard Harding Davis, from whom so many Americans learned what they would know about the conflict in Cuba.

O glorious to be a human boy!
CHARLES DICKENS

---

3 : AT PLAY IN THE FIELDS OF FORCE

: I :

Roger Burlingame's tribute to Richard Harding Davis in 1927 is included in his introduction to a collection of Davis's short fiction, and while the editor kept Davis's "heroic figure in the background of my mind," he also kept "the younger reader . . . in the foreground of my thought." As the literature of romance had given way in the 1920s to that "strong bias toward realistic fiction" shared by Burlingame, he felt that if Davis was to survive as a writer, it would be because his "appeal is primarily to youth," an epitaph of sorts that contains a complexity of implications (Burlingame viii).

The inescapable conjunction of Davis and Roosevelt toward which we are moving should remind us that much as RHD's contemporaries testified to the eternal boy in the man, it was a tribute often (at times in derision) accorded TR as well. In Mark Twain's blighted view, occasioned by the U.S. presence in the Philippines, Roosevelt was an overgrown Tom Sawyer, whereas Davis's friends put a kindly construct on RHD's essentially juvenile character. We have Anthony Hope Hawkins's amusement over Davis's penchant for collecting medals of dubious origins, and there is the testimony of Charles Dana Gibson, RHD's friend and illustrator, recalling his first meeting with Davis: "I can see Dick now dressed [for boating] in a rough brown suit, a soft hat, with a handkerchief about his neck, a splendid, healthy, clean-minded, gifted boy at play. And so he always remained" (*R.H.D.* 31).

Davis was, testified a friend and a contemporary, "almost too good to be true," for whom life was always something of a game. In the year before Dick Davis's death, the friend testified that "we have played at pirates together, at the taking of sperm whales; and we have ransacked the Westchester Hills for gunsites against the Mexican invasion" (*R.H.D.* 3). "He was youth incarnate," wrote his fellow war correspondent and novelist John Fox Jr., "ruddy, joyous, vigorous, adventurous, self-confident youth" (63).

Here again we can acknowledge Robert Louis Stevenson's priority, not only in his celebrated youthfulness but in the author's own association of literary romanticism with the games and daydreams of youth. At the start of Stevenson's career as a novelist, boys made up a large percentage of his readership, beginning with his young stepson, for whom *Treasure Island* was originally written. In this Stevenson anticipated those other authors associated with the new romanticism, including Anthony Hope Hawkins, Arthur Conan Doyle, and H. Rider Haggard, whose unlikely but fast-paced tales of adventure most certainly attracted if they did not actually court a youthful readership.

Boys' books, after all, are a traditional vehicle for romance, a kind of permitted territory, as the continuity of Defoe, Scott, Fenimore Cooper, Captain Marryat, and R. M. Ballantyne suggests, those writers to whom the new romanticists, following Stevenson's lead, looked for inspiration. We may add Richard Harding Davis to that list, for although he has had no lasting fame as a writer for young readers—despite the younger Burlingame's prediction—his first book, published in 1891, was a collection that advertised itself in its title—*Stories for Boys*. Although it appeared early in Davis's career, the book has a value well beyond it intended appeal for young readers, thanks to one story in the collection, "The Reporter Who Made Himself King." Looked at closely, it demonstrates the author's awareness of the expansive geopolitics of his day, albeit placed in a humorous frame.

The title of the story was obviously taken from Rudyard Kipling's famous tale of imperial ambitions balked by the primitive realities of Afghanistan, a narrative that was in Davis's list of stories he admired. Kipling's tale had been given a brief (and dismissive) synopsis by Andrew Lang in 1890 as "the legend of the wanderer with the head of his crowned and dead comrade in his wallet" (688). But in Davis's hands Kipling's situation was given a light and comic treatment, making the subject appropriate for a youthful readership even while preserving the anti-imperialistic burden.

Written at the start of Davis's dual career as reporter and writer of fiction, the story evidences the factual basis of his most imaginative flights. Equally important, it mingles elements of farce derived from current international events while evoking the exaggerated notion of the Monroe Doctrine that would characterize U.S. policy in years to come. Though hardly a celebration but rather a burlesque of the new imperialism, it brings together elements that soon enough would characterize the war that made its author the king of reporters and the United States an international presence. All in all, the story is an amazing performance, which young readers could enjoy but which had a serious message for a mature audience.

Burlingame included "The Reporter Who Made Himself King" in his collection of Davis's short fiction in 1927, and it remains a story well worth consideration, whereas the other tales with which it first appeared can for the most part be justly neglected. But all stories in the collection were about athletic competition, a subject that reflected the growing interests of boys in the 1880s and 1890s. Whether sailing or tennis or swimming or baseball or football, organized sports is the common theme, and the cover of the first edition of *Stories for Boys* was decorated with tennis rackets, baseball bats and balls, and "three little sloops under full sail," with the title embossed in gold inside a football (Quinby 19). The subjects both attest to Davis's own participation in college football and cricket and provide a suitable frame for the most important story in the collection, which not only had to do with sports but also was chiefly concerned with war, a distinction not easily made by prominent writers of Davis's generation.

Theodore Roosevelt regarded both athletics and warfare as regenerative exercises, and he included as frontispiece to *The Strenuous Life* (1900) a photograph of himself on horseback leaping over a split-rail fence on his daily ride across the then untenanted reaches of Chevy Chase. This picture was undoubtedly included lest the reader forget Roosevelt's famous ride up San Juan Hill, but it served too as a reminder of his western adventures and was symbolic also of his commitment to the benefits of strenuous exercise, a stress essential to the emerging Roosevelt myth.

During 1893, the last year of Davis's editorship, there appeared in *Harper's Weekly* an essay by Roosevelt on the value of athletic training, which, while lamenting needless violence on the playing field, regarded sports as promoting "the virtues which go to make up a race of statesmen and soldiers, of pioneers and explorers by land and sea, of bridge-builders and road-makers, of commonwealth builders—in short, upon those virtues for the lack of which, whether in an individual or in a nation, no amount of refinement and learning, of gentleness and culture, can possibly atone. These are the very qualities which are fostered by vigorous, manly out-of-door sports, such as mountaineering, big-game hunting, riding, shooting, rowing, football, and kindred games." In passing, Roosevelt noted "the career of Washington, who was a devoted fox-hunter, and whose fox-hunting doubtless helped to make him a good general in after-life," but his emphasis finally was on football, of which "there is no better sport," promoting not only "the qualities of manliness and fair play, but especially in those of courtesy and generosity to the vanquished," virtues necessarily associated with the chivalric tradition (37: 1236).

Equally to the point was a full-page illustration published in *Harper's*

Out of the Game. *This illustration from* Harper's Weekly *suggests the closeness
of playing fields and fields of battle in the popular mind during the 1890s.*

Weekly on October 31, 1891, titled *Out of the Game,* showing a player lying unconscious on the field as an injured teammate raises his hand for help, an
image clearly martial in implication. Davis accompanied the illustration
with an editorial commentary in which he assured anxious parents of players that the boy was not seriously hurt. He urged his readers to save their
pity for those former college stars, now grown men, who are forced to watch
from the sidelines, players now truly "out of the game": "They envy this
youth who has just been borne off the field limp and a little bloody, because
they know he will be back on it in a day or two, while they must keep behind
the ropes for the rest of the season, and for all the other seasons to come"
(35: 843).

On the page opposite the picture is an essay by Yale's famous (and Frederic Remington's) coach Walter Camp, titled "Team Play in Foot-ball."
Camp's contribution is another reflection of Davis's interest as editor in promoting college sports, especially "the Game" that so closely mimicked the
danger and excitement associated with warfare. "The day will come," Davis
warned present-day football players who were scornful of the "has-beens"
watching from the sidelines, "when you would give all you have earned on

the street that month to be out on the frozen field in your dirty patched uniform, and to feel the blood tingle with the cold, and hear the roll and shock
of the college yells as they sweep over your head, and to see out of the corner of your eye the high black masses at the sides . . . and the sudden rise
and fall of the flags, and to delight once again in your own strength and in
the resistance to it."

On July 4, 1891, there had appeared in *Harper's* a profile by Davis of two
college athletes, comparing the first, Arthur Cummock, the plucky captain
of the Harvard football team, to Lieutenant C. J. W. Grant, a courageous
British officer in India who had recently been awarded the Victoria Cross for
conspicuous gallantry in battle. Davis had previously honored Grant in
a May 16, 1891, article, describing Grant's story "as too good . . . to be
true," reading "like one of those Mr. Rudyard Kipling invents" (35: 363). The
July 4 story was also about Frederick Brokaw, a player on the Princeton
team, who lost his life trying to save one of his mother's female servants
from drowning: "The mother who saw him die must know that there are
mothers whose sons are alive to-day who will perhaps outlive them, and
who yet envy her seeing her son die, dying as her son did" (35: 495). The
subtle association here between organized sports and warfare is undeniable, reinforcing Roosevelt's point made in 1893.

In his *Stories for Boys,* Davis emphasized over and again the ideal of good
sportsmanship, that winning the game is not the main idea; rather, playing
it to the best of one's ability without cheating or complaining when one
loses is what sports are all about. To drive home the point he has older
youths, college athletes, taking the time to instruct younger boys in sports
and sportsmanship, and one of the best of the tales, "The Story of a Jockey,"
is about a young rider who refuses to throw a race for gain, his love for his
horse and fair play overruling any temptation.

We cannot dismiss this emphasis merely as the result of the didacticism
demanded by editors of children's books and periodicals of the day; it seems
to have been essential to RHD's character, indeed was endemic to contemporary mores, as the emergence of team sports during the 1890s indicates.
If idealism was a characteristic of the new romantic writers, so it manifests
itself also in this repeated insistence on fair play by Davis and his contemporaries and is essential to the version of chivalry that was emerging in tan-
dem with the new American empire, which gives the testimony of Theodore
Roosevelt in 1893 further weight.

In 1890 RHD was something of an innovator in choosing sports as the
subject matter for a boy's book. At the age of fourteen Davis had boasted to

his father the he was "going to write a story that will raise my name to fame above that of Mark Twain," but if Davis thought of Mark Twain as his chief competition as a writer for boys, we look in vain for games or sports in Twain's stories (Lubow 27). The simple fact is that Sam Clemens based his most important novels on personal recollections of boyhood in Missouri in the 1830s and 1840s, a place and a time where organized sports were non-existent. Even in New England before the Civil War, games were largely im-provised, like the great snowball fight in T. B. Aldrich's autobiographical *Story of a Bad Boy* (1870).

Paradoxically, it is only in Louisa Alcott's *Little Women* (1868) that a game with rules plays an important function, the croquet match that reveals the poor sportsmanship of a visiting English boy, perhaps inspired by Great Britain's equivocal behavior during the recent war. I say "paradoxically" be-cause the book was aimed at girls and because good sportsmanship was as-sociated with British boyhood, thanks in large part to Thomas Hughes's *Tom Brown's Schooldays* (1857). And it was Hughes's popular book that surely contributed to the rise of organized sports in the United States following the Civil War, associated in the case of football—the American version of rugby—with life in college, where the game was gaining national atten-tion, which Davis would assist through the pages of *Harper's Weekly*.

By 1890 the new generation of writers, including not only Davis but also Crane and Norris, had played sports in college, but it was Davis who first saw the literary potential of sports competition, being a demonstration of the "red-blooded vigor" that an exponent of the new romanticism regarded as a chief and admirable characteristic of the new romantic heroes (Burton 89). These implicit links between romance and organized sports and be-tween games and warfare would provide a chain of association that con-tributed greatly to the popular enthusiasm for U.S. involvement in the Spanish-American War, which by RHD's account was a version of what Kip-ling called "the Great Game," though it was perhaps chess, not field sports, that the British writer had in mind.

Moreover, it was in "The Reporter Who Made Himself King" that Davis began the process of writing the Spanish-American War, for the story is amazingly prophetic even if told for humorous effect. The hero is a young reporter named Albert Gordon (a tribute to Davis's Anglophilia, evoking both the prince regent and the martyr hero of Khartoum), and is clearly modeled after the author, in combination with Stephen Bonsal. For, having left college and football (Yale) for a career in journalism at age eighteen, Gordon, like Davis and Bonsal, has had considerable success. By the time he

PUCK.

Who cares if old J. B.
Is monarch of the sea?
I'm not afraid if his Free Trade scoops all my biz from me.

I seek a greater fame,
And get there all the same,
I can knock creation to all tarnation at the glorious National Game!
Play Ball!

Cartoon from the humor magazine Puck, *1890s, in which the "National Game" of baseball (obviously a rough sport in its day) serves as a consoling equivalent to Britain's reputation as ruler of the high seas, which the United States would soon challenge.*

Cover illustration from the humor magazine Judge, June 1898, clearly inspired by the U.S. victory over Spain and celebrating the nation's acquisition of the Philippines, so recent a territory as to result in a misspelling.

turned twenty-one he "had become a great reporter, and had been to Presidential conventions in Chicago, revolutions in Hayti, Indian outbreaks on the Plains, and midnight meetings of moonlighters [i.e., Klansmen] in Tennessee, and had seen what work earthquakes, floods, fire, and fever could do in great cities, and had contradicted the President, and borrowed matches from burglars" (8).

The young reporter regrets, however, not having found the opportunity to become a war correspondent, no war having obliged him for that purpose, an omission "very disappointing to young Gordon, and he was more and more keenly discouraged" (9). Thinking instead to turn his hand to writing a novel, the reporter signs on as assistant to the newly appointed consul to a mid-Pacific island called Opeki. The older man is a veteran of the Civil War seeking an easy berth, but when he finds out his official residence is a hut in a crude native village, he immediately decamps, leaving all responsibilities and honors (including his dress uniforms) to young Gordon.

There are three other white men on the island, including another young American named Stedman and a father and son named Bradley, who are deserters from a British man-of-war. Stedman is stationed there to handle the far end of an uncompleted transpacific cable. Being from Connecticut, he is something of an inventor, having installed a water system made of bamboo pipes (superfluous in the rainy season, which occupies much of the year) and street lamps not as yet brought to full operating condition. The inventor and his reporter friend decide to bring further blessings of civilization to the island, impressing the king of the villagers with their diplomatic uniforms and many medals as a start in the right direction and instructing the natives in the art of baseball, the all-American game.

Learning that traditional hostilities exist between the villagers and a much wilder tribe that lives in the neighboring mountains, Gordon takes the side of the local king, who appoints him prime minister of war. With Stedman and the two Bradleys bearing rifles, Gordon sets out to negotiate with the king of the "hillmen." Though he is successful in impressing the mountain tribe with his firepower, the situation becomes more complex when Gordon learns that the other king has already sold the island to a representative of the German empire, the captain of a warship, who shortly thereafter raises his nation's flag in front of the village. This is done over the objections of the youthful United States consul, who cites the Monroe Doctrine and the intolerance of the United States for a foreign power "near her coast" (83).

Thanks to Gordon's coaching, the native kings are equally unhappy with the threat of a heavy German presence and in desperation surrender their monarchies jointly to the reporter, thus warranting the title of the story. While the warship is still in the harbor, Gordon hauls down the German flag and raises the Stars and Stripes, accompanying his gesture of defiance with a blast from an antique brass cannon. But a single shell fired from the battleship destroys both cannon and flagpole, then ricochets through the village. The Germans depart, but the war, as it were, has only begun:

> "Great Heavens, Gordon!" cried Stedman; "they are firing on us."
> But Gordon's face was radiant and wild.
> "Firing on us!" he cried. "On us! Don't you see? Don't you understand? What do we amount to? They have fired on the American flag. Don't you see what that means? It means war. A great international war. And I am a war correspondent at last!" (91)

Though the German warship has left the harbor, Gordon anticipates that it will land its marines elsewhere on the island. He therefore orders Stedman to report the situation to his newspaper by cable and dictates a much expanded and dramatized account of the incident, in which the native king demands of "the American people that the Monroe doctrine will be sustained" (97). But all such messages must be relayed to the United States by another cable operator on the neighboring island of Octavia, and since that operator has invested heavily in the fading fortunes of the cable company, the story is further magnified en route to Gordon's home office.

The additions include an account of the massacre of American citizens, and when printed in the United States they create a great deal of excitement, resulting in cabled demands for more details. The German marines having failed to land, Gordon must make up a substanceless story with the negative news as its one fact, but the operator on Octavia dismisses the report as nonsense. He thwarts any attempt by Gordon to communicate the boring truth that nothing has happened on Opeki remotely resembling the wild stories already in circulation.

Instead, seeing the stock in his cable company rising and his personal fortunes with it, the Octavia operator has made up further fictitious news of the island war: "I killed off about a hundred American residents, two hundred English, because I do not like the English, and a hundred French. I blew up [the king] and his palace with dynamite, and shelled the city, destroying some hundred thousand dollars' worth of property. . . . I leave Octavia this afternoon to reap my just reward. I am in about $20,000 on your little war, and I feel grateful" (114–15).

The operator also informs Stedman and Gordon that the German warship had already arrived at San Francisco and that its captain had explained the truth of the matter, offering restitution for any damages, but too late, for "warships belonging to the several powers mentioned in my revised dispatches, had [already] started for Opeki at full speed, to revenge the butchery of the foreign residents. A word, my dear young friend, to the wise is sufficient. . . . Leave Opeki. If there's is no other way, swim. But leave Opeki" (116). In 1890 the wireless was as yet Marconi's dream, and once warships weighed anchor they in effect severed communications with their home base until they reached a port with a cable connection.

The young Americans and their British friends take the cable operator's advice that very evening, setting sail from Opeki in a small boat. And as the sun sets that evening, it illuminates the great hulls of six warships, heaving toward the island with smoke and sparks shooting from their stacks and flying the flags of Great Britain, France, and the United States, with "vengeance . . . written on every curve and line, on each straining engine rod, and on each polished gun muzzle" (117). The boys watch, "their faces lit by the glow of the setting sun and stirred by the sight of the great engines of war plunging past them on their errand of vengeance. . . . 'Stedman,' said the elder boy, in an awestruck whisper, and with a wave of his hand, 'we have not lived in vain'" (117–18).

Though a comic exercise, Davis's story is not the mere jeu d'esprit that it might appear, being much in debt to current geopolitics in the Pacific. It is this aspect that not only gives the presumed story for boys an adult dimension but also makes an even stronger connection between "The Reporter Who Made Himself King" and the emerging expansionist mood of the United States during the 1890s. That the troubles on Davis's imaginary island of Opeki begin with the arrival of a German warship keys his fanciful parable to very real events that had been unfolding on a very real Pacific island for a decade.

: II :

American attention had been drawn in the late 1880s to the Pacific zone because of the instability in Hawaii, a result of the activities of King Kalakaua, a corrupt monarch with imperialistic ambitions, but the closest contemporary parallel in 1890 was the situation in Samoa. Because of its convenient mid-Pacific location, by the 1870s the archipelago had attracted considerable interest on the part of Germany, Great Britain, and the United States. During the Grant administration, Colonel A. B. Steinberger was sent to

Samoa as a special agent but so embroiled himself with native political intrigues that (like Davis's Albert Gordon) he was made prime minister to the king.

Repeatedly calling for annexation of the islands by the United States, Steinberger became an embarrassment to the American consul and was removed with the help of a British warship. The native government nonetheless kept up the appeal for American protection, worried that Great Britain or Germany would increase their control over the archipelago. In response, President Rutherford Hayes signed a treaty with the Samoans that included the Americans' right to maintain a naval base at Pago Pago, thereby giving substance to a statement of goodwill regarding any threatened incursions by other powers, a document with considerable resonance for future U.S. foreign policy in tropical regions.

There followed in 1879 a conference on Samoa of the consuls representing the United States, Germany, and Great Britain, which in effect set up a tripartite arrangement calling for negotiations should any conflict between the great powers ensue, an agreement that was never ratified by the U.S. Senate but remained in effect for a number of years. But in 1884 Germany began to experience imperial ambitions and, with the leadership of Otto von Bismarck, pushed for greater control in Samoa, noting the preponderance of German residents there. The wily chancellor lured the British government into a formal agreement that would create separate zones of influence throughout the Pacific, with a view toward tightening Germany's grip on Samoa, implicitly with British concurrence.

This partnership left American interests in jeopardy, and indignant declarations were forthcoming from the U.S. State Department, which, lacking naval power to back them up, relied chiefly on moral suasion. This took the form of what John M. Dobson has called "mission statements" emphasizing "the moral interest of the United States with respect to the islands of the Pacific," identified with the independence of the Samoan population, which was endangered by the heavy presence of a foreign power on the island (43).

Receiving this declaration of principle, the United States consul at Apia took it further than had been intended and promptly but prematurely (again like Albert Gordon) ran the American flag up a pole and declared the Samoan islands a protectorate of his country. For their part, the Germans busied themselves sowing discontent among the natives, employing the ancient Caesarean maxim about division and conquest, and the Samoans themselves began to think of forming some sort of transpacific league of islands, an illusion fed by the imperialistic plans of Hawaii's King Kalakaua.

In 1887 yet another conference of the three powers was held, this time in Washington, and though nothing concrete resulted—Germany, Great Britain, and the United States each held out for its own interests—the failure was certainly an educational experience for U.S. geopoliticians, who began to realize that conversation, though civilized, had little weight if not backed by mechanisms of force. By now, moreover, Germany was popularly regarded in the United States as dangerously ambitious in its plans for imperial expansion and, if given a strong foothold in the Pacific, might actually prove a threat to the west coast of North America.

Further declarations by the United States on behalf of native independence were forthcoming but were again ignored by the Germans, who began to meddle in Samoan internal affairs, deporting a king hostile to their presence and placing a friendly puppet on the throne, a blatant display of power designed to gain control of the entire island. Moral suasion alone was an insufficient force against an expanding empire, and President Cleveland dispatched warships to Samoa in a final effort to forestall German aggression. But when they arrived the U.S. fleet found an equivalent force had been sent by Germany and Great Britain as well. In sum, the situation was very similar to the conclusion of RHD's "story for boys," except that nature intervened: a tropical storm hit Samoa with such destructive power that the warships of both Germany and the United States were beached or demolished: "The sailors," observed Dobson, "worked so hard to rescue one another that any thought of conflict dissipated" (45).

But at last Germany began to take seriously the threat of hostilities with the United States: Bismarck called for yet another three-power conference, this time in Berlin, and though no one was particularly pleased by the outcome, it reinstated the informal tripartite division that had been in effect until Bismarck began to flex his imperial muscles. The agreement did not end the unrest. Nothing but a strong United States (or German or British) presence would have accomplished that, but the U.S. authorities, including Secretary of State James G. Blaine, were unwilling to make any such commitment, and the Germans and the British were for their part reluctant to force the United States to do so.

"It was too soon for colonialism," Dobson concludes, and yet the Samoan matter was "an early indication of how the United States would respond when its expansion directly conflicted with that of powerful European nations" (46–47). Which is to say that without sufficient naval forces, the United States could only issue "mission statements," and it is of some interest that in 1890 the Congress at last authorized the modernization of the

U.S. Navy by funding the construction of a limited number of battleships. In effect the national hand had been forced by Germany, which is the substance of RHD's parable, as well as the subtext of Captain Mahan's big book, published that same year.

It should now be obvious that "The Reporter Who Made Himself King" is not simply a "boys' story" but was informed by what John Dobson, following the lead of Walter LaFeber, has viewed as a critical moment in the emergence of the United States as a "great power." Kipling's similarly entitled tale is about two ambitious con men who carry imperialism backed by Martini rifles and Freemasonic signs and symbols into a barbaric land bordering Afghanistan and are destroyed when their subjects discover they are not gods but mere men (an echo of Captain Cook's fate). Kipling's is more a fantasy than a story reflecting the machinations of the British Empire in the Far East—which would be the proper subject of *Kim,* yet another putative "boys' book."

By contrast, Davis picked up as if by instinct an episode for a short story that would serve as a prelude to the Spanish-American War a decade later, a conflict from which he would, to turn his own phrase, emerge as the king of reporters. His warring native tribes, the manipulative American presence, the definitive arrival of a German warship (named *Kaiser*), and the impromptu alliance between the United States and Great Britain (thanks to the presence of the two British deserters)—all have clear equivalents in the Samoan situation, which in 1889 had not reached its resolution.

But ten years later, with the Cuban troubles behind him, Hawaii annexed, and the Philippines in the process of being secured, President McKinley agreed to the formal partition of the archipelago between the three interested nations. By then the United States was a nation with a much stronger naval presence in the Pacific, and McKinley was backed by a popular mandate for expansion, always to be exercised in the name of promoting world peace and morality, the "blessings," as McKinley liked to say, of "our flag."

But in 1889, like the two young Americans fleeing the outcome of the situation they had precipitated, the United States was in no such strong position and had not yet made up its collective mind to undertake expansionist adventures, hence the comic tone of Davis's parable, which needs to be read as a caution against American interference in tropic zones. Of especial interest is Gordon's frequent references to the Monroe Doctrine, which in 1889 had no obvious relevance to a tiny island in the mid-Pacific and is therefore another comic touch. And yet by the end of the century the

Doctrine will have been cited to sanction the American presence in the Philippines, in reaction to an expressed interest in those islands by Germany.

Davis's story somewhat resembles R. M. Ballantyne's popular boys' book *Coral Island,* an imperial fable with a strong evangelical message. Ballantyne demonstrated how the conversion of Pacific islanders from paganism to Christianity turns them into docile future subjects of the queen, a missionary impulse that Davis pokes fun at in his burlesque by identifying the mechanics of civilization with baseball, not baptism. But by 1898, jingoes in the United States Congress were espousing Ballantyne's missionary idealism in an updated form, one having less to do with religious than with ideological evangelism.

Thus the reason for declaring war on Spain in 1898 was only superficially the explosion of the *Maine,* a new battleship of the kind authorized by Congress in 1890 and a paragon of modern war machinery, equivalent to the mock-up displayed at the Chicago World's Fair. The rationale for war was underwritten by the conviction that Spain, that ancient feudal empire, had been an abusive and repressive presence in the Western Hemisphere and should be driven off so that the native insurgents could form their own democratic republic on the model of the United States.

But then another evangelical program took over, fueled by the conviction that the natives in both Cuba and the Philippines were incapable of governing themselves and needed the assistance of the United States to bring them into the twentieth century. It was this jingoistic logic that outraged Mark Twain, who in 1901 fulminated against the imperial racketeering not only of the United States in the Philippines but also of Belgium in the Congo. Yet the presence of these colonial powers in tropic zones can be seen as having been warranted by Hank Morgan's explanation ten years earlier, in *A Connecticut Yankee in King Arthur's Court,* that he was going to haul a primitive (i.e., King Arthur's) people into the nineteenth (soon the twentieth) century by introducing to them the advantages of civilization. That is, Arthur's Britain during the Dark Ages can be seen as a reasonable equivalent to those benighted regions toward which Belgium and the United States were carrying the blessings of modern technology—the pole, as it were, for the flag.

Which brings us to RHD's borrowings from Twain's novel, first published in 1889, shortly before Davis wrote his own story for boys. The connection is chiefly centered in young Stedman, the cable operator from Connecticut with a gift for ingenious mechanical improvements. And Albert Gordon's desire to intervene in the affairs of a native island, so as to raise the standard of living close to a civilized level, is also equivalent to Hank Morgan's plan.

But changed circumstances allow Gordon to realize his other dream, of becoming a war correspondent, with consequences that come perilously close to the ending of Twain's novel, in which the flower of chivalry is destroyed, thanks to the horrible mechanisms of destruction introduced by the "Boss" toward the benign end of "improvement."

For Gordon's ambitious plans likewise lead to disaster, as the six great warships converge on Opeki, presumably with the intention of ridding it of the German menace by blowing the island to pieces. Where Twain's book is darkly savage in its satire, RHD's is lighthearted and is intended as a spoof of the ineptitude of American imperialism in the Pacific, not as a serious critique. Yet it does suggest that at least one perceptive contemporary read Mark Twain's medieval parable not as an imaginative fantasy, an experiment in time travel, but as an allegory of imperialism. "Mark Twain's Connecticut Yankee could not have done more," notes Emily S. Rosenberg, having given a list of the improvements brought to Cuba in 1899 by its American military commander, General Leonard Wood, following the defeat of Spain—everything from telephone and telegraph lines to public toilets (46).

Even as Davis was drawing on Twain's *Yankee* and the contemporary troubles in Samoa, he was proving remarkably prophetic regarding his own subsequent career as a war correspondent in Cuba. There is a familiar resonance in the situation that results in Gordon's cables being inflated by the agent on the island of Octavia, which in turn sets up a popular hysteria in the United States, inspiring what is now called a feeding frenzy on the part of American journalists: "Your paper beat them on the news, and now the home office is packed with San Francisco reporters, and the telegrams are coming in every minute" ("Reporter" 101).

As RHD would learn to his distress, a similar inflation and distortion was caused during the war in Cuba, not by cable operators but by lazy reporters in Tampa and zealous editors in New York. They made up stories when no news was coming in and wildly exaggerated what they did receive in order to boost circulation, a motive similar to that of the cable agent who sought to raise the value of his stock. Albert Gordon's hoped-for war is a result of his ambitions to report it, making it necessary that he leave the island before it is blown away, and no one can deny the influence that journalism had on the Spanish-American War, to which Richard Harding Davis would contribute his certain share.

Even in the smaller touches, "The Reporter Who Made Himself King" has much to recommend it as an expansionist burlesque. When Albert Gordon packs for departure to Opeki, he is careful to add "a supply of articles with which to trade with the native Opekians," including "a large quantity of brass rods, because he had read that Stanley did so" (13). The example of the great explorer-journalist provides a suitable send-off for the young man, and when as a substitute for the departed consul he sets about making a good impression on the native king, he outfits the Bradleys, father and son, with "a blue jersey apiece, with a big white Y on it," given to him by "a great man" named "Walter Camp" (34). Davis thus added one more allusion to sports in his story "for boys," while incidentally elevating the notion of "game" to Kipling's imperial level. Gordon and Stedman likewise decorate their diplomatic uniforms with "the bicycle medals" won by the youthful Yankee when he was "the fastest bicycle-rider in Connecticut" (35).

There is at times something detectably Tom Sawyerish about these boys, as when, the two having prepared themselves to meet the native king by dressing in gaudy fashion with uniforms and medals, Stedman observes that "Democratic simplicity is the right thing at home, of course; but when you go abroad and mix with crowned heads, you want to show them that you know what's what" (36). Such touches remind us that as an imperial parable, the story is being played out for fun. Nor are we to take the consequences of Gordon's ambitions seriously, even as the six gunboats race toward the unstated but implicit conclusion of the story. Nonetheless, the United States is represented by "three magnificent hulls of the White Squadron," which would eventually be replaced by the White Fleet sent around the world by Theodore Roosevelt in 1908, purportedly as a gesture of goodwill but in truth a flexing of the nation's newfound imperial muscle (117).

It must be said that although Davis shared Roosevelt's love of organized sports, he was not sympathetic to TR's expansionistic bellicosity. In late November 1891, after he had assumed the editorship of *Harper's Weekly,* Davis wrote an article reviewing the embarrassing situation in Chile, which involved the U.S. minister, a deposed would-be dictator, and the crew of the USS *Baltimore,* stationed in Valparaiso. The minister was Patrick Egan, who had become an American citizen after fleeing to the United States from Ireland, where he had taken such an active role in promoting Home Rule that he was in danger of being arrested by the British government.

Egan became a Republican Party worker and was so valuable to Benjamin Harrison's successful campaign for the presidency that he was rewarded with the post in Chile by Secretary of State James G. Blaine, a close friend. It was a controversial appointment, seen by some as a shockingly open example of patronage. Blaine was interested in strengthening Latin

American ties, and Egan supported President José Manuel Balmaceda when the virtual dictator suppressed an attempt by liberal elements in the national assembly to oppose his rule, continuing his support after civil war broke out. Egan had the uneasy backing of Blaine and Harrison, which put the United States in a painful position when the Congressional Party was successful in overthrowing Balmaceda. A Chilean mob sympathetic to the new government attacked sailors on shore leave from the *Baltimore,* resulting in the arrest and confinement of the Americans, two of whom were killed and many badly injured in the melee.

Davis's article was an outspoken attack on Egan, who "publicly declared that this would-be dictator should not be overthrown, and the United States government, misled by his representations, refused to recognize the Congressionalists as belligerents," which would have given them legitimacy. According to Davis, Egan "in every way, though unofficially, worked into Balmaceda's hands, and against the party fighting for constitutional liberty and representation by the people" (35: 801). These actions by the United States inspired the attack on the American sailors, blame for which Davis placed at Egan's feet, noting that "what our government will do about these murdered sailors will be determined by the action of the new government of the Chilean republic, but while it waits for that tardy apology and restitution, it can do one thing without waiting, and cannot do it too quickly—it can recall Minister Egan" (802).

At President Harrison's insistence, Chile reluctantly apologized and paid an indemnity, much to the disgust of Theodore Roosevelt, who, as John Hay noted to Henry Adams, was so eager to effect a reprisal against Chile that he was willing to declare war on his own behalf. Roosevelt's impulsiveness was as typical of the terrible Teddy as reasoned discourse was natural to Dick Davis, although it should be noted that RHD's attack on Patrick Egan may have had as much to do with the minister's Irish background as with his actions in Chile. Davis interpolated in his article a veiled aside about "the circumstances which surrounded the departure of Mr. Egan from Ireland," a reference to charges of corruption, even murder, that were eventually disproved.

Davis's own politics are not easy to define. He seems to have voted for Grover Cleveland, but then that Democratic stalwart was a family friend, and in 1896 Davis supported McKinley against the silver-lined specter of Bryan. Still, Davis's sympathies were clearly with the new Chilean government, which stood for republican virtues, as opposed to the heavy-handed and arrogant administration of the deposed president; while Roosevelt overlooked these finer points in his outrage at the murder and mistreatment of American sailors.

Historians have been more kind than was Davis to Egan, who, as in his earlier troubles in Ireland, was cleared of any wrongdoing. But the Chilean imbroglio is now seen by Walter LaFeber and other delineators of the emerging new American empire as a step toward much more serious involvement by the United States in South and Central American affairs. As for Davis, his article on the situation in Chile is also a preview of his sympathies for the oppressed people of Cuba, much as Roosevelt's eagerness to declare war for whatever reason provides a gloss on his bellicose attitude toward Spain, the sort of thing Davis satirizes in "The Reporter Who Made Himself King."

"Something lost behind the Ranges.
Lost and waiting for you. Go!"
RUDYARD KIPLING

4 : WESTWARD, HA!

: I :

In January 1892, as the buildings signaling a new American empire were still rising over Lake Michigan, Richard Harding Davis decided to take a break from the New York weather and the onerous duties of being managing editor of *Harper's Weekly* by traveling to what had for so long been the region identified with American empire, the Far West. The journey was the first of several he would take while working for *Harper's,* and his account of that trip, as with the others that followed, appeared in serial form in the magazine. The book that resulted, *The West from a Car Window,* was one of Davis's most popular, yet it was in all ways an idiosyncratic performance, indicating the wide gap of sensibility between the author and contemporary celebrants of the western experience.

Davis's initial quest in search of material was an obvious one for a travel writer, for although, as Frederick Jackson Turner would announce, the frontier had closed for business, meaning that there was no longer free land for the taking, as a literary and artistic subject the West was booming. The Oklahoma land rush had just taken place, filling up the last of the available government lands, but a journalistic equivalent was now under way, animated in part by nostalgia for a simple and courageous life already fenced out by barbed wire, and in part by the quest for novelty itself, always a journalist's chief consideration.

The wave of popular interest had been led by Frederic Remington, a native of upstate New York, who after several ill-advised careers, including a western venture in raising sheep, had come back from the land of cowboys and Indians with a portfolio packed with sketches and paintings of life on the range. His western work first appeared in *Harper's Weekly* as early as 1882, and Remington would illustrate Theodore Roosevelt's *Ranch Life and the Hunting Trail* in 1888, parts of which were serialized in periodicals before the book was published.

Roosevelt would work his own very brief western experience for all the political capital it would provide, but he was sincere in his enthusiasm. He had undergone a physical and mental regeneration through total immersion in the Dakota Badlands in the summer of 1884 and, more important, during the spring and summer of 1885, when he participated in the yearly roundup and brought in his bad man at gunpoint. It was he who encouraged his friend Owen Wister to go west for his health in 1885, the first of the trips that would provide local color for the stories Wister began to write in 1891, the first of which was "Hank's Woman," published in *Harper's Weekly* a year later, shortly after RHD's account of his western travels appeared.

Remington himself had taken up journalism to provide copy for his illustrations, and during the year before Davis took over as editor of *Harper's Weekly,* it regularly published the artist's accounts of his adventures with the U.S. Cavalry as the magazine's official war correspondent. Riding with General Nelson Miles into South Dakota, Remington sketched one of the Ghost Dances that were preludic to the last Sioux uprising, was on hand when Sitting Bull was murdered, and was virtually within gunshot of the Wounded Knee massacre that soon followed. All this was published in *Harper's,* with pictures in which Remington himself figured, as well as other articles and illustrations covering the activities of the publicity-conscious General Miles that continued to appear throughout 1891.

But Remington's most ambitious western painting of that period, *The Last Stand,* reproduced in the January 10, 1891, issue of *Harper's* as a full two-page illustration, showed Custer surrounded by his men on the height at Little Big Horn. The event had taken place in 1876, and the subject was a departure from the artist-reporter's customary eyewitness emphasis. It seems to have been warranted by the massacre at Wounded Knee, which was viewed by the officers in charge and by sympathizers such as Remington as retribution for the deaths of Custer and his men.

The timing and title of *The Last Stand* were doubly significant, for as Ben Merchant Vorpahl has made clear, the idea of a contemporary heroic West, along with many innocent Native Americans, died at Wounded Knee. Remington's painterly treatment of cavalry and cowboys would become increasingly nostalgic, much as Wister's western stories would self-consciously record a way of life that had largely passed away. Notably, RHD's own contribution to the western literature of the 1890s, which appeared in *Harper's Weekly* through March, April, and May of 1892, would pretty much put an end to the magazine's coverage of western matters.

Davis's account of his travels through Texas, Colorado, and Oklahoma was in tone and subject matter perfectly in keeping with its valedictory function. As material for a journalist—as opposed to a nostalgic artist or novelist—the "storied" West had already disappeared by the time Davis arrived, an absence which, with the ingenuity that was typical of his writing, he made into the unifying theme of his book. Moreover, he steered wide of Roosevelt's territory—the Dakotas and Wyoming—following his own route, which was largely through a wasteland that served as a stark backdrop to his negative take on the no-longer-wild West. What he reported back was therefore a salutary remedy for the version being touted by Roosevelt and Remington, a disparity ironically emphasized by the illustrations the artist prepared for Davis's book.

The inspiration for RHD's western trip may perhaps be credited to Roosevelt himself, who seems to have kept a ready eye out for potential American "Kiplings" and had encouraged both Wister and Remington to assume that title. Davis had first met Roosevelt when TR was working on the Civil Service Commission in Washington but living in New York City. He included a profile on Roosevelt in a piece for *Harper's* on rising young men in Manhattan, and it was about this time that the young editor-journalist was invited to the Roosevelt home for a dinner party.

On that occasion Davis appalled the self-adopted westerner by his ignorance regarding the history of the Alamo, that shrine sacred to the notion of Texan independence and the overthrow of the Spanish American control of the Southwest. Roosevelt educated him on the spot, and Davis made sure that an account of the place where Davy Crockett and Colonel Bowie died for Texas appeared early on in his account of his western travels. It may have been Roosevelt who that evening put the idea of the trip into Davis's head, but whatever the source of the inspiration, it enabled him to get the jump on Wister in getting his experiences into print.

: II :

Where Remington and Roosevelt had conveyed the depths of their personal immersion in the Wild West, the very title of Davis's report on his travels conveys in a pleasantly facetious way the framed distance maintained between the reporter and his subject. Although Davis had plenty of firsthand exposure to the hard facts of life in Texas, Oklahoma, and Colorado, it was that of a visitor, indeed something of a tourist. Moreover, his brief passage dictated a pattern of encounter that he worked into the sustaining theme of his book, a wry consistency that was part and parcel of the humorous glance the author cast over the western scene. The West as he saw it was a series of disappointments, in which expectations nurtured by such mythmakers as

Roosevelt and Remington were repeatedly (if not explicitly) reversed. In effect, Davis wrote from the point of view of a tourist who had believed the brochures.

Like all visitors to Texas, RHD was duly impressed by its sheer size, and the reality of entry was made vivid when he was given nine silver dollars as change when he bought something with a ten-dollar bill, a signifier of a different style of life and a reminder that the free silver issue was as "large and vital" in the West as Texas itself (*West* 5). But it was while traveling by rail between Laredo and Corpus Christi that Davis felt that he had at last left the civilized world behind him.

For the famous "picturesque and lawless side of the Texan existence" seemed to be validated by a sunburned young man in a sombrero who was seated in front of him by an open window and who with a pistol began "to shoot splinters out of the passing telegraph poles with the melancholy and listless air of one who is performing a casual divertisement" (6). But this apparent act of random vandalism was soon explained: the youth was no outlaw but a deputy sheriff passing the time by improving his marksmanship.

Indeed, only lawmen were allowed to carry revolvers in public places in Texas; all others, as Davis found out firsthand, were politely told to divest themselves of their sidearms or face arrest: "This, I think, illustrates a condition of things in darkest Texas which may give a new point of view to the Eastern mind. It is possibly something of a revelation to find that instead of every man protecting himself, and the selection of the fittest depending on who is 'quickest on the trigger,' he has to have an officer of the law to protect him if he tries to be a law unto himself." The phrase "darkest Texas" is a turn on Stanley's coinage, "darkest Africa," yet another signal of Davis's indebtedness to the famous explorer and correspondent, here used ironically to explode the myth of western lawlessness.

Davis was also surprised by the degree of excitement aroused by the murder of a deputy sheriff, which commanded the kind of attention in the local newspapers that only "a railroad disaster or a Johnstown flood" would get back east. The murdered man was neither "celebrated" nor "popular," yet the day after his death "every ranchman and cowboy and Texas Ranger and soldier we chanced to meet on the trail . . . took up the story of the murder of Rufus Glover, and told and retold what some one else had told him, with desperate earnestness and the most wearying reiteration" (8).

That Davis's reputation as a journalist had received a very large boost as a result of his coverage of the Johnstown Flood is not incidental to the reference, but the point being made is that much bigger, more newsworthy

events are a regular occurrence in the East, while in the West the mere murder of a deputy sheriff causes a great sensation, a point used by Davis for humorous effect. Beyond the joke, however, lies a principle that Davis as an insulated easterner did not grasp: the murder of a lawman in a desert region
always on the verge of unrestrained outlawry was a serious matter in Texas.

Public meetings were held to demand that an end be put "to such lawlessness—that is, the killing of one man in an almost uninhabited country."
When RHD left for the West, a total of twenty-five accused murderers were
awaiting trial in New York City, with hardly a ripple of public comment or
attention. It was time, Davis conjectured, for the East to "reconstruct a new
Wild West for itself, in which a single murder sends two committees of indignant citizens to the State capital to ask the Governor what he intends to
do about it" (11).

Just such a reconstruction, with an obvious poke at the pretensions of
William Cody's ongoing promotion of what was purported to be the "old"
Wild West, seems to have been Davis's overall intention as he reported his
experiences in a country that was no longer wild but rather mild and for
long stretches simply boring. As a venture in reconstruction it was also de-
constructive, and in the manner of *Roughing It*, Mark Twain's account of life
in Virginia City during the great silver bonanza, Davis imposed an eastern
perspective on western matters.

In effect, that train car window through which he peered acted as an aesthetic frame, though as RHD observed a number of times, the picturesque
was not an abundant aspect of the western scene. Owen Wister himself had
reacted with shock when he first encountered the raw facts of Wyoming,
and his journal reveals how he was appalled by the crudity and casualness
of life in the cattle country. With repeated exposure came tolerance, even
understanding, yet it must be said that Wister's cowboys and cavalrymen
were also filtered through an eastern cultural sieve; many, including his
cowboy hero, Lin McLean, are transplanted easterners themselves.

Moreover, Wister's West was forever fixed at the moment of the author's
first encounter, in 1885, a time when the market in beef was booming and
much of the range remained as yet unfenced. It was still the heroic age of
the cowboy and, with rebellious, well-armed Indians escaping reservations
and carrying on a kind of partisan warfare against white settlers, the heroic
age of the cavalryman as well. The passage of seven years had changed all
that, resulting in Davis's deconstructed West, which appeared just as Wister
began to publish the short stories that would make him famous. Wister's
western tales would preserve the heroic cowboy and cavalryman in literary

aspic, a more sophisticated version of Buffalo Bill's Wild West Show, much as Bret Harte's stories were a living museum of California mining life.

The irony is that in his account of his travels, Davis both anticipated and invalidated Wister's West, and though it was popular in its day, *The West from a Car Window* has not survived whereas the other man's writings are still viewed as essential components of the western myth. Such neglect is perfectly understandable, for not only did Davis invite eventual oblivion with his supercilious title and tone, but keepers of the western myth would naturally shun any account that did not sustain the heroic ideal, preferring always—as the newspaper editor's line in *The Man Who Shot Liberty Valance* has it—the legend to the fact. And yet, if only for his departures from the conventions of the genre, Davis's account of his western trip is well worth consideration.

But it has a further value as well. For if Davis's account of the West was dismissive not celebratory, thereby emphasizing the differences that define him as a chronicler of his age, if he saw western life as something of a hoax and a joke—carrying forward the essential burden of Mark Twain's *Roughing It*—he also was able, like Wister, to detect a heroic quality still vibrant and alive, much as he regarded the cowboy, with pistol or without, as a distinct and picturesque aspect of American life.

Like Wister, he was drawn to those westerners who through gritty determination or the exercise of vested authority were able to lend a certain order to an otherwise chaotic environment. Like Wister, he more often than not identified those westerners and that authority with representatives of the United States Army, one of whom eventually emerges as the right man in the right place, foreshadowing the hero of *Soldiers of Fortune,* on the one hand, and the hero of the battle for San Juan Hill, on the other. For this reason alone, Davis's *The West from a Car Window* merits serious attention.

: III :

The title of Davis's book is misleading, in that it suggests a distant and detached perspective, when in fact the book is a realistic, up-close look at western regions. As he insisted in his conclusion, the West, "as seen from the car window," is a place "where beautiful scenery and grand mountains are separated by miles of prairie and chaparral." It is also false to assume that one can step "from ranches to army posts, and from Indian reservations to mining camps with easy and uninterrupted interest," for in truth long and boring travel separated one place of interest from another: "Indians do not necessarily join hands with the cowboys, nor army posts nestle at the feet of mountains filled with silver. The West is picturesque in spots, [but] as the dramatic critics say, the interest is not sustained throughout" (242). Clearly, Davis did not learn that truth from guidebooks; he learned it by emulating his great model, Stephen Bonsal, by immersing himself in his subject, briefly but intensely. But as the allusion to the drama suggests, he did it on his own, not Bonsal's, terms.

Davis's account of the Chicago Exposition demonstrates how his perspective as a traveler is characteristically dominated by aesthetic considerations. But where he found much to admire at the fair, the controlling theme throughout his account of his western travels is one of disappointed expectations, based on the popular notions of the West with which he himself had set forth:

> I confess I had an idea that after I had travelled four days in a straight line due west, every minute of my time would be of value, and that if each man I met was not a character he would tell stories of others who were, and that it would merely be necessary for me to keep my eyes open to have picturesque and dramatic people and scenes pass obligingly before them. I was soon undeceived in this, and learned that in order to reach the West we read about, it would be necessary for me to leave the railroad, and that I must pay for an hour of interest with days of the most unprofitable travel. . . . The soldiers who guard this land, the Indians who are being crowded out of it, and the cowboys who gallop over it and around their army of cattle, are interesting, but they do not stand at the railroad stations to be photographed and to exhibit their peculiar characteristics. (222–25)

As in RHD's sketch of the correspondent's beau ideal, "interesting" is the key word, and he went on to cite Matthew Arnold's opinion that the United States was "uninteresting," which had outraged Americans but with which Davis agreed, so long as one applied the adjective to the western landscape: "If Matthew Arnold travelled from Pittsburg to St. Louis, from St. Louis to Corpus Christi, and from Corpus Christi back through Texas to the Indian Territory, he not only has my sympathy, but I admire him as a descriptive writer" (225).

It is dry exaggerations like this, along with the overall strategy of disillusionment, that call to mind Mark Twain's *Roughing It*. But in this concluding assessment of his western experience, Davis is also mounting a challenge to himself, for in traveling over the route just described he has done his best to make the experience "interesting," even if, as he admits, it means promoting the illusion that western travel is a steady sequence of spectacular scenery and unusual characters.

From the start, RHD encountered obstacles placed in the way of travelers in quest of the picturesque, a frustrating experience that began in San Antonio. Though theirs was an old city with a depth of history and many "picturesque show-places," the residents of San Antonio preferred to point visitors to "the new Post-office and the City Hall" and let the old Spanish missions outside of town remain unseen (15). But in the midst of these modern structures "on which the mortar is hardly yet dry," there stood the Alamo, the importance of which Commissioner Roosevelt had driven home to Davis, who strove to convey the proper, indeed requisite, awe: Even if surrounded by "modern efforts that tower above it," the ancient mission "dwarfs" everything in the neighborhood by its "grace and dignity" (17).

Though "thrice-told," the story of the Alamo as Davis declared bears yet another retelling. It forever recaptures the heroic and self-sacrificing spirit of the elder West, making up for the perceived deficiencies of modern Texas, from its "passing taste in literature" (which tended toward dime novels) to its desolate landscape, with "its cactus and dying cattle" (23). When the visitor found "his patience and understanding tried" by such inconveniences as having his dinner served at noon instead of in the evening as in the East, he can derive some compensation by remembering the Alamo. This facetious note was hardly Roosevelt's emphasis, but it reveals the eastern prejudice that controlled Davis's perspective throughout.

According to RHD, some elements of the heroic West still existed in the Southwest: Sharing breakfast with a detachment of Texas Rangers "under the only tree within ten miles," Davis was treated to an exhibition of trick shooting, reminding him of "the picturesqueness of [Buffalo Bill's] Wild West show and its happiest expression" (11). Davis also joined a troop of cavalry that was in pursuit of a Mexican revolutionary named Catarina Garza who had slipped over the border into the United States. This meant that the reporter had to cross a dreary and monotonous wasteland of "red sandy soil covered with cactus and bunches of gray, leafless brush, marked with the white skeletons of cattle" (27).

His escort was "Trumpeter Tyler," a soldier whom Davis found covered with alkali dust, with "blue shirt open at the breast, his riding breeches bare at the knee," and his military blouse torn into rags by the cactus and chaparral (28). Tyler was something less than those trig cavalrymen depicted in the pages of *Harper's Weekly* by Frederic Remington, and even the depiction of Tyler by Remington in Davis's book shows a much neater soldier than the man described, with an open shirt but neither dusty nor ragged in apparel. It would be difficult to find a more effective demonstration of the difference in attitude between the two men toward the West as fact and legend, though further differences would reveal themselves when, six years later, Remington and Wister would travel together to Cuba on assignment.

Tyler proved both able guide and acute philosopher, and the quality of his conversation was also something of a shock, in effect anticipating the cultured cavalrymen of Owen Wister:

> He was very young, and came from Virginia, as his slow, lazy voice showed; and he had played, in his twenty-three years, the many parts of photographer, compositor, barber, cook, musician, and soldier. He talked of these different callings as we walked our horses over the prairie, and, out of deference to myself and my errand, of writing. He was a somewhat general reader, and volunteered his opinion of the works of Rudyard Kipling, Laura Jean Libbey, Captain Charles King, and others with confident familiarity. . . . Of Mr. Kipling he said, with an appreciative shake of the head, that "he knew the private soldier from way back;" of Captain Charles King, that he wrote for the officers; and of Laura Jean Libbey, that she was an authoress whose books he read "when there really wasn't nothing else to do." I doubt if one of Mr. Kipling's own heroes could have made as able criticisms. (31–32)

King was a veteran of both the Civil War and the Indian wars, an author popular at the time who specialized in Cooperesque fiction with a military setting, and Laura Jean Libbey was a writer of romantic novels who has suffered the sort of posthumous fate suggested by Trumpeter Tyler's evaluation. In 1892 Kipling had only recently appeared on the scene, having first exploded in print with *Departmental Ditties* in 1886, though it was undoubtedly *Soldiers Three* (1888) that Trumpeter Tyler had in mind. Once again, for American authors ambitious to write about the West, Kipling was the mark, a truth reinforced by the guide who led RHD to his rendezvous with the cavalry troop.

Davis discovered that many of the soldiers had a range of earlier careers matching Tyler's; the typical cavalryman was both "intelligent" and because of his relative sophistication "unpicturesque"—hence disappointing as subject matter even if entertaining as a companion (34). Even more disillusioning was the wasteland crossed by the cavalry troop, characterized as

TRUMPETER TYLER

Frederic Remington's rendition of Trumpeter Tyler, somewhat tidied up so as to reinforce the emerging myth of the cavalryman hero. From The West from a Car Window.

"the back-yard of the world. It is to the rest of the West what the ash-covered lots near High Bridge are to New York. It is the country which led General Sheridan to say that if he owned both places, he would rent Texas and live in hell. It is the strip of country over which we actually went to war with Mexico, and which gave General Sherman the opportunity of making the epigramme, which no one who has not seen the utter desolation of the land can justly value, that we should go to war with Mexico again, and force her to take it back" (41–42).

What most impressed Davis was the unlikelihood that the troop would succeed in apprehending the fugitive, for they spent their time running down reports of sightings brought back by their Mexican guide, only to find lonely campfires warming "revolutionists" who bore the unmistakable signs of shepherds or antelope hunters (51–52). But the cavalrymen never gave up hope, which was "especially invented for soldiers and fishermen," and hope acted as a stimulant for physical activity: "They never grew weary; they rode on many days from nine at night to five the next afternoon, with but three hours sleep . . . but the hot, tired eyes of the enlisted men kept wandering over the burning prairie as though looking for gold; and if on the ocean of cactus they saw a white object move, or a sombrero drop from sight, or a horse with a saddle on its back, they would pass the word forward on the instant, and wait breathlessly until the captain saw it too" (54). There is a Quixotic dimension to this admirable dedication to duty, fueled not only by the cavalrymen's chivalric code but also by a desire to obtain the reward for Garza's capture, a complex impulse that Davis would find assuming alternative forms throughout his western journey.

In 1888 Frederic Remington had accompanied a troop of "buffalo soldiers" on an arduous scouting expedition through hostile Apache country in Arizona, resulting in a well-received account of his experience that was published in the *Century Magazine* the following year. Davis undoubtedly regarded this kind of involvement as de rigueur for western correspondents, which of course was the model set by Bonsal in Europe and the Near East. And yet the futility of the search in which he participated, which he compared to Lewis Carroll's hunt for the fabulous Snark, was not the emphasis of the article by Remington.

But in 1898 Remington wrote "Massai's Crooked Trail" for *Harper's Monthly,* a story about a fugitive Apache for whom several troops of U.S. Cavalry had long searched in vain. The chief of scouts telling the story claims to have once caught a glimpse of Massai, limited to the Apache's "G string flickering in the brush," a flash of hinder parts suggesting not the

Snark but Moby-Dick (Remington 283). Where Davis emphasizes the stubborn persistence of the cavalrymen searching for Garza, Remington underscores the skill of Massai in evading capture. Thus the "bronco Chiricahua . . . manifested himself like the duststorm or the morning mist—a shiver in the air, and gone" (277).

It is a telling difference, revealing Remington the artist's abiding fascination with the primitive aspect of man, essential to the mythic West, as opposed to Davis's sophisticated take on the deluded quest in a wasteland of sagebrush and alkali dust, essential to the grim facts. By 1898 the Apache threat had been removed, along with Geronimo, the real-life model for Massai, allowing for Remington's shift of emphasis, the fugitive Indian being essentially a ghost, a relic of a heroic past now gone.

Davis's reference to Lewis Carroll is indicative of both the lightheartedness with which he viewed the deadly earnest pursuit and the essential absurdity of the situation, being a hunt by "a file of ghosts" for another ghost, "always sure that this time it meant something" (54). Indeed, we may wonder what RHD would have made of it had the search been successful, had the shabby reality of the ghostly fugitive been paraded before him. Somehow it was the failure of the quest that gave the story its point, conveying the essential meaning of the West in a parable without closure.

: IV :

If Davis sought to behold the soldiers of the border cavalry through Kipling's spectacles as stalwart representatives of American military power on the frontiers of empire, he found instead a ragged troop of cavalrymen in pursuit of a mirage. Likewise, when he headed for a mining camp newly set up in Creede, Colorado, it was, as he claimed, with ideas "derived from an early and eager study of Bret Harte" (59). It was an expectation much like the illusion Mark Twain brought to Nevada thirty years earlier, when he thought he would find Indians like those celebrated by Cooper.

Not that Davis really expected to find a replica of Poker Flat or Roaring Camp, but he would have liked nevertheless to encounter "John Oakhurst, in his well-fitting frock-coat . . . and Yuba Bill pulling up his horses in front of the Lone Star saloon." Of course he was disappointed, as he knew he would be: "All that I found at Creede which reminded me of these miners and gamblers and the chivalric extravagant days of '49 were a steel pan, like a frying-pan without a handle, which I recognized with a thrill as the pan for washing gold, and a pick in the corner of a cabin" (59–60).

Like San Antonio, the world of the mining camp had lost something in transition, an aesthetic rather than a historical transformation, one signaling decline, not urban growth and prosperity. Though he could detect resemblances between the modern miner and his fabled antecedents, "they were dim and commonplace, and lacked the sharp, clear-cut personality of Bret Harte's men and scenes. They were like the negative of a photograph which has been under-exposed, and which no amount of touching up will make clear" (60).

The simile is fitting: RHD carried with him a Kodak camera, and in place of the Remington sketches that illustrated his Texas rambles, he provided his own pictures for his account of Creede. As a rule these are not of picturesque individual miners but of the town itself, as well as the mine called Holy Moses (after the exclamation of the prospector who discovered the lode), illustrating the crude mechanics and rustic architectonics of the modern mining experience.

The kind of travel writing practiced by RHD depends on repeated surprises, whether reversals of expectations or persons and events amazing, even spectacular, in novelty. The allusion to Bret Harte's miners is of the first sort; to the second belongs Davis's description of Creede: "hundreds of little pine boxes of houses and log cabins" strung along a water-worn gully, "pine shanties" clinging "for support to the rocky sides of the gulch into which they have squeezed themselves," with all the permanence of "a city of fresh cardboard" (65).

Although Davis does not remind the reader of the association, the expected summer flood like the one in Harte's famous story would "carry with it fresh pine houses and log huts instead of twigs and branches" (62). The prospect of destruction enhances the imagery of impermanence, as do the heaps of "furniture and kegs of beer, bedding and canned provisions, clothing and half-open packing cases, and piles of raw lumber" stacked along the muddy street, in front of stores made of "canvas tops and foundations of logs" (64, 65). With all this canvas, the town resembles "a circus-tent, which has sprung up overnight, and which may be removed on the morrow . . . and you cannot but feel that the people are part of the show."

A great shaft of rock that rises hundreds of feet above the lower town gives the little village at its base an absurdly pushing, impudent air, and the silence of the mountains around from ten to fourteen thousand feet high, makes the confusion of hammers and the cries of the drivers swearing at their mules in the mud and even the random blasts from the mines futile and ridiculous. It is even more strange and fantastic at night, when

it appears to one looking down from half-way up the mountain like a
camp of gypsies at the foot of a cañon. On the raw pine fronts shine electric lights in red and blue globes, mixing with the hot, smoky glare rising
from the saloons and gambling houses, and striking upward far enough
to show the signs of The Holy Moses Saloon, The Theatre Comique, The
Keno, and The Little Delmonico against the face of the great rock at their
back doors, but only suggesting the greater mass of it which towers ma-
jestically above, hidden somewhere in the night. It is as incongruous as
an excursion boat covered with colored lights, and banging out popular
airs at the base of the Palisades. (65–66)

This last is a typical Davis touch, rendering the unfamiliar vivid by means
of an analogy or simile framed in terms recognizable to the reader. He was,
noted Booth Tarkington, "an American writing to Americans," who often
"told us about things abroad in terms of New York; and we have all been to
New York, so he made for us the pictures he wished us to see. And when he
did not thus use New York for his colors he found other means as familiar to
us and as suggestive; he always made us see" (*R.H.D.* 26–27).

What Davis is attempting to convey in this passage is the idea of the
ephemeral clinging to the surface of the sublimely permanent, the mountains that will remain long after the brightly lit gypsy camp has been washed
away by floods or time. In his journals Owen Wister likewise recorded his
impression of the main streets in western towns as stage sets, in large part
because of the false fronts of stores, what RHD calls a "Leadville front,
where the upper boards have been left square instead of following the slop-
ing angle of the roof" (*West* 65).

Yet this shabby, fragile community is enjoying great wealth, thanks to the
prospector for whom the town was named, who first discovered silver in
what was a place empty of houses some twenty months earlier: "When I was
in Creede that gentleman was offered one million two hundred and fifty
thousand dollars for his share of this mine, and declined it. After that my interest in him fell away" (68). Here again, RHD's account of his western journey is reminiscent of Mark Twain's travel writings in not only the combination of the marvelous and the mundane but also the use of understatement
for humorous effect.

As in Twain's *Roughing It,* Davis's description of bonanza days depends
on illustrative anecdotes to convey the bizarre and often violent way of life
that such a sudden eruption of prosperity and population can produce:

At the time I visited Creede, it was quite impossible to secure a bed in any of the hotels or lodging houses. The Pullman cars were the only available sleeping-places, and rented out their berths for the night they laid over at the mining camp. But even in these, sleeping was precarious, as one gentleman found the night after my arrival. He was mistaken for another man who had picked up a bag of gold-dust from a faro table at Little Delmonico's, and who had fled into the night. After shooting away the pine-board façade in the Mint gambling-house in which he was supposed to have sought shelter, several citizens followed him on to the sleeping-car, and, of course, pulled the wrong man out of his berth, and stood him up in the aisle in front of four revolvers, while the porter and the other wrong men shivered under their blankets, and begged them from behind the closed curtains to take him outside before they began shooting. The camp was divided in its opinion on the following morning as to whether the joke was on the passenger or on the hasty citizens. (72)

But where this is a scene reminiscent of Twain's account of Virginia City, with its eastern distaste for western violence, Davis also found men in Creede with whom he felt very much at home. He was given a bunk in a cabin occupied by a number of "younger sons from the East," youths of wealth and privilege. The contrast in the setting provided another humorous episode, as RHD notes the "satisfaction" he felt while "watching the son of a president of the Somerset Club light the fire with kerosene while the rest of us remained under the blankets and asked him to be careful" (72–73). The use of blankets for protection unifies the two episodes, yet the causes of the potential danger are quite different, the one traditional gunplay, the other unique to the situation of wealthy greenhorns sharing a cabin.

Pleased to find himself in the company of the "right sort," Davis's emphasis was in the spirit of Teddy Roosevelt, who had stressed the regenerative effects of his sojourn in the Far West. Davis noted the speed with which "such carefully bred youths as one constantly meets in the mining camps and ranches of the West can give up the comforts and habits of years to fit into their surroundings. It is instructive and hopeful . . . to see how neatly a Yale graduate of one year's standing can sweep the mud from the cabin floor without spreading it" (73–74). Davis would return again and again to the presence in the West of men of privileged backgrounds, versions in their way of Bret Harte's genteel gamblers, but variations as well on the experience of Theodore Roosevelt: "It is," says Davis, quoting the anonymous authority of faraway fathers and brothers regarding the wealthy young emigrant, "the best thing for him," and is undeniably one version of the "strenuous life."

Other kinds of men were to be found in a place like Creede, among whose "prominent citizens" was "Bob Ford, who shot Jesse James" and who in no way resembled a "desperado" but had "a loutish, apologetic air, which is explained by the fact that he shot Jesse James in the back" (82–85). Bat Masterson (misspelled "Masterden" by Davis), employed as a faro dealer in a gambling saloon, was more true to form. "One night when he was off duty I saw a drunken man slap his face, and the silence was so great that we could hear the electric light sputter in the next room; but Masterden only laughed, and told the man to come back and do it again when he was sober" (85). That electric light comes as something of a shock. Not the sort of thing we associate with the mining (or any) frontier, it literally enlightens us as to the differences between Mark Twain's Virginia City of the 1860s and Davis's Creede some thirty years later. Needless to say, no electric lights sputter in the West of Roosevelt and Wister.

Some things remain consistent, like the ever present gunplay. Again in the vein of Twain, Davis distinguishes between "very good shots" and "very bad shots." Notably, it is the representatives of this latter group whom he emphasizes, like "Mr. James Powers, who emptied his revolver and Rab Brothers' store at the same time without doing any damage. He explained that he was crowded and wanted more room." Such displays were relatively rare, however, and RHD characterized the town as not very dangerous, with lawlessness tending toward the "scattered and mild." The gambling saloons were chiefly gathering places, where people went for social purposes, and "there were no sudden oaths, nor parting of the crowd, and pistol-shots or gleaming knives—or at least, but seldom. The women who frequented these places at night . . . were a most unpicturesque and unattractive element. They were neither dashing and bold, nor remorseful and repentant. . . . The men occasionally gave glimpses of the life which Bret Harte made dramatic and picturesque—the women, never" (86).

Davis admits that he saw little of the "inner life" of the mining town, "the speculation in real estate and mines" (90). His encounter, after all, was a brief visit, with no participation in the day-to-day life of the miners. What he saw lay on the surface, the camp life itself—"a prize fight at Billy Woods', a pie-eating match at Kernan's, a Mexican circus in the bottom near Wagon Wheel Gap, a religious service at Watrous and Bannigan's gambling-house, and the first wedding in the history of the town." There were the prospectors, the town's chief citizens, swarming over the mountains every day, leaving behind "their little heaps of stone and their single stick, with their name scrawled on it in pencil, [which] made the mountains look like great burying grounds," claims that were as "effectual as a parchment sealed and signed" but no guarantors of future wealth. Davis was shown samples of promising ore but "no silver nuggets," despite his expectation of seeing "delicate veins of white silver" from which he could pry out with his penknife a souvenir piece to be made into "scarf-pins and watch guards" (81).

Here once more Davis may be compared with Mark Twain, who had similar expectations of finding quick and easy riches, a Quixotic hope that was constantly frustrated. Many of these coincidences were undoubtedly matters of fact and not the result of Davis's writing with *Roughing It* open before him, but it is clear that Mark Twain provided the wry perspective with which Davis viewed the West. It was a point of view inimical to promoting myth and discounts the heroic version being promulgated by Remington and Roosevelt, much as Twain wrote to devalue James Fenimore Cooper's romantic image of the frontier, on the one hand, and Francis Bret Harte's glamorized version of mining life, on the other.

Like Twain also, RHD as always was quick to grasp the picturesque potential of the scene: While wandering deep in the mountains, in the midst of "wonderful beauty and silence," a sublimity that seemed to make "words impertinent," he would come across "a solitary prospector tapping at the great rock in front of him, and only stopping to dip his hot face and blistered hands into the snow about him, before he began to drive the steel bar again with the help which hope gave him. His work but for this ingredient would seem futile, foolish, and impossible"—for always before the prospector was the hope of becoming "a millionaire like Creede, and so he makes the next stroke, and the next, and the next" (78).

Despite the work of Bret Harte, the miner never gained the mythic stature accorded the cowboy, nor were Roosevelt or Remington attracted to the type. Davis here suggests the reason, for there is no idealism at work in the unrelenting quest for wealth, and that he would choose to emphasize this unglamorous fact is a clue to his view of the West. It is of a piece with the life that Davis found elsewhere on his western trip, where an often futile hope was the dominant note, a temporal expectation of great material gain, whether in the form of reward money or a lucky strike, inspiring a terrific expenditure of labor and displays of courage, but with no certain future at the end. It was, like the miner's dream, not an abstract ideal, not labor for the sake of some virtuous end, and for all the chivalrousness of western men, what they sought was not a mystical but a material grail. As in the stories of Bret Harte, the dominant institution in the mining town was the gambling hall; the owner of one such in Creede permitted church services, but he made his money back, as he boasted to Davis, by allowing the bar to remain open, although the gaming tables were closed for the time.

This is hardly a gambler modeled after Harte's John Oakhurst or Jack Hamlin, idealized creations who manifest in all their dealings a chivalric nobility and a generosity of soul. It is in the vein of the narrowest kind of American commercialism, cynical to the core, with no room for the exercise of spirit. Nor are noble outlaws resident in Creede, only the dirty little coward named Ford who shot the legendary Jesse James in the back, and Bat Masterson reduced to dealing cards at a faro table. It was Mark Twain who proposed that the gold rush destroyed the pastoral idealism of an earlier America, and his account of Virginia City in the 1860s, like RHD's description of Creede, served to substantiate Twain's notion that mining was an exercise in rapacity and folly with little room left for transcendent ideals.

Hope, as RHD insisted, may have survived in the West, but it was the kind of optimism that drove the conquistadores onward, the pursuit of material reward, not some chivalric goal. It was a bond that joined together the cavalry troop searching for a fugitive revolutionary for the sake of reward money and the persistent miners in the Colorado mountains, staking their claims with the expectation of striking it rich. For a romantic such as Davis, these were contemporary realities that held out no promise for literature beyond the journalistic account in which they appeared, nor as his western travels continued did he find much that appealed to his idealistic or aesthetic propensities.

Davis came west seven years too late, and five more years would intervene before he found a territory and a spirit that sparked his creative interests. Yet to understand and appreciate those qualities in Davis's journalism that appealed to his contemporaries, the Twain-like ironies that irradiated the passing scene, requires consideration of the remaining chapters of *The West from a Car Window*. In doing so, we should keep in mind that what Davis was looking for but did not find is as important as the realities of the West he encountered, because when he finally found a subject suitable for romantic literature, it was thoroughly invested with what he assumed was the true western spirit.

We'll build a sweet little nest
Somewhere out in the west,
And let the rest of the world go by.
POPULAR SONG

5 : WESTWARD, WHO?

: I :

The first three chapters of *The West from a Car Window* deal with aspects of the region associated with what might be called the ephemeral scene, from cavalrymen pursuing rumors across a wasteland of sand and sagebrush to miners crowding into what was essentially a temporary center of opportunism. The remaining five chapters treat more permanent aspects of the West—cattle ranch and army post life, for example—but always with an emphasis on the changes that in bringing stability have created stasis. By Davis's account, what was most interesting about the region was what had disappeared.

If RHD saw little in the modern-day West of interest to writers, he was equally unenthusiastic about the West as a place in which to settle, a point of view he shared with another unregenerate easterner of an earlier generation, Francis Parkman. Parkman's account of his travels along the Oregon Trail at the outset of the Mexican War not only validated Fenimore Cooper's notion that the trans-Mississippi territory was a virtual desert but also presented a picture of westering settlers that did not sustain the emerging romantic myth of hardy and visionary pioneers. Instead, Parkman suggested that emigrants were an eternally restless people perpetually in quest of personal advantage associated with free land, which the victory of the United States over Mexico would greatly augment.

Likewise, Davis's account of the Oklahoma land rush, although written three years after the last great expanse of government land had been opened for settlement, is a classic of its kind, describing the hysterical scramble that was the last and surely the most notorious spasm of frontier expansion. Having started on April 22, 1889, the rush itself was long over when Davis arrived, but its spirit continued to manifest itself in Oklahoma City, where opportunism took a somewhat different but no less rapacious form than in the temporary town of Creede.

In 1893 Frederick Jackson Turner could talk of the democratic institutions that owed their origins to the frontier experience, but in 1892, with the dust of the scramble for free land barely settled over Oklahoma City, the origins of the frontier seemed demonstrably materialistic. Davis's account of the land rush recorded no evidence of natural nobility or generosity, and the democratic spirit took the form of anarchy that required the imposition of martial law. Like Francis Parkman, Davis packed an eastern set of attitudes in his mental baggage, and where another might have praised the rapid urban growth that had characterized the sudden emergence of Oklahoma City from a desert region previously inhabited primarily by Indians, Davis saw a community completely lacking in what he defined as cultural advantages.

Rather than sharing Turner's view, that the westering process was responsible for the evolution of American ideals, Davis defined the frontier as one of devolution, in which the pious idealism of the Forefathers had degenerated into naked, uncontrolled greed: "The history of its pioneers and their invasion of the undiscovered country not only shows how far the West is from the East, but how much we have changed our ways of doing things from the days of the Pilgrim Fathers, to those of the modern pilgrims, the 'boomers' and 'sooners' of the end of the century" (94). By 1891, the word "pilgrim" as a designation for a newcomer to the West—parlance that would fourscore years later become associated with the western characters played by John Wayne—was fairly common usage, which Davis may or may not have had in mind as he went on to draw a distinction between "pilgrims" old and new:

> We have seen pictures in our school-books, and pictures which Mr. Boughton has made for us, of the Mayflower's people kneeling on the shore, the long anxious voyage behind them, and the "rock-bound coast" of their new home before them, with the Indians looking on doubtfully from behind the pine-trees. It makes a very interesting picture—those stern-faced pilgrims in their knickerbockers and broad white collars; each man strong in the consciousness that he has resisted persecution and overcome the perils of the sea, and is ready to meet the perils of an unknown land. I should like you to place in contrast with this the opening of Oklahoma Territory to the new white settlers three years ago. (94–95)

Davis had it all wrong in historic particulars, for not only did George Henry Boughton never render a depiction of the arrival of the *Mayflower*— he was famous instead for his portrayal of the departure of that ship from Plymouth the following spring, leaving a forlorn band of exiles behind—

but as most historians now agree, the landing of the Pilgrims as described by Davis never occurred. It is a myth promoted by New Englanders who sought to derive a measure of sanctity thereby. But he got it right when he turned to the "modern pilgrims" of 1889, a scene that he makes as vivid as if he had been there to witness it. As Arthur Lubow testifies, the day that the territory was opened to settlement, Davis was hard at work as a reporter in New York City and was about to become famous for his coverage of the Johnstown Flood, which with its anecdotal account of the effects of a natural rampage provided the model for his postmortem account of the land rush.

We must assume that RHD depended on secondhand sources for his information, and yet surely no more graphic an account of the event has been written, starting with the tableau of April 22, 1889, a scene that Davis substitutes for that traditional picture of the prayerful Pilgrims on December 22, 1620:

> These modern pilgrims stand in rows twenty deep, separated from the promised land not by an ocean, but by a line scratched in the earth with the point of a soldier's bayonet. The long row toeing this line are bending forward, panting with excitement, and looking with greedy eyes toward the new Canaan, the women with their dresses tucked up to their knees, the men stripped of coats and waistcoats for the coming race. And then, a trumpet call, answered by a thousand hungry yells from all along the line, and hundreds of men and women on foot and on horseback break away across the prairie, the stronger pushing down the weak, and those on horseback riding over and in some cases killing those on foot, in a mad, unseemly race for something which they are getting for nothing. (95)

Unlike their predecessors, including "Columbus according to the twenty-dollar bills," iconography inspired by the anniversary that was even then being celebrated in Chicago, these modern pilgrims do not drop on their knees to pray but kneel only to "hammer stakes into the ground and pull them up again, and drive them down somewhere else, at a place which they hope will eventually become a corner lot facing the post-office, and drag up the next man's stake, and threaten him with a Winchester because he is on *their* land, which they have owned for the last three minutes."

Over the past decade, historical scholarship in the United States has gone through a revisionary cycle, perhaps most noisily regarding the heroic myth of the frontier. But the famous exhibit in our nation's capital that defined "The West as America" as violence and rapacity personified was mounted exactly one hundred years after RHD wrote his description of the Oklahoma land rush. Yet even while ignoring *The West from a Car Window,* the exhibition catalogue had very little to add to his account of rampant opportunism. And as for the Native Americans who had previously occupied the Oklahoma Territory, Davis accounts for them as well: As opposed to the traditional depictions of the arrival of Columbus or the Pilgrims, "there are no Indians in this scene. They have been paid one dollar and twenty-five cents an acre for the land, which is worth five dollars an acre as it lies, before a spade has been driven into it or a bit of timber cut, and they are safely out of the way." By 1889 the Muskogees, who had given Oklahoma its name in 1866, were gone from the Indian Nation toward which Huck Finn headed in 1884, only five years before it disappeared.

The pilgrim problem was exacerbated by the "sooners," so called because they "'beat the pistol'"—jumped the gun—and infiltrated the territory "too soon." These were mostly land-company employees who had sneaked onto the site of the future Oklahoma City with the aim of staking out claims before the mass of settlers arrived. On the morning of April 22, the place was little more than a water tower and a railroad siding, crowded with freight cars loaded with lumber and other materials to be sold to the future citizens of the town yet to be built. Beyond lay what appeared to be "an empty green prairie of high waving grass," located fifteen miles from the gathered line of pilgrims. When the trumpet sounded at noon, the soldiers stationed there to guard the cars saw the surrounding desert suddenly spring into bloom, as "five hundred men sprang from the long grass, dropped from the branches of trees, crawled from under freight cars and out of cañons and ditches." In moments the "blank prairie became alive with men running and racing about like a pack of beagles that have suddenly lost a hot trail" (99–100).

Within fifteen minutes, land-company surveyors were already dragging rods and chains "up the street on a run, the red and white barber poles and the transits were in place all over the prairie, and neat little rows of stakes stretched out in regular lines to mark where they hoped the town might be." But the apparent orderliness of the suddenly triangulated landscape was illusory: the peremptory claims made by the "sooners" (sometimes three to a claim) ended up in law courts, where the race was run all over again, albeit at a much slower pace, thereby keeping "Oklahoma City from growing with even more marvellous rapidity than it already has done" (98–99).

The mob scene that resulted after the trumpet sounded became a near riot when the first train arrived, disgorging twenty-five hundred souls greedy for free land and the profits to be made from its sale. Yet "there was no blood shed even during the greatest excitement of that feverish after-noon" (103). This was perhaps less a tribute to the character of the "pil-grims" than the result of all arms and liquor having been confiscated by the provost marshal on the scene, Captain D. F. Stiles of the Tenth Infantry.

Davis credited Stiles with single-handedly maintaining law and order during "the founding of Oklahoma," the captain being an instance of "the right man in the right place" (108). So far as RHD's eventual use of his west-ern experience, Captain Stiles is of particular interest, for like Trumpeter Tyler he emerges as a figure equivalent to the military men who are the he-roes of Owen Wister's fiction. But Stiles is also an early prototype of Davis's own heroic types, both fictional and real, those strong leaders who enforce law and order in turbulent places.

As a Union officer during Reconstruction, Stiles had the ruling hand in Waco, Texas, "and the questions and difficulties that arose after the war in that raw community fitted him to deal with similar ones in the construction of Oklahoma." One predictable result was Stiles's intense unpopularity "with the worst element," while the "better element call him blessed." The provost marshal was just the kind of authoritative figure admired by Theodore Roosevelt, who would have seen something of himself in the "personal bravery" with which Stiles "met the difficulties he had to solve at a moment's consideration. Several times he walked up to the muzzles of re-volvers with which desperadoes covered him and wrenched them out of their owners' hands" (109).

It was, RHD reflected, a great nation that could engender such a man, who kept his head when all around him were losing theirs. With consider-able irony, Davis "rejoiced to think how well off our army must be in majors, that the people at Washington can allow one who has served through the war and on the border and in this unsettled Territory, and whose hair has grown white in the service, to still wear [a captain's] two bars on his shoulder strap" (110). Stiles's portrait accompanies Davis's account, a photo-engraving of a lean, mustached man in uniform, with his two bars and gray hair clearly on display.

Most of the illustrations in the chapter on Oklahoma City are of con-trasting scenes in 1889 and 1892, such as the post office, a ramshackle ag-gregate of boards and logs replaced by a modern, four-story gabled struc-ture built of stone. This last was the Oklahoma City Davis visited, the end result of a truly amazing period of growth, but we should not confuse his ac-count of the town's rise with a brochure encouraging emigration to that place. For all the signs of an orderly, civilized life, "churches of stone and

CAPTAIN D. F. STILES

Woodcut from The West from a Car Window, *providing a portrait of the man Davis regarded as the hero of Oklahoma City during the riotous days of the land rush.*

brick and stained glass, and a flour-mill, and three or four newspapers, and courts of law, and boards of trade," according to Davis the rapacious spirit of 1889 still thrived in Oklahoma City.

Captain Stiles acted heroically during the first days of the new community, but the spirit of greed for free land survived his efforts, resulting in a rampant restlessness "which in a community founded by law and purchase would not exist. For speculation in land . . . and the battle for rights in the courts, seem to be the prevailing and ruling passion of the place. . . . Every one in Oklahoma City seems to live, in part at least, by transferring real estate to some one else, and the lawyers and real-estate agents live by helping them to do it. It reminded me," Davis concludes, "of that happy island in the Pacific seas where every one took in every one else's washing" (112).

These open displays of greed and litigiousness RHD blames not only on the character of the original settlers but also on the act of Congress authorizing the opening of the territory, which was rushed through "the hot, hurried end of a session." Davis was especially angered by the failure of the government to distinguish between bona fide settlers, who arrived with their families and intended to set up new homes in the farther West, and those who rushed in with the hope of making a quick profit by selling their claims. Captain Stiles could maintain law and order, but he was not empowered by that "bungling, incomplete bill" to sort out honest pilgrims from the greedy strangers among them who were chiefly responsible for the instability of the new community and the litigious spirit that prevailed (112).

In winding up his account of the land rush, RHD addressed his closing words to those "many persons in the East" who may be attracted to Oklahoma by "the announcements and advertisements of the 'boomers,'" for the West "is always full of hope to the old man as well as to the young one, and the temptation to 'own your own home' and to gain land for the asking is very great" (113). The key word here, once again, is "hope," that golden promise which lured so many persons to the West.

Davis counsels his readers to consider the large sign posted at the train station in Sedalia, which advises "Go East, Young Man, Go East," a play on the famous advice attributed to Horace Greeley. For all of the visible signs of progress, the town promises very little that is attractive to a city-dweller from the East, the cultural life being limited largely to gambling or endless discussions of real estate speculation. What the "young man" should also know is that "the schools are not good for his children as yet, and the society that he is willing his wife should enjoy is limited" (114).

Like many an eastern traveler to the West, RHD believed that "any man who can afford a hall bedroom and a gas-stove in New York City is better off than he would be as the owner of one hundred and sixty acres on the prairie, or in one of these small so-called cities," whose leading men are not responsible citizens "but are now as men playing with children's toys or building houses of cards" (114). It is not always a matter of growing up with the West; one may also shrink down with it: "It depends altogether on the man" (116).

Davis saw Oklahoma City as no place for persons of talent or abilities. Instead, he declared it a community well-suited to those people who "are just big enough to be leading citizens of a town of six thousand inhabitants," for such are "meant for nothing else" and will be "satisfied with the unsettled existence around them." They will find happiness in a place "where the organ in the front room is their art gallery, book-store, theatre, church, and school, and where the rustling grass of the prairie greets them in the morning and goes to bed with them at night" (116).

We may dismiss Davis's caveat as having come from a snob who left Philadelphia for the social, professional, and cultural opportunities of New York City and who drew what creative energies he possessed from the urban scene, which he could never leave for long. Still, even Remington, Roosevelt, and Wister, those celebrants of the western scene, had their homes in New York and Philadelphia and were never more than sojourners in the West, in search of big game or literary and artistic subject matter. It was not New York's Horace Greeley who coined that advice to young men in the East but an editor in Terre Haute, and Frederick Jackson Turner grew up in Portage, Wisconsin.

Moreover, as we stand where Davis stood in 1892 and look ahead to the next half century, we may acknowledge that his criticism of what was then the modern western scene would hold true for later writers, even those born in towns located beyond the Mississippi. In a certain, very valid sense that broad, red-clay thoroughfare along which Oklahoma City rose up, with a populace filled with raw energy and expressing a commercial spirit, may be seen as aligned both east and west.

It would run on in literature to become the Main Street of Sinclair Lewis's fictional Gopher Prairie, providing the selfsame cultural limitations set against an infinite horizon and a very large and empty sky. In sum, the American West is a very big place in which there is nowhere to go. As Gertrude Stein would observe of Oakland, California, when you get there, there is no there there. As soon as they were of age, both Lewis and Stein, as well as many other writers who were born or grew up in the West, heeded the advice posted in Sedalia, Oklahoma.

: II :

In succeeding chapters of his book on the West, Davis rendered accounts of that trinity sacred to the idealized version of the frontier experience—the Cowboy, the Indian, the Cavalryman—and in all three instances he stopped well short of the mythic types. Thus the fabulous King Ranch in Texas was spectacular in size, covering seven hundred thousand acres, but the lives of the men who worked there were considerably diminished in heroism from earlier days. The ranch was now the residence of the widow of Captain Richard King, and the business part of the operation was administered by her son-in-law, Robert J. Kleberg, who bore more resemblance to a captain of industry than to a rancher. Likewise, the cowboys in his employ were little more than glorified factory hands, whose amazing skill with the lariat was in the service of beef production.

The King Ranch "is as carefully organized and moves on as conservative business principles as a bank." Cowboys are found here by the score, but these are not the wild, uncombed, illegitimate sons of the sagebrush and coyote of popular lore, for they "do not ride over its range with both legs at right angles to the saddle and shooting joyfully into the air with both guns at once. Neither do they offer the casual visitor a bucking pony to ride, and then roll around on the prairie with glee when he is shot up into the air and comes down on his collar bone. . . . Neither do they shoot at his feet to see if he can dance. In this way the Eastern man is constantly finding his dearest illusions abruptly dispelled. It is also trying when the cowboys stand up and take off their sombreros when he is leaving their camp" (125).

For a frontispiece to Davis's book, Frederic Remington supplied a picture of a cowboy astride a "bucking broncho," which would eventually be worked by the artist into one of his most famous bronzes, substantial reinforcement of a mythic West. But for the chapter on the King Ranch he rendered an illustration much more in the spirit of Davis's text, an early cowboy in a fringed buckskin shirt and sombrero, with a pistol in his belt and a huge mustache decorating a squinty, hard-jawed face, a composition entitled *A Shattered Idol.*

Remington also supplied an illustration showing two ranch hands "fixing a break in the wire fence" that ran for three hundred miles around the King Ranch, illustrating Davis's point that "the coming of the barb-wire fence and the railroad killed the cowboy as a picturesque element of recklessness and lawlessness in southwest Texas. It suppressed him and localized him and limited him to his own range, and made his revolver merely an ornament" (136). In a subsequent version of this same subject, Remington rendered in

A BUCKING BRONCHO

Remington's frontispiece to The West from a Car Window, *rendering the heroic version of the cowboy which the artist would help make famous.*

A SHATTERED IDOL

Remington's version of the "old-time" cowboy, the passing of which he commemorated in countless paintings of the "Old West." From The West from a Car Window.

FIXING A BREAK IN THE WIRE FENCE

Remington's illustration for The West from a Car Window *of cowboys mending a barbed-wire fence on the famous King Ranch, something less than a heroic task.*

oils his fenced-in cowboys, this time placed in a winter landscape and not mending a fence but stopping to drop the bars in a gate that provides an opening in a barbed-wire barrier that stretches toward a point on the horizon line.

Painted in 1895, *The Fall of the Cowboy* is tragic in implications, the men clearly stripped of any heroic potential and dejected in mood. After 1892, Remington's depiction of the West became increasingly nostalgic, a change in subject matter from contemporary to historical, necessitated by the kinds of changes recorded by RHD's chapter on the King Ranch. But he seldom depicted the cowboy in decline, instead preferring to delineate the images we associate with his work, men in sombreros and buckskins galloping with pistols drawn across an open range or taking a stand against Indians, all images celebrating a lost glory.

By Davis's account, system and order have come to the range, along with the fences that sectioned it off in rectangles and squares, closing it to free grazing and making the great cattle drives of the golden age of the cowboy impossible, even if they were still necessary. In Kleberg's office hangs a map, on which the various areas of the ranch are marked off in colors, each area stationed by a cohort of cowboys who can on short notice round up cattle

The Fall of the Cowboy. *(Oil on canvas. By permission of the Amon Carter Museum.
1961.230.) Painted by Remington in 1895, this composition associates the passing
of the heroic version of the cowboy with the fencing off of the formerly open range,
a point also made by RHD in* The West from a Car Window.

according to breed and number, an operation run so efficiently that ten men
are able to herd together a thousand head within two days.

The rancher can receive orders from Chicago in his home office and fill
them readily without sending his men and beef any farther than the local
railroad station. Although RHD seems to have been impressed with the efficiency of the King operation, he makes clear from his description that the
romance has gone from the range, much as Mark Twain only ten years earlier had observed the same thing about life on the Mississippi, technology
having displaced and devalued the skills of river pilots, formerly the gods of
the river.

The nostalgic spirit, as F. Scott Fitzgerald observed in *The Great Gatsby,*
forever bears us back into the past, the territory where the spirit of romance
thrives. But for romantics of the type represented by Richard Harding
Davis, what is needed is a more exciting present. Thus the point being made
implicitly by Davis in his book on the West is that if Americans wish to have

a heroic image of American enterprise for the new century, they need to go somewhere else to create it. For with the passing of the great cattle drives, the heroic aspect of the cowboy had disappeared, which had been warranted by the hazards of moving huge herds of fractious beeves to market over hundreds of miles of open land.

"One of the most interesting and distinctive features of the West," the great drives were for the cowboy both a dangerous and boring chore, resulting in his reputation for wildness when he finally arrived at Dodge City, riding into town "with both guns going at once, and yelling as though the pent-up speech of the past six months of loneliness was striving for proper utterance." Still, the cowboy has not changed his costume and "cannot be overestimated as a picturesque figure; all that has been written about him and all the illustrations that have been made of him fail to familiarize him, and to spoil the picture he makes when one sees him for the first time racing across a range outlined against the sky" (140).

With his sombrero and chaps, his spurs and lariat and neckerchief, "he is a fantastic-looking individual," and "one suspects he wears the strange garments he affects because he knows they are becoming," although the parts of the assemblage do have definite functions, "in spite of rather than on account of their picturesqueness" (142–43). The exception is the cartridge belt and revolver once deemed a necessity but now regarded as something of an indulgence: "Cattle-men say they have found that on those days when they took this toy away from their boys, they sulked and fretted and went about their work half-heartedly, so that they believe it pays better to humor them, and to allow them to relieve the monotony of the day's vigil by popping at jack-rabbits and learning to twirl their revolver around their first finger." Davis noted that "of the many compliments I have heard paid by officers and privates and ranch-owners and cowboys to Mr. Frederic Remington, the one which was to sure to follow the others was that he never made the mistake of putting the revolver on the left side" (143).

It was Remington who was responsible for aestheticizing the cowboy, and it is chiefly as an aesthetic object that Davis presents him, galloping over the range, "with his handkerchief flying out behind, his sombrero bent back by the wind, and his gauntlets and broad leather leggings showing above and at the side of his galloping pony." Yet the aside about the revolver is the defining touch, for if the cowboy is still a picturesque object, he is defanged, his once deadly revolver now a "toy" chiefly used to reduce the jackrabbit population. Here again Remington obliged with an illustration of a cowboy at full gallop, with hat, chaps, and neckerchief, carrying a lariat at the ready

GATHERING THE ROPE

*Remington's cowboy here is armed with his lariat only, in accordance
with Davis's observation regarding the absence of pistols on the
modern range. From* The West from a Car Window.

but with no pistol visible at his side. On the other hand, in the frontispiece
showing a bucking bronco, a pistol is plainly in evidence on the correct side
of the cowboy's belt, thereby sustaining the myth that Remington the artist
would carry into the twentieth century.

But if the modern cowboy retains something of his traditional profile, his
traditional adversary, the Indian, has suffered a considerable decline. In his
next chapter, "On an Indian Reservation," RHD reveals the grim realities
imposed on the Native American by the same government that so recently
bought Oklahoma for one-fifth of the land's value. It is not that Davis was especially sympathetic toward the Indian, but his sense of fair play, which is
to say sportsmanship—that modern-day version of chivalry—was deeply
offended by what he saw, a bloody and ignoble display that like the rampant
greed of the Oklahoma land rush suggested that there were better ways of
running the West than those mandated by the U.S. government.

"The Indian," Davis declares early in the chapter, "will only be considered
here lightly and as a picturesque figure of the West," but this aesthetic

emphasis, maintained throughout the book, is somewhat misleading (151). In the very next paragraph, RHD follows the precedent set by Mark Twain and dismisses the notion of the Indian derived "from Cooper's novels and 'Hiawatha.'" He acknowledges that travelers in the West have called the Native American a "problem," whether as "a national nuisance or as a much-cheated and ill-used brother," a bipolarity that Davis manages to unify, but only by severely reducing the aesthetic aspect of the Indian (151–52).

As in his treatment of the modern cowboy, Davis initially deals with the picturesque qualities of the Native American, describing "a blanket Indian walking haughtily about in his buckskin, with his face painted in many colors and with feathers in his hair." It is such a self-conscious and theatrical spectacle that, as with the cowboy, the traveler is tempted to regard the Indian as having "dressed for the occasion" or to conclude that he goes about "thus equipped because his forefathers did so, and not because he finds it comfortable" (153).

Whatever the reason, to see in the flesh what one has previously known "only in pictures and photographs" provides an aesthetic shock of recognition. When the tourist witnesses an Indian on horseback riding across the prairie, "where the red buttes stand out against the sky, and show an edge as sharp and curving as the prow of a man-of-war," it is a "view of the West one seems to have visited and known intimately through the illustrated papers" (153). As if in validation of Davis's impression, we are provided another picture by Remington, already famous because of his work for "illustrated papers," showing an Indian in war dress astride a prancing pony.

The scene RHD is describing above is set in Fort Reno, Oklahoma Territory, for the moment still a reservation for Cheyenne and Arapaho, "but the Government has bought it from the Indians for a half-dollar an acre, and it is to be opened to white settlers. The country is very beautiful" but is no longer reserved for Native Americans, save in the very restricted sense conveyed by the word "reservation" (153). By way of reinforcing the difference, Davis traveled to the fort to witness the issuing of beef, a biweekly event, but having arrived too late, he traveled on to Anadarko, where a beef issue was scheduled to take place in three days.

Davis accounted this journey away from Fort Reno an inconvenience, for he "met few men more interesting and delightful than the officers at the post-trader's mess" at the fort (154). To make matters worse he was forced to travel in one of the stages "owned by a Mr. Williamson," which were so uncomfortable that "everyone who has travelled . . . over Mr. Williamson's routes wishes that sad things may happen to him; but no one, I believe,

BIG BULL

A Remington Indian, dressed as for battle, by 1892 a costume reserved chiefly for
Buffalo Bill's Wild West Show. From The West from a Car Window.

would be so wicked as to hope he may ever have to ride in one of his own
stages" (157–58). Once in Anadarko, Davis put up in the City Hotel, which he
thought to be "the worst hotel in the Indian Territory," and "the officers at
Fort Sill, who have travelled more than I, think it the worst in the United
States" (158). Here again, Davis as a journalist departs from the model established by his friend Bonsal and, while willing when necessary to put up
with the inconveniences of western travel, is often acutely conscious of the
low level of accommodations. He seems at times more a disgruntled tourist
than an adventuresome correspondent, but then it can also be said that the
further Davis gets from Bonsal, the closer he gets to Mark Twain, whose
grumpiness always had a humorous edge.

The next morning Davis witnessed the handing out of rations to the Indians on the reservation, the women receiving due measures of flour, soap,
sugar, and baking powder, all scooped from barrels into their open aprons,
to be sorted out after each woman left the line. Next came the beef ration,
administered on the hoof, or barely so, the steers being in such poor condition that "when they tried to run, [they] stumbled with the weakness of

starvation." Each steer was supposed to provide sufficient beef for twenty-five people for a period of two weeks, but the calculation is based on an animal weighing between "one thousand to one thousand and two hundred pounds," whereas it was very clear to Davis that the ration fell far short of the promised weight (162).

"The steers that I saw issued weighed about five hundred pounds," wrote Davis, for they had been purchased at full weight but then were allowed to winter over on the reservation, when forage was scarce. This resulted in a net saving for the contractor but was a decided loss for the intended recipient: "The agent is not to blame for this. This is the fault of the Government, and it is quite fair to suppose that some one besides the contractor benefits by the arrangement," someone, moreover, other than the person for whom the steer was intended (167). Davis the idealist here puts on his crusader's helmet, anxious to right wrongs by identifying the true culprit, in this case the Indian policy of the U.S. government, the same government that authorized an indiscriminate settling of the Oklahoma Territory.

Not that Davis was an apologist for the Native American: "A beef issue," he warns at the start, "is not a pretty thing to watch." Instead of mercifully slaughtering the cattle before turning the beef over to the Indians, the government has determined that it is somehow kindest to the beneficiaries to let them emulate the killing of the long vanished buffalo. Therefore, after each steer is turned loose, little boys under the approving smiles of their elders shoot many small arrows into its hide, wounding it but not mortally so. Next, it is shot at by its claimant with a Winchester, often many times over, so that the cow takes a long time in dying, a pack of dogs snapping at its wounds as it staggers about slowly bleeding to death:

> The field grew thick with these miniature butcheries, the Winchesters cracking, and the spurts of smoke rising and drifting away, the dogs yelping, and the Indians wheeling in quick circles around the steer, shooting as they rode, and hitting the mark once in every half-dozen shots. It was the most unsportsmanlike and wantonly cruel exhibition I have ever seen. A bull in a ring has a fighting chance and takes it, but these animals, who were too weak to stand, and too frightened to run, staggered about until the Indians had finished torturing them, and then, with eyes rolling and blood spurting from their mouths, would pitch forward and die. And they had to be quick about it, before the squaws began cutting off the hide while the flanks were still heaving. (166)

"This is," notes RHD grimly, "the view of the beef issue which the friend of the Indian does not like to take." Nor was Remington apparently interested in illustrating this chapter in Davis's book, there being nothing noble in this display of savagery. The whole affair is a bloody mess, one that could be remedied by a fair and humane handling of the procedure, but then that would reduce the profits of the contractor and the fun enjoyed by the Indians, presumably as compensation for the reduction in their rations. A further measure of irony is provided by the presence and participation in the affair of Native American policemen, in uniforms with brass buttons, each of which is engraved "with the figure of an Indian toiling at a plough in the centre," encircled with the motto "God helps them who help themselves" (166).

Davis draws a distinction between the two representatives of the U.S. government who oversee the reservations, the army officers and the Indian agents. The first are "men who have absolutely nothing to gain, make, or lose, by the Indians, and their point of view is accordingly the fairest." The agents, on the other hand, are political appointees who are frank to admit that they "are not here for their health." Yet these are the men put in charge of "hundreds of sensitive, dangerous, semi-civilized people, whom they are as capable of understanding as a Bowery boy would be of appreciating an Arab of the desert" (179).

Davis ends his chapter with a story about an agent who, having issued to the Indians in his charge wagons painted green, refused their request that the wagons be painted red, on the ground that he would be pandering "to their absurdly barbaric taste. . . . He was a man who had his own ideas about things, and who was not to be fooled, and he was also a superior person, who preferred to trample on rather than to understand the peculiarities of his wards. So one morning this agent and his wife and children were found hacked to pieces by these wards with barbaric tastes, and the soldiers were called out, and shot many of the Indians" (180).

Some of the soldiers were also killed, leading Davis to conclude "that it would be cheaper in the end to place agents over the Indians with sufficient intelligence to know just when to be firm, and when to compromise in a matter; for instance, that of painting a wagon red" (181). If RHD seems consistent in his journalist's pursuit in the West of novel and picturesque elements, so also does he emphasize throughout his book the need for proper and equitable methods of handling those situations unique to the region, a matter of fair dealing and fair play, elements essential to good sportsmanship.

Davis's realism shows itself not only in his occasional emphasis on the gritty, even bloody and violent aspects of the region but also in his pragmatic suggestions regarding the right way of doing things by demonstrating how badly they are handled at present, whether the subject is unregulated grants of free land or ill-advised issues of starving cattle. And his chivalric nature reveals itself in his championing of the virtues of army officers such as Captain Stiles and the cavalrymen stationed at western forts, all being soldiers who are skillful and dedicated in their service and untainted by the kinds of corruption extending westward from Washington, D.C. They are, in their profession, equivalents to the ideal correspondent Davis celebrated in Stephen Bonsal and attempted himself to emulate.

But here too Davis promotes a different emphasis from that found in the stories of Wister and the paintings by Remington, which generally depict cavalry life as exclusively male. For army wives had early on joined their husbands on western army posts, a fact attested to by the popular published account of "tenting on the plains" by the widow of General George Armstrong Custer. The presence of women, moreover, had not resulted in situations that might bring discredit to the U.S. Army.

"There are," notes RHD, "many in the East who think life at an army post is one of discomfort and more or less monotony, relieved by petty gossip and flirtations," but he saw very little of the latter (200). It was a lack explained to him by an officer's wife as being chiefly due to "the railroads":

> I had heard of many great advances and changes of conditions and territories brought about by the coming of the railroads, [but] this was the first time I had ever heard they had interfered with the course of more or less true [i.e., adulterous] love. She explained it by saying that in the days when army posts lay afar from the track of civilization the people were more dependent upon one another, and that then there may have existed Mrs. Hauksbees and Mrs. Knowles, but that to-day the railroads brought in fresh air and ideas from all over the country, and that the officers were constantly being exchanged, and others coming and going on detached services, and that visitors from the bigger outside world were appearing at all times. (201)

These references to women of flirtatious and seductive character are to stories of married life on army posts in India written by Kipling, which Andrew Lang in his essay in *Harper's Weekly* found shocking because of their frankness in dealing with sex. They were certainly negative in conveying an idea of the moral tone on the frontiers of the British Empire.

But as RHD tells it, any writer who wishes to set up as the American Kipling should perhaps look elsewhere for material than on a western army post, where the quality of life so "impresses a stranger as such a peaceful sort of an existence that he thinks that must be its chief and great attraction, and that which makes the army people, as they call themselves, so well content." Such a proposition might seem "absurd" on the face of it, "to speak of an army post of all places in the world as peaceful," but the West in 1892 is no longer associated with Indian wars, leaving the officer population with not much to do, save to "enjoy that blessing which is only to be found in the army and in the Church of Rome—of having one's life laid out for one by others, and in doing what one is told, and in not having to decide things for one's self" (201).

Cavalry officers in the West dwell in a male cloud-cuckoo-land, in which they are relieved of the anxieties of other professions and are free to hunt and fish in what amounts to a vast and necessarily exclusive game preserve. Moreover, the social life on an army post is a replication of the sort of thing RHD knew back in New York City, even to the comforts of the officers' homes and the multiplicity of place settings at a formal dinner table. He was surprised by this high level of social graces and hoped only that "the army people will not resent this, and proudly ask, 'What did he expect to find?' but I am sure that is not the idea of a frontier post we have received in the East. There was also something delightfully novel in the table-talk," as when he heard "one pretty, slight woman, in a smart décolleté gown, casually tell how her husband and his men had burned the prairie grass around her children and herself, and turned aside a prairie fire that towered and roared around them" (204–5). Small wonder that most of the officers on an army post were married, "when there are women who can adapt themselves as gracefully to snow-shoes at Fort Brady as to the serious task of giving dinners at Fort Houston" (205).

If life on an army post is a well-regulated utopia where all the social graces are observed, then Fort Sam Houston, "one of the three largest posts in the country," is a veritable heaven on earth for "the army people." Close to the city and enjoying a mild climate year-round, the fort is furnished with palm trees and in the summer "white uniforms—which are unknown to the posts farther north, and which are as pretty as they are hard to keep clean," making "the parade-ground look like a cricket-field" (205–6). Dances are held twice a month, with music provided by the regimental band and the officers are arrayed in colorful uniforms, matching the signal flags and banners that decorate the hall. By contrast, there is the army post at Oklahoma

City, a small, literally one-company affair, "built of logs and mud." There one finds few wives if any, and no dances or dinner parties.

Some slight advantages exist in such places if they lie near a town, but there are none at all on army posts farther out along the frontier, "where there are no towns, and where every man knows what the next man is going to say before he speaks." These forts house "single companies which the Government has dropped out there, and which it has apparently forgotten, as a man forgets the book he has tucked away in his shelf to read on some rainy day. They will probably find they are remembered when the rainy days come" (206).

It would be an incomplete story of life at a post which said nothing of the visits of homesickness, which, many strong men have confessed to me, is the worst sickness with which man is cursed. And it is an illness which comes at irregular periods to those of the men who know and who love the East. It is not a homesickness for one home or for one person, but a case of that madness which seized Private Ortheris, only in a less malignant form, and in the officer's quarters. An impotent protest against the immutability of time and of space is one of its symptoms—a sick disgust of the blank prairie, blackened by fire as though it had been drenched with ink, the bare parade-ground, the same faces, the same stories, the same routine and detailed life, which promises no change or end; and with these a longing for streets and rows of houses that seemed commonplace before, of architecture which they had dared to criticise, and which now seems fairer than the lines of the Parthenon, a craving to get back to a place where people, whether one knows them or not, are hurrying home from work under the electric lights, to the rush of the passing hansoms and the cries of the "last editions," and the glare of the shop windows, to the life of a great city that is as careless of the exile's love for it as is the ocean to one who exclaims upon its grandeur from the shore; a soreness of heart which makes men while it lasts put familiar photographs out of sight, which makes the young lieutenants, when the band plays a certain waltz on the parade at sundown, bite their chin straps and stare ahead more fixedly than the regulations require. Some officers will confess this to you, and some will not. It is a question which is the happier, he who has no other scenes for which to care, and who is content, or he who eats his heart out for a while, and goes back on leave at last. (211–12)

This extended paragraph ends RHD's account of life on army posts. It serves as another demonstration of his mastery of prose (written again as if with an ear tuned to the spoken word), as well as his use of sentimentality to arouse sympathy for the subject, whether it be lonely young women in New York City or lonely young men on the outposts of American empire.

The passage also emphasizes two themes worth noting. First, there is the allusion to one of Kipling's "Soldiers Three," the enlisted man who went berserk while on his frontier post in India. It serves as a further tie between Davis's western journey and that felt necessity somehow to rival the writer who had enjoyed such a rapid ascent in popularity and critical reputation from his stories about the farther reaches of the British Empire. Second, in defining the difference between life on remote outposts in India and western army forts in America, Davis is careful to associate the madness resulting from isolation with the "less malignant" forms taken in the "officer's quarters."

The distinction drives home the obvious point that when RHD refers to "army people," he means the only kind of people of interest to him, namely, those who live in the "officers quarters," for he made no attempt to single out equivalents to Trumpeter Tyler on the western army posts he visited. Davis was perfectly content to enjoy the comforts of officer life when they were made available to him, routinely (and openly) complaining when journalistic necessity took him out into less pleasant surroundings.

It would be Owen Wister who would render the most memorable account in fiction of enlisted army life in the West, creating a hero out of Specimen Jones, who resembles Tyler in a number of ways, being well educated and having a marvelous singing voice. Moreover, though wearing only a sergeant's stripes, Jones has qualities of leadership that are associated with elites. Wister, that is to say, had it both ways, much as in his cowboy hero, the Virginian, he created an uneducated but charismatic leader, an updated George Washington. Like Specimen Jones, his cowboy was a natural aristocrat, fulfilling the hopes of Thomas Jefferson for the American people.

It was Wister, therefore, who became the American Kipling, deriving from his many visits to the West an idealized territory, set in an immediate past that was nonetheless quite different from the life RHD encountered, for the reasons I have given. But that is Davis's own conclusion, that writers who sought romantic material in the modern West were bound to be disappointed. Not himself drawn to historical subjects but with contemporary writers such as Norris and Crane concerned with depicting modern times—

the journalistic mandate—RHD would leave the West as unlikely material. He would leave it, that is to say, to Owen Wister, who would create a territory almost entirely of his own imagining.

Wister seems not to have been particularly grateful for the favor. Rudyard Kipling came to the United States in that same year of 1892, with the intention of taking up permanent residence. Through the agency of Theodore Roosevelt, the British writer eventually made the acquaintance of the writer who was TR's favorite candidate for the American Kipling, which by that time Kipling himself was fast becoming, having by then built a home in his wife's native Vermont.

The two writers hit it off famously when they were first introduced by Roosevelt at his own home in Washington in 1895, and later Wister visited Kipling on his new estate, where the two men took long walks through the woods and talked late into the night, discovering that they agreed on everything. Among the many things they agreed on was Richard Harding Davis, toward whom Wister expressed "disappointment and distrust," despite having recently received from Davis a friendly notice of the forthcoming *Red Men and White,* along with an admiring note (Payne 163).

But Kipling and Wister seem to have agreed mostly on negative views of their contemporaries, and Davis was put into the unlikely company of Hamlin Garland, whose *Main-Travelled Roads* had just been published, while Kipling and Wister declared a mutual reverence for the works of Sir Walter Scott, an attitude they jointly defined as "wholesomely orthodox." Wister's biographer, Darwin Payne, does not tell us what it was about RHD that inspired such negative reactions on the part of writers he so admired. Nonetheless, in *The West from a Car Window* Davis mapped out for Wister the territory he would famously populate with western heroes, then left it for the other man to claim.

: IV :

"The West," Davis declared, in bringing his book to a close, "is a very wonderful, large, unfinished, and out-of-doors portion of our country, and a most delightful place to visit. I would advise every one in the East to visit it, and I hope to revisit it myself." Some who make that trip, he conjectured, would remain, and in time "the course of empire will eventually Westward take its way. But when it does, it will leave [this] one individual behind it clinging closely to the Atlantic seaboard" (242).

In his penultimate line Davis declared that "little old New York" was "good enough for him," a preference that his western visit had only reinforced: "If any one doubts this, let him leave it for three months, and do one-night stands at fourth-rate hotels, or live on alkali water and bacon, and let him travel seven thousand miles over a country where a real-estate office, a Citizen's Bank, and Quick Order Restaurant, with a few surrounding houses, make, as seen from the car window, a booming city, where beautiful scenery and grand mountains are separated by miles of prairie and chaparral" (242).

In his final chapter, "The Heart of the Great Divide," in which these opinions appear, Davis begins with a description of Denver, which being a modern metropolis surrounded by charming suburbs most recommends itself because of its resemblance to an eastern city. If indeed empire moves westward, it clearly had arrived at the foot of the Rocky Mountains. Although there still is a chance that a visitor might "enjoy the picturesque excitement of being held up by train robbers," a tourist is "in much more constant danger of being held up by commercial travellers and native Western men, who demand that you stand and deliver your name, your past history, your business, and your excuse for being where you are" (225–26).

The West that was populated by pioneers and desperadoes lives on mostly in "stories" told about such "characters," tales that provided "the most vivid and most interesting memories I have of the trip."

> But these men have been crowded out, or have become rich and respectably commonplace, or have been shot, as the case may be. I met the men who had lynched them or who remembered them, but not the men themselves. They no longer over-run the country; they disappeared with the buffalo, and the West is glad of it, but it is disappointing to the visitor. The men I met were men of business, who would rather talk of the new court-house with the lines of the sod still showing around it than of the Indian fights and the killing of the bad man of earlier days when there was no courthouse, and when the vigilance committee was a necessary evil. These were "well-posted" and "well-informed" citizens, and if there is one being I dread and fly from, it is a well-posted citizen. (226)

Davis's distinction here is the "great divide" that Wister would become famous by celebrating, his stories and novel being an extended postmortem on a West that no longer existed.

In Davis's only western short story, "The Boy Orator of Zepata City," published in *Harper's Magazine* late in 1892, he framed his plot around the trial for murder of the last of the desperadoes. A youthful district attorney (the "boy" of the title, a gratuitous poke at the young William Jennings Bryan, already prominent as an orator for his speeches in Congress favoring free silver) seeks to have the outlaw imprisoned forever, thereby burying him with the rest of the Wild West. But the last of the bad men is set free when he pleads that he be allowed to redeem himself in the eyes of his wife, a sentimental conclusion of a sort that Owen Wister never used in his own western stories, which render a hard-bitten, male-dominated world.

Wister did give a sentimental ending to *The Virginian,* and by marrying his handsome cowboy to a schoolteacher inspired outrage in Frederic Remington and wistful regret in Henry James. But Davis chose to write a fan letter of sorts, claiming that he had been inspired by Wister's novel "to go to New Mexico and Arizona on my own to get 'local color' at the fountainhead. So could you tell me where I ought to go to see cowboys, indians, army posts, and ranches" (Payne 207).

It was a request the sarcastic point of which anyone familiar with *The West from a Car Window* would have understood, and Davis's demurral concerning the regional origins of Wister's hero was in the same debunking spirit: "The last time I saw a first family Virginian he was hitting a bell and saying 'Take two towels and a pitcher of water to 296'" (Payne 207). This wry humor, so typical of Davis in his travel writing, is the kind of thing that causes romantic myths to wither away. Though the thinly veiled reproof was written in 1902, it provides some warrant to that unfavorable opinion of RHD shared by Wister and Kipling seven years earlier. He could no more be trusted than, as his letter suggests, can Wister's celebrated account of an impossibly romantic, intensely picturesque, and thus an "interesting" West.

But if in *The West from a Car Window* Davis did not contribute to the legend that Wister and his friend Roosevelt labored so hard to promote, that is what makes the book valuable to us today. Not only did Davis render an account of a transformed, "new" American West the year before Turner announced that the frontier was officially closed, he vividly portrayed a region lacking those qualities which nourish the romantic impulse. Wister, in his introduction to *The Virginian,* acknowledged that the cowboy, like Columbus's caravels, would return no more. But by then Davis's book had been in print for a decade, his own contribution to the Columbian anniversary having provided concrete evidence that the frontier had indeed disappeared, not so much as available land but as a sustainable myth.

Davis, remember, belonged to a new class of romance writers, who looked to the present moment for their materials, not the recent or remote past, as did Wister. Kipling may have shared Wister's reverence for Scott, but he was the leader in this new movement, and when RHD went west he seems to have been screening the region as a possible setting for Kipling's kind of fiction but found little to encourage a writer ambitious to set up as Rudyard's American rival. In his short story "Boy Orator of Zepata City," Davis gave fictional and highly seasoned shape to the idea that dominates his account of the modern West, that the adventuresome frontier is gone, a vacancy that is the point of the thing entire. Likewise, as a journalist looking for material, Davis had discovered that there was nothing left to report other than that there was nothing left to report.

Though Davis would not find in the West what he needed for his kind of fiction, it is notable that his most famous romantic hero is from that region, an emphasis that validates the emerging myth while fulfilling Davis's sense that a modern romance needed to seek out new regions, in his case Central America, for the display of heroic virtues. This is not to say that in his subsequent travel writings Davis was constantly on the lookout for the possibilities for fiction. But when he came across what seemed to him likely settings and situations, he was quick to turn them into short stories and novels, a continuity that, like Roosevelt's career, leads inevitably to Cuba.

He's an Anglo-Saxon messenger—and those are Anglo-Saxon attitudes.
LEWIS CARROLL

6 : IN DARKEST BRITAIN

: I :

Throughout *The West from a Car Window,* Richard Harding Davis reveals the snobbery that was habitual with him, an open preference for the company of elites, whether army officers or persons of wealth and privilege, like the young men he bunked with in Creede. For Davis, a commission, an Ivy League diploma, or a private club membership was like the sterling stamp on a piece of silver, symbols of immediate and unquestioned value. He was himself a member of the Players, a club in New York founded by actors and theater people, with whom he was fond of associating. Ironically, though it was the exclusiveness of club life in general that attracted him, when he became famous he collected honorary memberships in clubs as assiduously as he did foreign medals and decorations.

G. Edward White has demonstrated the importance of private clubs as an extension into the West of the privileged life associated with eastern colleges and universities, a conduit between Manhattan and such places as Cheyenne. The closed society offered sanctuary to transplanted easterners like Theodore Roosevelt and his friend Wister, and had Davis remained for a time in the West, we may be sure that he would have taken advantage of the opportunities to mingle with his fellow clubmen.

As it was, he recalled encountering "the part owner of a ranch, whom I supposed I had left looking over the papers in the club," and whose partner "was 'Jerry' Black, who, as I trust no one has forgotten, was one of Princeton's half-backs" (*West* 229). Like most institutions in the United States that sustained the privileged lives of elites, private clubs were inspired by the British example, and the membership of cattlemen's clubs in the West was a mixture of native-born U.S. ranchers and those who had come over from Great Britain.

Perhaps by chance, the only Englishmen Davis seems to have met in the West were those who had fallen on hard times, providing interesting examples of privileged persons suddenly divested of their wealth. According to RHD, "San Antonio seemed particularly rich in histories of those who came there to change their fortunes," but often for the worse, and it was the Englishmen who provided "the most conspicuous examples of those unfortunates—conspicuous in the sense that their position at home had been so good, and their habits of life so widely different" (229–30). Here again Davis anticipated Wister, whose long short story "The Right Honorable the Strawberries" is about a British nobleman down on his luck in the West. The prevalence of Englishmen in that region was so notable that Wister hardly needed Davis to point them out: "The proportion of young English gentlemen who are roughing it in the West far exceeds that of the young Americans" (230).

They did so not from choice but from necessity. Most of them either had been swindled out of what money they brought with them or had gambled it away. Unlike their American counterparts, these young men had not been trained to earn a livelihood and "take to driving horses or branding cattle or digging in the streets, as one graduate of Oxford, sooner than write home for money, did in Denver" (230). Davis told of hearing "stories of this sort on every side, and we met faro-dealers, cooks, and cowboys who have served through campaigns in India or Egypt, or who hold an Oxford degree. A private . . . who was my escort on several scouting expeditions in the Garza outfit, was kind enough and quite able to tell me which club in London had the oldest wine-cellar. . . . He did this quite unaffectedly, and in no way attempted to excuse his present position" (231).

Englishmen were not the only persons who found themselves fallen from high place in the West, and Davis encountered a "brakeman on a freight and passenger train in Southern Texas . . . whom I remembered at Lehigh University as an expert fencer. . . . Another man whom I remembered as a 'society' reporter on a New York paper, turned up in a white apron as a waiter at a hotel" (229). But clearly it was the Englishmen in the West who provided the most picturesque contrast, much as the landscape differed so starkly from that of Great Britain: "Hundreds of miles of level mud and snow followed by a hot and sandy soil and uncultivated farm lands are not as interesting as hedges of hawthorn or glimpses of the Thames or ivy-covered country-houses in parks of oak" (225).

Moreover, we can credit Davis's interest in these unfortunates to his own deep-seated Anglophilia. His love of all things English was hardly unique to him but was particularly strong in the eastern United States in the late nineteenth century, a time when Anglo-Saxon origins were regarded as all the more precious for being under demographic challenge by the flood of

middle and southern European immigrants. The Republican stalwart Senator Henry Cabot Lodge, whose very name leaked blue, attempted in 1896 to
push through Congress a bill that would restrict immigration to "desirable"
persons, an idea that had gained increasing momentum in the wake of the
1886 Haymarket Riots. In 1885, while still enrolled at Johns Hopkins, Davis
himself delivered a speech proposing a tax on immigrants in order to halt
the influx of impoverished foreigners, a response to what many intelligent
(and well-placed) Americans considered a threat to the stability of national
institutions.

Perhaps the clearest evidence of Davis's Anglophilia was the series of
short stories he wrote, starting in 1890, about the adventures of Cortlandt
Van Bibber, a sophisticated, high-living young New Yorker and a member of
the exclusive Knickerbocker Club. Van Bibber is generally regarded as a projection of what RHD at the time regarded as his ideal self. A number of the
stories were illustrated by Charles Dana Gibson, using his friend as a model,
further cementing the connection. Though obviously from an old Dutch
family, the young man is determinedly English in manner, as were many
New Yorkers associated with the exclusive set to which Davis longed to gain
entry. Anthony Hope Hawkins singled out the Van Bibber stories for especial
praise, suggesting their (and his) essential bias toward British ideals. Davis's
eponymous hero is a "swell" with a social conscience—or a snob with a
heart of gold—and the stories in which he figures have a uniformly sentimental tone and plot, with endings that anticipate the happy reversals in
O. Henry's tales.

In most of the Van Bibber stories the young hero is associated with acts
that emphasize his essential chivalry, bright gleams of nobility in an otherwise wastrel existence. It is this contrast that suggests RHD's indebtedness
to Bret Harte's heroic gambler, John Oakhurst, who like Van Bibber is a projection of the author's self-image, which was in both instances inspired
by an exaggerated reverence for the British example. Van Bibber's self-
indulgent, indolent existence—he is given to attending boxing matches,
betting on horses, dining and drinking out until early in the morning and
sleeping in the next day—contrasts with his essentially idealistic and romantic view of life. It thereby provides a disguise for his chivalric acts of
generosity and courage, and in this he resembles the comic book superheroes of recent times.

Where Harte's hero is a creature of the demimonde, whose privileged
past is only hinted at, Van Bibber is authentically a son of the wealthy class
and as such emphasizes the worth of moneyed persons, this at a time when

'EVEN TO-DAY. THERE IS THE CHANCE SAMARITAN.'"

Davis's young cosmopolitan hero Cortlandt Van Bibber, dressed
in his habitual costume of formal evening dress, opera cape, and silk
hat, as rendered by the artist-illustrator Charles Dana Gibson,
who here as elsewhere used his friend Davis as his model.

radical protest and labor unrest were on the rise. Equally important, unlike Oakhurst, who is associated with adulterous affairs, Van Bibber, while attractive to women and fond of their company, evinces a Davis-like chasteness in keeping with his chivalric image, despite his Byronic propensity for late-night carousing.

Though he is most definitely an American youth, operating in a definably American setting, Van Bibber is a testimony to the transatlantic influence of Victorianism, with its chivalric ideals. For all his wastrel ways he is pure at heart, being innocent of sexual escapades and thereby as "clean" as the man who created him. He is of a class with that courageous football player from Princeton who lost his life trying to save the life of a servant girl, a modern Galahad, with a top hat for a helmet and a boiled shirt for armor plate.

Van Bibber may be a creation of the early 1890s, but he is also a prefiguration of later Davis heroes, who will be associated with climates much more exotic than Manhattan can offer. Like the Englishmen Davis encountered in the West, these adventurers seek their fortunes in dangerous places, but they emerge triumphant from their experiences, morally if not financially. Yet it is clear that the virtues they portray are, like Van Bibber's, derived from the British tradition, on current display in the stories by Kipling, in which tropic zones provide the new arena for the demonstration of heroic qualities. It is there that the emerging hero of Davis's romances will head, carrying with him the traditions of British chivalry while bearing a banner emblazoned with the Stars and Stripes.

: II :

The British connection is especially strong in one of the best of Davis's short pieces, "An Unfinished Story," first published in *Harper's Magazine* in October 1891, which unfolds during a dinner party set amid "the great mass of stucco and brick of encircling London" (224). The story contains a number of elements that will be reworked in *Soldiers of Fortune,* his most famous romance and the one with a strong Cuban connection, thus the implications of its plot and character, which are sufficiently complex to warrant a novella, merit consideration. Central to the action is an American explorer recently returned from Africa who dominates the dinner table conversation with a story of his own, a narrative frame we associate with both Conrad and Henry James.

Arthur Lubow regards the narrator-protagonist of "An Unfinished Story" as the first manifestation of "the classic Davis hero" (81). He believes that the tale, while influenced by both Kipling and Stevenson, was inspired by the real-life adventures of RHD's wealthy and blue-blooded friend William Astor Chanler, whose exploits would inspire a piece by Davis published in *Harper's Monthly* in March 1893, "An American in Africa." That article contains a portrait of the handsome young man who had been educated at Exeter and Harvard and who displays a firm-jawed, athletic profile to match, an indication of his Anglo-Saxon heritage.

At the time Davis wrote his article, Chanler was just starting out on the great adventure suggested by the title of the piece, thereby giving Davis a dandy opening line: "About four months ago young William Astor Chanler went into Africa, to be gone two years," and "when he returns," RHD promised, "his story will be well worth the telling. But even should he never return, his story, unfinished as it is to-day, has certain values," starting with "that value which attaches to the work of those who explore the few territories still unknown to us." To this may be added the "value in the intense personality of the young man himself," as well as that obtained from the fact "that he is the first man born in this country to carry the American flag into Africa at the head of so important an expedition" (632). In sum, Chanler's career is a display of heroism with nationalistic overtones, providing a model for other wealthy youths.

According to Davis, the adventure in question was not Chanler's first venture into the "Dark Continent." Barely out of Harvard in 1887, he left for Africa with "only one white companion, his servant," leading a party of 180 men "around the mountain of Kilima-Njaro and through the land of the Masai, where Henry M. Stanley has said it is not safe to go with even a thousand rifles." As Chanler breezily told another, senior explorer he met while making his way through the African wild, he was doing it "for fun," and the experience had "whetted his appetite for more." It was between the first and second of Chanler's expeditions that Davis wrote "An Unfinished Story," even as his young friend was making plans for his much greater adventure, which entailed even more risk but promised large, if not monetary, rewards.

After a year and a half of preparations, Chanler set out "on September 16, 1892," from Lamu, leading "a caravan . . . for Somali Land, a country in East Africa extending along the coast from Abyssinia to Cape Guardafui. In about two months after the date of his departure he expects to reach Mount Kenia, where he will halt for some weeks to ascend the mountain, which is estimated to be over 18,000 feet high. From Mount Kenia he purposes to push north through the desert to the southern extremity of Lake Rudolph, and after this lake region is explored, will enter with his caravan from Lake

Stephenie into 600 miles of utterly unknown territory, which lies between
the lakes and the Juba River. If he reaches this river, Chanler will follow it to
the ocean, and then journey along the sea-shore to Lamu" (634).

Chanler's journey was to be some three thousand miles and would take
at least two years to accomplish, during which no word was expected from
the young explorer, who, as Davis's pivotal "if" suggests, may never return.
It is a route through regions that have cost the lives of earlier explorers and
with goals that have not been reached by men with much greater experience. This time Chanler is not traveling "for fun" but with a serious aim, for
"the benefits to science, if it be accomplished, will be of incalculable value."

His is not the quest of a man leaving home "for the love of the adventure
or for fame" but with the "earnest aim" revealed by the scientific equipment
he is carrying. These include "his telescopic cameras, which enable him to
photograph an object half a mile distant, and yet make it look when devel-
oped as though it had been taken at a few yards' range," as well as "a search-
light, which is to be used to show the position of a certain tribe which always
attacks at night" and "a stock of war-rockets which go through the air in various colors and in irregular lines, and with which he intends to pursue retreating foes."

Such an expedition requires a leader of exceptional qualities, both
courage and knowledge. He must know "the endurance of a man as compared with the endurance of a camel" and be informed in the fields "of med-
icine and of agriculture, of engineering and of war, of geography and of
diplomacy." Chanler not only had to negotiate with the East Africa Company
but also with several governments for permission to undertake this enterprise, and "had to know enough of agriculture, for one thing, to properly
plant certain cereals, so that on his return journey he might be able to enjoy
their fruit; of surgery, to care for the sick or wounded in his outfit; of pho-
tography, to reproduce the scenes and people which he will be the first
white man to see; and of military tactics, to organize and discipline a force
of three hundred men" (634–35).

And yet "if you should meet Chanler as I met him last he would appeal to
you as a most live, interesting, and entertaining youth, and not at all the sort
of young man you would expect to meet at the head of three hundred negroes in the heart of Africa." Like Stephen Bonsal, and for similar reasons,
Chanler is good company, a man who can regale his friends "with reminis-
cences of Harvard or the boulevards" of Paris one minute, then amaze them
as "the worldly, idle, and conscientiously dressed youth . . . told how men

look who are dying of thirst, or how an elephant is liable to act when you fire at it" (633–34).

The same man who spent part of his day "testing smokeless powder and repeating-rifles, or choosing canned meats and bottled medicines," among other extensive and detailed preparations for his expedition, could "still later walk past Stanhope Gate and critically inspect the gowns [of the women] on the lawn, or order a dinner at the Savoy with enviable taste." Chanler was equally interested in discussing "the coming Presidential election in our own country or the selection of a button-hole at Simpson's," a famous British tailor (633).

This is an important criterion of the emerging Davis culture hero: that he be perfectly at home whether dealing with African kings or conversing with fellow clubmen, that he be, above all else, "interesting," thanks to the multiplicity of his experiences and accomplishments. It is an ideal that, as his contemporaries testified, Richard Harding Davis would himself exemplify in a few short years, by which time his carefully cultivated public image would merge with those fictional heroes with profiles cut along his own firm-jawed silhouette, both close in outline to that of William Astor Chanler.

Chanler, moreover, is an exemplar of quiet modesty, slipping away on his second trip to Africa without any public notice:

> Young men who do important things for the sake of the things themselves, and not for the afterclap of applause, are so few that it seems almost a pity to spoil Mr. Chanler's modest departure by even this reference to it. But there are other reasons why his story should be written, the chief one being, to my mind, the chance that what Chanler has done and what he hopes to do may suggest to other young men who do not have to work that there are more dangerous as well as more profitable sports than following hounds across country, and that they may get much amusement, and may benefit the world, and gain experience and strength for themselves, not by following his footsteps, but by making their own footsteps mark the way into new countries and among strange peoples. (637–38)

Equally admirable, because of Chanler's dedication to useful enterprise, when (and if) the young man returns he plans not "to rest on his lion-skins, or pose upon lecture platforms," but to "serve his country by representing it and the city of New York in Congress," an ambition "natural" for "the great-great-grandson of John Jacob Astor, who opened up the great Northwest, or

in the son of John Winthrop Chanler, for three consecutive terms a Democratic congressman of New York City." With this distinguished paternity and
his abundant energy and abilities, Chanler is an exceptional member of his
generation: "To most young men it would be quite enough to have opened
up a new country; their ambition, or restlessness, or desire for power and responsibility, or whatever it is which makes young men exert themselves,
would be amply satisfied by this; but Chanler treats himself to this expedition into Africa, and thinks his serious work in life lies after his holiday in
that strange country is over. But then when you have said that, you have told
the whole story. Chanler is not content to be like most young men" (635). By
Davis's account, Chanler is something of a superhero, the master of any
number of specialized skills, the polymath that the complex, technology-
controlled world revealed in the World's Fair of 1893 would need, but who
carried all that knowledge in a head with a hero's profile. He was, in short,
the ideal leader that a United States seeking to enter the imperial lists, "carrying the American flag" into as yet unexplored, unmapped territories,
would need.

So also the explorer in "An Unfinished Story," who has been like Bonsal
(and Davis) a journalist but who has also filled a number of heroic roles re-
quiring specialized skills: "He had been an engineer, a newspaper correspondent, an officer in a Chinese army, and had built bridges in South America, and led their little revolutions there, and had seen service on the desert
in the French army of Algiers. He had no home or nationality even, for he
had left America when he was sixteen; he had no family, had saved no
money, and was trusting everything to the success of this expedition into
Africa to make him known and to give him position" (238). Like the journalist in "The Reporter Who Made Himself King," this man is named Gordon, for Davis obviously intends this "vagabond" to evoke not only the hero
of Khartoum but also the romantic rootlessness of the grand original,
George Gordon, Lord Byron. Gordon's multifaceted and heroic life is, however, untainted by Byronic hypersexuality. It is instead a chivalric expression of both freedom and courage, which proves a very attractive mixture to
a wealthy young woman from New York.

As Gordon himself puts it, entertaining his British hosts with a purportedly true story that projects his own history through an invented second
party, also an African explorer:

It was the story of Othello and Desdemona over again. His blackness lay
from her point of view, or rather would have laid from the point of view

of her friends, in the fact that he was as helplessly ineligible a young man as a cowboy. And he really had lived a life of which he had no great reason to be proud. He had existed entirely for excitement, as other men live to drink until they kill themselves by it; nothing he had done had counted for much except his bridges. They are still standing. But the things he had written are lost in the columns of the daily papers. The soldiers he had fought with knew him only as a man who cared more for the fighting than for what the fighting was about, and he had been as ready to write on one side as to fight on the other. He was a rolling stone, and had been a rolling stone from the time he was sixteen and had run away to sea, up to the day he had met this girl, when he was just thirty." (238–39)

As Lubow tells us, Gordon was undoubtedly inspired in part by William Astor Chanler, but his background is quite different from that of the wealthy young American, a man free to pursue his adventuresome career because he can afford it. Therefore, while acknowledging the connection, we should also note the extent to which the hero as described merges with the outlines of the explorer briefly mentioned in Davis's account of Chanler's first expedition in Africa, Henry M. Stanley. For Stanley loomed large in the public imagination in 1893 and as a famous war correspondent served Davis as a model for emulation as his own career took off.

: III :

Born in Wales in 1841, Stanley was virtually orphaned at an early age and, after a Dickensian childhood, in 1859 moved to the United States, where he worked for a benevolent employer, who informally adopted him but died before the connection was made legal. When the Civil War broke out, Stanley enlisted in the Confederate Army, was imprisoned at Shiloh, nearly died in a prison camp, then upon his release volunteered to serve with the Union forces. At war's end, Stanley became the famous correspondent who, after covering Indian wars in America and the British invasion of Abyssinia, went on, under assignment from James Gordon Bennett of the *New York Herald,* to find Livingstone in Africa.

After discovering the true source of the Nile, among other subsequent feats of exploration, Stanley brought civilization, King Leopold, and a rail line to the Congo. Like Chanler's, Stanley's is a strongly gendered ideal, but it is far more than that, as the allusion to Othello in "An Unfinished Story" should suggest. That is, the "blackness" of Davis's heroic soldier-correspondent-engineer-explorer stems from his social status, which being in effect classless and without elite origins equates him with the heroic Moor, on the one hand, and with Stanley, on the other.

Stanley's social status was considered so negligible by British geographers as to discount the reports of previously unexplored areas of Africa he brought back in 1872 after his successful journey in quest of Livingstone. His connection with Bennett aroused suspicion, and he was publicly disgraced by having his lowly birth revealed. Stanley was eventually proven right, but he spent almost twenty years attempting to gain the respect of British elites, an ambition that was eventually successful, resulting in honorary degrees and a knighthood in 1899, the year RHD visited him on his hard-earned country estate. Single for most of his adventurous life, Henry Stanley married after his accomplishments were recognized in England and his writings had brought him considerable wealth. This was in 1890, when Stanley was almost fifty: Until then his adventures were coupled with a purportedly celibate existence that contributed to his chivalric image.

The explorer made two triumphant tours in America: the first in 1886, after a decade spent in Africa in the service of King Leopold, and the second in 1890, riding the wave of his fame after rescuing Emin Pasha. He was introduced to a Boston audience by Mark Twain, who stressed Stanley's "indestructible Americanism." At a time "when it is the custom to ape and imitate English methods and fashions, it is like a breath of fresh air to stand in the presence of this untainted American citizen who has been caressed and complimented by half of the crowned heads of Europe." Patently ignoring Stanley's British origins, Twain insisted that he was "a product of institutions which exist in no other country on earth—institutions that bring out all that is best and most heroic in a man" (Clemens 132).

Likewise, in 1890, introducing Stanley to an audience that filled the Metropolitan Opera House in New York, Chauncey Depew identified him as an "American traveler and explorer" whose "great discoveries and wonderful achievements have been made and performed by him as an American citizen. . . . It is a career intensely American and dramatic" ("Great Forest" 377). Depew noted that Stanley had been prepared for the hazards of African exploration by his earlier experience as a war correspondent, which immunized him to hardship even while calling forth "fertility of resource in perils of savages, perils of flood, and perils of the wilderness" (378). We may be sure that Richard Harding Davis was not unaware of this last emphasis, having in 1886 commenced his own career as a famous correspondent by covering the Johnstown Flood. Then in 1890 he wrote his story for boys about the young reporter who wanted to be a war correspondent and ended up by imitating Stanley in bringing civilization to the residents of a remote and tropical land—albeit more civilization than he had intended.

Of equal importance was the insistence by Twain and Depew that Henry Morton Stanley was an instance of American initiative and courage, hence a ready model for the emerging Davis hero. Unlike the wealthy and privileged William Astor Chanler, Stanley was a self-made man and therefore comes much closer in profile not only to the American prototype for success but also to Davis's fictional explorer, Gordon. Like him, Stanley had a multifaceted career, combining military service with war reporting, and having opened "darkest Africa" by his explorations, remained there to build a railroad, becoming in effect a civil engineer.

The Stanley connection is further cemented in Gordon's virtual lack of nationality, his orphan status as he travels about the world—a "rolling stone"—and the hope that his proposed African expedition would bring him fame and fortune, thereby qualifying him for marriage with the upper-class American woman he loves. She is drawn to him because of "the daring of his present undertaking . . . and the picturesqueness of his past life," but she belongs to a level of society even more unattainable to him than the interior of Africa so long as he is without wealth and position: "It came to him like a sign from the heavens. It was as if a goddess had stooped to him. He told her when they separated that if he succeeded—if he opened this unknown country, if he was rewarded as they had promised to reward him—he might dare to come to her; and she called him her knight-errant, and gave him her chain and locket to wear, and told him whether he failed or succeeded it meant nothing to her, and that her life was his while it lasted, and her soul as well" (Davis, "Unfinished Story" 239–40).

Manhood is the issue here, as it is in so much of Davis's writing, but far more important is the matter of class, underlined by a subtler consideration, certainly of interest to Davis, who when he wrote this story was himself an author identified with the most ephemeral kind of work and who had accomplished nothing equivalent to the engineer's "bridges." What was required of a "man" was a "work" of some substance and permanence, whether in the arts, the mechanical sciences, or, as here, profitable discovery. The necessary chivalric link is provided by the heart-shaped locket, a token of plighted troth like that carried by a knight, equating the explorer's quest with the Arthurian errand, never mind the adventures of Rider Haggard's Allan Quatermain, another fictional version of Henry Stanley.

Gordon's audience is a dinner party of guests gathered on the eve of their departure from London for their summer places. "It was a most delightful

choice of people, gathered at short notice and to do honor to no one in particular," but "if there was a guest of the evening, it was one of the two Americans," either Gordon or "Miss Egerton, the girl who was to marry Lord
Arbuthnot," a young nobleman ambitious to succeed in politics (224).
The dinner party also includes a general, a novelist, the Austrian minister, and
a society painter—Trevelyan, the host—as well as "some simply fashionable smart people who were good listeners" (224). Having recently spent
time in London, where he was accepted by the highest social circles because
of his editorship of *Harper's Weekly,* RHD knew whereof he wrote.

The centerpiece of this gathering is Miss Egerton, "a most strikingly
beautiful girl, with a strong, fine face, and an earnest, interested way when
she spoke, which the English found most attractive." She had been likened
by Trevelyan, who was working on her portrait, "to a druidess, a vestal vir-
gin, and a Greek goddess." But the attention of the guests is drawn to the
other American, the explorer, who seems reluctant to join the conversation:
"The worst of Gordon was that he made it next to impossible for one to li-
onize him," being skilled (like Chanler) at dodging the attentions of his
hostesses at the many functions to which he had been invited (224–25). The
assumption of Mrs. Trevelyan, being English, is that Miss Egerton and Gordon must know one another, not only because they are both Americans but
also because "they had both been made so much of, and at the same houses"
(227). It turns out that the hostess is both right and very wrong.

Gordon has accepted the invitation only because his host was an old
friend, having known him when Trevelyan "was a travelling correspondent
and artist for one of the great weeklies" (226). Trevelyan had "found him at
the club the night before, and had asked him to his wife's impromptu dinner." The club connection serves to reinforce Gordon's social status, much
as his friendship with the artist connotes his cosmopolitanism, and the conversation at the dinner brings out another of Gordon's heroic qualifications,
as well as his narrative skill.

After some superficial exchanges the talk turns to the matter of art versus reality, a subject introduced by Philips, the novelist, who has been arguing a point brought up by Sir Henry, the general, "that fiction is stranger
than truth" (227). The general then appeals to Gordon, a man who has seen
so much of the world, to corroborate his point that "what happens only suggests the story; it is not complete in itself" and that it is the duty and the responsibility of the novelist to give definitive shape ("closure," as the Austrian minister calls it) to the plain and unadorned facts of life (232).

Because he is directly challenged, the American is forced to disagree with

Sir Henry, maintaining that stories, complete and well-shaped in themselves, do occur in real life: "We all know such a story, something in our own lives or in the lives of our friends," and he goes on to tell such a one, "'a particular story . . . as complete, I think, and as dramatic as any of those we read. It is about a man I met in Africa. It is not a long story,' he said, looking around the table tentatively, 'but it ends badly'" (233). This, then, is the frame of the story within a story, a fiction within a fiction designed to demonstrate that life on occasion assumes the shape of art.

: IV :

Considering the circumstances—a group of privileged people gathered around a dinner table in London as a famous explorer entertains them with a tale about a man he met in Africa—it is difficult to think not only of Henry Stanley but also of Conrad's *Heart of Darkness,* which RHD declared one of the greatest stories of the modern period. The similarity is even more fascinating when one recalls that Davis's African story first appeared in 1891, more than a decade before Conrad's would be published. Nor is the story's frame and setting the only correspondence between Gordon's and Marlow's tales, much as there is a great deal of Sir Henry Stanley in Conrad's Kurtz.

The man Gordon met in Africa was discovered along the trail "from Lake Tchad to the Mobangi," lying wounded and nearly dead. Thinking he is going to die, the man asked Gordon to return the locket to his beloved: "Tell her I wore it ever since she gave it to me. That it has been a charm and a loadstone to me. That when the locket rose and fell against my breast, it was as if her heart were pressing against mine and answering the beating and throbbing of the blood in my veins" (236). But the man recovered from his ordeal, and Gordon tells how he was able finally to learn his story.

The wounded man "had been trying to reach Lake Tchad. . . . He had undertaken the expedition on a promise from the French government to make him governor of the territory he opened up if he succeeded, but he had no official help. If he failed, he got nothing; if he succeeded, he did so at his own expense and by his own endeavors" (236). As a result, his expedition was underequipped and undermanned. His Senegalese porters and soldier-escort had finally turned against the explorer, beating him unconscious and stealing his arms and food, leaving him in the condition in which he had been discovered by Gordon and his party.

Having been motivated by his love for the girl who gave him the locket, on the return trip the man lived for nothing, as Gordon declares, but "getting back alive to this woman with whom he was in love. . . . I have read about men in love, I have seen it on the stage, I have seen it in real life, but I never saw a man so grateful to God and so happy and so insane over a woman as this man was. . . . She must have been a very remarkable girl" (237). Gordon testifies that the man had put the expedition and his ambitious plans completely out of his mind, dwelling to the point of endangering his life on getting back to his beloved: "All the time the poor devil kept saying how unworthy he was of her, how miserably he had wasted his years, how unfitted he was for the great happiness which had come into his life. . . . It used to frighten me to see how much he cared" (241–42). But as Gordon goes on to reveal, though the man survived his terrible experience in Africa, on the boat returning to England he suffered a relapse and died: "He had no home and no country and no family, as I told you, and we buried him at sea." All he had left worth saving was the locket given him by the girl, "which he had told me to take from his neck when he died" (243).

As proof and conclusion, Gordon produces a leather pouch from which he takes the heart-shaped gold locket and silver chain: "'This is it,' he said gently. He leaned across the table, with his eyes fixed on those of the American girl, and dropped the chain in front of her. 'Would you like to see it?' he said. The rest moved curiously forward to look at the little heap of gold and silver as it lay on the white cloth. But the girl, with her eyes half closed and her lips pressed together, pushed it on with her hand to the man who sat next her, and bowed her head slightly, as though it was an effort for her to move at all" (244).

The reader now knows the secret Miss Egerton and Gordon share, that she is the dead explorer's love, who has either forgotten her pledge or, worse, dishonored it by becoming engaged to the young Lord Arbuthnot. But that is not the message received by the other dinner guests, whose opinion is represented by the army general, Sir Henry: "If all true stories turn out as badly as that one does, I will take back what I said against those the story-writers tell. . . . I call it a most unpleasant story" (244). But Gordon declares that the story has not yet reached "closure," that there is still more to tell, a conclusion that will make the story even more unpleasant.

He goes on to relate his efforts to contact the girl so as to return the locket, only to discover "that her engagement had just been announced to a young Englishman of family and position, who had known her only a few months, and with whom she was very much in love. So you see . . . it was better that he died, believing in her and in her love for him. . . . Nature is kinder than writers of fiction, and quite as dramatic" (245). This is the end of Gordon's story but not of Davis's, which will merge the two tales into one.

Later in the evening, Gordon encounters Miss Egerton in the darkened privacy of a balcony overlooking a garden and once again offers her the locket, only to be denounced for having caused her so much pain: "'Are you . . . satisfied? Was it brave? Was it manly? Is that what you have learned among your savages—to torture a woman?' She stopped with a quick sob of pain, and pressed her hands against her breast" (246–47). Miss Egerton goes on to tell her side of the story, how she had been informed that her lover had died, then that he had survived, "and then the French papers told of it again, and with horrible detail, and how it happened."

Unmoved by her explanation, Gordon turns on her in a fury: "And does your love come and go with the editions of the daily papers. . . ? Is that the love, the life, and the soul you promised the man who—" They are here interrupted by the girl's fiancé, who peers out of a lighted drawing-room into the darkness, which has concealed Gordon and Miss Egerton. She joins young Arbuthnot, and the two make a pretty picture, so that even Gordon is struck by "how handsome they were and how well suited" (248). But then, as the matched pair is about to leave, Arbuthnot turns and asks Gordon whether his story is absolutely true to the facts or he had "helped the true story out a little" (249).

The explorer admits to having made one small change: "The man did not die."

> Arbuthnot gave a quick little sigh of sympathy. "Poor devil!" he said, softly; "poor chap!" He moved his left hand over and touched the hand of the girl, as though to reassure himself of his own good fortune. Then he raised his eyes to Gordon's with a curious, puzzled look in them. "But then," he said doubtfully, "if he is not dead, how did you come to get the chain?"
>
> The girl's arm within his own moved slightly, and her fingers tightened their hold upon his hand.
>
> "Oh," said Gordon, indifferently, "it did not mean anything to him, you see, when he found he had lost her, and it could not mean anything to her. It is of no value. It means nothing to any one—except, perhaps, to me." (249)

Once again, this is perhaps the best of RHD's early short stories, with a skillful balancing of formulas that brings events to a close with an audible click, not unlike those with which the far greater stories of Henry James often end.

We may remember how similarly yet with what a difference Conrad's

African fable ends. Marlow returns to Brussels to tell Kurtz's beloved of his death, but rather than grieving, the woman receives the news coldly, thereby emphasizing the terrible waste of Kurtz's life. The burden of the story is devoted to discounting the evangelical enthusiasm with which the idealistic Belgian had set off up the Congo, inspired by a faith in civilized progress which is soon devoured by his surroundings. His chivalric devotion to a woman has also sustained him, although it too is betrayed by the force of "darkness," in the form of a beautiful native girl, a fact that Marlow tactfully conceals from Kurtz's fiancée.

By having Kurtz die in Africa, Conrad stops where Gordon leaves off in telling his story to his dinner companions. Davis, typically, brings his man back alive, Gordon having carried out his errand—unlike the tragic hero of his story. Like Stanley, Gordon has been a successful Kurtz, and his "savagery" is obviously a well-warranted indignation over the betrayal of the dead man by the woman he loved. In paying his visit to Brussels, Marlow acts out the role Gordon plays for his dinner party audience, that of a messenger telling the tale of another man's death to his fiancée. But where Davis exploits the situation for its melodramatic potential, Conrad by contrast frames it with quiet irony.

In the recent film *Cast Away* we have had a retelling of Davis's story. This time a young man named Chuck Noland is able to survive a terrible ordeal of suffering and isolation on a desert island because of his love for a lovely woman named Kelly, whose picture he keeps in an antique pocket watch she has given him. Driven by his love as well as loneliness, after four years on the island he manages to construct a crude raft and makes it over the barrier reef to the open ocean. Like the lost explorer in Davis's story, Noland is rescued at the point of death, only to discover that the woman he loves has married another man, not a British aristocrat but a dentist, a profession that in these modern times is often used to denigrate by association.

Though Kelly is portrayed sympathetically, we tend to fault her for her lack of fidelity, and the reasons she gives for having married another man echo those of Miss Egerton. Unlike Gordon, Noland maintains an admirable restraint, entirely in keeping with the sentimental tradition, which the woman has violated by marrying another. On the other hand, by remaining with her dentist husband and child, despite her great passion for the man she thought dead, Kelly does redeem herself in sentimental terms. Indeed, I mention this contemporary instance to demonstrate that the popular audience to which Davis was addressing his story still exists, that sentimentalism is very much alive and well, although the context has somewhat changed. The implications of the switch from an African explorer bringing civilization to the "dark" continent to a FedEx efficiency expert striving to convert Russian workers to time-conscious work habits are worth considering, but not here.

What is important to our discussion is what Davis's story and the script of *Cast Away* do with the chivalric matter, which is to identify it exclusively with the hero. Only the dead explorer and the FedEx executive are true to their declared love, and though their adventures may be a demonstration of their manliness, that is hardly the final emphasis of the stories. Both plots are rounded off by accounting the heroes' ordeals as relatively worthless, in that the point made is the unfaithfulness of the woman. In the film, that unfaithfulness is mitigated by Kelly's obvious suffering, torn as she is between duty and passion, as well as by the hero's resolve to derive from his experience the psychic strength to keep on living. But in Davis's story, as in Conrad's, the woman is clearly not worthy of the explorer's love.

Davis's ending is uncharacteristic of his fiction, where plots are often resolved by a union between perfectly matched lovers, as in Shakespeare's romantic comedies, after a prolonged misunderstanding. Typical is another early short story, "A Walk up the Avenue," which begins as a young man has just ended a romantic relationship and vows in Tom Sawyer fashion to "strike . . . into Africa, and come back bronzed and worn with long marches and jungle fever, and with his hair prematurely white. He even considered himself, with great self-pity, returning and finding her married and happy, of course. And he enjoyed, in anticipation, the secret doubts she would have of her later choice when she heard on all sides praise of this distinguished traveller. And he pictured himself meeting her reproachful glances with fatherly friendliness, and presenting her husband with tiger-skins" (*Gallegher* 60–61). All these vows come to nothing when, at the end of his "walk" up Fifth Avenue, the young man by chance meets and reunites with his sweetheart in their favorite Central Park grove.

But in "An Unfinished Story" this frivolous situation becomes serious, with a motivation quite different from a lover's quarrel and an ending that, as the general suggests, is "unpleasant." Moreover, Miss Egerton will appear again and again in Davis's fiction as the unworthy woman who is a foil for the one who finally gets the man. Indeed, much of that fiction is devoted less to a definition of true manhood, which is a given constant, than that of true womanhood: as here, the controlling figure of knight-errantry, as in the Arthurian matter, is set against social disarray, one signal of which is often a woman who has broken her pledged troth, or worse.

A curious thing about "An Unfinished Story" is the setting, the London dinner party with which it begins, especially because the "story" concerns two Americans. RHD had recently himself been honored by similar affairs, and being such an intense Anglophile and a snob, perhaps he set the story against a cosmopolitan backdrop so as to display his familiarity with the details of such a gathering. In making the American explorer a lion in London, he is obviously staging events so as to enhance Gordon's heroism, but by having Miss Egerton give up her American lover for a wealthy and titled Englishman, Davis is adding further weight to her disgrace. Simply put, being a hero to the English makes Gordon more heroic, while being engaged to an Englishman disqualifies Miss Egerton as a heroine.

The increasing frequency with which American heiresses were seeking to marry foreign noblemen was regarded as a problem in the United States, having inspired a number of James's stories and novels and provided numerous opportunities for RHD's friend Charles Dana Gibson to devote his skills as a satiric cartoonist by portraying the scandalous situation. Then too, American readers may have derived a certain measure of satisfaction from the inability of such a brilliant company of Britons to get the true drift of the story, a point underscored when Lord Arbuthnot asks the right question but is unable to fathom the answer. The English have their superior qualities, but the implication is that they can on occasion be bested by an American, the British lion, as it were, bearded in his den.

In contrast to his reception in London in 1891, Davis's first exposure to upper-class life in England had been brief and bitter: As Arthur Lubow tells us, in 1889 RHD had a terrible experience in Great Britain when he went there as a reporter with a cricket team from Philadelphia, having been badly treated not only by the snobbish British but by the upper-crust Philadelphians as well. The incident hardly cured him of his Anglophilia, much as it may have added impetus to his ambitions to be accepted by the higher reaches of American society, but it perhaps explains the superiority of young Gordon to his English hosts.

As for William Astor Chanler, left by Davis in *Harper's Monthly* bearing the flag of the United States into "darkest" Africa, he did make it back to America, wrote a book about his experiences, and fulfilled his stated ambition by serving his state and his country as a U.S. congressman, albeit briefly, from 1899 to 1901. His political career may have benefited from his contemporary fame as an explorer, but his election to Congress followed his service as an army officer in the Spanish-American War, where he fought in the battle of Santiago with sufficient bravery to warrant a special commendation from his commanding general.

There is more, including a report by the biographer of the Astor scions that gives us a tantalizing hint of further Chanler heroics in the Davis vein: Tired of legislative routine, unhappy that he could not join the Boers fighting the British in South Africa, Chanler subsequently was heard from in Arabia, "roaming the Sahara as a Moslem holy man inciting an Arab revolt" (Thomas 287). Chanler thereby persisted in acting out Davis's fantasies of African adventures, merging with the mythic shadow of that ultimate adventurer, T. E. Lawrence. But what happened to Chanler after 1898 is of no real importance to us here, the African and the Cuban adventures providing the important sequence. As Davis wrote in *Harper's Monthly* about Chanler's plans for a career of public service following his return from Africa, "When you have said that, you have told the whole story" (154).

: V :

Davis no sooner returned from his western tour in May 1892 than he set off once again for Great Britain, with the assurance that his newfound fame as a writer as well as his association with *Harper's Weekly* would guarantee another friendly reception. American writers, like American explorers, could expect a certain celebrity if not complete acceptance in Great Britain. Davis's plan was to encounter the English at the height of the social season, counting on his status to open doors normally closed to touring Americans, nor was he disappointed. Warmly welcomed at Oxford and elsewhere, he ended up by making lifelong friends and important contacts. The book that resulted, *Our English Cousins,* suggests that he had a good time, but it also provides a very convenient display of his complex attitude toward the place from which Matthew Arnold had come to America and to which he had happily returned.

Though the English spoke essentially the same language as Americans, their customs and manners were quite different, a truth that remains consistent throughout the five chapters that make up RHD's book. The differences between Americans and their English cousins are essential to the very spirit of travel writing, which derives its interest from novelty. Important to the art and practice of journalism is the other operating consistency in the book, that what Davis found in England was not what Americans might expect. No longer an aristocratic occasion, Derby Day has been taken over by a colorful but orderly mob of commoners; the Henley Regatta is a polite gathering of the upper classes that gives way to a shouting melee of men of all ages running along both sides of the river in support of their boats; a general election is a display not so much of party principles as anarchic confusion; Oxford is less a seat of higher learning than a setting for undergraduate pranks; and the social "season" in London is not so much a matter of exclusiveness as a public show, tantamount to a parade. Most surprising of all, according to Davis, what Americans think of as class snobbery is really a heightened sense of personal freedom.

Davis's account of his British tour is for the most part favorable to the English people, further evidence of his own high regard for the Anglo-Saxon continuity. This Anglophilia will manifest itself in his later writings, where the connection is treated as essential to defining America's imperial ambitions. Most important, perhaps, for our purposes is his deep respect for British institutions, an awe that transcends his occasional criticisms of modern England. Thus we find very few of those ironic witticisms that characterize *The West from a Car Window*. Instead, throughout his book RHD maintains a balanced viewpoint and good-natured tolerance toward the British, obviously striving to prove himself a gracious guest of the empire.

Still, if the natural inclination toward orderliness is by Davis's account the chief virtue of the English, the habitual reserve of the British upper classes results in an apparent lack of hospitality. This can often (as Davis learned in 1889) leave Americans in tears, feeling, "as they supposed," that they had been "snubbed and insulted and neglected" when the opposite was true (*Our English Cousins* 200). If American visitors feel ignored, it is not because of their place of origin "but because we are strangers, and London is a very busy place, and a very big place, and those who go about there have their time more than taken up already, and have but little to spare for the chance visitor. They treat their own people in the same way" (203). Again, the chief paradox of English life is that restrictions and repressions of the class system promote a kind of freedom unknown in the United States, and when the guest of an English family finds himself left alone, that is so that he may follow his own inclination, not his hosts' bidding.

As both an American and an individual who had experienced the often brutal cruelty of an English snub, Davis was not entirely at home in Great Britain, but it is clear from what he writes that he would have liked to be. What he appreciates, ever and again, are the assurances that rigidly observed order brings, the uniform sense of all things being in their proper places. Though he acknowledges that the "slums" of the East End of London are "the back yard of the greatest city in the world, into which all the unpleasant and unsightly things are thrown and hidden away from sight, to be dragged out occasionally and shaken before the eyes of the West End as a warning or a menace," this is distinctly a minority note in RHD's group portrait of his English cousins (215). Like the starving men Davis saw scrambling for garbage tossed from carriages at Derby Day, the London slums are things the upper classes choose to ignore, a darker manifestation of that freedom which a rigid social system permits.

But Davis did not prolong his tour through the East End, his politeness perhaps not permitting any prolonged exposure to (or of) the underside of Great Britain. By his accounting the queen is on her throne and all is right with her world. But much as the strict boundaries of the class system permit social iniquities, so the extended order of the British Empire has its price, a truth defined in RHD's next book of travels. There he explored the Victorian world order as displayed in that most ancient of traveled places, the Mediterranean, a journey over the ancient, even epic pathways of early empire that brought him into confrontation with the imperial presence of Great Britain. His reaction to those encounters is essential to understanding RHD's complex attitude not only toward England as a colonial power but also toward the way the specifics of British power were exercised in foreign places. More important, it inspired in Davis thoughts about his own country's rapidly expanding role in regions beyond its shores, a nascent imperialism that could benefit from the English example, not always, however, by imitating it.

Our English cousins, as he would discover, may cherish their freedom at home, but at times they ignore the freedom of those people over whom they exercise control, imposing an order that is quite different from that found in England. As a consequence, it became increasingly difficult for Davis to maintain his characteristic Anglophilia, and we find him repeatedly retreating to his native American sense of common decency. Equally important, along the way Davis drops occasional hints that where Great Britain failed, the United States might succeed, this at a time when such jingoistic champions of extending the American sphere of influence as Henry Cabot Lodge regarded England with envy and suspicion as their chief rival in the field.

So here's your Empire.
RUDYARD KIPLING

7 : A WAVE AT BRITANNIA'S RULE

: I :

Davis's account of his travels abroad in 1893 would be published a year later as *The Rulers of the Mediterranean,* and it does not take one long to recognize that the plural is misleading. The rulers of the Mediterranean are themselves all subjects of Great Britain, whose presence is ubiquitous, not only at Gibraltar, that sentinel post by the gateway to the inland sea, but also along the greatest of its tributaries, the Nile. And where *Our English Cousins* was generous toward the British, Davis's subsequent travel book is less so, and even his praise is couched in ambivalent terms. What's more, perhaps because he was conscious that he was traveling over a route already laid down by Mark Twain, perhaps because the Near East presented a spectacle often offensive to his tastes, Davis recovered that sense of the ridiculous that makes *The West from a Car Window* so amusing.

Typical is RHD's account of his stopover in Port Said, the city made great by the opening of the Suez Canal, which he regarded as occupying "the same position to the waters of the world as Dodge City once did to the Western States of America—it is the meeting-place of vessels from every land over water, just as Dodge City was the meeting-place of the great trails across the prairies." In his book on the West, Davis alludes to Dodge City's late reputation as a wild place, thanks to the physical needs of young men who arrived in town at the end of a long and arduous cattle drive. He reminds his readers that the cowboy who had been deprived of companionship other than steers for six months "wanted wickedness in its worst form—such being the perversity of man. And you are told that Port Said offers to travellers and crew the same attractive features after a month or weeks of rough voyaging that Dodge City once offered to the trailsman" (*Rulers* 95).

Kipling's shadow looms large over RHD's travels through the Near East, and Davis reminds us that in Kipling's *Light That Failed,* Port Said is described as "the wickedest place on earth, that it is a sink of iniquity and a

hole of vice, and a wild night in Port Said is described there with pitiless detail." Spread by Kipling's great popularity, the dubious reputation of Port
Said cannot be ignored, and "almost every young man who leaves home for
the East is instructed by his friends to reproduce that night or never return
to civilization" (96).

That Davis is exaggerating for comic effect is obvious, and for verification
we need only turn to Kipling's actual account of Port Said, a passage that
hardly lives up to its reputation. "There is," Kipling wrote, "iniquity in many
parts of the world, and vice in all, but the concentrated essence of all the iniquities and all the vices in all the continents finds itself at Port Said": And
yet the "wild night" to which Davis refers is something less than promised
(*Light That Failed* 31). Described as "an orgy" staged for the benefit of Kipling's artist-hero, it offers only a momentary glimpse of "naked Zanzibari
girls danc[ing] furiously by the light of kerosene lamps" while a piano plays
"the tin-pot music of a Western waltz" (33). It is against this bare fact that
we must place RHD's claim of expecting to find a spectacle of blazing shame
in Port Said.

"When guides in Continental cities and in the East have invited me to see
and to buy strange things which caused me to doubt the morals of those who
had gone before, I have always put them off, because I knew that some day
I should visit Port Said. I did not want second-best and imitation wickedness, but the most awful wickedness of the entire world sounded as though
it might prove most amusing" (*Rulers* 96). We know from the start that this
tourist in quest of unspeakable debauchery is bound to be disappointed, a
certainty against which Davis's ingenuous efforts to replicate the episode in
Kipling's novel must be placed.

> So I went on shore and gathered the guides together, and told them for
> the time being to sink their rivalry and to join with loyal local pride in
> showing me the worst Port Said could do. They consulted for some time,
> and then said that they were sorry, but . . . as it was now nearly half-past
> twelve, every one was properly in bed. I expressed myself fully, and they
> were hurt, and said that Egypt was a great country, and that after I had
> seen Cairo I would say so. So I told them I had not meant to offend their
> pride of country, and that I was going to Cairo in order to see things al-
> most as old as wickedness, and much more worth while, and that all I
> asked of Port Said was that it should live up to its name. I told them to hire
> a house, and wake the people in Port Said up, and show me the very
> worst, lowest, wickedest, and most vicious sights of which their city

boasted; that I would give them four hours in which to do it, and what money they needed. I should like to print what, after long consultation, the five guides of Port Said—which is a place a half-mile across, and with which they were naturally acquainted—offered me as the acme of riotous dissipation. I do not do so, not because it would bring the blush to the cheek of the reader, but to the inhabitants of Port Said, who have enjoyed a notoriety they do not deserve, and who are like those desperadoes in the West who would rather be considered "bad" than the nonentities that they are. I bought photographs, a box of cigarettes, and a cup of black coffee at Port Said. That cannot be considered a night of wild dissipation. Port Said may have been a sink of iniquity when Mr. Kipling was last there, but when I visited it it was a coaling station. I would hate to be called a coaling station if I were Port Said, even by me. (99–100)

Though Kipling is the target, Davis's point of view and even his technique are reminiscent of Mark Twain, recalling similar episodes in *Innocents Abroad,* including the ragging of the guides, whose attempts to defend the honor of their country are set against their failure to validate the scandalous reputation of their town.

In 1893, after attending a formal dinner in New York where the famous humorist was present, Davis wrote to his mother that "Mark Twain told some very funny stories, and captured me because I never thought him funny before" (*Adventures* 133). It is difficult to reconcile this statement with what seem to be a number of indebtednesses by Davis to Twain's travel writings and fiction, never mind that youthful boast about becoming more famous than Twain himself.

Much as Port Said at the entrance to the Suez Canal was a bust in the wickedness market, RHD found that the great canal itself was something less than sublime, being a matter of "sandy banks and . . . strange odors of fish and mud. . . . You have heard so much of the Suez Canal as an engineering feat that you rather expect, in your ignorance, to find the banks upheld by walls of masonry, and to pass through intricate locks from one level to another, or at least to see a well-beaten towpath at its side. But with the exception of dikes here and there, you pass between slipping sandy banks, which show less of the hand of man than does a mill-dam at home, and you begin to think that Ferdinand de Lesseps drew his walking-stick through the sand from the Red Sea to the Mediterranean, and twenty thousand negroes followed him and dug a ditch" (*Rulers* 100).

Even the fabled Sphinx, to which Davis made the required pilgrimage after arriving in Cairo, "is disappointing," but here he was in plentiful company: "So many who have seen it say so that I feel I am . . . not individually lacking in reverence or imagination."

> I have seen photographs of the Sphinx . . . much more impressive than the Sphinx itself. Lying in a hollow of the sand hills as it does, the farther you move away from it in order to get a better focus, the less you see of it, and as you draw nearer to it it loses its meaning, as does the scenery of a theatre when you are on the wrong side of the foot-lights. I know that it is an unpopular thing to say, and that there are many who feel thrills when they first look upon the face of the Sphinx, and who describe their emotions to you at length, and who write down their impressions in their diaries when they get back to the hotel. But they have come a long way expecting to be thrilled, and they do not intend to be disappointed. (131–32)

On the other hand, Davis did admit that he was impressed by the Sphinx as seen at night. Without the daytime swarm of tourists, guides, and photographers, "the moonlight threw the great negro face and the pyramids back of it into shadows of black and lines of silver, and the yellow desert stretched away on either side." Davis would make the same point later that year, when he would go into raptures over "the illumination of the Court of Honor at night" at the Columbian Exposition, comparing it to the Sphinx seen by moonlight. Here, however, his attitude is not only aesthetic at base but also keyed to the antiquity of the scene; the emptiness of the landscape allows him to feel he "was alone and back two thousand years in the past, discovering the great monuments for myself, and for the first time" (133).

Let us at this point leave RHD's immersion in antiquity and return him to the modern moment, which was always his preference, and to his first sight of the Rock of Gibraltar with which his account of the Mediterranean begins and which provides an alternative monolith. First of all, according to Davis, the Rock of Gibraltar is best seen not at night but in the full light of day, for in the dark of the early morning hour when he first saw it, the Rock was disappointing: "Its black outline against the sky, with nothing to measure it with but the fading stars, is dwarfed and spoiled."

> It is only after the sun begins to turn the lights [of the city] out, and you are able to compare it with the great ships at its base, and you see the battlements and the mouths of cannon, and the clouds resting on its top, that you understand it; and then when the outline of the crouching lion,

that faces all Europe, comes into relief, you remember it is . . . the lock to the Mediterranean, of which England holds the key. And even while you feel this, and are greedily following the course of each rampart and terrace with eyes that are tired of blank stretches of water, some one points to a low line of mountains lying like blue clouds before the red sky of the sunrise, dim, forbidding, and mysterious—and you know that it is Africa.

This distant and alluring prospect of Africa diminishes the famous Rock, for its "grim show of battlements and war become somehow of little moment," being familiar because so often described, whereas "this other land across the water looks as inscrutable, as dark, and as silent as the Sphinx that typifies it" (7).

But much as Davis revised his initial opinion of the Sphinx, so he will come to regard the Rock of Gibraltar as mysterious and powerful, albeit hardly inscrutable in connotations. As a guardian gatehouse to the Mediterranean, it serves also as a symbolic entrance to his narrative and a key of sorts to Davis's geopolitical discourse, much as it was and still is a dominant symbol of British empire. Like much of what he saw in England, the fortress rock was a manifestation of order, but of quite a different sort from that evinced at Derby Day and the Oxford regatta.

: II :

The town of Gibraltar satisfied RHD's desire for novelty and fulfilled his usual aesthetic criteria, as so often put forth in terms of setting and costume: "It is a fortress as imposing as the Tower of London, a winter resort as pretty as St. Augustine, and a seaport town of free entry, into which come on every tide people of many nations, and ships flying every flag" (12). As such, it is "the clearing-house for three most picturesque peoples—the Moors, in their yellow slippers and bare legs and voluminous robes and snowy turbans; the Spaniards, with romantic black capes and cloaks and red sashes, the women with the lace mantilla and brilliant handkerchiefs and pretty faces; and mixed with these, the pride and glory of the British army and navy, in all the bravery of red coats and white helmets, or blue jackets, or Highland kilts" (12).

But the composition is necessarily dominated by the Rock, which towers over the town, "naked and bare above, stretching for several miles from north to south, and rearing its great bulk up into the sky until it loses its summit in the clouds. . . . At times a sunset paints the rock a martial red, or the moonlight softens it, and you see only the tall palms and the graceful balconies and the gardens of plants, and each rampart becomes a terrace and each casement a balcony. Or at night, when the lamps are lit, you might imagine yourself on the stage of a theatre, walking in a scene set for Fra Diavolo" (13–14). We can recall the great rock towering above the mining camp at Creede, but here the Rock serves less as contrast than reinforcement, being integrated into the scene, for a scene it is, keyed when Davis evokes his favorite simile, the world of the theater: "Outside of stage-land . . . there are no streets or houses" like those found in Gibraltar (14).

And the drama is the kind called "high," being imperial in implication, for everywhere are signs of the British military presence, from the officers and soldiers crowding the main street to the sentinels on guard. From the town's immaculate cleanliness to the "high, heavily carved Moorish doorways and mysterious twisting stairways in the solid rock," it all resembles a stage set, "where dark figures suddenly appear from narrow alleyways and cry 'Halt, there!' at you, and then 'All's well' as you pass by" (14).

From a purely aesthetic point of view, these men in uniform are only part of the spectacle: "All of these things, troops and goats and yellow cabs and polo ponies and dog-carts, and priests with curly-brimmed hats, and baggy breeched Moors, and huntsmen in pink coats and Tommies in red, and sailors rolling along in blue, make the main street of Gibraltar as full of variety as a mask ball." Though British in nationality, the sentinels are the most superficial evidence of empire. The true function of the Rock, "the Gibraltar militant, the fortress and the key to the Mediterranean," is largely invisible: "You can see but the little that lies open to you and to every one along the ramparts," and "of the real defensive works of the place you are not allowed to have even a guess" (18).

The head of the "crouching lion"—nor need we question which lion it is—faces north toward Spain and "shows two long rows of teeth cut in its surface by convicts of long ago." These extensive "dungeons" are open to the public, allowing the tourist to "look down upon the Neutral Ground and the little Spanish town at the end of its half-mile over the butts of great guns. . . . Lower down, on the outside of this mask of rock, are more ramparts, built there by man, from which infantry could sweep the front of the enemy were they to approach from the only point from which a land attack is possible" (19–20).

Further protection is provided by a line of sentries, a kind of "watchdog" posted along the North Front of the Rock: "Their red coats move backward and forward night and day, and any one who leaves the straight and narrow road crossing the Neutral Ground, and who comes too near, passes a dead-line and is shot." Facing them, half a mile away, are the Spanish sentries guarding the frontier to their own country, "and so the two great powers watch each other and say, 'So far shall you go, and no farther; this belongs to me'" (21).

"There is," declares RHD, "nothing more significant than these two rows of sentries," a significance that lies in defining differences. The English soldier is "rather short and very young, but very clean and rigid, and scowling fiercely over the chin strap of his big white helmet." His boots are polished brightly, his white shoulder straps glisten with pipe clay, and his rifle shines with oil. He is the British Empire in miniature, "one of a great system that obtains from India to Nova Scotia, and from Bermuda to Africa and Australia," and the sentry seems aware of his importance, kicking out his feet as he marches back and forth "guarding the big rock at his back" (21).

His counterpart, across the neutral ground, is "a tall handsome man seated on a stone, with the tails of his long coat wrapped warmly around his legs, and with his gun against another rock while he rolls a cigarette." Here is the personification of Spain, sitting at his ease, and wondering when he will draw his pay, the peseta he gets each day "for fighting and bleeding for his country." The contrast between these two guardian soldiers "helps to make you understand how six thousand half-starved Englishmen held Gibraltar for four years against the army of Spain" (22). Even as the four hundredth anniversary of Columbus's voyage was being celebrated in Chicago, Davis suggests that Spain, in whose service Columbus had sailed, was now a demoralized and degenerate empire, in which the national spirit was in severe decline. Great Britain's was the mark to match, and Gibraltar was that nation in miniature, much as each red-coated sentry was a single "atom" in the great imperial system on which the sun never set.

Like the Sphinx of the guidebooks, the Rock of Gibraltar had its mystery, for "no stranger has really any idea of the real strength of this fortress, or in what part of it its real strength lies. Not one out of ten of its officers knows it." The Rock, as RHD defines it, is something of a "practical joke," for its appearance is belied by the reality, whatever that reality might be: "What looks like a solid face of rock is a hanging curtain that masks a battery; the blue waters of the bay are treacherous with torpedoes; and every little smiling village of Spain has been marked down for destruction." Gibraltar is a granitic semblance of "the wooden horse of Troy," being hollow within by virtue of its tunnels and vaults (23).

At every point are placed modern technological devices, from telephones to searchlights, to aid in its defense, "and only the Governor knows what other modern improvements have been introduced into the bowels of this mountain or distributed behind bits of landscape gardening on its surface" (23–24). But it does not take a Odysseus to read the riddle of this Sphinx: the secret of empire is preparedness to defend. When Davis's account of his Mediterranean travels was published serially in *Harper's Weekly,* each chapter was decorated by a headpiece showing the British lion confronting the Sphinx across a narrow stretch of water, the icons of the modern and the ancient empire brought into meaningful juxtaposition.

But Davis was no geopolitician, and his touch is characteristically light. He digresses on the pleasant life of a junior officer on Gibraltar, which resembles the happy mixture of the social and the military enjoyed by junior officers stationed outside Houston more than it does the rigors endured by those posted along the frontiers of American empire: "As far as I could see, his most trying duty was the number of times a day he had to change his clothes, and this had its ameliorating circumstance in that he each time changed into a more gorgeous costume." We are reminded yet again of RHD's penchant for theater and costuming. He deemed the dinner jackets of the officers most impressive, being scarlet in color, "with high black silk waistcoats bordered with two inches of gold lace" and "gold buttons sewed along every edge that presents itself. . . . When eighteen of these jackets are placed around a table, the chance civilian feels and looks like an undertaker" (27).

It is not only in the variety and sumptuousness of its uniforms that the British army has an advantage. Essential to the spirit and morale of the garrison on Gibraltar is the regimental unit: "In the English army regimental feeling is very strong; father and son follow on in the same regiment, and now that they are naming them for the counties from which they are recruited, they are becoming very close corporations indeed" (28–29). The unity of the British regiment is transcendent, its collective sense strengthened by a consciousness of its history. In Davis's description the regiment resembles a fraternal organization in the United States: "Each regiment has its peculiarity of uniform or its custom at mess, which is distinctive to it, and which means more the longer it is observed" (29). There are those who hope to get rid of these traditions, "signs and differences in equipment" that distinguish one regiment from another. In Davis's opinion such men "are writing themselves down asses as they do so" (30).

But the chief point RHD seeks to make has less to do with the British army than with its American equivalent: "We have no regimental headquarters in America, and owing to our officers seeking promotion all over

the country, the regimental esprit de corps is lacking" (28). This was a sore
spot only briefly touched on by Davis, for proponents of increasing the
armed strength and preparedness of the United States often pointed to the
army's lack of regimental organization. This deficiency was the result of a
lack of personnel, the army being spread out all along the western frontier,
in the kinds of small garrisons described in *The West from a Car Window*.
Davis may not have been an exponent of increasing the size of the U.S.
Army, but those Americans who were would have received strength and encouragement from his description of the might and manpower found on the
Rock of Gibraltar. That and the indolent Spanish sentry, smoking his cigarette and staring dreamily through the cloud of his own making, are points
on a vector clearly drawn toward the last bastion of Spanish power in the
Caribbean.

As always, RHD livens his discourse with a humorous story, here, as often
elsewhere, at his own expense. One night on Gibraltar he found himself
locked outside the North Front after hours: "I had seen the officer of the keys
pass every night, and the guards turn out to salute the keys, and I had rather
imagined that it was more or less of a form, and that the pomp and circumstance were all there was of it. I did not believe that the Rock was really
closed up at night like a safe with a combination lock. But I know now that
it is." After much effort he managed to gain admittance and in so doing
learned that the post was guarded by a whole phalanx of sentries: "They
were not nice sentries, either, like those on the Rock, who stand where you
can see them, and who challenge you drowsily, like cabmen, and make the
empty streets less lonely than otherwise" (35).

Davis's account of his stay on Gibraltar ends with the preceding anec-
dote, which further emphasizes the rigor and punctiliousness maintained
by the British guardians of empire, the final paragraph of which I quote here
for the sake of its last sentence: "This was the only trying experience of my
stay in Gibraltar, and it is brought in here as a compliment to the force that
guards the North Front. For of them, and the rest of the inhabitants and
officers of the garrison, any one who visits there can only think well; and
I hope when the Rock is attacked, as it never will be, that they will all cover
themselves with glory. It never will be attacked, for the reason that the
American people are the only people clever enough to invent a way of taking it, and they are far too clever to attempt an impossible thing" (36). We
may account this a compliment of sorts, but in 1893 it was something more
(or less) than that, for in the anniversary year of the Columbian voyage, the
United States was clearly at a turning point necessitated by the closing of

the western frontier. When the nation finally turned, it faced the way Captain Mahan had suggested, and in looking south it necessarily confronted the threat of a British presence in the Caribbean.

There would never be any question of taking Gibraltar. But in announcing, however facetiously, that only in the United States could England find its military match, Davis was making the kind of polite noises that would become more insistent as the decade wore on. We will remember that in his account of the rise of the White City on the banks of Lake Michigan, written after he returned from his Mediterranean tour, he declared that Chicago was quite capable, if it wished, of raising a Gibraltar there as well.

: III :

Davis would, moreover, be still less polite in *The Rulers of the Mediterranean* when dealing with the British presence elsewhere than on Gibraltar. "In the next chapter," he promises at the end of chapter 4, "I shall try to tell something of the men who have their fingers on Egypt's pulse, and who are agreed in only one thing—that there are too many fingers for Egypt's good" (138). In that chapter, "The Englishmen in Egypt," Davis traces the recent and troubled history of the country, in which "the foreign element" had obtained "a footing. . . , which footing has now grown to a trampling under foot of what is native and properly Egyptian" (151).

Originally called the "Dual Control" and jointly shared by France and England, the situation in Egypt was revised when the French departed, leaving the English in sole control. This was not in Davis's view a good thing: "The English remained . . . to 'restore order,' and to see the 'organization of proper means for the maintenance of the Khedive's authority.' They have been doing that now for ten years, and it is interesting to note that they have made so little progress that the last 'disorder' in Cairo was due to the action of the British consul-general himself in allowing the young Khedive just twenty-four hours in which to dismiss one of his cabinet. This can hardly be described as 'maintaining the authority of the Khedive,' which the English had promised to do" (156).

In effect the British are in place as an army of occupation: "For the last ten years the English have been as tardy in getting out of Egypt as they were in going after Gordon into the Sudan. They have repeatedly declared their intention of evacuating the country, not only in answer to questions in the House, but in answer to the inquiries of foreign powers. But they are still there" (162). Davis has nothing but praise for the courage of General Charles George Gordon, the hero of "a campaign which has been unequalled within the last twenty years in picturesqueness, heroism, and dramatic surprises" (163). Yet his emphasis is less on Gordon's courage than on the failure of the British to relieve the besieged general in time to save him and his men at Khartoum.

What is more, although in that campaign the British suffered losses tantamount to defeat, inspiring some to feel "that Egypt has cost them too much already, and more than they can ever get back," the army remained hopeful of recouping its losses (163). To this needless expense Davis added not only the diminished independence of the Egyptian people because of the heavy hand of British rule but also the incalculable loss borne by the reputation of England for improving the countries its colonial administrators control.

Davis admits that the English have done much good since the Sudan debacle "and have brought benefits innumerable to Egypt," including the rescue of the country from financial ruin. But the English have also profited from this arrangement, Egypt being well known for its comfortable "billets" for Britons, and yet the English want credit not only for what they have done but also "for having done it unselfishly and without hope or thought of reward, and solely for the good of mankind and of Egypt in particular. They remind me of those of the G.A.R. who not only want pensions and medals, but to be considered unselfish saviors of their country in her hour of need" (163).

With that sense of fair play that is so characteristic of his ethical evaluations, Davis is inclined to take a hard line toward both the Union army veteran in America and John Bull in Egypt: "Let him have either the honors or the money, but he should not be so greedy as to want both" (163). The English, having "made a very good thing out of Egypt," should forgo their hoped-for reputation "as an unselfish and enlightened nation that is helping a less prosperous and less powerful people to get upon their feet again" and order their army home, its job being over and done (163–64).

From this argument, we have to conclude that despite his subsequent association with the expansionist spasm we call the Spanish-American War, RHD was in 1892 making the sounds of an anti-imperialist. In like fashion, he went on to insist that the Egyptians no longer needed the help of the English, because despite the opinions expressed in "the English press," the present khedive and his prime minister were men of ability. According to Davis it is "absurd" to say that such leaders need "the advice or support of an English resident minister. . . . These men are not barbarians nor despots; they have not gained their place in the world by favor or inheritance . . . and if they care for their country and the authority of their Khedive, it is certainly hard that they may not have the right of serving both undisturbed" (169–70). The present minister in residence, Lord Cromer, may be the most pleasant kind of companion "in his own room, with a pipe in his mouth," but when "advising a minister of the Khedive or the Khedive himself, he can be as intensely disagreeable in his manner and as powerfully aggressive as a polar-bear" (171).

By contrast, the young khedive is a gentle youth with peaceful tastes, rather much a Prince Albert in a fez, "and is said to find his amusement in the garden and among flowers and on the farm lands of his estates." He is also a cosmopolite who speaks several languages and in dress and appearance resembles "any other young man of twenty-three or twenty-four in Paris or New York." He is said by those who know him best to have a "high spirit, and one that, as he grows older and will be guided by greater experience, will lead him to firmer authority for his own good and for the good of his people" (175). The question then is who or what is best for Egypt, the self-interested tyranny of a resident minister from England or the gentle, enlightened administration of the duly appointed leader: "It is true that the Khedive still sits on the box and holds the reins, but Lord Cromer sits beside him and holds the whip" (177).

Such an opinion may seem at odds with RHD's usual Anglophilia, his admiration for the English people and the British army, but it is consistent with the idealism that animates so much of his work, the love of fair play that is essential to the Anglo-American tradition. The British, at least in Egypt, are not good sports but sore losers and bullies, the sort of thing that Tom Brown was famous for putting down with a well-placed fist. And yet some subtle undercurrents are at work here: in Davis's private audience with the khedive, he learned one thing "of interest to Americans," namely, the influential role played by the "American officers who entered the Egyptian army after the end of our Civil War." In the opinion of the khedive they were "the best-trained men in their particular department in his army. This is the topographical work, and the making of maps and drawings," but "the Americans who are in charge of Egyptian troops on the frontier are also well esteemed" (175).

The khedive's praise of American officers on the Egyptian frontier inspired Davis to suggest to his host "that he should borrow some of our officers, those who have succeeded so well with the negroes of the Ninth Cavalry and with the Indians, for it seemed to me that this would be of benefit to both the officers and the Egyptian soldier" (176). The stunning racism of this remark underlines Davis's American ingenuousness, which allowed him to suggest to the ruler of Egypt that his soldiers are equivalent in intelligence and capacity to peoples regarded by Davis and his fellow Americans not of color as characteristically deficient in same. His drift could hardly have escaped the intelligent young khedive, who by remaining silent proved himself as polite as Davis claimed. But RHD's insensitive chauvinism does not obliterate the larger point, for no such arrangement could be made so long as the English were in charge.

There are detectably prophetic sounds made by Davis in this key chapter, remarks critical of British imperialism and suggestions of the benefits to be derived from replacing the English soldier with American equivalents. Mingling acute perceptions with a certain obtuseness, these comments are typical of RHD's confused view of the world beyond the American shore, but they also reflect the increasing ambition expressed by a minority of powerful men in the United States regarding the nation's future role abroad. "Of course," he tactfully adds, "it is none of our business (at least it is our policy to say so) when England stalks forth like a roaring lion seeking what she may devour all over the world" (164).

Yet, like other Americans who travel "into out-of-the-way corners of the world," RHD noted "how little there is left of it that has not been seized by the people of Great Britain," and for his own part, "I find one grows a little tired of getting down and sailing forth and landing again always under the shadow of the British flag." If the United States should actually get around to playing the game of empire, beginning "with Hawaii" and then going on "to annex other people's property, we should find that almost all of the best corner lots and post-office sites of the world have been already preempted" (164).

Davis says this tongue in cheek, as the figures of speech should suggest, but those figures of speech are taken from his experiences in the American West and are derived specifically from the recent history of the great Oklahoma land rush, which signaled the end of free land in the West. In 1892 the annexation of Hawaii was as yet a remote possibility chiefly promoted by American businessmen on the island. While in his private correspondence Davis noted that "if we took Hawaii" it "would be just as mean" as the "bullying insolent way" of the British authorities in Egypt, in the published version his viewpoint is more complex: "If the United States had taken away the little princess's island from her and continued to plunder weaker nations, she would have found that England wants the earth too, and that she is in a fair way of getting it if some one does not stop her very soon" (164; cf. Lubow

97). Similar noises, uttered without tongue in cheek, were being made around Washington, D.C., at this time, as champions of the extension of U.S. interests beyond its shores began to look hard at the omnipresence and possible expansion of the British Empire.

As early as 1884, while RHD was in college, the humor magazine *Life* (to which Davis would contribute some of his first published work) celebrated July 4 by featuring a cover cartoon by its artist-editor, John Ames Mitchell, showing John Bull facing a rather hefty representation of Columbia and expressing amazement at her growth. The perspective of the cartoon suggests that although she has not as yet attained her full height, Columbia is already taller than the traditional personification of Great Britain, and her pose prefigures Bartholdi's gigantic *Liberty Enlightening the World,* shortly to be set up in New York harbor. And after 1890, when Congress approved the building of a few battleships, Columbia would grow heftier yet, in the shape of the Great White Fleet that would be a signal expression of U.S. power abroad. But if our country wanted to grab its share of the imperial action, as Davis suggests, it had better get busy as a promoter of enlightenment in "dark" places of the world and set up as a competitor to the English "in redeeming" countries like Egypt "as a form of missionary work" (164). In putting forward this notion, Davis was anticipating President McKinley's benevolent view of American expansion, expressed in his phrase "the blessings of the flag."

In assessing the present-day value of Davis's reflections on his encounter with the British in the Mediterranean, consider the extent to which they were circulated in the United States, thanks to the popularity of *Harper's Weekly*—and of the author himself. Davis's observations on the British Empire in *Rulers of the Mediterranean* appeared in serialized sequence with the stories reporting the construction, building by building, of the great fair in Chicago and with the parallel build-up of the U.S. Navy, with illustrations depicting each warship under construction. It must therefore be accounted as a significant contribution to the growing enthusiasm for American empire, a "Sunday supplement" to Captain Mahan's big book.

We may also recall that graph comparing the relative size of the navies of the world, with a British tar towering over the tiny American sailor. This is the larger frame of reference in which Davis's account of the British presence in the Mediterranean needs to be placed, a collective sense expressed on many levels of discourse that something great was stirring in the United States, which as Henry Adams reflected needed only a proper focus to take definitive shape. The rivalry with Great Britain was already established; the

Cover of the humor magazine Life, *which used the Fourth of July in 1884 to celebrate the growing stature of Columbia, in proportion to the paternal (and somewhat apprehensive) John Bull.*

only thing left was to find some strategic spot of land as yet unclaimed by Victoria's empire.

: IV :

Despite his jingoistic noises regarding the British precedent, Davis often evinces what Emerson would have regarded as a open-minded inconsistency regarding the beauties of empire. En route to Port Said, RHD had visited Tangier, his first stop in Africa, and his account of that experience is another display of self-contradictory attitudes we can only call American. The chapter opens with a meditation on Africa itself, that immensity about which little more is known than when "Hercules built the mountain of Abyla and its twin mountain which we call Gibraltar."

> Men have crept into Africa and crept out again, like flies over a ceiling, and they have gained much renown at Africa's expense for having done so. They have built little towns along its coasts, and run little rocking, bumping railroads into its forests, and dragged launches over its cataracts, and partitioned it off among emperors and powers and trading companies, without having ventured into the countries they pretend to have subdued. But from Paul du Chaillu to W. A. Chanler, "the Last Explorer," as he has been called, just how much more do we know of Africa than the Romans whose bridges still stand in Tangier?

Davis's brief mention of the man he would that same year celebrate as an amalgam of heroic qualities somewhat diminishes Chanler's great adventure by placing it in context, a point of view that is here distinctly Conradian: "There are still," Davis observes dryly, "a few things for us to learn" (37).

Over the four hundred years since Columbus first landed in America, the Spaniards and the English had spread across the two great Western continents, "but Turks and Romans and Spaniards, and of late, English and Germans and French, have been pecking and nibbling at Africa like little mice around a cheese, and they are still nibbling at the rind, and know as little of the people they 'protect,' and of the countries they have annexed and colonized, as did Hannibal and Scipio."

> The American forests have been turned into railroad ties and telegraph poles, and the American Indian has been "exterminated" or taught to plough and to wear a high hat. The cowboy rides freely over the prairies; the Indian agent cheats the Indian—the Indian does not cheat him; the Germans own Milwaukee and Cincinnati; the Irish rule everywhere;

even the much-abused Chinaman hangs out his red sign in every corner
of the country. There is not a nation of the globe that has not had its hold
upon and does not make fortunes out of the continent of America; but
the continent of Africa remains just as it was, holding back its secret, and
still content to be the unknown world. (38)

This would seem to be a call for the United States to turn its inventiveness
and enterprise toward Africa, exploiting the untapped resources of that
unknown continent by following the lead of Henry Morton Stanley, who
showed the way by building a rail line that considerably extended civilized
access to the interior provided by the fabled but inadequate Congo.

And yet, on the very next page, Davis suggests that an untapped Africa
might be a very good thing, for Tangier serves as a vivid example of the unfortunate effect of civilization on the fringes of that continent. Lying "but
three hours off from Gibraltar," the colonial outpost "can teach you how
little we or our civilized contemporaries understand of these barbarians
and of their barbarous ways." The city lies on "the nearest coast of Africa"
and appears from the sea "like a mass of drifted snow on the green hills below" (39). On closer encounter it proves to be "a fine place spoiled by civilization. . . . The first thing which meets your eye on entering the harbor at
Tangier is an immense blue-and-white enamel sign asking you to patronize
the English store for groceries and provisions. It strikes you as much more
barbarous than the Moors who come scrambling over the vessel's side" in
such a ferocious manner as to "remind you of their piratical ancestors" but
who are merely "hotel porters and guides" seeking custom (40).

Davis expresses a great deal of admiration for the Moor, who when encountered in towns other than Tangier, "in Tetuan or Fez," is seen at his best
and gives some idea of "what Tangier once was. . . . There he lives in the exclusiveness which his religion teaches him is right—an exclusiveness to
which the hauteur of an Englishman, and his fear that some one is going to
speak to him on purpose, become a gracious manner and suggest undue familiarity." Here again RHD seems to have Mark Twain's manner resonating
in his writerly ear, the ironic exaggeration that can irradiate the commonplace scene of a Moroccan bazaar. For even the Moors who keep shop in
Tangier preserve "a haughty contempt for a passing Christian," RHD observes, taking solace from the wisdom that "there is always something beneficial in feeling that you are thoroughly despised; and when a whole community combines to despise you, and looks over your head gravely as you

pass, you begin to feel that those Moors who do not apparently hold you in contempt are a very poor and middle-class sort of people" (45).

"The Moorish gentleman," wrote Davis, "is the most perfect type of a gentleman that I have seen in any country. He is seldom less than six feet tall, and he carries his six feet with the erectness of a soldier and with the grace of a woman. The bones of his face are strong and well-placed, and he looks kind and properly self respecting, and is always courteous. When you add to this clothing as brilliant and robes as clean and soft and white as a bride's, you have a very worthy-looking man" (62). Davis's description of the "barbaric" Moor recalls Melville's description of Typee warriors, both being versions of primitivism essential to the romantic spirit and both used to argue against the colonial presence, whether in Morocco or the Marquesas. When Davis was privileged to meet the Bashaw of Tangier, he thought him "the finest-looking Moor he had seen," an superb specimen of the Moorish gentleman, with "the air of a man of the world," who "looked exactly like Salvini as Othello" (63).

Davis, by contrast, expresses no admiration for the Englishman in Tangier, who when back in Great Britain is "always preaching that [his] house is his castle, and yet he invades this country . . . and demands that not only shall he be treated well, but that any native of the country . . . who chooses to call himself an American or an Englishman shall be protected too. Of course he knows that he is not wanted there; he knows he is forcing himself on the barbarian, and that all the barbarian has ever asked of him is to be let alone. But he comes, and he rides around in his baggy breeches and varnished boots . . . and complains because he cannot get his bath, and all the rest of it, quite as if he had been begged to come and to stop as long as he liked" (46). This is not the viewpoint of a writer friendly to the idea of imperialism.

Indeed, most of what Davis has to say about Tangier is humiliating to the pretensions of the civilized world, which has not improved but spoiled the city: "Barbarism with electric lights at night is not attractive. Tangier to every traveller should be chiefly interesting as a stepping-stone towards Tetuan or Fez. Tetuan can be reached in a day's journey, and there the Moor is to be seen pure and simple, barbarous and beautiful" (71). It is easy enough to criticize RHD for his condescension here, akin to his recommendations to the khedive of Egypt concerning the use of American officers from western garrisons. We no longer are sympathetic to the notion of barbarism, even in the service of a primitivist aesthetics that regards the Moor as a noble

savage superior to those who would civilize him. And yet we can hardly disagree with Davis's larger argument that the Moor is not only happiest but
also best off when left alone.

Davis had read stories in the British papers concerning "the cruelty
shown to the inmates" of the jails and prison in Tangier, that within their
walls could be found "madmen and half-starved murderers and rebels,
loaded with chains, dying of disease and want, who are tortured and
starved until they die" (56–59). As a reporter, he felt it incumbent upon him
to check on prison conditions, especially because no outsider had been
allowed inside its walls for a decade. The prohibition made him all the more
certain that "there was something there that the Sultan did not want seen,"
hence convinced that he should gain admittance. Davis's persistence assures
us that American journalists have not much changed in attitude over the intervening century: "I . . . dragged the Consul-General into it, and brought
things to such a pass that I could see no way out of it but my admittance to
the prison or a declaration of war from the United States" (59).

Davis took advantage of his interview with the bashaw to press his request, which was finally but reluctantly granted, with the warning that as
an infidel he might be torn apart by the fanatic Muslims incarcerated there.
But once inside, Davis not only went unharmed by the prisoners—who
merely gratified "their curiosity by staring at us"—but also saw no signs of
abuse. Although "very dirty and poorly clothed," as well as haggard and pale
from long confinement, the prisoners seemed in rather good shape. The
"iron bars around their legs" which made it necessary that they crawl, not
walk, about, with a great clanking of chains, even added an element of picturesque "interest" (66–69).

"Indeed, I was not so much impressed with the horrors of the Sultan's
prison as with the fact that our own are so little better, considering our advanced civilization" (69). Moreover, any comparative evaluation should
take into account the cultural context: "To be fair, you must compare a
prisoner's condition in jail with that which he is accustomed to in his own
home, and the homes of the Moors of the lower class are as much like stables
as their stables are like pig-sties." Here again, we can only take Davis at his
word, which is that of a privileged American insulated by a very thick skin.

As with his other demonstrations of national naïveté, we must focus on
his larger and quite valid point. In concluding his account of this visit to the
Moroccan prison, RHD wonders in print why the foreign legations in Tangier, if they truly believed the stories they told "of the horror of these jails,"
had not done something about it, why they had not "used their influence to

try and better the condition of the prisoners, rather than to introduce the game-laws for the protection of partridges and wild-boars" (70–71). Davis was accompanied in his visit to the prison by Colonel Matthews, the resident consul general of the United States, along with another compatriot and fellow tourist "the Rev. Dr. Henry M. Field, the editor of the *Evangelist,* and a distinguished traveller in many lands" (60). As a result, the first foreigners to have visited the prison in ten years were all Americans. It was a situation that reflects badly on the British residents who are the majority in Tangier's foreign colony and who circulated the horror stories while making no effort to check out their truth. Here, as with Davis's report on matters in Egypt, the clear implication is that what the English do well, the Americans could do far better.

To be sure, the U.S. consul general was not at all eager to press the bashaw to allow Americans into the prison. Before Dr. Field and Davis were done with their visit to Tangier, "Colonel Mathews wished we were both in the United States" (60). As with his behavior in Port Said, Davis pokes fun at himself, importuning the authorities in order to discover that his suspicions about the conditions in the Tangier prison were wrong. He manages to make his point about the faults of the English colony at his own expense and on occasion is willing to portray himself as less an innocent than an ignoramus abroad.

For example, Davis notes that in the books he has read about Morocco, tourists are instructed always to haggle with shopkeepers and to offer only a third of the asking price. Supposedly, the Moorish merchant "would cry aloud to Allah to take note of the insult, and would ask you to sit down and have a cup of coffee, and . . . he would then beat you up and you would beat him down, and . . . at the end of two or three hours you would get what you wanted for two dollars" (53). So advised, RHD sallied forth to the bazaar in search of one of the ornately decorated, long-barreled muskets seen in those parts. He soon found one, for which the merchant was asking twelve dollars:

> I offered him eight. I then waited to see him tear his beard and unwrap his turban and cry aloud to Allah; but he did none of these things. He merely put the gun back in its place and continued the conversation, which I had so flippantly interrupted, with a long-bearded friend. And no further remarks on my part affected him in the least, and I was forced to go away feeling very much ashamed and very mean. The next day a man at the hotel brought in the gun, having paid fourteen dollars for it, and

said he would not sell it for fifty. We would pay much more than that for
it at home, which shows that you cannot always follow guide-books. (54)

Here as elsewhere, RHD casts himself as a late-nineteenth-century version of what has been called the Ugly American (by persons who have not
read the book of that title). But he is not up to the measure of ugliness displayed by any number of those foreigners permanently residing in Tangier,
whose behavior seems to warrant the superior attitude of the Moors. Davis
attributes the decline of morality in the exile community to the climate and
isolation of the place, which relaxes the restraints of civilized lands: "There
is something about these hot, raw countries, hidden out of the way of public opinion and police courts and the respectability which drives a gig, that
makes people forget the rules and axioms laid down in the temperate zone
for the guidance of taxpayers and all reputable citizens. As the sailors say,
'There is no Sunday south of the equator'" (48).

Davis seems once again close to the viewpoint of Conrad or, in more modern instances, Graham Greene, Alec Waugh, and Malcolm Lowry, for whom
"hot countries" is a byword for the loss of civilized veneer, which reacts to
heat and humidity by peeling away from the raw and uncertain wood beneath: "It is hard to tell just what it is, but the sun, or the example of the barbarians, or the fact that the world is so far away, breeds queer ideas, and one
hears stories one would not care to print as long as the law of libel obtains
in the land" (48).

Whenever Davis hears a character in a novel or on the stage cry out,
"Come let us leave this place, with its unjust laws and cruel bigotry. We will
go to some unknown corner of the earth, where we will make a new home.
And there, under a new flag and a new name, we will forget the sad past, and
enter into a new world of happiness and content," he invariably knows "that
he is going to Tangier," the foreign equivalent of Texas, long a refuge for discontent and disreputable Americans (48–49).

It is seldom some Utopian scheme that motivates the refugees in Tangier,
who are less often in search of freedom from oppression than in flight from
the law:

It may be that he goes there with somebody else's money, or somebody
else's wife, or that he has had trouble with a check; or, as in the case of
one young man who was feted and dined [in Tangier,] had robbed a diamond store in Brooklyn, and is now in Sing Sing; or, as in the case of a recent American consul, had sold his protection for two hundred dollars to
any one who wanted it, and was recalled under several clouds. And you

hear stories of ministers who retire after receiving an income of a few hundred pounds a year with two hundred thousand dollars they have saved out of it, and of cruelty and bursts of sudden passion that would undoubtedly cause a lynching in the chivalric and civilized states of Alabama or Tennessee. And so when I heard why several of the people of Tangier had come there, and why they did not go away again, I began to feel that the barbarian, whose forefathers swept Spain and terrorized the whole of Catholic Europe, had more reason than he knew for despising the Christian who is waiting to give to his country the benefits of civilization. (49)

This is not the Richard Harding Davis we find in revisionist accounts of America in the 1890s, whose romances of foreign adventures like *Soldiers of Fortune* are regarded as avatars of the imperialist spirit. Nor is it the Davis who in his coverage of the war in Cuba seems the tacit spokesman not only of intervention but annexation as well. Davis here, moreover, seems at odds with the Davis who earlier challenged the United States to get busy if it hoped to buy into the empire business. Like his criticism of the English presence in Egypt, Davis's account of the exile community in Tangier condemns the effects of civilization on countries which seem not to need its blessings and are spoiled rather than improved by its presence. Moreover, the influence seems to work in reverse in tropical lands, as colonists tend to lose their own civilized manners instead of teaching them to supposed barbarians.

Davis's account of Tangier can hardly be seen as advocating the movement of the United States toward an imperial destiny. On the contrary, he would seem to be dissuading his readers from dreaming of American adventures in tropic zones. This Conradian theme would provide the basis for one of Davis's short stories of this period, "The Exiles," an extended illustration of the demoralization of Americans who flee the United States and take up residence in Tangier. And yet, his next book of travels will find RHD in a land much less traveled than the coasts of the Mediterranean, where the conditions inspire him to argue for extending the sphere of the United States's influence into the region, sentiments in harmony with Captain Mahan's geopolitical theories.

Still, Davis's viewpoint lacks the rigid consistency of the Mahan cast of thought. A journalist, not a geopolitician, his opinions are influenced by the scene through which he was passing at any given moment. His was not the big picture but the vivid, small scene, much as he was better at the short story than the extended romance. Passing through Gibraltar, he waxed enthusiastic over British empire; visiting Egypt, he lamented the heavy hand of British empire; and touring Tangier, he found the evidences of British tenancy tawdry and out of place in an otherwise magnificent setting.

Yet a steady drift exists in his viewpoint, for Davis approved of imperialism when it seemed to fulfill his love of order, whether social or aesthetic, which he associated with England and the British Empire. He was always ready to override his animadversions against the effects, aesthetic and otherwise, of introducing civilization into savage places when the occasion seemed to demand it. And whether he was for or against a specific colonial presence, RHD's inconsistency was unified by the deep sense of decency and fair play that was essential to his character.

We may never determine whether Davis was an imperialist, but we can surely define him as an idealist, an instinctive proponent of the Emersonian brand of benevolence, which came packaged with a leavening of pragmatism. Indeed, it was Davis's chivalric activism that was root and branch of what it meant to be a certain kind of American at a certain time in U.S. history. It not only goes a long way toward explaining Dick Davis's popularity during his lifetime but also helps to clarify his championing of the U.S. invasion of Cuba.

Your "Never-never country."
RUDYARD KIPLING

8 : IMPERIAL LESSONS

: I :

Davis's idealism was one aspect of his romantic nature, but it was inseparable from his love of travel to exotic places, his hunger for the novel more
than for the familiar. It was an impulse essential to his journalism and his fiction. Moreover, Davis's love of novelty was in harmony with the national enthusiasm for progress, whether as invention, architecture, or bringing order
to messy places, a trinity that the proposed Nicaraguan Canal, so much in
the news throughout the 1890s, was intended to combine. It is not surprising, then, that Davis's travels eventually carried him to that fabled isthmus
from which Keats's Cortez first caught sight of the great western sea.

In his letters to his mother from the Mediterranean, Davis complained of
the lack of new material so essential to his journalistic quest, for his route
retraced the one taken by so many tourists, from Ulysses to General Grant.
Catching his first sight of the African coast, he wrote "all the fascination of
King Solomon's Mines seems to be behind those great mountains." Calling
"Willie Chanler . . . the most sensible individual I have yet met," Davis entertained the fantasy of "disappearing for years and years in the Congo." But
he quickly assured his mother (as he always did after making such threats)
that he would not yield to the temptation of leaving those parts of the world
which were so familiar, in order "to go on where it is older, and new" (*Adventures* 108).

Eventually, RHD did catch up with Willie Chanler, where his friend sat
waiting in Tampa for the promised invasion of Cuba. That island was certainly an "old" place if measured by American time but was soon to become
as new as any journalist could hope. In the meantime, Davis returned home
from the Mediterranean by way of France, which resulted in yet another
travel book, *About Paris,* published in 1895. His sketches of Paris life have
little bearing on the advancing line of reflections and reactions that leads to
his coverage of the United States's invasion of Cuba. But in the year that
book was published, Davis took yet another trip, one that would carry him

as inexorably as a plot in one of his romances to the hotel porch in Tampa
and his reunion with Chanler.

For the remainder of 1893 and much of 1894, RHD followed a familiar
routine, even while suffering from periodic depression and bouts of chronic
sciatica. In September 1893 his editorship of *Harper's Weekly* was termi-
nated by the Harper brothers, although for a time he would continue his
connection with the periodical. He attended plays regularly and kept up his
social contacts with theater people. He also wrote a romantic novella, *The
Princess Aline,* inspired by a chance encounter with Princess Alix of Hesse-
Darmstadt (soon to marry Czar Nicholas) while in Athens, at the far end of
his Mediterranean journey. His first venture beyond the short story, it was
favorably received and sold well.

Declaring himself tired of European travel, with its muchness of same-
ness, Davis nonetheless traveled to Paris again in June 1894. He returned to
America at a time when the papers were full of stories about the Japanese
invasion of Korea, then Chinese territory, news that awoke his old ambition
to cover a war. There were stories as well about the effects of a severe economic depression in the United States, but Davis never seems to have been
much attracted to such controversial local material, which would require
his taking a stand on the hot issue of labor versus capital. Instead, he made
plans to take a train to San Francisco and travel from there to China.

Davis got only as far as Ottawa before his excitement was swallowed up
in the anticipated boredom of a very long journey by rail and ship. Once
again he had heard the seductive call of Kipling's "long trail" from across the
distant hills, only in this case the call came from too far away for consummation, and he returned home. But then, early in 1895, RHD undertook
what was perhaps the most significant of the many travels of this period, for
if there is a prelude to his coverage of the Spanish-American War, it is the account of his rambles through Central America and the novel that was nour-
ished by that experience.

Davis had already started writing what would become *Soldiers of Fortune*
before leaving the country, and he would finish it while seeing the account
of his Central American trip through the press. It is a connection that when
properly considered becomes a framework of considerable heft. Though his
experience was hardly a match for the danger and enterprise of young
Chanler's expedition into Africa, Davis too may be said to have carried the
American flag into little-known places. Moreover, Chanler's expedition led
where few Americans would follow, while Davis made his way through

places where the Stars and Stripes soon would become a familiar if not always welcome sight.

Davis's record of his Central American journey, *Three Gringos in Venezuela and Central America,* belongs to an Anglo-American genre that starts with John Smith's *True Relation,* is continued in William Byrd's two-sided version of his experience surveying the colonial boundary between Virginia and South Carolina, and extends through the published account of the Lewis and Clark expedition. To this we can add Richard Henry Dana Jr.'s *Two Years before the Mast,* a writer who shared both Davis's initials and his biased view of Spanish American culture, which the Harvard undergraduate turned sailor had encountered on the coast of California.

Then there is Francis Parkman's *California and Oregon Trail,* another travel narrative that benefited from contemporary circumstances for its initial popularity. All these earlier books are accounts of journeys through regions that lack any coherent pattern of settlement, territory that can be properly—which is to say profitably—exploited only through the imposition of some kind of law and order, often by a military presence. In Dana's book, orderliness was also coupled with what was thought of as Yankee enterprise, an emphasis shared by Davis's work.

Davis's Central American venture was inspired by a chance encounter in Delmonico's with a man he had earlier met while in Texas gathering the material for his western book. He told RHD about a scandal brewing in Honduras that "was better than any you'll find lying around here in New York" (Lubow 117). Because this was the same individual who had told him how best to make contact with U.S. Cavalry troops pursuing the Mexican revolutionary Garza, it seemed a likely lead to pursue, and although the "scandal" did not amount to much, the overall result of the Honduran junket was certainly rewarding. What Davis literally stumbled into (or through) was the kind of "new" material he had been searching for ever since beginning his career as a traveling correspondent, set against the exotic tropical backdrop Davis associated with the adventures of William Astor Chanler.

When Davis arrived in Honduras, an international incident was in progress in neighboring Venezuela, not the war which he had long hoped to cover but conditions that at the time threatened to result in armed conflict. Entirely unrelated to the purpose of Davis's trip but influential on the reception of the book that resulted, there was an ongoing border dispute between British Guiana and Venezuela that President Cleveland had inherited from the Harrison administration. The resulting brouhaha between Great

Britain and the United States had implications far more important than anything Davis encountered in Honduras.

Under pressure from jingoistic politicians and editors and with Venezuela pleading for U.S. protection, Cleveland (or rather his secretary of state,
the pugnacious Richard Olney) continued Harrison's policy of favoring
Venezuela's side of the boundary dispute. When the British foreign secretary, Lord Robert Salisbury, refused to negotiate the matter, the president
delivered a strong message, citing the Monroe Doctrine in a situation incidental to its original purpose but hardly irrelevant to its subsequent use
by such as Theodore Roosevelt. In it Cleveland made clear that the United
States was willing to go to war over the dispute.

As a Democrat, Cleveland was hardly a champion of extending the
sphere of U.S. influence, which was the province of such Republican statesmen as Henry Cabot Lodge. However, Great Britain's overbearing actions
did seem to require strong language, and though the situation was dip-
lomatically resolved without interference by the United States, it was, as
Walter LaFeber and other students of U.S. expansionism have maintained,
a prelude to much more serious business to come.

The border dispute came to a head in December 1895, long after Davis had
returned home, indeed as his account of the trip was appearing serially in
Harper's Magazine. Because of this contretemps between the United States
and Great Britain and its consequences, Davis's report on conditions in Central America would be published at a critical time in our history, as the United
States began to take an increased interest in Latin American matters. And
like his other travel writings of the 1890s, it provides a useful gauge to the
emerging imperialistic temper in the United States. But unlike most of those
earlier books, *The West from a Car Window* excepted, it caught the public's
imagination, popularity not due solely to its current newsworthiness.

Although, as Davis lamented to his mother, he was once again traveling
over familiar ground, he had with him amusing companions, and they encountered persons, both public and private, who gave his narrative a picturesque and at times picaresque quality. The famous Davis luck not only
held but thrived, for the popular reception of *Three Gringos in Venezuela and
Central America* undoubtedly prepared the audience for *Soldiers of Fortune,*
Davis's first full-length novel. And that romance of love and revolution set in
a tropic zone in its turn heralded the intervention of the United States in
Cuba, in which Davis again played a significant role.

The perceivable difference between the realism of Davis's reporting and
the fancifulness of his romances is no more obvious than in the disparities

between the novel whose composition was interrupted by his travels in Central America and his account of that experience. He undertook the trip in part to obtain background for the novel, realistic detail of the sort that would loan verisimilitude to romantic fiction. And yet one is hard-pressed to find any but the most superficial connections between the two narratives. Indeed, the romance is in many ways contradicted by the realities of Central American life that Davis encountered.

Both were written with a bias against the political temper of Hispanic countries, seen as volatile and unstable, much as their residents were depicted as indolent and wasteful, making little use of the rich potential of their region. But where the romance holds out some hope in these regards, the travel narrative suggests that if matters are left in the hands of native peoples, nothing positive by way of progress can be expected. Nor would Davis's next novel, *Captain Macklin,* which was clearly derived from his Honduran trip, provide anything that would mitigate his pessimism regarding the situation in Central America.

: II :

Davis's first stop on his Caribbean journey, en route to Puerto Cortés, was Belize in British Honduras, like Gibraltar in the Mediterranean an outpost of England and to Davis's mind a model of its kind: "A British colony is always civilized; it is always the same, no matter in what latitude it may be, and it is always distinctly British. Every one knows that an Englishman takes his atmosphere with him wherever he goes, but the truth of it never impressed me so much as it did at Belize" (*Three Gringos* 5–6). A British man-of-war lay in port, its officers "playing cricket with a local eleven under the full tropical sun," verifying Noel Coward's famous line about "mad dogs and Englishmen" (9). It was Sunday, "and Sunday in an English colony is observed exactly as it should be, . . . so the natives were in heavily starched white clothes, . . . all apparently going somewhere to church in rigid rows of five or six" (9).

Davis recalled Belize fondly, not only because " in its way it was one of the prettiest ports at which we touched" but also because "its cleanliness and order, while they were not picturesque or foreign to us then, were in so great contrast to the ports we visited later as to make them most remarkable (16). Leaving the miracle of orderly governance behind when he boarded a boat loaded with bananas, RHD exulted in a letter to his mother that thenceforth he would "see Conrad, Conrad, Conrad!!" (*Adventures* 141).

It is a suggestive but seemingly puzzling remark given that the writer best known for his studies of white men in the tropics had in January 1895 not yet published his first novel; *Almayer's Folly* appeared in March of that year, the month Davis returned from his Central American journey. It is perhaps less of a puzzle if we recall that Conrad is also the name of the hero in Byron's *Corsair,* a gallant pirate and type and symbol for the nineteenth century of romantic restlessness and daring.

On the other hand, the adventures of Byron's Conrad take place on the Aegean Sea and have nothing to do with tropic zones, whereas what Davis found in Spanish Honduras and the other places he visited in Central America anticipated the Conradian world of tropical disarray, created by the imposition of Western notions of progress. His viewpoint was reinforced by the orderly grid imposed by British rule in Belize, for what RHD subsequently witnessed bore out his notion that in hands other than the English, the process of civilization is less than redemptive.

As in Tangier, the modern European presence in Central America does not so much lend the evidence of order to tropic climes as impose the ugliness of utilitarian expedience: "There are two opposite features of landscape in the tropics which are always found together—the royal palm, which is one of the most beautiful of things, and the corrugated zinc-roof custom-house, which is one of the ugliest. Nature never appears so extravagant or so luxurious as she does in these hot latitudes; but just as soon as she has fashioned a harbor after her own liking, and set it off at her best so that it is a haven of delight to those who approach it from the sea, civilized man comes along and hammers square walls of zinc together and spoils the beauty of the place forever" (*Three Gringos* 19–20). The native population dwells in structures that harmonize with the landscape, being built of adobe and covered with thatch or tiles; the "gringo," on the other hand, "is in a hurry, and wants something that will withstand earthquakes and cyclones, and so wherever you go you can tell that he has been there before you by his architecture of zinc" (21).

Davis is here describing Livingston, a Guatemalan seaport that compared with Belize "was like a village on the coast of East Africa," a paragon of ugliness that would be followed by many more. Instance Port Barrios, on the river Dulce, a Guatemalan town sitting "at one end of a railroad, and surrounded by all the desecration that such an improvement on nature implies, in the form of zinc depots, piles of railroad-ties, and rusty locomotives" (25). Davis's Dulce brings to mind Marlow's account of the stations along the Belgian Congo, from which Conrad himself had only recently returned, and Davis shares the same wry perspective.

Thus the native huts in town are papered inside "with copies of the New York Police Gazette, which must give the Guatemallecan a lurid light on the habits and virtues of his cousins in North America." It was here that the most of Davis's fellow passengers left the ship, "wandering about the place with blank faces, or smiling grimly at the fate which condemned them and their blue-prints and transits to a place where all nature was beautiful and only civilized man was discontented" (26).

Clearly, in RHD's view, consistent with his report on Tangier, the presence of the British Empire may lend admirable order to tropic places, but the activities of civilized man in general create only an aesthetic affront to persons seeking the exotic beauty of the tropics. The transit and chain, instruments of humankind's control over nature, seem less symbols of rectilinear order than icons of an insane determination to reduce tropic luxuriousness to a wasteland of zinc. The impulse that is the heart of imperialism may be counted on to create a Conradian shambles, not the outlines of an emerging civilization.

The supposedly hot tip given Davis in New York involved corruption in the dealings of the Louisiana Lottery, which, having been outlawed in the United States, was now doing business in Puerto Cortés on the coast of Spanish Honduras, to which Davis sailed from Guatemala. The promised story, however, turned out to be less a matter of scandal than of desuetude: the once thriving and profitable lottery was now an operation in decline. What Davis discovered was a lot of local color but not much corruption, for the lottery was guilty of nothing illegal beyond using the U.S. mails to lure dollars from overly hopeful Americans. It had lost much of its celebrity and had become pretty much a mom-and-pop operation. Because Davis out of necessity had put up in the headquarters of the lottery itself, he was hardly in a position to pump up the story beyond what it deserved, which was not much.

Accompanying RHD on this trip were two other young men, and they were joined in Honduras by a third. First in rank was Somers Somerset, the future Duke of Beaufort, Davis's friend since his visit to Oxford, who was in it for the adventure. The second man was Lloyd Griscom, a young American whose father had been asked to head a company that would build the long-awaited Nicaraguan Canal. Griscom therefore joined the party to report on the conditions, political and geological, of the region. In Puerto Cortés the three met up with American-born Charles Jeffs, a colonel in the Honduran army who offered to serve as a guide over the mountains to the capital city, Tegucigalpa. Jeffs's help was necessary because the rail line over the mountains had never been finished and gave way to a road in name only, a trail that had to be negotiated on muleback through very rough and insect-rich terrain.

Davis had encountered similarly rough country in the arid regions of southern Texas, but travel in tropical countries brought with it added discomforts. Indeed, the hazards and nuisances of his journey over the mountains to Tegucigalpa were a reasonable equivalent to the sort of thing he had associated with young Chanler and proved a contrast to the lack thereof on the tourist-crowded routes he had taken though England, the Mediterranean, and France. In reporting his first encounter with the Honduran jungle to his mother at home, Davis declared that "I never expect to see such a country again unless in Africa" (*Adventures* 145).

To these difficulties was added the usual problem of familiarity, for at this point in his journey the experience "was pretty much as you imagine it is from what you have read, that covers it, and I have discovered nothing new by coming to see it. I only verify what I have seen. . . . I do not mean that I did not do well to come for I am more glad that I did than I can say only I have not, as I have been able to do before, found something that others have not seen." Davis's confused syntax perfectly expresses his attitude at this stage in the journey, but his pessimism was unwarranted. As it turned out, RHD was more successful than he had anticipated in finding something new in Central America; as a reviewer noted of *Three Gringos in Venezuela and Central America,* "Mr. Davis always has a way of giving an air of novelty to what he has seen, and in this book, as the scenes which he descries are wholly novel to most of us, he is doubly interesting" (quoted in Lubow 123).

Ironically, it was following his Central American travels that the Richard Harding Davis celebrated by such younger writers as Booth Tarkington first emerged, the tanned and rugged correspondent striding out of jungles into the Waldorf, only to stride out of the Waldorf back into other jungles. This is the mythic RHD, a man who was as much at home surrounded by savages as he was in the midst of polite society, a hero clearly derived from his admiring account of the adventuresome Stephen Bonsal. Yet at the start of his experience in Honduras, he seems anything but a man in control of his destiny; indeed, he seems to be wondering what he was doing there at all.

It might even be said that Davis's trip over the mountains in Honduras was a rite of passage, by means of which he was able to assume the identity he had earlier associated with Henry Morton Stanley, becoming what he had been writing about and what he would forever be associated with in his subsequent writings. Perhaps what he saw was nothing new, but Davis himself was becoming something of a novelty, a revised, updated version of that explorer-reporter in whose footsteps he was treading.

The train tracks ended in San Pedro Sula, and the three travelers put up in a hotel built in expectation that the railroad would be continued "across the continent," despite the mountains that loomed into the clouds to the west. It was not a town distinguished by much local enterprise. The only hotel was kept by a widow of recent vintage, "an American woman, who was making an unappreciated fight against dirt and insects, and the height of whose ambition was to get back to Brooklyn and take in light sewing and educate her two very young daughters" (*Three Gringos* 65).

A portrait of her late husband dominated the hotel dining room, and the admirable qualities of the man himself were the subject of much of the widow's conversation. She kept up the tone of her establishment by refusing to accommodate Hondurans, only gringos, with the result that she had so far saved only "eight dollars of the sum necessary to convey her and her children home, and to educate them when they got there; and as American travellers in Honduras are few, and as most of them ask you for money to help them to God's country, I am afraid her chance of seeing the Brooklyn Bridge is very doubtful" (66). I quote this as typical of Davis's mildly sardonic manner throughout much of his narrative, as well as the tenor of what he had to say, in which squalor and hopelessness seem to be the dominant themes. If one is occasionally reminded of Conrad in reading Davis's account of Central America, here Graham Greene seems closer to the mark.

As Davis and his party left San Pedro Sula in company with eleven mules, they were followed out of town by well-wishers, a local custom but one that made RHD feel "as though I were an undesirable citizen who was being conveyed outside of the city limits by a Vigilance Committee" (70). This was yet another allusion to Bret Harte, though Davis admitted that his escort consisted of only two men, the railroad manager and his baggage master. The trail they were to follow startled the travelers at first sight, for "it led almost directly up the face of the mountain, along little ledges and pathways cut in the solid rock, and at times was so slightly marked that we could not see it five yards ahead of us" (73).

Honduras is made up mostly of high mountains, so many in number that they bear no names: "A Hondurian deputy once crumpled up a page of letter-paper in his hand and dropped it on the desk before him. 'That,' he said, 'is an outline map of Honduras.'" (In *Hot Countries*, Alec Waugh credits this gesture to Columbus, in reference to the island of Dominica.) And it was over this precipitous trail that the commerce between the capital city and the Atlantic coast of Honduras was forced to travel: "whether it be a postal card or a piano, or a bale of cotton, or a box of matches," everything was carried "on the back of a mule or on the shoulders of a man" (75).

Accommodations for travelers along this route were correspondingly primitive and consisted chiefly of the homes of people who were used to putting up (and putting up with) strangers, though an alternative was provided by the local town hall, invariably "a large hut with a mud floor, and furnished with a blackboard and a row of benches, and sometimes with stocks for prisoners; for it served as a school or prison or hotel, according to the needs of the occasion" (79). We will recall Davis's preference for comfortable quarters while traveling and his delicate palate as well, characteristics that do not jibe with the mythic image of the adventurer at home anyplace in the world. But it must be said that as always he put a humorous frame around such inconveniences, as in his description of the staple of the Honduran diet:

> The black-bean habit in Honduras is very general; they gave them to us three times a day, sometimes cold and sometimes hot, sometimes with bacon and sometimes alone. They were frequently served to us in the shape of sandwiches between tortillas . . . the national bread [which is] made of cornmeal, patted into the shape of a buckwheat cake between the palms of the hands and then baked, [though] generally given to us cold . . . burned on both sides, but untouched by heat in the centre. . . . At first, and when [the black beans] were served hot, I used to think them delicious. That seems very long ago now. When I was at Johnstown at the time of the flood, there was a soda cracker, with jam inside, which was served out to the correspondents in place of bread; and even now, if it became a question of my having to subsist on those crackers, and the black beans of Central America, or starve, I am sure I should starve, and by preference. (80)

The Hondurans used hammocks for sleeping, "on account of the insects and ants and other beasts that climb up the legs of cots and inhabit the land," another national habit with which Davis was unhappy, as the hammock kept his body at an uncomfortable forty-five-degree angle: "There are men who will tell you that they like to sleep in a hammock, just as there are men who will tell you that they like the sea best when it is rough, and that they are happiest when the ship is throwing them against the sides and superstructure, and when they cannot sit still without bracing their legs against tables and stanchions" (82). He observed with satisfaction that when he had visited an American warship anchored at Colon, the sailors who could find space to sleep on the decks did so, their hammocks swinging empty above them.

As well as a sense of humor, RHD characteristically displayed an active aesthetic sensibility, and if accommodations along the trail were dreadful, he was clearly charmed by the scenery they passed through, "trees with a pale-green foliage, and covered with the most beautiful white-and-purple flowers," as well as "many birds of brilliant blue-and-black or orange-and-scarlet plumage. . . . This was the most beautiful and wonderful experience of our journey" (84). The luxuriant growth of palms kept in clay pots at home was awe-inspiring, towering over the travelers, so that they felt they had somehow shrunk to the height of garden gnomes. "Hundreds of orchids clung to the branches of the trees, and from these stouter limbs to the more pliable branches of the palms below white-faced monkeys sprang and swung from tree to tree, running along the branches until they bent with the weight like a trout-rod, and sprang upright again with a sweep and a rush as the monkeys leaped off chattering into the depths of the forest." It was, Davis maintained, an "enchanted wilderness," and coming out of it into an open plain "was like an awakening from a strange and beautiful nightmare" (88).

In contrast to the fantastic and exotic scenery was the character of the Hondurans dwelling amid such tropical abundance, the "country people" as Davis calls them, whose lives were led on a level "as near an approach to the condition of primitive man as one can find on this continent . . . not because the people are poor, but because they are indolent" (92–93). They are also pious, if the little altars found in their homes are any indication, though the iconography of the objects decorating them is highly unconventional, being "almost always china dolls, with no original religious significance, but which they have dressed in little scraps of tinsel and silk, and which they have surrounded with sardine-tins and empty bottles and pictures from the lids of cigar-boxes. Everything that has color is cherished," noted Davis, and many of the icons had been scavenged from what travelers had left behind: "Sometimes the pictures they use for ornamentation are not half so odd as the fact that they should have reached such a wilderness. We were frequently startled by the sight of colored lithographs of theatrical stars . . . pinned to the mud walls and reverenced as gravely as though they had been pictures of the Holy Family by a Raphael or a Murillo" (93).

Something closer to Davis's notion of civilization was provided by the village of Santa Barbara, boasting paved streets but little else to recommend it. The travelers were granted an audience with General Louis Bogran, "who has been President of Honduras for eight years and an exile for two" and who, when questioned about his greatest accomplishment while in office, replied "Peace for eight years." Davis found this a most appropriate response "when you consider that in the three years since he had left office there have been four presidents and two long and serious revolutions, and when we were in the capital the people seemed to think it was about time to begin another" (104).

Davis was clearly impressed by the deposed president, for he was "a very handsome man, with a fine presence, and with a great dignity of manner," and a photograph of Bogran was included to prove the point, shown standing behind a railing, dressed in a white suit and sporting a graying Vandyke. He was the prototype of the kind of leader who for Davis seemed to hold out the most hope for progress in Central America, although the odds provided by events during the brief period since the general had left office indicated that the hope was not substantial.

: III :

What seems to have impressed RHD most about Spanish Honduras was its abundance of insect life, which made sleeping outdoors a virtual impossibility: "There is nothing green that grows in Honduras that is not saturated and alive with bugs, and all manner of things that creep and crawl and sting and bite. It transcends mere discomfort; it is an absolute curse of the country, and to every one in it. . . . You cannot sit on the grass or on a fallen tree, or walk under an upright one or through the bushes, without hundreds of some sort of animal or other attaching themselves to your clothing or to your person . . . and after they have once laid their claws upon you, your life is a mockery, and you feel at night as though you were sleeping in a bed with red pepper" (111–12). To this ever present nuisance Davis added the activities at night of vampire bats, who fed so voraciously on the mules that they were often soaked with blood in the morning, and when the travelers attempted to saddle up the animals "they would stagger and nearly fall" (112). This was certainly the "new" kind of country that Davis envied his friend Chanler for having traveled, but if it was a route seldom taken by tourists, his account gave little encouragement to anyone who might think of following him through it.

After a hard journey of more than ten days, the travelers at last spied from a height the capital city, Tegucigalpa. Though an urban center in the heart of the Honduran mountains, it provided something less than an inviting prospect, having been built "in a bare, dreary plain, surrounded by five

Photo engraving from Three Gringos *showing General Louis Bogran, the former president of Spanish Honduras, whose chief pride was that he was able to keep his country at peace during his administration.*

hills that rose straight into the air, and that seemed to have been placed
there for the special purpose of revolutionists, in order that they might the
more exactly drop shot into the town at their feet" (126–27).

Advised of the travelers' arrival by telegraph, the foreign residents of the
town turned out with a brass band and a military guard, a promising welcome that ended in yet another shocking disappointment, for the hotel accommodations reserved for them had just been vacated by an invalid who
had left his medicines and the smell of a sick chamber behind. The gringos
chose instead a small dirty room with three dirty cots, an experience that
had the advantage of making "anything that savoured of civilization" encountered thereafter in Tegucigalpa a delightful surprise (130).

In the Honduran capital there was little of note to be found. The "only
suggestion of energy that the town furnishes" is the sight and sound of
washerwomen doing laundry in the river running through the capital city:
"The other residents seem surfeited with leisure and irritable with boredom." Tegucigalpa has shops, a large cathedral, a government palace, a
penitentiary, a university, and a cemetery and boasts an attractive plaza,
"where the band plays at night and people circle in two rings, one going to
the right and one going to the left. " Otherwise, Davis despaired, "there is no
color nor ornamentation nor light nor life nor bustle nor laughter. . . .
Everyone seems to go to bed at nine o'clock," and then the place is as silent
as its own graveyard, "except when the boy policemen mark the hour with
their whistles or the street dogs meet to fight" (131).

The only "interesting thing" about the capital city is the fact that everything in it that could not be dug from the ground or made from wood had
been hauled there on mule back, including not only the mailboxes (once the
property of the U.S. Postal Service) and the gas street lights but also "the
great equestrian statue of Morazan the Liberator," which had been carried
in pieces to the plaza and assembled. "These things were not interesting in
themselves, but it was interesting that they were there at all," an opinion
Johnsonian in periodicity and condescension (133).

While in the capital, the visitors called on the newest president, Bonilla,
brought to office by yet another revolution and surrounded by officials who,
although very young for their responsibilities, had the merit of having
"fought and bled" for the privileges they now enjoyed: "You cannot help
feeling more respect for the man who has marched by the side of his leader
through swamps and through jungle, who has starved on rice, who has slept
in the bushes, and fought with a musket in his hand in open places, than for
the fat and sleek gentlemen who [in the United States] keep open bar at the

headquarters of their party organization, who organize marching clubs, and who by promises or by cash secure a certain amount of influence and a certain amount of votes" (134).

If gaining office in Honduras is a dangerous game, holding on to it has its hazards as well. Where in American a defeated politician loses only a job, in Central America he may find himself "with his back to a church wall, and looking into the eyes of a firing squad, or he digs his own grave by the side of the road, and stands at one end of it, covered with clay and sweat, and with the fear of death upon him, and takes his last look at the hot sun and the palms and the blue mountains, with the buzzards wheeling about him, and then shuts his eyes, and is toppled over into the grave, with a half-dozen bullets in his chest and stomach" (134–37). If such was the fate of "half of our professional politicians at home," muses Davis, "then the other half might understand that holding a public office is a very serious business, and is not merely meant to furnish them with a livelihood and with places for their wives' relations" (137).

This Jeffersonian sentiment should be taken as criticism of the American spoils system rather than as praise for the way politics were conducted in South America, being yet another example of Davis's wry sense of humor. For he went on to reckon that the cost of the recent revolution had been less in lives lost than in the economic ruin that resulted, in part because the ousted men are already busy planning a counterrevolution, making "any sort of continued prosperity . . . impossible. Native merchants will not order goods that may never reach them, and neither do the gringos care to make contracts with men who in six months may not only be out of office, but out of the country as well" (139).

Worse, "it follows . . . that a government which is created by force of arms, and which holds itself in place by the same power of authority, cannot be a very just or a very liberal one, even if its members are honest, and the choice of a majority of the people, and properly in office in spite of the fact that they fought to get there, and not on account of it" (140). As in his previous reactions to a foreign culture, Davis renders a balance sheet, in which the good is computed against the bad. He seems to feel that although undeniable qualities of hardihood and courage are required to participate in Central American politics, any system that depends on a constant sequence of revolutions hardly guarantees economic and political stability.

Davis doubted that the Honduran people were capable of any other course, such as honoring their own constitutional requirement that the president remain four years in office. Instead, they prefer to limit his term to whatever period is ended by the rise of someone with sufficient strength to overthrow and replace him: "The value of stability in government is something they cannot be made to understand. It is not in their power to see it, and the desire for change and revolution is born in the blood" (143). Davis's conclusion is hardly unique to him, but his lengthy account of the instability of Central American governments, which fills a number of pages, certainly appeared at a critical time in the history of his own country. For the economic investment of capital in South and Central America by businesses in the United States would be an essential element of the new imperialism, with a consequent interest in insuring that local governments were not momentary creations of popular impulse.

"The republics of Central America are republics in name only," Davis declared, having found that all strangers passing through are regarded as potential enemies of the state: "The only time in Central America when our privacy was absolutely unmolested, and when we felt as free to walk abroad as though we were on the streets of New York, was when we were under the protection of the hated monarchical institution of Great Britain at Belize, but never when we were in any of these disorganized military camps called free republics" (146). These are sentiments that harmonize with what would emerge as the policy of the United States regarding the political instability of its South and Central American neighbors, and Davis's tribute to the good effects of the British presence has a detectably imperialistic implication.

Even more explicit in this regard is Davis's opinion that a citizen of any Central American country is "no more fit for a republican government than . . . for an arctic expedition, and what he needs is to have a protectorate established over him either by the United States or by another power; it does not matter which, so long as it leaves the Nicaragua Canal in our hands" (146). Davis gives symbolic point to his disparaging comments about the inadequacy of Central American republics by describing a statue that stands in the capital of Costa Rica. It shows "the Republic in the form of a young woman standing with her foot on the neck of General Walker, the American filibuster," whereas in Davis's opinion "it would have been a very good thing for Costa Rica if Walker, or any other man of force, had put his foot on the neck of every republic in Central America and turned it to some account" (146–47).

By "some account" Davis means productivity, for the potential wealth of Central America is untapped and will remain so as long as power there stays in the hands of the Central Americans, who "are like a gang of semi-barbarians in a beautifully furnished house, of which they can understand neither its possibilities of comfort nor its use" (147). Nature has poured forth its bounty throughout the land, in terms both of fruitfulness and minerals concealed beneath the earth, resources that remain unexploited. Nature has also placed the lakes in Nicaragua in such proximity that only a little effort would be necessary to eliminate the long and dangerous voyage around the Horn, "but it will have to be some other man than a native-born Central-American" who will undertake the project (148).

In 1895 the United States was still hopeful of finding that person, having benefited from a treaty that gave it exclusive control over any such artificial waterway, and periodicals as well as politicians extolled the benefits that would pour from the long-projected canal as from a great cornucopia. Its completion was regarded by Captain Mahan as a certainty, so much so that his argument for augmenting the U.S. naval presence in the Caribbean was as early as 1890 contingent on the presence of the isthmian waterway.

A lengthy article appeared in *Harper's Weekly* in 1891 that argued for digging the Nicaraguan Canal, along with a map showing how it would alter the trade routes in both hemispheres. Davis included an almost identical map in his book on Central America, further testimony to the derivativeness of his geopolitics. His was the geopolitical position maintained by the persons who made up Henry Adams's expansionist circle, but aside from material derived from sources such as *Harper's,* Davis seems to have come to his own conclusions independent of the Adams coterie.

Having arrived on the Pacific coast of Honduras, Davis and his two companions bid farewell to Jeffs and traveled on to Corinto in Nicaragua itself. There they boarded a train to Lake Managua, and next took a boat to the capital city itself. Nature may have been kind to human purposes by its dispersal of lakes in that country, but Davis was unimpressed by the accomplishments of the Nicaraguans. Managua had all the picturesqueness of "a baseball diamond," having been built "on a plain of sun-dried earth, with houses of sun-dried earth, plazas and parks and streets of sun-dried earth, and a mantle of dust over all. Even the stores that have been painted in colors and hung with balconies have a depressed, dirty, and discouraged air" (178).

The visitors were granted an interview with the president of the country, Zelaya, who impressed Davis as "a very able man, and more a man of the world than Bonilla . . . and much older in many ways." As an example of the president's mature wisdom, Davis cited Zelaya's enthusiasm over the prospect of having the United States dig the canal through his country, for if he was "somewhat of a philosopher," it was as a student of the Spencerian

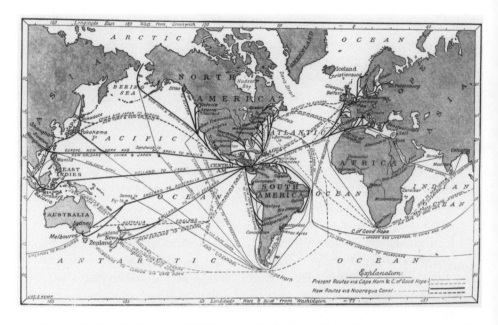

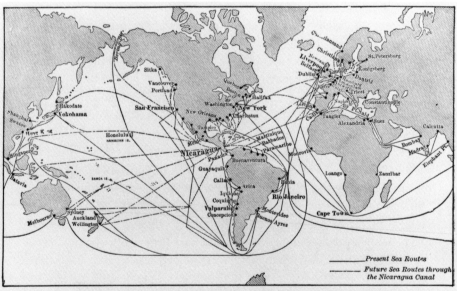

MAP OF THE WORLD SHOWING CHANGE IN TRADE ROUTES AFTER THE COMPLETION OF THE NICARAGUA
CANON

The top map is from an article in Harper's Weekly;
the bottom is from Davis's Three Gringos, *published at about the
same time. Influenced by Captain Mahan's book on seapower,
the* Harper's *piece stressed the importance of an Isthmian canal.*

school who could see the imperial handwriting on the wall: "He . . . believed, or said he did, in the survival of the fittest as applied to the occupation of his country. He welcomed the gringos, he said, and if they were better able to rule Nicaragua than her own people, he would accept that fact as inevitable and make way before them" (182).

President Zelaya also echoed the philosophy of Captain Mahan and declared that the best "argument in favor of the Nicaragua Canal" was that "it would enable the United States to move her ships of war quickly from ocean to ocean" (181). Here again, in RHD's view, was the kind of leader Central America needed, one willing to step aside and let the United States play through. This was the kind of good sportsmanship that appealed to the man who played football at Lehigh and cricket at Johns Hopkins.

But as Walter LaFeber tells us, there were very good reasons for President Zelaya's enthusiasm for cooperation with the United States. At the time of Davis's visit, Nicaragua was under the threat of British armed invasion, with the stated purpose of collecting an indemnity for Zelaya's earlier expulsion of the British vice-proconsul. Previously unfriendly toward the United States, Zelaya's change in attitude was a result of his assumption that the Monroe Doctrine would protect Nicaragua from the British. He was still entertaining that notion when the two young Americans dropped by for a visit but would be disappointed shortly thereafter (LaFeber 225–27). Davis, unaware of these exigencies, took Zelaya's statements of goodwill toward U.S. interference at face value.

Here, as elsewhere, Davis resembles those fictional caricatures of ingenuous if courageous Americans of later times, whether as played by Joel McCrea in Hitchcock's *Foreign Correspondent* (1939) or Joseph Cotten in Carol Reed's *The Third Man* (1949). While visiting Europe, these innocents blunder into very complex international situations the implications of which they do not understand and therefore draw unsubstantiated conclusions before finally seeing the light. At the same time, it is RHD's very innocence that recommends him to us, for his take on affairs in Nicaragua conveys a chauvinism that is representative of the much better informed champions of expansionism in the United States. He may have been wrong as to particulars but was entirely in harmony with what would emerge as the new imperialism regarding South and Central American countries.

Lloyd Griscom, having accompanied Davis and Somerset with the purpose of reporting back to his father concerning the advisability of digging the Nicaraguan Canal, came to the conclusion that Captain Mahan's pet project was ill advised. His findings were largely based on the instability of the region—not political but geological—which was subject to frequent earthquakes. David McCullough has given us an entertaining and detailed account of the debate regarding the Nicaraguan Canal, arguments both tangled and obscure, involving great financial interests and devious plots and counterplots. But certainly young Griscom's opinion was in harmony with the final decision to locate the canal elsewhere.

The proponents of completing the Panama Canal won the debate, choosing to carry out the aborted plan of the famous French engineer, Ferdinand-Marie de Lesseps. In arrogance and ignorance, Lesseps had insisted that a level, lockless canal like his own Suez could be easily dug through the isthmus, while engineers of considerable experience argued otherwise and were proved right. In 1894 Davis was in harmony with the major opinion in the United States, still in favor of the Nicaraguan route, and yet his description of the stalled Panama operation is of some interest. It may have contributed something to the change in plans, for it contradicted his own expectation, based on information then current regarding the present condition of the abandoned project.

After the French gave up work on the canal in 1887, the population of the town of Panama had declined to such a degree that it reminded Davis "of a Western county-seat after a boom had left it" (*Three Gringos* 202). Though still standing, it was a "ruin" inspiring "melancholy and disgust" because of the enormous extravagance and corruption associated with the project; Davis felt that "the relics of this gigantic swindle can only inspire you with a contempt for yourself and your fellow-men" (197). The place had been a scene of activity on an epic scale, equivalent to the Battles of Waterloo and Gettysburg in terms of sacrifice and loss of life. It reminded Davis of the Crusades, being a display of zeal by "these young soldiers of the transit and sailors of the dredging-scow," who had "no promises or sentiment to inspire them; they were not fighting for the boundaries of their country, but redeeming a bit of No Man's Land; not doing battle for their God, but merely digging a canal" (197).

So many workers succumbed to yellow fever that their fate suggested that if the isthmus was "holy ground . . . there was a curse upon it" (198). The story of the Panama Canal was a "legend" of sorts, which endowed "the city, and the people in it," with great "interest," for "even the ruins of the Spanish occupation, and the tales of buccaneers and of bloody battles and buried treasure, cannot touch you so nearly as do the great, pretentious building of the company and the stories of De Lesseps' visit, and the cere-

monies and feastings and celebrations which inaugurated the greatest failure of modern times" (202).

But if Panama the town was a metaphorical ruin, what Davis found during his tour of the uncompleted canal was something quite different. Seeing
"what the other writers who have visited the isthmus saw" would have provided considerable "interest" of the kind found in Panama, for his descriptive powers would have been inspired "had I found the ruins of gigantic
dredging-machines buried in the morasses, and millions of dollars' worth
of delicate machinery blistering and rusting under the palm-trees; but, as
a rule it is better to describe things just as you saw them, and not as it is
the fashion to see them, even though your way may be not so picturesque"
(205–6). Here again we have Davis's credo as a reporter stated in full, his dedication to reporting as realistically as possible the facts as he found them,
as usual heightened by his characteristic style.

What Davis found along the canal was not the promised spectacle of
"thousands of dollars' worth of locomotive engines and machinery lying
rotting and rusting in the swamps," in effect a technological Gothicism, but
just the reverse: "All the locomotives that we saw were raised from the
ground on ties and protected with a wooden shed, and had been painted
and oiled and cared for as they would have been in the Baldwin Locomotive
Works. We found the same state of things in the great machine works . . .
and climbed to shelves twenty and thirty feet from the floor, only to find that
each bit and screw in each numbered pigeon-hole was as sharp and covered
as thick with oil as though it had been in use that morning" (205).

David McCullough quotes in full this passage at a key place in his story of
the Panama Canal as further evidence that Lesseps's project was regarded
at the time as a total failure unworthy of resumption. However, it can be
read as evidence too of the great value not only of what had already been
accomplished by those heroes of transit and dredge but also of the machinery left behind, needing only enterprise and vision to set it once again in motion. Those were the qualities that Theodore Roosevelt would bring to the
project once he was in the White House.

In that connection, McCullough gives an interesting aside regarding the
delicate negotiations in 1903 between Secretary of State John Hay and
Philippe Bunau-Varilla, a civil engineer representing the French interests in
the canal, that resulted in a revolution breaking out in Colombia, creating
the independent Republic of Panama, a key to Roosevelt's grand strategy.
Remaining vague as to the willingness of the United States to recognize any

new government, Hay in parting gave the engineer-diplomat a copy of *Captain Macklin,* a recent novel by "Hay's friend, Richard Harding Davis," and urged him to read it (McCullough 354). That novel is a highly seasoned romance about a young American trained at West Point who joins an older French officer in raising a revolution in Honduras. Having read it, Bunau-Varilla understood that he had been handed what amounted to an encoded message: Hay, without explicitly agreeing to lend U.S. support to a revolution in Colombia, was doing so in effect.

As McCullough reports, it was clear to Bunau-Varilla—who would soon become the minister to the United States from the newly created Republic of Panama—that Davis's novel was "'the subtle symbol, the password exchanged between Mr. Hay and myself." As such it was the signal to start an uprising that would free a critical section of the isthmus from Colombian control. Though RHD's actual connection with John Hay seems to have been slight—an acquaintance derived from the friendship between Hay and Davis's father—we find him playing a role at both ends of the process by means of two books a decade apart. Whatever the reputation *Soldiers of Fortune* may have in these recent days as a document of American imperialism, surely in the hands of John Hay *Captain Macklin* was the thing itself.

Given the ongoing debate over whether the isthmian canal should be dug through Nicaragua or what was then Colombia, it is interesting to find Davis's own opinion divided. Thus while he encouraged "every citizen of the United States" to support opening "the Nicaragua Canal to the world under the protection and the virtual ownership of his own country," Davis could not help observing that "it looks to . . . ignorant eyes as though only a little more energy and a greater amount of honesty would be necessary" to complete the Panama Canal (*Three Gringos* 211). Like other supporters of the latter project, Davis was overly optimistic regarding the necessary effort and cost, but in calling for "energy and honesty" he was in effect sounding the kind of trumpet to which Theodore Roosevelt characteristically responded in the manner of the biblical warhorse.

Moreover, while he was in Panama, "where," as he ingenuously wrote his mother, "we may be said to be absorbing local color," Davis got somewhat more deeply involved in local matters than he acknowledged to Rebecca (*Adventures* 61). He conspired with his fellow travelers to effect the escape of "a young lawyer and diplomat," a Panamanian who had been placed under house arrest on suspicion of "being one of the leaders of the revolution" then threatening the Colombian government—albeit not the one encouraged by President Roosevelt (212). Conceived by the three adventurers as a "sporting act," the scheme was frustrated when the young man was taken off to prison. Still, it was a gesture in keeping with Davis's chivalric nature, as well as with his love of sports.

Perhaps more important, the episode demonstrates the very thin line that divided the reporter of facts and the heroes of romance Davis would write. And in plotting his private intervention in Panamanian matters, he undoubtedly was reassured by the presence of the USS *Atlanta* at Colon, for he felt "that comforting sense that comes to a traveler from the States when he knows that one of our White Squadron is rolling at anchor in the harbor" (216). This was sentiment that would be translated from his account of Central America to *Soldiers of Fortune,* where the idea of revolution takes a much more serious form.

: IV :

While waiting for a boat to Corinto, Davis and his party spent a brief period on the island of Amapala, one hardly short enough for the travelers, the place being "the hottest" RHD had ever visited. His account of the "one cool spot in Amapala" perfectly captures the surreal qualities of Central America, which characterizes the stories about the region by O. Henry, who followed Davis to Honduras two years later. Davis and his friends found a refuge from the heat on "a point of land that the inhabitants had rather tactlessly selected as a dumping-ground for the refuse of the town, and which was only visited by pigs and buzzards."

This point of land ran out into the bay, and there had once been an attempt to turn it into a public park, of which nothing now remains but a statue to Morazan, the Liberator of Honduras. The statue stood on a pedestal of four broad steps, surrounded by an iron railing, the gates of which had fallen from their hinges, and lay scattered over the piles of dust and débris under which the park is buried. At each corner of the railing there were beautiful macaws which had once been painted in brilliant reds and greens and yellows, and which we tried to carry off one night, until we found that they also were made of iron. We would have preferred the statue of Morazan as a souvenir, but that we doubted its identity. Morazan was a smooth-faced man with a bushy head of hair, and this statue showed him with long side-whiskers and a bald head, and in the uniform of an English admiral. It was probably the rejected work of some English sculptor, and had been obtained, no doubt, at a moderate

price, and as very few remember Morazan to-day it answers its purpose
excellently well. We became very much attached to it . . . and if we did
plot to convert Honduras into a monarchy and make Somerset king, no
one heard us but the English edition of Morazan smiling blandly down
upon us like a floor-walker in the Army and Navy Stores, with his hand on
his heart and an occasional buzzard soaring like Poe's raven above his
marble forehead. The moonlight turned him into a figure of snow, and
the great palms above bent and waved and shivered unceasingly, and the
sea beat on the rocks at our feet. (168–69)

The humor here, as in similar passages in the book, discounts the seriousness and hence the worth of Central American culture. Moreover, there are
hints of the subversive imperialism which Davis, in person and through his
fiction, would advocate. Thus the facetious "plot" to overthrow the Honduran government would provide the story line for *Captain Macklin,* which
in turn would serve to signal the U.S. approval of the Panamanian revolution, a plot of considerable heft.

Nor was Davis an innocent regarding the identity of the persons actually
in control of affairs in Central America. They were not local officials but representatives of foreign commercial interests, chiefly German, who worked
as consuls for countries other than those from which they came. The companies often operated under assumed corporate identities: "You have only
to change the name of the Rossner Brothers to the San Rosario Mining Company, to the Pacific Mail, to Errman Brothers, to the Panama Railroad Company, and you will identify the actual rulers of one or of several of the republics of Central America." So powerful were the Rossner interests that
they could, "if they wanted, purchase the entire Republic of Honduras in
the morning, and make a present of it to the Kaiser in the course of the
afternoon" (162).

It needs to be said that RHD's negative account of Central America is balanced by his description of Venezuela, which reads at times like a tourist
brochure: "I do not know of a place that will so well repay a visit . . . or a
country that is so well worth exploring as Venezuela" (266). In a chapter
titled "The Paris of South America," on Caracas, Davis begins with a lengthy
discussion of Simón Bolívar, the "Liberator of Venezuela," whose statue
may be found in New York's Central Park and who—taking into consideration differences in temperament—deserves the traditional comparison with
George Washington, "the North American Bolívar" (222). Unlike the towns
in Honduras, Nicaragua, and Colombia, Caracas is a beautiful and pleasant

city, and Davis's arrival there "was like a return to civilization after months on the alkali plains of Texas" (245).

Davis expressed excitement over the potential wealth of Venezuela, in whose "interior there is a vast undiscovered and untouched territory waiting for the mining engineer, the professional hunter, and the breeder of cattle" (269). His enthusiasm may in part be explained by his brief interview with Joaquín Crespo, the recent dictator but now the newly elected president of Venezuela, who impressed him as being "very polite . . . and very large," as well as a promoter of "freedom that betokened absolute democracy" (262). Davis was also pleased with his visit to Caracas, as he confided to his brother, because he and his two friends headed home wearing "the Order of the bust of Bolivar the Liberator of Venezuela of the 4th class . . . although I still sigh for the third class with its star and collar" (*Adventures* 164). He also brought back with him "a basket of alligator pears," avocados in 1895 being unknown to American cuisine; thanks to Davis's efforts, they were soon a regular item on the menu at Delmonico's (Lubow 123). But then, as the friendly *Bookman* reviewer noted of *Three Gringos,* Davis was adept at nosing out "novelty" of whatever kind.

It is doubtful that during his short stay in Caracas Davis learned much about the ongoing boundary dispute between Venezuela and England, which had resulted from the inexorable expansion of British Guiana over many years. Pressure on President Cleveland's administration to intervene on behalf of Venezuela had been mounting since the previous summer, when William Scruggs, the former U.S. minister in Caracas, had published a pamphlet on behalf (and in the service) of the Venezuelan government. However, it was not until April, after RHD had returned to New York, that Richard Olney sent an outspoken note to Lord Salisbury regarding the situation in Venezuela and demanding the opening of negotiations between the two countries.

Olney's communiqué ended with a thinly veiled threat of direct intervention by the United States, in accordance with the terms of the Monroe Doctrine. It was Salisbury's long delay in responding to Olney, as well as his high-handed refusal to acknowledge the relevance of the Monroe Doctrine, that inspired President Cleveland's angry message to Congress on December 17, 1895. Cleveland once again cited the Monroe Doctrine and spoke in such militant language that his speech aroused an outpouring of American sympathy; there being no equivalent arousal on the part of the English people, the British government finally agreed to an arbitrated negotiation with Venezuela.

Since 1876 the Venezuelans had been making tacit or direct appeals to the United States, in the hope of inspiring interference in the boundary dispute under the aegis of the Monroe Doctrine. That Davis, regarded as a visiting American of some importance, may have been approached in Venezuela much as he was by the Nicaraguan president, who likewise hoped to elicit American sympathy, is possible. But there is no mention of any such appeal in his letters home. And in his account of the dispute, which first appeared in the December issue of *Harper's Magazine,* where his book on Central America was being serialized, Davis (like many Americans) felt that the "Doctrine as we understand it is a very different thing from the . . . Doctrine as they understand it" (*Three Gringos* 273).

Yet Davis's understanding of the conflict seems to have been imperfect. It was his impression that the situation had been worsened by Venezuela's "hasty action in sending three foreign ministers out of the country for daring to criticise her tardiness in paying foreign debts and her neglect in not holding to the terms of concessions" (269). No historical study of the boundary dispute mentions any such matter. Venezuelan authorities had arrested two inspectors of the British Guiana police, with their subordinates, for having trespassed on presumed Venezuelan territory, and subsequently released them, an incident that did exacerbate relations with Great Britain and presumably influenced Olney's note to Lord Salisbury.

According to Davis, Venezuela was apprehensive that its action would bring armed retribution by warships of Great Britain, France, and Germany and therefore looked to the United States for protection. But Davis "did not think the Monroe Doctrine meant that south American republics could affront foreign nations with impunity" (275). However, in Davis's view the boundary dispute was another matter. Great Britain had "pushed her way westward," taking advantage of conflicting land claims inherited from other nations, until her boundary had advanced "over a territory of forty thousand square miles," which included the strategic "Barima Point at the entrance to the Orinoco" (276).

At the time Davis was writing his account of the situation, in mid-1895, Great Britain had not yet responded to Secretary Olney's hostile letter, and warhawks in the United States were beginning to make shrill noises. The rival territorial claims might well have provided what Henry Adams thought of as an "educational" opportunity, not only for Venezuela but also for Great Britain concerning "what the Monroe Doctrine really is." As Davis maintained, "If the Monroe Doctrine does not apply in this case, it has never meant anything in the past, and will not mean much in the future" (276–75). Here, he seems to be in sympathy with both Olney and Senator Lodge, who anticipated the letter sent by the secretary of state to Lord Salisbury in a blustering article in the *North American Review* on the Venezuelan situation in which he stated forthrightly that "the supremacy of the Monroe Doctrine should be established and at once—peaceably if we can, forceably if we must" (Garraty 155).

But having drawn his line in the sand, Davis immediately took a few steps backward. "I cannot think the principle of this doctrine should be applied in this instance. For if it does apply, it could be extended to other disputes much farther south, and we might have every republic in South America calling on us for aid in matters which could in no possible way affect either the honor or the prosperity of our country" (278–81). Davis was not even sure if he approved of the Doctrine itself, which he regarded as "selfish" in nature, "as all rules for self-preservation must be selfish."

On the other hand, Davis opined, should the United States decide to intervene in the dispute, "I should prefer to think that we are interfering in behalf of Venezuela, not because we ourselves are threatened by the encroachments of Great Britain but because we cannot stand by and see a weak power put upon by one of the greatest." The best course, however, would be to stay clear of the quarrel, but once "being in, we must bear ourselves so that the enemy may beware of us, and see that we issue forth again with honor, and without having stooped to the sin of war" (281).

There is a certain amount of fishtailing here, for if Richard Harding Davis was no Alfred Thayer Mahan, neither was he a Henry Cabot Lodge, who, encouraged by Cleveland's angry message to Congress, rose up on the Senate floor on December 30 and delivered a long, learned, and comprehensive review of the Monroe Doctrine. In the spirit of his earlier article, Lodge's speech was specifically designed (even warped) to encourage U.S. intervention in Venezuela. It fairly bristled with Lodge's hatred of Great Britain, which dated from that country's tacit support of the Confederacy.

Lodge and his friend and fellow jingo Theodore Roosevelt had long lusted for war with England, which would excuse an invasion of Canada, and in the service of that desire Lodge continued to beat the Monroe Doctrine into a sword. He used for his anvil "the great law of self-preservation," precisely the emphasis to which Davis took exception (Lodge 235). It was shortly afterward that Henry Adams prepared his own updating of the Doctrine, licensing U.S. intervention in Cuba. Things were certainly warming up in Washington, to the point where, as the popular song associated with the Spanish-American War had it, there would be "a hot time in the old town" in 1898.

It was the excitement over the situation in Venezuela that may have warranted the addition of that country's name to the title of Davis's book, as a half century earlier Francis Parkman's publishers had been inspired by the gold rush to add "California" to the title of a book that took the reader no farther west than the foothills of the Rockies. Yet Davis's position was hardly expansionist and agreed with that of President Cleveland at the time he wrote it, which was prior to the president's angry message to Congress.

On New Year's Eve in 1895, Davis wrote to his brother, Charles, that "several of the papers here jokingly alluded to the fact that my article on the Venezuelan boundary," the last chapter of his forthcoming book having been published in the December *Harper's Magazine,* "had inspired the President's message" (*Adventures* 171). As he noted in the same letter, it was Salisbury's rudeness that resulted in Cleveland's militant position, which Davis regarded as a mistake, being "a cast iron ultimatum" lacking "a loophole for diplomacy and a chance to back out." He seems to have revised the concluding paragraphs of this chapter at about this time, referring to "President Cleveland's so-called 'war' message," which Davis thought would encourage Venezuela "to go much further than she would dare go" otherwise (*Three Gringos* 269). He made no mention of Lodge's speech, but we may doubt he approved of it, given his remark about the selfishness of any rule that was based on self-preservation.

If the serialization and subsequent publication of Davis's book insured that his discussion of the Venezuelan dispute would make its contribution to the on-going debate regarding the proper use of the Monroe Doctrine, it was hardly as an expansionist tract. As he wrote to his brother, all the talk in the United States in December had been of "war and Venezuela and the Doctrine of Mr. Monroe," and yet, despite Davis's yearning to become a war correspondent, he noted that the jingoism had influenced the stock market, resulting in a loss "of one thousand of millions of dollars." Now that eyes had been suddenly opened to the economic consequences of war, all the talk was of peace, and Davis knew "of but one jingo paper, The Sun, and war talk is greeted with jeers" (*Adventures* 171).

Thus in 1895 Davis, unlike Lodge and Roosevelt, had little interest in promoting imperial adventures by the United States. Likewise, we need to recognize the extent to which Davis thought of the situation in Venezuela in chivalric terms, of defending a weak nation against a strong but in such a way as to avoid violence while acquitting oneself with honor. That is, he comes much closer to what would be the position of President McKinley regarding Cuba than to that of Adams, Lodge and Roosevelt. Remembering how RHD had earlier praised the effects of Britain's orderly presence in Belize, we can compare his position regarding the Monroe Doctrine with his discussion of the overbearing role England was playing in Egypt. It was clearly one thing for Great Britain to bring order and civilization to indolent Hondurans; it was something else to push around the country associated with the George Washington of Central America.

Students of U.S. imperialism, following Walter LaFeber, regard the Venezuelan incident as an important turning point, an extension of the Monroe Doctrine that would soon enough, as Henry Adams intended, allow for the attack on the Spanish in Cuba and the Philippines. It is toward that eventuality we must see *Three Gringos in Venezuela and Central America* also moving. Unlike Lodge and Roosevelt, RHD may not have been hoping for war, but if the dispute in Venezuela had come to blows, Davis would have been among the first to head out as a correspondent to cover the fight.

On February 4, while cooling his heels in the capital of Nicaragua, Davis read in a Panamanian paper about "the trolley strikes in Brooklyn, a crisis in France, War in the Balkans, a revolution in Honolulu, and another in Colombia." Davis despaired of not being "in it" and wrote to his family of his discontent, envying those reporters who in the case of the trolley strikes would tell "how the militia fired on the strikers and how Troop A fought nobly" (*Adventures* 152). The sentence probably reveals less about Davis's sentiments toward labor unrest than about his frustrated yearning to witness the sight of soldiers in action.

But the letter home also reveals his innocence regarding the direction in which events in Central America were moving. He was "in it" much more deeply than he realized. In attempting to free the political prisoner from Panamanian authorities, he had in effect already committed himself to the party of revolution in Colombia (*Three Gringos* 215; cf. Lubow 122). "Never mind," he wrote to his family, "our turn will come someday and we may see something yet" (*Adventures* 152), little realizing that he and the United States were being carried by events in Central America toward the kinds of consummation he had for so long desired, if not exactly in the terms he might have anticipated.

Clear the land of evil, drive the road and bridge the ford.

RUDYARD KIPLING

9 : SOLDIERS OF THE TRANSIT

: I :

Even as he prepared *Three Gringos in Venezuela and Central America* for publication, Davis was finishing the manuscript of *Soldiers of Fortune,* and the contrast between the two works, the journalistic travel book and the romantic novel of adventure, is remarkable. There would seem to be a disjunction between RHD's pragmatic view of the proper use of the Monroe Doctrine in account of Central and South America and his apparent championing of armed interference there by the United States that characterizes his romance, which might better be titled "Three Jingos in South America." It would be difficult to find a better example of Davis the realist as opposed to Davis the romantic.

Writing fiction seems to have released a certain recklessness in the author, an indulgence in imaginary hairbreadth adventures whose popularity suggests that his dreams were not private fantasies. Revisionist critics have been quite right in singling out *Soldiers of Fortune* as an epitome of masculine aggressiveness, a novel that not only underwrote an emerging American imperialism but in effect also licensed the Spanish-American War, both of which operated under the protective aegis of the Monroe Doctrine. It would seem an inarguable thesis, if not as new as its proponents seem to think: Grant Knight, nearly fifty years ago, noted that Davis's novel was "a romance of Nordic supremacy and of American economic imperialism so entertaining that it must have stirred American fighting blood and been an unintentional preparation for the war we were about to wage" (*Critical Period* 122).

Economic imperialism aside, one can hardly deny the gendered basis of Davis's notion of heroism; his friend, the dramatist Augustus Thomas, also testified to the masculine emphasis found in RHD's most popular novel. In his introduction to *Soldiers of Fortune* in 1916, Thomas wrote that Davis "liked enthusiastically to write of men doing men's work and doing it man fashion with full-blooded optimism" (ix; cf. *R.H.D.* 43). But then, Thomas was merely approving a posture made popular by Kipling's "kingly boys" (as Van Wyck Brooks would call them in this connection [106]).

Certainly Robert Clay, the hero of Davis's romance, has "done things." By the time he appears, still a young man, he has been very busy. In Grant Knight's summary of his achievements, Clay "had been a sailor at sixteen; from the diamond mines of South Africa he had gone to Madagascar, Egypt, and Algiers; he had been an officer in the British army in the Soudan, had received a medal from the Sultan of Zanzibar, and had won the Legion of Honor fighting as a Chasseur d'Farique against the Arabs; he had built a harbor at Rio and had been made a German baron; he had been President of the International Congress of Engineers; he had visited Chile and Peru; he had been a cowboy on our western plains; he had helped build the Jalisco and Mexican Railroad" (*Critical Period* 121–22).

Clay moreover is a self-made man, having like Henry Stanley been orphaned early and denied the privilege not only of class but also a college education. He is a composite type, thoroughly American, with additions provided by a number of other bona fide heroes later celebrated in Davis's companion volume, *Real Soldiers of Fortune* (1906), in which a number of heroic Americans figure who found fame in foreign countries. Robert Clay is a piece of work of the kind that we can only call highly imaginary, a superhero whose accomplishments as summed up by Grant Knight above are impossible for a person of his youthful years and lack of formal education. Like Cortlandt Van Bibber, he looks forward to the comic book superheroes of a later period as well as to the protagonists of Ayn Rand's romances.

In constructing his superman, Davis was careful to parcel out the details of Clay's history in bits and pieces, a slow revelation attributable to the hero's natural modesty, so that they seem more believable than when summarized in a breathless paragraph. For our purposes, moreover, Clay is chiefly notable for what he is not: Unlike his predecessor Gordon, whom he closely resembles, Clay is not a correspondent or explorer; as Knight's résumé reveals he is a trinitarian combination, being equal parts cowboy, soldier, and civil engineer.

It is the last identity that is the most important. Robert Clay is a fictional embodiment of those "soldiers of the transit" who laid out the Panama Canal and as such is given romantic expansion and elevation. Like the heroic wastrel Courtlandt Van Bibber and the Stanley-like explorer-correspondent Gordon, Robert Clay is another stretch of the author's imagination designed to accommodate a larger-than-life masculine ideal. It is not surprising that Cecelia Tichi's description of the emergence of the heroic civil engineer in popular literature at the turn of the century reads like a portrait of Davis's hero:

> The heroes of these novels are typically civil engineers living roughneck lives in the American (or Latin American) outback. They design and construct railroads, mines, bridges, dams, and ironworks in such places as West Virginia, Kentucky, Alaska, Cuba, and California's Imperial Valley. Neither crude nor parochial, these men straddle the eastern clubroom and the western camp. In fact, they must. They are ruling class figures. If eastern by birth . . . they must imbibe the western spirit to become certifiably American. If western born, they must venture east to be civilized. . . . A visit to the East, in fact, becomes a device by which the novelist authenticates the civil engineer's civility in stories enacted in primitive conditions. . . . Mobile, adaptive, tough yet gentlemanly, these engineers are literally all-American men, integrating the nation's regions as birthplace and workplace conjointly manifest the national character in them. They are American stability incarnate. (118–19)

Tichi acknowledges that the hero of *Soldiers of Fortune* epitomizes the type. Having been "born in the shadow of Pike's Peak," Clay spends his youth "as sailor and cowboy" but "intuitively seeks acculturation in the capitals of Europe and is professionally renowned in Edinburgh, Berlin, and Paris, as well as the eastern United States" (118).

There is something in this that recalls Henry James's Christopher Newman, another self-made American who, having accumulated a fortune, sails for the Old World to acquire culture and, while he is at it, a wife of great beauty, charm, and ancient lineage. Clay, too, is ready for marriage, but typically for Davis, his ideal woman, though wealthy and beautiful, is an American, not an aristocratic European. Nor is Davis's hero associated with manufacturing but with a profession that had been given a very high American profile by the 1890s, thanks to the fame engendered by such marvels as the Union Pacific and the Brooklyn Bridge.

As Alan Trachtenberg has shown in his book on the Brooklyn Bridge, civil engineers during the years following the Civil War were responsible for works that assisted in realizing the ideal of national unity by literally bridging and binding a continent. But by the 1890s, as corporate America revised Hamilton's precept and began to think intercontinentally, the function of civil engineers underwent a transformation, epitomized by Robert Clay's activities in Mexico and Central America. As Van Wyck Brooks noted, *Soldiers of Fortune* served as a "memorial" of a time "when American traders financed revolts" in South and Central America "to control the nitrate beds and the rubber forests," activities that civil engineers facilitated, if not with quite the ardor of Davis's hero (107). Having hastened the western advance of the United States, civil engineers now assisted the spread of American commerce into Mexico and Central America.

Contemporary oratory often provides clues to popular beliefs, and in ascertaining the value put on the civil engineer in the 1890s we can begin with a quotation from Chauncey Depew, in his day a byword for elegant public discourse, who has already been cited in connection with Henry Stanley's tour of the United States. His collected addresses and orations fill twelve volumes, from which Edward Sundell mined *Mottoes, Aphorisms, and Nuggets,* in which we find the following excerpt:

> We have now no Tennysons, nor Longfellows, nor Hawthornes, nor Emersons. Perhaps it is because our Michael Angelos are planning tunnels under rivers and through mountains for the connection of vast systems of railways, and our Raphaels are devising some novel method for the utilization of electrical power; our Shakespeares are forming gigantic combinations of corporate bodies, our Tennysons are giving rein to fancy and imagination in wild speculations in stocks, and our Hawthornes and Emersons have abandoned the communings with and revelations of the spirit and soul which lift their readers to a vision of the higher life and the joy of its inspiration, to exploit mines and factories. (91)

This "nugget" immediately follows a passage headed "Our Responsibilities to Cuba," inspired by the victory over Spain in 1898, which speaks of the "wonderful agricultural and mineral resources" of the newly acquired protectorate: "We must give her the help and encouragement of beneficial concessions for her leading products. The wealth we thus create will be spent here for the railway and electrical supplies, the machinery and tools, the textile fabrics and agricultural implements required for her increasing population and wants" (91).

As if in anticipation of Depew's call, Clarence King, the geologist and mining engineer Tichi regards as a prototype of the "engineer heroes of the popular novels," especially "a Richard Harding Davis novel," visited Cuba in the early 1890s so as to assess the country's mineral wealth (Tichi 167–68). Henry Adams, King's friend and ardent admirer, defined him as a man who "directed his life logically, scientifically, as Adams thought American life should be directed," and by 1896 American life was directed at Cuba as through a surveyor's transit (Adams 312). In that year King joined Adams and wrote in support of intervention by the United States in the ongoing insurrection.

In 1897, the year in which *Soldiers of Fortune* appeared, Joseph H. Choate, a prominent New York lawyer, addressed the American Society of Civil Engineers in terms that echo Adams's appraisal of King: In comparing the engineer with his own and other callings, Choate noted that "we are all engaged alike in studying and applying laws to the uses and convenience of mankind, and in that respect the engineers, as it seems to me, have a very decided advantage over the other and older professions. They work from known and certain premises to inevitable conclusions. Theirs is an exact science, based not upon opinion, based not upon judgment, but upon absolute and fundamental facts in respect to which they ought not and cannot be allowed to err" (786).

Choate went on to insist that where "the breath of the lawyer is the measure of his fame," the very image of mutability, "the works of the engineer live after him as an enduring monument to carry down to a distant posterity his merits and his defects." He cited the testimony of the great public works erected by the Romans that were still standing a thousand years later. So also "the work of those great engineers of to-day, the men who build our great bridges, our great docks, our great tunnels, our great railroads, will be carried down to a posterity that will long since have forgotten the doctor, the lawyer, and even the clergyman, who are now ruling over us" (787).

Like Depew, his fellow New Yorker and clubbable friend, Choate was an influential lawyer and a popular speaker, but though an active Republican he never sought public office. In 1899 President McKinley would appoint him ambassador to the Court of St. James, where he would be instrumental in securing for the United States absolute control over the Panama Canal, another marvel of applied science and American energy, as yet incomplete. In 1897 Choate went on to recite the great accomplishments of civil engineering in the United States, labors that made possible the integrity of a union that was far greater in extent than that envisioned by the founding fathers. "Now, how did they do all this?" he asked rhetorically. "Well, I think it was only—to borrow a phrase of Emerson's—by hitching a wagon to a star." In the manner of Depew, Choate authenticated the work of the modern civil engineer with the example of Emerson, who as the champion of self-reliance was so often cited in the 1880s and 1890s to give credence to the commercial ethos (Choate 792; cf. Emerson, l:630).

When we add together the tributes of Depew and Choate, the sum suggests that the civil engineer, in addition to providing an example of the linear rectitude with which Tichi associates the type, was a mythic amalgam perfectly suited to the enterprising and romantic spirit of the age. Perhaps because Davis was himself beginning to usurp the profile of his earlier heroic ideal, the cosmopolitan traveler-correspondent; perhaps because as a writer he needed to find a new kind of hero to celebrate; or perhaps because of his stated admiration for the accomplishments of those who had built the first stage of the Panama Canal, Davis in effect coined the civil engineer as a romantic literary figure for his age.

Much as the economic depression of the mid-1890s inspired politicians and editors to champion the opening of foreign markets and encourage investments in Mexican and Central American products, so Davis in Robert Clay provided an entirely different kind of hero, virtually created out of that rising enthusiasm for a new kind of empire. Clay from the start is associated with the American West, like James's Christopher Newman and Owen Wister's Virginian, but he has qualities that distinguish him from those other distinctly American types, derived from his profession and the unique position he is put in by his South American location. Clay is closest to Wister's hero, being a compound of commercial enterprise and chivalric values, a knight enrolled in an distinctly modern crusade. He is Captain Stiles, as it were, transferred to an assignment better suited to his abilities, in that it has rewards more substantial than frozen rank and pay.

: II :

Robert Clay's career may differ somewhat from Gordon's in "An Unfinished Story," but as Arthur Lubow notes, the literary genesis is very clear. Thus Gordon too "had been an engineer" who "built bridges in South America, and led their little revolutions there," a provocative mixture given the plot of *Soldiers of Fortune* ("Unfinished Story" 238). Gordon had also been a soldier, having "seen service on the desert in the French army of Algiers" and like Robert Clay "had no home or nationality even, for he had left America when he was sixteen."

At one point Gordon even compares himself to a "cowboy," whose background and poverty make him ineligible to court the woman he loves. Clay is also given a cowboy past, but in contrast to the bitter finale of Davis's short story, *Soldiers of Fortune* ends happily, with the man from the West having triumphed over evil and won the hand of a beautiful and wealthy young woman. As a romance, the story is a modern and extended version of a fairy tale in which the hero, after proving his intelligence and courage, wins a fortune and an equivalent princess.

Like Wister and in anticipation of *The Virginian,* Davis realized that for his novel to attract the necessary female readership, it would have to involve a love story. That part of the plot may be incidental to what might be called the imperialistic game plan, but it cannot be easily separated from the whole, and Davis clearly thought of his plot as a coordinated collection of interrelated parts. Notably, the cover of the first edition is embossed with a picture of a beckoning young woman done in C. D. Gibson's familiar style. But I shall try to be brief in my discussion of those sections of the book that small boys would be sure to skip.

The novel, like "An Unfinished Story," opens with a dinner party, but in New York, not London. Likewise, it pairs a handsome, mysterious adventurer with a beautiful, wealthy, and cosmopolitan young woman, Alice Langham. At the time, Alice is interested in another man, the wealthy Reggie King, who had voyaged with his yacht all over the world and "was as well known and welcome to the consuls along the coasts of Africa and South America as he was at Cowes or Nice. His books of voyages were recognized by geographical societies and other serious bodies" (6–7).

It is not difficult to see in King a semblance to the privileged Anglo-American male ideal that dominates Davis's earlier fiction—Van Bibber in a yachting cap. But Alice Langham, though attracted to Reggie, feels that perhaps he has become too familiar a figure in her life and fantasizes that one day "the man would come who would pick her up on his saddle and gallop off with her, with his arm around her waist and his horse's hoofs clattering beneath them and echoing the tumult in their hearts" (5). A reference to Scott's "Lochinvar" (one of the tentative early titles Davis gave his novel as it was being written), this romantic dream is a prelude to Alice's meeting Robert Clay, the man she has been paired with as a dinner companion by her hostess, who has described him only as a "cowboy."

During the party that precedes the dinner but before she has been introduced to Clay, Alice sees across the crowded room "a tall, broad-shouldered youth, with a handsome face, tanned and dyed, either by the sun or by exposure to the wind, to a deep ruddy brown, which contrasted strangely with his yellow hair and mustache and with the pallor of the other faces about him" (8). Clay is here the Nordic ideal as defined by Grant Knight, keyed by his blondness, and as such is a novelty not only in Alice Langham's life but also in Davis's fiction.

Clay's predecessor, the explorer Gordon, is given no physical description, but the "cowboy" is rendered in detail, emphasizing "the ease of manner which comes to a person who is not only sure of himself, but who has no knowledge of the claims and pretentions to social distinction of those about him. His most attractive feature was his eyes, which seemed to observe all that was going on, not only what was on the surface, but beneath the surface, and that not rudely or covertly but with the frank, quick look of the trained observer" (9).

Alice, being observant herself, realizes that here is the man she is to be paired with at dinner, whom earlier she had imagined as arriving "in leather leggings and long spurs." Her first reaction is to wonder "how any one who had lived the rough life of the West could still retain the look, when in formal clothes, of one who was in the habit of doing informal things in them" (9). Unlike Clay, Alice concentrates on superficial attributes, and she is less comprehending than bewildered by what she sees. She is the counterpart to Miss Edgerton in "An Unfinished Story" and chiefly serves to emphasize the hero's superior qualities.

Clay is carrying a picture of Alice Langham, cut from a newspaper announcement of her "coming out" some years ago, and has also been following the news of her social life, both in America and abroad. It is clear that he has fallen in love with Alice from afar, and yet he takes advantage of their meeting by bluntly declaring that he disapproves of her life, which seems to him a terrible waste of her beauty and talents. She is a woman, he declares, who could in Europe "have a salon, or . . . influence statesmen" in America (20).

This assessment is Emersonian in its moral values, a mixture of idealism and pragmatism, but Alice professes to be puzzled by this frank if hardly tactful appraisal of her situation: "And have you come out of the West, knowing me so well, just to tell me that I am wasting myself? . . . Is that all?" (21). As Alice seems to recognize, this is the Lochinvar of whom she has been dreaming, but put off by Clay's judgmental attitude, she rudely rebuffs him. She tells him that the picture he carries is of a girl who no longer exists, whom Clay therefore could never meet, and in dismissing the girl, she dismisses the "cowboy" as well.

Robert Clay is, of course, no longer a cowboy, an identity mistakenly conveyed by his hostess, Mrs. Porter, in describing how he had been helpful to her son, George, when he was hunting in Mexico. As Clay himself describes it, he had met young Porter at what was then "the terminus of the Jalisco and Mexican Railroad. . . . he came out over the road and went in from there with an outfit after mountain lions. I believe he had very good sport" (11). Reggie King remarks that the rail line in question "is a very wonderful road . . . quite a remarkable feat of engineering." Clay merely acknowledges, "indifferently," that the railroad "will open up the country, I believe" (12).

Where his bluntness with Alice reflects his honesty, his diffidence here results from his modesty, for as the reader learns he is the engineer who put through the rail line in question. Ignorant of the connection, King goes on to state his high opinion of civil engineers, "picturesque" individuals whose work is unfortunately not much appreciated. He had met the men putting through the Mexican line when his yacht docked at Pariqua, the port where they received their materials, and was impressed by "their work and its difficulties."

> Now those men I met . . . were all young fellows of thirty or thereabouts, but they were leading the lives of pioneers and martyrs. . . . They were marching through an almost unknown part of Mexico, fighting Nature at every step and carrying civilization with them. They were doing better work than soldiers, because soldiers destroy things, and these chaps were creating, and making the way straight. They had no banners either, nor brass bands. They fought mountains and rivers, and they were attacked on every side by fever and the lack of food and severe exposure. They had to sit down around a campfire at night and calculate whether they were to tunnel a mountain, or turn the bed of a river or bridge it. And they knew all the time that whatever they decided to do out there in the wilderness meant thousands of dollars to the stockholders somewhere up in God's country, who would some day hold them to account for them. They dragged their chains through miles and miles of jungle, and over flat alkali beds and cactus, and they reared bridges across roaring canyons. We know nothing about them and we care less. When their work is done we ride over the road in an observation-car and look down thousands and thousands of feet into the depths they have bridged, and we never give them a thought. They are the bravest soldiers of the present day, and they are the least recognized. I have forgotten their names, and you never heard them. But it seems to me the civil engineer, for all that, is the chief civilizer of our century. (12–13)

King's pronouncement is in keeping with the praise heaped on engineers by orators of the day. But because Clay—one of the men whose names King has forgotten—is sitting unrecognized across the table from him, the praise is framed with a certain humor, revealed when Clay admits a few minutes later that he is the engineer who had built "that road Mr. King is talking about" (14). Moreover, Clay does not regard himself as a martyr. He declares that he looks forward to the greatest of difficulties because he "has the fun of overcoming them," the kind of modest courage that Davis habitually credits to his romantic heroes (14).

Like Gordon—which is to say like Stephen Bonsal and William Astor Chanler—Clay is a man at home both in tropical jungles and the drawing rooms of the upper classes in great cities. It is a facility that puzzles Reggie King once the "cowboy" has revealed his true identity: "What I can't understand . . . is how you had time to learn so much of the rest of the world. You don't act like a man who had spent his life in the brush . . . talking about England and Vienna and Voisin's." Clay responds by attributing his cosmopolitanism to a combination of "accident and design," his having "'worked for English and German and French companies, as well as for those in the States, and I go abroad to make reports and to receive instructions." He pronounces himself "what you call a self-made man; that is, I've never been to college," and having to educate himself, he resolved to put his holidays to good advantage, spending them "where civilization was the furthest advanced—advanced, at least, in years" (15).

Clay plans, once he has become sufficiently expert in his profession, to settle down in New York and work as an engineering consultant. But until that time arrives, "I go where the art galleries are biggest and where they have got the science of enjoying themselves down to the very finest point . . . so, though I hope I am a good American, it happens that I've more friends on the Continent than in the United States" (16). It is only after this introduction to his character and career that Clay reveals to Alice Langham his interest in her; the "cowboy's" combination of heroic enterprise and sophistication would seem to be an attractive blend, but put off by his frank appraisal of her wasted life, Alice sets aside her initial fascination and delivers her rebuke.

But despite her curt "good night," as any reader familiar with the conventions of romance will anticipate, the first encounter between Alice Langham and Robert Clay is not the last. Although he can impress Reggie King with his sophistication, a dinner party in New York is not Clay's proper terrain, and he is best seen on his home ground, where Alice will next meet him. The territory in question is not the West of cowboy fame, already dismissed by Davis as unromantic terrain, nor Africa, but Latin America, the tropical and exotic location with which Clay's greatest accomplishments have been associated.

Alice returns home from the dinner party to find her widowed father and her younger sister, Hope, alone together. She soon learns that Mr. Langham knows Robert Clay and has hired him to open "the largest iron deposits in South America" (26). For the Valencia Mining Company, named for "the capital of Olancho, one of those little republics down there . . . is your beloved father," a quietly self-promoting claim that leaves Alice speechless beyond a startled if quiet "Oh!" The information may also surprise the reader, but the net effect is to begin the process by which Clay is made over into an integral part of the American capitalist's extended empire, an association that also sets up the romantic possibility that he will become part of Mr. Langham's family. That is, the reader might anticipate that Robert Clay will in the end prove to be just the sort of knight in shining armor that Alice has been waiting for, and indeed he will, but not in the way that the reader might expect. Still, it is Clay's work in the service of the Valencia Mining Company that is the chief burden of the novel.

Though obviously a leader in the new world of international corporate capitalism, Mr. Langham plays a relatively passive role in what follows. The active part is played by his agent, Robert Clay, and the action takes place in Olancho, where the hero devotes himself to promoting the progress and profitability of the Valencia Mining Company, the center of gravity about which his romantic interest in Langham's daughter coincidentally revolves. Once again, what happens thenceforth is a modern fairy tale, a demonstration of initiative and courage that is finally rewarded, an American fable ever since the emergence of Ben Franklin.

As an engineer Clay is truly civil, who in "opening up the country," as he puts it, will insure that the land having been opened will enjoy political stability, because duly constituted local authority has been enforced. That is, having made the way straight for American commerce, he intends to keep it on the level. Most important, Robert Clay has no interest in remaining in foreign places or even in bringing them under U.S. control by annexation. His only desire is maintaining the security and safety of Mr. Langham's investment, in which he demonstrates the courage and initiative of a conventional romantic hero, as well as displaying that mixture of Emersonian idealism and pragmatism associated with emerging American champions of capitalistic enterprise.

In the case of Robert Clay it is a display that, because of the background of the hero, is given a coloration derived from the American West, much as Clay will emerge as an avatar of the Strenuous Life. Davis's hero was defined by Grant Knight as "an embodiment of the American Spirit of fling and swing, a man whom even Theodore Roosevelt might envy" (*Critical Period* 122). He is even more than that: it is as if the many sources of this conglomerate man had been melted down and then cast in the model provided by Roosevelt himself, indeed in such a way as to prove prophetic. By the end of the book we are very close to Cuba and San Juan Hill, thanks to a strategic revision of the author's attitude toward Manifest Destiny.

: III :

Supposedly a South American country, the mythical Olancho draws to some extent on Davis's travels through Central America, but it was chiefly inspired by a much earlier trip RHD took to Cuba, while still a college student. This was in 1886, as the guest of William W. Thurston, the president of the Bethlehem Iron Company, with whom, despite their difference in age, Davis had often played tennis while attending Lehigh. Thurston's firm had recently opened an iron mine in Siboney, a village a few miles outside Santiago de Cuba, and he invited Davis to accompany him on a tour of inspection, entertaining the youth at his luxurious home with a magnificent view of the city and its harbor.

The mining operation was supervised by an engineer named Dave Kirkpatrick, who had been in charge of clearing the land and constructing a rail line from the mine. The rails ended at a pier jutting out into the ocean at Daiquirí, constructed to facilitate the loading of iron ore on ships that would carry it back to the States. It was, as Arthur Lubow testifies, a memorable experience for the young man, the recollection of which would furnish the chief details of the setting in *Soldiers of Fortune*. It is clear that Kirkpatrick provided the inspiration not so much for Robert Clay—that highly imaginative construct—but for Clay's chief subordinate at the mine, MacWilliams, a civil engineer who lacks Clay's sophistication and broad-gauge views.

Like Kirkpatrick, MacWilliams supervises the building of a railroad from the port to the mine site, but though a vital link in the operation, its construction plays no important part in the novel. In "The Bridge Builders," a story that also celebrates the civil engineer as a bringer of order to turbulent worlds, Rudyard Kipling renders in loving detail the technical details of the project being carried out by Findlayson, the man in charge. In Davis's novel, by contrast, the chief engineer is a man more of projects than of actual practice. The work going on at the mine serves chiefly as an accepted fact rather than the focus of the story, which is mainly concerned with Clay's handling of the threat posed by a Central American revolution.

MacWilliams, having come "from some little town in the West" and worked his way up in his profession from a lowly apprentice "cutting sage-brush and driving stakes," has had a varied but hardly as heroic a life as Robert Clay. Like his friend and superior, MacWilliams is an example of a self-made man but without the added benefit of world travel, having spent his adult life "in Mexico and Central America," where cultural advantages are sparse (47). Though ten years away from home, MacWilliams still prefers canned vegetables from the States to the exotic and delicious produce of the tropics.

MacWilliams's abundant sense of wry humor balances Clay's serious-mindedness. It has protected him from "experiences that would have shattered the nerves of any other man" and "served to make him shrewd and self-confident and at his ease when the occasion or difficulty came" (47). A deft hand with the guitar as well, MacWilliams is much more the cowboy than Clay, who has long since transcended his humble origins. He is a familiar fixture in the emerging genre of adventure fiction, being the brave but less enterprising companion of the hero, a prototypical sidekick.

It was Clay who, a year before the dinner party that begins the story, noticed the evidence of iron ore in Olancho while passing along the coast in a tramp steamer. It is at this point that Davis's hero merges with Henry Adams's, for Clarence King assessed the mineral wealth of Cuba in 1894, even while pursuing Cuban women and consorting with Cuban men who were plotting revolution against the Spanish government. It is a suggestive mix, given the tangled plot in *Soldiers of Fortune,* so perhaps Davis got wind of King's activities, given that they were both members of private clubs in New York. Certainly as Tichi tells us, King resembled "the engineer-heroes of the popular novels," being "at his ease in clubrooms, galleries, and at dining tables" (166). Though born in the East, King was associated by Adams with the adventuresome western life, and he figures in *Education,* "in terms reminiscent of a Richard Harding novel" (167).

Relying on that power of intuition that is the usual accoutrement of a superhero, Clay decided to leave the steamer at Valencia. Shortly afterward he "disappeared into the interior with an ox-cart and a couple of pack-mules, and returned to write a lengthy letter from the Consul's office." Sent unsolicited to Mr. Langham on the basis of the industrialist's known interest in mines, the letter described the five mountains and stated that they were "filled with ore . . . which should be extracted by open-faced workings. . . . I should call the stuff first-class Bessemer ore, running about sixty-three per cent metallic iron. The people know it is there, but have no knowledge of its value, and are too lazy to ever work it themselves." Clay volunteered to "look into the political side of it and see what sort of a concession I can get for you. I should think ten per cent of the output would satisfy them" (30). Convinced by Clay's account and obviously impressed by the man himself, Langham established his mining company in Valencia, and Clay returned to work on the Mexican rail line.

At first the work at the mine site was put under the direction of "a man named Van Antwerp," who proved not up to the job, being unwilling to delegate authority and inept at dealing with local laborers and the wealthy residents of the place, the planters through whose lands the rail line had to be run. His rule lasted six months, after which Clay, who had by then finished the railroad in Mexico, was sent by Langham south to take over the mine. He was "given the title of General Manager and Resident Director, and an enormous salary," which Clay attributed not only to the difficulties that lay ahead but also to the possibility that he had at last "reached that place in his career when he could stop actual work and live easily, as an expert, on the work of others" (32).

Having spent three days exploring the mountains where the mines were located, still rough and difficult terrain, Clay next confronted the engineers gathered at the camp with a stern ultimatum. Dismissing their work as negligible and wasteful, he denounced them for laziness and mismanagement as well as "incompetency upon . . . a magnificent and reckless scale." He gave the entire staff a month to get moving or else leave at the first opportunity with a character reference so bad "that you'll be glad to get a job carrying a transit" (37).

Clay made an exception of MacWilliams, put in charge of building the railroad from the mine but prevented from doing so because of Van Antwerp's inability to obtain from the owners a right-of-way across their lands. With that instinctive sense of worth—mineral or personal—that distinguishes the superhero, Clay made the self-taught engineer his chief associate. A man primarily of concepts, Clay is also an able manager, as his new title suggests, and is really more an administrator than an engineer. As a literary creation he may have been inspired by the high popular esteem bestowed on the civil engineer, even while borrowing from the reputation of Clarence King, but in action he seems closer to that other emerging literary figure, the entrepreneurial businessman. The American engineer like Kipling's Findlayson is a bridge-builder between an advanced nation and a backward one, but with a view not toward promoting understanding but facilitating exploitation, as the unfolding action of the novel reveals.

Needless to say, the new resident director is successful in his efforts, earning first the grudging and then the open respect of the engineers in his service, establishing good relations with the Olanchoan soldiers provided by the government as workers in the mine as well as with the rich planters whose lands the railroad is to cross. Clay and MacWilliams are soon joined by the son and heir of Mr. Langham, Teddy, a Yale student and football player "who came ostensibly to learn the profession of which Clay was so conspicuous an example, and in reality to watch over his father's interest" (39). During this critical episode, the director proves to be a dynamic, fair-minded administrator and something of a diplomat, but he has no opportunity to display his talents as a civil engineer, that responsibility being assumed by MacWilliams.

Despite the rhetoric of Depew and Choate, the daily work of the civil engineer is not the stuff of which romance fiction is written, nor did Davis absorb much in the way of technical training during his elegant passage through Lehigh that could inform his novel. What he did acquire at college was the friendship of Mr. Thurston, whose guided tour of his iron mine in Cuba provided the slim factual basis for *Soldiers of Fortune.* Thus although the rail line is run and the pier erected, the most detailed account of construction is devoted to describing the elegant "bungalow" designed and built by Clay when word arrives that Langham senior, for reasons of health, is soon to arrive in the company of his daughters. Like Thurston's, the house is placed on a height providing a view of Valencia, at night a fairyland of twinkling lights.

These labors are inspired not only by Clay's desire to shelter his employer's family in something better than the rough shack that serves as home for himself and his two chief subordinates but also by his intention to provide a proper setting for continuing his courtship of Alice Langham: "It delighted Clay to find that it was only the beautiful things and the fine things of his daily routine that suggested her to him, as though she could not be associated in his mind with anything less worthy, and he kept saying to himself, 'She will like this view from the end of the terrace,' and 'This will be her favorite walk'" (43). Notably, Davis here leaves off referring to the woman in question as either Alice or Miss Langham, using "she" and "her," which is less a matter of pronoun choice than an intensification of worshipfulness on the part of the hero typical of the sentimental novel.

Thus "her" promised arrival transforms the engineer's way of viewing his surroundings, so that he sees them "as she would . . . when she came, even while at the same time his own eyes retained their point of view. It was as though he had lengthened the focus of a glass, and looked beyond at what was beautiful and picturesque instead of what was near at hand and practicable." As Davis's figure suggests, Clay's devotion to Alice serves as a version of a Claude glass, revising his sensibility so that it more closely approximates that of Davis himself, always alive to the aesthetic aspects of a scene. The three men meanwhile continued to live in their splintery wooden shack at the end of the rail line, kept hidden from "the fairy palace" by "an impenetrable rampart of brush and Spanish bayonet," there to wait for the great day when the Langham family would appear (40).

The juxtaposition of the palace on the hill and the shack down below is a clue to a structural division central to the novel, for in carrying Mr. Langham and his daughters to Olancho, Davis is manipulating events so as to maintain a love story that is traditional to the romance genre, even essential to its commercial success given the preponderance of women in the readership of that kind of fiction. And yet the love story in *Soldiers of Fortune* is in no way essential to the plot, for though the initial meeting between Robert Clay and Alice Langham certainly helps define the hero's sterling qualities, once he has set sail for Olancho the entire Langham family could have been left in New York and done little harm to the main part of the story, which is about men in action. Moreover, it is the masculine heroics that provide a continuity between *Three Gringos in Venezuela and Central America* and Davis's coverage of the Spanish-American War, a bridge and a bond that is male in gender.

In "An Unfinished Story," the love Gordon feels for the undeserving Miss Egerton is essential to his motivation in going to Africa in the first place, where he hopes to find the wealth that will enable him to marry her. The story takes its meaning from the contrast between the noble, chivalric explorer and the selfish, self-pitying woman he loves. This is not the case in *Soldiers of Fortune,* where Clay has already found his mine and contracted with his employer to manage the enterprise before he meets Alice. That his newfound love for Alice Langham brings out Clay's more sensitive side—his RHD side—is undeniable, but bringing it out has nothing to do with what follows. It is not Clay's feminine side that will save the day.

Alice, having arrived in Valencia and taken up residence in the lovely cottage prepared for her, continues to snub the engineer, thinking she will gain even greater power over him thereby. Instead, Clay becomes more and more attracted to Mr. Langham's younger daughter, Hope, who as he realizes resembles the girl in the photograph he has been carrying, the one of an Alice

Langham that no longer exists. Alice pressures Clay to leave off civil engineering and take a position that is more "worthy" of his talents, an obvious
echo of the disapproval he expressed of her way of life; by pointed contrast,
Hope declares her admiration for his professional accomplishments: "He's
built thousands of miles of railroads . . . and he built the highest bridge in
Peru. It swings in the air across a chasm, and it rocks when the wind
blows. . . . He put up a fort in the harbor of Rio Janeiro during a revolution . . . and the Germans built one just like it, only larger, on the Baltic, and
when the Emperor found out whose design it was, he . . . made him a baron"
(122–23).

Hope also becomes fascinated with the operations of the mine, to the admiration of MacWilliams clambering over the machinery without regard to
grease and dirt; in all ways she plays the part of a woman who will make an
ideal companion and wife for the ambitious, enterprising hero. Her interests, including a well-informed enthusiasm for football, suggest that Hope
is essentially male in gender. We will remember that she was inspired by
Cecil Clark, the woman with a sexually ambivalent name and nature who
was to be Davis's first wife, much as Hope will marry Clay.

The novel's emerging heroine is therefore given qualities that fit into the
definably masculine activities that take place on Olancho, but not even
Hope is essential to the core story, which has to do with an emerging conflict
in Olancho between insurrectionist elements among the natives and the
preservation of Mr. Langham's investment in the mine. Having been hired
to manage the mine, Robert Clay must now guard it against those forces that
threaten the enterprise. It is not the preservation of the chastity of a fair
maiden that provides the main action; what must be preserved is the sanctity of a contractual agreement.

A new hero for a new imperialism, Clay is not only a visionary engineer
but an able administrator and a capable soldier as well. And though, as in
a traditional, fairy-tale romance, he will be rewarded with the hand of a
lovely and wealthy maiden, Davis puts an interesting spin on that conventional closure, reasserting the intensely male aura that surrounds the creation of his new American hero. The screen of Spanish bayonet is intended
to make the ugly shack invisible from the elegant mansion, but it also (as the
name suggests) acts as a gendered division, separating the feminine-
centered world of the mansion from the masculine-centered world of the
shack. The essential drama of the new imperialism will be acted by a cast
of men.

: IV :

In the days of William Gillette, a drama needed an easily detected villain, preferably dark in complexion and duplicitous in behavior. Before Mr. Langham and his daughters arrive in Valencia, the three Americans are visited by a less welcome figure, "General Mendoza, the leader of the Opposition in the Senate," who is also, as it turns out, spokesman of the opposition to the American presence in Olancho (50). The general will disrupt the engineers' anticipated ease, now that the mine and its railroad are in operation; he will provide both dramatic tension as well as an objective correlative for Davis's revised notion concerning the meaning of the Monroe Doctrine.

The general pays his visit so as to express his people's discontent with their contracted share of the profits, the 10 percent that Clay had suggested to Mr. Langham. The resident director explains to General Mendoza the costs to his employer of making the mines a paying proposition: "Three millions of dollars; that's a good deal of money. It will be some time before we realize anything on that investment" (52). Moreover, as Clay argues, before the American company had made the necessary improvements, the iron ore was unobtainable and therefore worth nothing. Now it is worth a great deal, 10 percent of which the Olanchoan government receives without having invested a peso.

But General Mendoza is not a reasonable man and threatens to overturn the present administration in Olancho, which has, in his view, received not a fair percentage but a bribe, giving away "the richest possessions in the storehouse of my country, giving it not only to aliens, but for a pittance" (53). As the new president of Olancho he will insist on 50 percent as a fair share of the profits and has come to advise Clay of his intentions, so that he can warn "your people in New York . . . that they [will] have to deal with men who do not consider their own interests but the interests of their country" (54).

The general has recently returned from fighting in a war protecting the boundaries of Olancho to discover that the Valencia Mining Company is taking the lion's share of the profits. Moreover, his patriotism is offended by the government's cooperation in turning soldiers into common laborers, exchanging rifles for picks and shovels: "It is monstrous!" The modern reader sensitized by postcolonial revisionism tends to side with General Mendoza, but as the negotiation continues, the self-proclaimed patriot reveals that he is willing to be bought off for a mere sixty thousand dollars, which will make him and his powerful friends quite satisfied with the state of things in

Olancho, "no matter whether I be in Opposition or at the head of the Government" (60).

This is what Clay has been waiting for, and he informs the general that if he attempts to carry out his threatened revolution, the solicited bribe will be revealed. Having earlier blasted his engineers for their laziness and ineptness, Clay now turns on the corrupt general: "Try to break that concession; try it. It was made by one Government to a body of honest, decent business men, with a Government of their own back of them, and if you interfere with our conceded rights to work those mines, I'll have a man-of-war down here with white paint on her hull, and she'll blow you and your little republic back into the mountains. Now you can go" (61–62).

A hard-fisted projection of what would become the new imperialism in action, Clay's threat is a very particularized notion of the Monroe Doctrine. This sort of thing is what Davis would seem to have argued against in *Three Gringos,* where he objected to the use of U.S. forces to protect Venezuela and other South and Central American republics every time they came running for help. Here would seem to be concrete evidence that we have moved over from the hard-nosed realism of RHD's reporting to the kind of fantasy that sustains romance. On the other hand, the Venezuelan government had appealed to the principles of the Monroe Doctrine because of actions that had nothing to do with the affairs of the United States, where here American commercial interests are threatened. We will remember Davis's argument that it is the instability of Central American governments that discourages investment by U.S. companies. Indeed, it was Davis's point that Central and South American republics needed the active presence of Anglo-Saxon leaders, like General William Walker, men who are the personification of the spirit of get-up-and-go, precisely what Richard Henry Dana Jr. had observed of California some forty years earlier.

That Walker was an agent of slave interests when he led repeated invasions of Nicaragua is ignored by Davis, who celebrates him as the kind of strong man necessary to drag Central American republics into the modern age. The famous filibuster also figures also in Davis's *Real Soldiers of Fortune,* where his days in California are stressed: "In the days of gold in San Francisco . . . William Walker was one of the most famous, most picturesque and popular figures. Jack Oakhurst, gambler; Colonel Starbottle, duellist; Yuba Bill, stage-coach driver, were his contemporaries. Bret Harte was one of his keenest admirers, and in two of his stories . . . Walker is the hero" (148). Where William Walker is the ideal celebrated in *Three Gringos,* it is Robert Clay in Davis's romance.

There is therefore a consistency and a continuity between the two books, although it must be said that in *Soldiers of Fortune* Davis demonstrates none of the careful, Hamlet-like meditation on the proper use of the Monroe Doctrine which he displayed in *Three Gringos*. There he declared that the Doctrine should be cited only when a foreign power interfered in Latin American affairs, which is not the case in the novel, where interference is threatened by a local revolution.

Like Walker, Robert Clay is a man of the American West, a hero handy with a pistol. After Mendoza responds to his threat of calling in the U.S. Navy by challenging the engineer to a duel, the American takes out his revolver, which lay "in the palm of his hand, into which it seemed to fit like the hand of a friend." Barely raising the weapon, he takes four shots at a table lamp inside the mining shack, the first of which "broke the top of the glass chimney, the second shattered the green globe around it, the third put out the light, and the next drove the lamp crashing to the floor. There was a wild yell of terror from the back of the house, and the noise of a guitar falling down a flight of steps. 'I have probably killed a very good cook,' said Clay, 'as I should as certainly kill you, if I were to meet you'" (63–64).

The general departs with no more talk of a duel, but he does fire off a Parthian insult concerning Clay's past history as a cowboy, which is "quite evident by your manners." He also informs the director that he has made a dangerous enemy, but Clay, "twirling the revolver around his middle-finger," reckons that should push come to shove he can command sufficient support from the native soldiers working in his mine to make himself the president of Olancho (64). Readers familiar with Wister's *The Virginian* will recognize the type, for Clay's face-off with Mendoza anticipates the Virginian's confrontations with Trampas, but Davis enlists his hero in a much bigger action than tidying up affairs on a cattle ranch.

We are treated here to a fictional version of the kinds of schemes even then being hatched by American jingoes, in which the commercial opportunities to be found in South American countries will be protected by a powerful, armed U.S. presence. It was, in effect, a revised version of filibustering, for like Walker, Clay assumes that he can easily take over a Latin American republic, but as we shall see his imagination here is outrunning his true inclination, which is in accord with the postfilibustering principles of the new imperialism. That is, Davis is letting his own romantic imagination run wild but will in time apply the reins.

Before the Langhams arrive, Clay gives a dinner party in the house he has built, to "test his girders" as the engineer puts it, inviting the President of

Olancho, Alvarez, with his wife, the former Countess Manuelata of Spain. During the dinner it is revealed that Alvarez has plans to throw over his presidency and become dictator of Olancho, a further wrinkle in the increasingly rumpled tranquillity of the scene. The dinner party also serves to introduce "Captain Stuart . . . an auburn-haired, fair-skinned young man" whose eyes are "blue and frank and attractive-looking" and who is "late of the Gordon Highlanders, and now in command of the household troops at the Government House and of the body-guard of the President" (110, 67). At times one gets the impression that Davis is making up his novel as he goes along, for this is the first we have heard of Stuart, yet we are told he "was a friend of Clay's and popular with every one present" (67). We should account this the second act in the drama, because Stuart will become a major actor in the unfolding action.

Why Stuart is in the service of President Alvarez in Olancho, rather than "serving his own Government in his own army," is a mystery inspiring gossip: "Some people said he had been crossed in love, others, less sentimental, that he had forged a check or mixed up the mess accounts of his company" (67–68). But ignoring these rumors, Clay remains loyal to his friend, much as Stuart proves to be faithful to the president he serves. He is also, perhaps, something more than that to Madame Alvarez, a Spanish countess who misses her homeland and the sophisticated life she has left for the primitive and boring confines of Valencia.

After the arrival of the Langham family, the love story continues its traditionally unsmooth path, further complicated by the arrival in Valencia's harbor of Reggie King and his great white yacht. Clay is made acutely aware by King's presence of his humble origins, which allows Davis to fill in even more details concerning his hero's background. But the point being made has little to do with the romantic complications and everything with the unfolding political situation in Olancho, which will bring forward Clay's paternal heritage in the service of new occasions.

Clay's mind went back to the days when he was a boy, when his father was absent fighting for a lost cause; when his mother taught in a little schoolhouse under the shadow of Pike's Peak, and when Kit Carson was his hero. He thought of the poverty of those days—poverty so mean and hopeless that it was almost something to feel shame for; of the days that followed when, an orphan and without a home, he had sailed away from New Orleans to the Cape. How the mind of the mathematician, which he had inherited from the Boston schoolmistress, had been swayed by the spirit of the soldier, which he had inherited from his father, and which led him from the mines of South Africa to little wars in Madagascar, Egypt, and Algiers. It had been a life as restless as the seaweed on a rock. But as he looked back to its poor beginnings and admitted to himself its later successes, he gave a sigh of content. (99–100)

The Wister-like combination of a schoolteacher mother from New England and the soldier-father who fought "for a lost cause" suggests that Clay combines in his genes the best of the North and the South, for in 1897 service in a "lost cause" would identify his father with the Confederacy, but it was not in defending states' rights that Clay's father had died.

The necessary revelation comes one evening when Clay is alone with Hope Langham and at her request not only describes his own considerable military experience but also tells her that his father had been "a filibuster, and went out on the *Virginius* to help free Cuba, and was shot, against a stone wall. We never knew where he was buried" (175). The *Virginius* episode occurred in 1873, when a vessel carrying arms to Cuban rebels which was sailing under the American flag and with an American captain was captured by the Spanish, who summarily executed the captain and a number of his passengers and crew.

Davis thereby links Clay to the ongoing insurrection in Cuba, sympathy for which by 1897 was rising in America, so that filibustering was no longer associated with the extension of southern slavery but the reverse—namely, lifting the heavy yoke of Spain from long-suffering Cubans. This, then, is Clay's paternity, the final line in the diagram of his unfolding history, and it is for our purposes the definitive one, pulling together his background as cowboy, soldier, and engineer and bringing it to bear on a revolution about to break out in Olancho. Son of a filibuster martyr, he is in effect a son as well of William Walker. He is a filibuster for the coming century, a representative of the new American imperialism, not a renegade attempting to establish an empire of his own.

The age of chivalry is never past, so long
as there is a wrong left unredressed on earth.
CHARLES KINGSLEY

10 : MEN WITHOUT WOMEN

: I :

I have attempted in the last chapter to trace the two-stranded plot of *Soldiers of Fortune,* in which the hero's imperial errand is given a romantic burden because of his attraction to his employer's daughters. It is the first strand that most interests us here, and as the novel gains headway, after General Mendoza's treachery and the political ambitions of President Alvarez are made known, the action becomes increasingly a story of political intrigue that finally explodes as revolution. In what follows, I pay particular attention to this latter element, in which the male emphasis is necessarily increased, although not to the complete exclusion of romantic elements.

Having given fair warning to General Mendoza that he should not attempt to break faith with Clay's American employer, the hero expresses indifference to the reported plans of Countess Alvarez to have her husband declared king, thereby making Olancho over "'into a sort of dependency of Spain, as it was long ago'" (134). Clay asks only that he be left alone to manage Mr. Langham's mine and pursue first his employer's older and then his young daughter, but this turns out to be impossible. Alvarez's activities remain in the background, but Mendoza proves to be a general nuisance. His henchmen are soon busy plastering posters around Valencia which denounce the Alvarez regime and call for a popular uprising to drive the president and his ambitious wife out of the country.

These posters become scurrilous when they accuse Captain Stuart of maintaining an intimate relationship with the woman from Spain, a charge he denies angrily to Clay when the two meet to make plans regarding the rising threat from Mendoza. "He serves her," Clay later explains to Hope, "with the same sort of chivalric devotion that his ancestors felt for the woman whose ribbons they tied to their lances, and for whom they fought in the lists" (215). But the woman who inspires him to fight "for men not worthy to hold his horse's bridle" is the wife of the president Stuart is sworn to protect

(214). In sum, Stuart is more a Lancelot than a Galahad, and this suggestion of sin will warrant his tragic death.

The confidential conversation between Clay and Captain Stuart takes place late one evening following a formal ball. The meeting is staged by Davis in the Plaza Bolivar in Valencia, "in what had once been the centre of the fashionable life of Olancho," a spot virtually abandoned when "the town had moved farther up the hill" (180). "The houses about it had fallen into disuse, and the few that were still occupied at the time Clay entered it showed no sight of life. Clay picked his way over the grass-grown paths to the statue of Bolívar, the hero of the sister republic of Venezuela, which still stood on its pedestal in a tangle of underbrush and hanging vines. The iron railing that had once surrounded it was broken down, and the branches of the trees near were black with sleeping buzzards. Two great palms reared themselves in the moonlight at either side, and beat their leaves together in the night, whispering and murmuring together like two living conspirators" (180–81).

This scene is transplanted from *Three Gringos,* the plaza a reconstruction of the neglected point of land on Amapala, once a park but now a garbage dump, over which brooded the fraudulent statue of "Morazan, the Liberator of Honduras." There the three travelers went to escape the heat and plot mock schemes "to convert Honduras into a monarchy and make Somerset king," safe in the assurance that "no one heard us but the English edition of Morazan smiling blandly down upon us" (169). In the concluding chapter on Caracas in that same book, Davis mounted his tribute to Bolívar, whose statue stands in New York's Central Park, and the two monuments are combined here in a suggestive fashion. Unlike the spurious "Morazan," we have a bona fide Bolívar, the George Washington of South America, but in abandoning the plaza in which he stands, the fashionable part of Valencia has obviously lost touch with the democratic spirit he represents.

Indeed, the best hope for the republic resides in the American engineer and the British soldier, who are not plotting the overthrow of the present regime but are devising the means to prevent it. The two men are determined to fight the good fight if the revolution threatened by Mendoza breaks out, defending the constitutional government. Captain Stuart then leaves, striding "away erect and soldierly through the débris and weeds of the deserted plaza," while Clay remains in the plaza, smoking a cigar and looking up at "the stern, smooth-shaven face of the bronze statue above him that seemed to be watching Stuart's departing figure": "'General Bolivar,' Clay said, as he lit his cigar, 'observe that young man. He is a soldier and a gallant gentleman. You, sir, were a great soldier—the greatest this God-forsaken country will ever know—and you were, sir, an ardent lover. I ask you to salute that young man as I do, and to wish him well.' Clay lifted his high hat to the back of the young officer as it was hidden in the hanging vines, and once again, with grave respect to the grim features of the great general above him, and then smiling at his own conceit, he ran lightly down the steps and disappeared among the trees of the plaza" (*Soldiers of Fortune* 187).

This scene, which serves to associate Stuart with the Bolivian hero well known for both physical courage and an often unwise love for beautiful women, was regarded as a great Davis moment in the novel by Augustus Thomas, who in his introduction to *Soldiers of Fortune* defined it as "Davis at his best" (ix; cf. *R.H.D.* 44). Thomas, as a dramatist, necessarily emphasized the theatrical side of RHD and was here implying a direct connection between the author and his created hero: "In the circumstance of this story . . . he could himself have been either Clay or Stuart and he had the humor of MacWilliams" (ix). The connection was reinforced by Charles Dana Gibson, who provided a frontispiece for the romance that showed Clay in formal evening dress (Davis's favorite costume), wearing his medals (another of Davis's theatrical vanities), and lifting his silk hat to the invisible statue.

Later in the book Gibson provided another illustration, this one showing Clay dressed in the informal uniform established by Davis for war correspondents in the field and soldiers of fortune in literary romances and movies—riding breeches, boots, and an open tunic—striding bareheaded up a flight of stairs carrying the dead body of Stuart, whose now empty scabbard drags uselessly behind. Here, Clay is a towering giant, with the blond hair and mustache that links him to the Nordic continuity. And the man whose body he is carrying establishes the Anglo-American link, a chivalrous youth who has hired out his sword to the Alvarez regime and died in defense of a lady whose grief suggests that she was something more to young Stuart than the wife of his employer.

The tableau, with a representative of the new American empire carrying the corpse of a representative of the old British Empire, comes in the midst of the revolution staged by General Mendoza. Clay, Stuart, and Hope are together in the presidential palace as a mob attempts to break down its doors, inspiring the palace guard to turn against its commander. After Stuart is treacherously killed, he is carried by his friend up the stairs and placed on "a great leather lounge" in a dining hall set for a celebratory dinner honoring Alvarez's new dictatorship. Not content with this arrangement, Hope

"YOU SIR, WERE A GREAT SOLDIER."

Frontispiece to Soldiers of Fortune. *Gibson's pen-and-ink illustration shows Robert Clay, dressed in Davis's favorite costume, saluting the state of General Bolívar. In the background, Clay's friend Stuart may be seen striding away, his sword in tow.*

HE STRODE ON UP THE STAIRS.

Davis's hero dressed for counterrevolutionary activities, in jodhpurs and riding boots, establishing the standard for men of adventure. In Gibson's composition, Clay seems a veritable giant, cradling the dead body of his friend Stuart in his arms, the now-empty scabbard dragging behind. From Soldiers of Fortune.

picks up Stuart's sword, and laying it on his body, "closed his hands upon its hilt," then heaped the dead soldier with "an armful of flowers" taken from the dining table (270–71).

Clay races from the building with Hope as the angry mob of revolutionists breaks into the palace, leaving Stuart in the company of the portraits of Olancho's dead general-presidents, who seemed "to be staring down less sternly now upon the white mortal face of the brother-in-arms who had just joined them. One who had known him among his own people would have seen in the attitude and in the profile of the English soldier a likeness to his ancestors of the Crusades who lay carved in stone in the village church, with their faces turned to the sky, their faithful hounds waiting at their feet, and their hands pressed upward in prayer" (272).

So impressive is the mortuary arrangement that when General Mendoza and his mob rush into the room, they are arrested by the sight: "The Spanish-American General strode boldly forward, but his eyes lowered before the calm, white face, and either because the lighted candles and the flowers awoke in him some memory of the great Church that had nursed him, or because the jagged holes in the soldier's tunic appealed to what was bravest in him, he crossed himself quickly, and then raising his hands slowly to his visor, lifted his hat and pointed with it to the door. And the mob, without once looking back at the rich treasure of silver on the table, pushed out before him, stepping softly, as though they had intruded on a shrine" (272). This scene is another effective piece of theater, emphasizing the common bond shared by all soldiers, whether a plucky little British officer with a tarnished past or a boastful and ambitious Hispanic general who sets aside his opportunism and greed in respect for the dead comrade in arms for whose death he is responsible. In taking off his hat, Mendoza repeats Clay's gesture to the statue of Bolívar, and though he is the villain of the piece who will be shot down by Clay and his impromptu army, the general reveals that like Stevenson's rogues, he has his gallant side.

These monumental moments provided by Bolívar's statue and the statuelike Stuart are symbolic accoutrements to the violence of the revolution and its successful suppression by Clay and his small army made up of sailors from King's yacht, American miners, and disaffected soldiers from Mendoza's army. This action, in which Clay displays the courage of his filibuster father, but without suffering the same fate, provides ample opportunity for the usual hairbreadth and harebrained escapades that are traditional in romantic literature of adventure. They include the successful flight of the Spanish countess with the help of Clay and his friends, as well as their seizure of a cache of weapons smuggled into Olancho by a picaro named Burke, a raffish Irish American filibuster whose profitable activities on behalf of South American revolutions seem to offend neither Davis nor his hero.

The revolution is put down and the rightful president placed back in the palace: not the self-appointed dictator Alvarez, who is killed by the mob, but his vice president, an official who, as in the United States, is designated by the republic's constitution as the president's successor. This is General Rojas, a man we see very little of but who is reputed to be an honest leader, a figure cut along the outline provided by General Louis Bogran, the former president of Honduras whom the three gringos met during their travels.

Bogran was a "good" leader and a man proud of his record of an extended period of peace, the sort of thing that encourages American investments in Central America. There are also overtones here of the situation in Chile in 1891, which Davis addressed in his article in *Harper's Weekly,* for both Alvarez and Mendoza are, like President Balmaceda, corrupt men who seek to set aside constitutional government, while Rojas, like President Jorge Montt, put in power by the Congressional Party in Chile, is a true republican leader.

The tangle of events that makes up the violent denouement of *Soldiers of Fortune* is too complicated for summary, but a few events and passages deserve mention if only because they clarify Davis's intention. First, there is Hope's participation in the dangerous drama, for she stays by her newfound lover's side throughout and assists in his escape when he is surrounded by Mendoza's riflemen, added proof of her spunk and mettle and assurance that she is a suitable mate for the hero. While Alice Langham remains safe with her father and Reggie in King's yacht, Hope and her brother, Teddy, take an active part in events. During one encounter the young man is wounded and is obviously disappointed when assured by MacWilliams that "it won't leave a scar," a quiet reference to the triumphant stigmata in *Red Badge of Courage* (304).

It is Teddy who, as General Mendoza and his army approach, observes, "It reminds me of a football match . . . when the teams run on the field," obviously drawing on his experience at Yale but laying down a metaphor that is sustained by the action that follows (253). Likewise, after Mendoza and his men have taken the palace, Clay and his people seize two buildings opposite, the "Theatre National and the Club Union," from which they fire on the enemy. These are suitable and quietly symbolic strongholds for an author who generally divided his time between the private club and the playhouse, and they serve to undergird the class divisions in the drama then under way (332).

For example, in putting down Mendoza's revolution, Clay is ably assisted by his miners, especially "the Irish Americans," who "showed a winning spirit, and stood in as orderly an array as though they were drawn up in line to receive their month's wages. The Americans in front of the column were humorously disposed"—being Irishmen they had little choice—"and inclined to consider the whole affair as a pleasant outing" (325). But Clay divides up the miners into units commanded by his subordinate engineers, officers for the occasion through virtue of their superior station, an assertion of elitism that serves a double function.

Thus, at a critical moment in the action, as the opposing armies fire on each other with the victory still in the balance, Davis notes that two of the assistant engineers "were kneeling at Langham's feet with the barrels of their rifles resting on the railing of the balcony. Their eyes had been trained for years to judge distances and to measure space, and they glanced along the sights of their rifles as though they were looking through the lens of a transit, and at each report their faces grew more earnest and their lips pressed tighter together" (334). Here, Davis has borrowed his own figure from *Three Gringos* and reversed the emphasis, so that the "soldiers of the transit" are here converted into soldiers of the rifle, multiple copies of the civil engineer who leads them to victory over Mendoza's forces.

Augustus Thomas observed of *Soldiers of Fortune* that it had "a quick and a deserved popularity," being "cheerily North American in its viewpoint of the sub-tropical republics" and therefore "very up to date" (*R.H.D.* 45). Grant Knight was much more specific, noting that Davis's romance was integral to the surge of sympathy for the beleaguered Cubans that inspired so many young Americans to go marching "cheerily" off to do battle with Spain, closely followed by Richard Harding Davis, as well as by other, younger writers, including Stephen Crane, Frank Norris, and Jack London, all of whom traveled to Cuba as war correspondents.

If *Soldiers of Fortune* did indeed contribute to the mood that inspired the Spanish-American War, it was thoroughly in synchronization with what Thomas blithely calls the "up to date" attitude of North Americans toward what was going on in places bordering the Caribbean. Published soon after RHD's popular account of his travels in Central America, the best-selling romance gave a militant edge to his conviction that only persons from the United States had the intelligence and drive to give productive order to "subtropical" countries. It was an imaginative exercise that lent color and drama to the dry geopolitics of Captain Mahan and Senator Lodge, and without specifically mentioning the Monroe Doctrine, the novel suggested that when American commercial interests were threatened, then Americans had a mandate to interfere in the affairs of Latin American republics.

But in answering the question about the reasons that so many American young men shared the enthusiasm of Robert Clay and his cohort for risking their lives to restore to a people their rightful rule, we need to heed another passage that comes toward the very end of Davis's romance. It is spoken by MacWilliams to Robert Clay as the novel's hero prepares to leave Olancho with Hope, soon to be his bride, and is the expression of a confirmed bachelor. "There were three of us," he tells his friend as they ride their horses out of Valencia after the battle, "and one got shot, and one got married, and the third—?"

> You will grow fat, Clay, and live on Fifth Avenue and wear a high silk hat, and some day when you're sitting in your club you'll read a paragraph in a newspaper with a queer Spanish date-line to it, and this will all come back to you,—this heat, and the palms, and the fever, and the days when you lived on plantains and we watched our trestles grow out across the canyons, and you'll be willing to give your hand to sleep in a hammock again, and to feel the sweat running down your back, and you'll want to chuck your gun up against your chin and shoot into a line of men, and the policemen won't let you, and your wife won't let you. That's what you're giving up. There it is. Take a good look at it. You'll never see it again. (348)

To grasp the full implication of MacWilliams's valedictory, it is perhaps best to look back at the little essay written by Richard Harding Davis in 1891 to accompany the full-page illustration in *Harper's Weekly* entitled "Out of the Game." Because in that essay "it" is football, the game which Stephen Crane and Davis among so many young men of their generation played in college and which taught them what they knew of war before they experienced war itself.

: II :

When Reggie King arrives unannounced in Olancho, his "long, white ship" is first mistaken by Teddy Langham for an American gunboat, a resemblance that is enhanced by the readiness of King's sailors to join in with Clay's miners in the attack on Mendoza's army, in effect serving as representatives of the United States without official sanction. Clay in denouncing Mendoza for

attempting to abort a legal contract had threatened him with the long arm
of the U.S. Navy, and we later learn of "an American man-of-war lying in the
harbor of Truxillo, a seaport of the republic that bounded Olancho on the
south" (209). The ship is summoned by Weimar, the German-born American consul in Valencia, but arrives too late to be helpful in the battle, yet the
belated presence of a detachment of sailors in arms contributes symboli-
cally to the victory drama.

These representatives of the United States march into town just after
Clay has declined the suggestion by the native officers who have served with
him that he be made the "military President" of Olancho, in effect the country's dictator, and the reaction of both the hero and his fellow Americans to
the arrival of the navy puts matters into a proper perspective:

> The cheering from the housetops since the firing ceased had changed
> suddenly into hand-clappings, and the cries, though still undistinguish-
> able, were of a different kind. Clay saw that the Americans on the bal-
> conies of the club and of the theatre had thrown themselves far over the
> railings and were all looking in the same direction and waving their hats
> and cheering loudly, and he heard above the shouts of the people the reg-
> ular tramp of men's feet marching in step, and the rattle of a machine gun
> as it bumped and shook over the rough stones. . . . The mob parted at the
> Palace gates, and they saw two lines of blue-jackets, spread out like the
> sticks of a fan, dragging the gun between them, the middies in their tight-
> buttoned tunics and gaiters, and behind them more blue-jackets with
> bare, bronzed throats, and with the swagger and roll of the sea in their
> legs and shoulders. An American flag floated above the white helmets of
> the marines. Its presence and the sense of pride which the sight of these
> men from home awoke in them made the fight just over seem mean and
> petty, and they took off their hats and cheered with the others. (341–42)

The officer in charge of the detachment of sailors is made to understand
the courageous role played by Clay, who admits wistfully to having "worn
several uniforms since I was a boy . . . but never that of my own country"
(345). The officer takes this as a cue to have Clay honored by the U.S. Navy
as he swings up onto his horse to leave the city: "The officer stepped back
and gave the command; the middies raised their swords and Clay passed
between massed rows of his countrymen with their muskets held rigidly
toward him. The housetops rocked again at the sight, and as he rode out into
the brilliant sunshine, his eyes were wet and winking" (346). The honor

paid Clay by his countrymen clearly means more to the hero than that paid
him by the officers of the republic he has just saved, which he had waved off
with a joke.

The author has it both ways, assigning his hero a dual role essential to the
meaning of his novel. By having Clay serve as "the Liberator of Olancho,
[and] the Preserver of the Constitution," Davis relieves the United States
of having to interfere in the affairs of a neighboring republic. Yet he also allows the Navy to arrive in time for the victory celebration, and by honoring
Clay the officers make him one of their own. Finally, by leaving Olancho,
Clay signals the difference between himself and William Walker, for like
his father he is a filibuster interested only in bringing democracy to Caribbean countries. The navy likewise will withdraw, leaving the Olanchans
to handle their own affairs until such a time as its presence in the harbor
is once again warranted by instability threatening American interests.

As Clay and MacWilliams stand on the deck of the steamer carrying them
to New York, the career bachelor attempts to lure the future bridegroom to
Macedonia, where a Greek uprising against Turkish tyranny is brewing.
"You, as an American citizen, ought to be the last person in the world to
throw cold water on an undertaking like that. In the name of Liberty now?"
(360). But Clay laughingly dismisses the proposition, without stating the obvious, that liberty in the abstract is one thing, but the particulars of American interest in political disturbances abroad is another. The fortunes in
which Clay as a soldier involves himself are for the immediate future solidly
anchored in Wall Street, much as New York is the place he now will call home.

Where in *Three Gringos in Venezuela and Central America* Davis expressed
concerns about the misuse of the Monroe Doctrine, in *Soldiers of Fortune* he
provided an implicit counterpart text, underwriting what would become
the official policy of the new imperialism. Because of the romantic machinery, it is easy to accept Clay as a traditional hero, taking up arms against a
sea of troubles, winning the heart of a fair maiden, and thereby gaining intimate access to the Langham fortune. Concealed below the romance conventions, however, we find a consistent ideology, albeit one that may be
called situational, in that the hero in overthrowing a revolution is merely
doing his job as a loyal employee of the Valencia Mining Company.

Starting with Grant Knight, revisionist critics have insisted that the novel
is virtual propaganda for America's interference in the Cuban insurrection,
and it certainly may help explain the popular enthusiasm for that conflict,
but the issues that sparked the Spanish-American War were quite different from the circumstances in *Soldiers of Fortune*. Indeed, they were much

closer to the situation in Venezuela in 1895, and the expressions of popular outrage in the United States over Great Britain's bullying of a small republic, exacerbated by the empire's indifference to American concerns, have clear parallels in the excitement of 1898 and its causes.

Still, Davis's novel expresses unqualified faith in the power of a few courageous U.S. citizens to rid a Latin American country of evil, an extension of his admiration for General Walker, and a foretaste of his celebration of real-life heroes yet to come. As Clay rides off in the company of Mac-Williams, who tells him to take a last look behind him, because once he is married he will never again have such a grand opportunity for adventure, the hero foreshadows another man on horseback, not only in his western background, his boundless energy, and fortitude but also with his sunburned hair and mustache. For Teddy Roosevelt, though officially serving in Cuba as a colonel in the U.S. Army, would enjoy an independent status as the leader of a regiment of volunteer cavalrymen, made up of cowboys and college athletes, an equivalent mix to that assembled by the civil engineer who is the hero of Davis's romance.

: III :

Before moving on to RHD's real-time Cuban adventure, I want to take a brief look ahead at a companion novel to *Soldiers of Fortune,* a work that undoubtedly helped cement the image of Davis as a projection of his fictional heroes but only because it was misunderstood by his contemporaries. Published in 1902, *Captain Macklin* derived directly from Davis's experiences in Honduras, work on which began soon after RHD completed his first South American romance. His writing was interrupted by his career as a war correspondent for a critical five years, so that by the time he returned to *Captain Macklin,* his view of men under arms had become strategically modified.

As a result, where *Soldiers of Fortune* has a relatively clean line of development, with conventional heroes and villains, beautiful women, both courageous and cruel—the whole panoply of romance fiction—*Captain Macklin* is sui generis. It is a confusing, because confused, work of fiction that suggests RHD was capable of a more complex view of imperialism than is sustained by *Soldiers of Fortune,* even if complexity was a matter of deepseated uncertainty. The novel has a number of apparent inconsistencies, suggesting that the author was not in complete control of his subject and theme, but it most certainly gives an acid bath to the idealism generally associated with Davis's version of romance.

According to Arthur Lubow, citing letters from Davis to his mother, *Captain Macklin* was conceived as an antiromance, being about the adventures of a young man who is "'always in love and always in trouble'" (Lubow 154). It was written in the first person, a fictional autobiography set down as lengthy journal entries, recounting the events over the course of a year in Royal Macklin's life soon after they occur. "It is rather amusing writing in the first person," Davis told his mother, "and making yourself out no end of a cad." As the sentence reveals, where Davis's earlier heroes were idealized versions of himself, this one was to be just the opposite, a compound of qualities that Davis deplored, yet the result turned out to be something of a self-caricature, or at least a caricature of a Davis hero. Unfortunately for the author's intention, the outline at times seems drawn too close to the familiar, idealized self-portrait, confusing so astute a critic as Van Wyck Brooks, never mind John Hay.

Royal Macklin is the orphaned maternal grandson of General Hamilton, who fought against American Indians and was a famous veteran of both the Mexican War and the War of the Rebellion on the Union side. Royal's father was an Irish army officer, "Fighting Macklin," a soldier of fortune who died in the service of the Confederacy, so that Macklin's is a dual heritage resembling that of Robert Clay (and Theodore Roosevelt). Brought up by his revered grandfather, the boy has no ambition beyond maintaining the family tradition of military service and sees his dream of martial fame becoming a reality when he receives an appointment to West Point. An indifferent student in the classroom, he is skilled in "drill, riding, marksmanship, and a knowledge of the manual" of arms, a narrow range of accomplishments that distinguishes him from Davis's other fictional heroes, who are virtual polymaths (18). When in his third year Macklin is dismissed from the academy for having attended a dance without permission, with a very limited future ahead of him, he elects to become a soldier of fortune.

Poring over a newspaper and an atlas, Macklin surveys the various trouble spots around the world, including "strained relations existing between France and China over the copper mines in Tonkin; . . . a tribal war in Upper Burmah with native troops; . . . a threat of complications in the Balkans, but the Balkans, as I have since learned, are always with us and always threatening" (44). He finds none of these possibilities of interest, but then, reading that a revolution has broken out in Honduras, with the aim of establishing a republican government free of corruption, Macklin decides that his future career lies there. For he had mastered Spanish at an early age, thanks to his grandfather, who learned the language while fighting in Mexico and who held "a fixed belief, that if the United States ever went to war, it would be with some of her Spanish-American neighbors, with Mexico, or Central America, or with Spain on account of Cuba. In consequence he considered it most essential that every United States officer should speak Spanish" (18). In 1902, this can hardly be accounted prophecy, but it does given the novel a contemporary frame.

Macklin sets sail for Central America and, having traveled into the interior of Honduras, joins a "foreign legion" commanded by a charismatic General Laguerre, a professional soldier of fortune of French and Irish descent. Because of his West Point training, Macklin is commissioned a captain, sudden authority that thrills him, as does the prospect of establishing an honest republic in Honduras. He is clearly an idealist with values not much different from those we associate with Robert Clay. But where Clay is a marvel of self-control, Royal Macklin, because of his Irish heritage, is passionate and headstrong in all that he does and soon comes to love Laguerre, who as an older man serves in the place of his grandfather. In return, the general regards the young man as his son.

Macklin is also passionate where beautiful women are concerned, starting with his lovely cousin Beatrice, left at home in Dobbs Ferry, but it is a chaste passion, and women play relatively minor roles in the novel. As a romance, it is very close to the Robert Louis Stevenson model, especially *Kidnapped,* in which David Balfour comes under the spell of the charismatic Jacobite rebel Alan Breck. Both romances are versions of bildungsroman, in which the hero's education is a matter of practical experience, yet despite the many hardships Royal Macklin endures in the service of his beloved General Laguerre, his enthusiasm for combat never fades.

As he says toward the end of the book, "the one thing I understood and craved, was the free, homeless, untrammelled life of the soldier or fortune. I wanted to see the shells splash up the earth again, I wanted to throw my leg across a saddle, I wanted to sleep on a blanket by a camp-fire, I wanted the kiss and caress of danger, the joy which comes when the sword wins honor and victory together, and I wanted the clear, clean view of right and wrong, that is given only to those who hourly walk with death" (325). Well, we wonder, what is wrong with that? Indeed, it is this very paragraph that Van Wyck Brooks drew upon in his characterization of RHD as a heroic figure.

Perhaps values have somewhat changed since 1900, but it is difficult to see how Royal Macklin is a "cad," a word Davis used in describing his antihero and one we will recall that Roosevelt once used in reference to Davis himself, though without explanation. Macklin at one point in the novel is called a cad, but mistakenly, when after drubbing a wealthy young American for having insulted General Laguerre he is accused by the youth's sister of having done so under the protection of his soldiers, thus being a "cad who went about armed, insulting unarmed people" (222). This is a central episode in the novel, for the young man in question is the son of Joseph Fiske, who owns the Isthmian Line of steamships, a powerful force in Honduran politics, and his sister is Fiske's daughter, so beautiful that the hero regards her as "a regal, goddess-like woman, one that a man might worship with that tribute of fear and adoration that savages pay to the fire and the sun" (220).

Macklin catches his first sight of this remarkable person as he rides through the Honduran capital at the head of his victorious regiment, dressed in "a wonderful uniform" of his own design, "a dark-green blouse with silver facings and scarlet riding breeches" (206). When he spies Fiske's daughter, he is overwhelmed by "a sudden deep flood of gratitude for anything so nobly beautiful. I was as humbly thankful as the crusader who is rewarded by his first sight of the Holy City, and I was glad, too, that I came into her presence worthily, riding in advance of a regiment. I was proud of our triumphant music, of our captured flags and guns, and the men behind me, who had taken them" (208).

There is something here of D'Artagnan riding into Paris, for it takes only one scornful look from this vision of beauty to make Macklin aware of the sordid reality of his ragtag army: "With her eyes, I saw the bare feet of our negro band, our ill-fitting uniforms with their flannel facings, the swagger of our officers, glancing pompously from their half-starved, unkempt ponies. . . . I saw that to her we were so many red-shirted firemen, dragging a wooden hose-cart; a company of burnt-cork minstrels, kicking up the dust of a village street; that we were ridiculous, lawless, absurd, and it was like a blow over my heart that one so noble-looking should be so blind and so unjust" (209).

For Macklin is aware of the suffering and deprivation that his men had undergone and the courage with which they had fought to seize Tegucigalpa from the armies of the corrupt President Alvarez. (Davis's vocabulary of Latin American proper names was obviously limited, nor does his hero ever demonstrate his mastery of Spanish.) It is at this critical point that Joseph Fiske's son makes his insulting remark: "Well, here's the army . . . but where's Falstaff? I don't see Laguerre" (210). When approached by an angry Macklin with a demand for an apology, young Fiske adds injury to insult by striking Macklin with his riding crop, and the well-deserved beating follows.

A fistfight in the streets of the capital city is admittedly improper for the "Vice-President, Minister of War, and Provost-Marshall" of the newly established republic, but it is certainly understandable given the provocation: "Because the girl had laughed at us I felt indignant with her, but for the same offence I was grateful to the man, for the reason that he was a man, and could be punished" (210). In sum, Macklin's Irish blood is up and his inherited sense of honor offended, overriding all other considerations. But do we blame him? And in what sense was his a caddish act?

The incident results in a duel between Macklin and young Fiske, who has a reputation as a crack shot, but the hero refuses to fire at his adversary, aiming his first ball at the ground and his second into the air. He receives a flesh wound from the first shot fired by Fiske, whose second goes wild, effectively laying to rest his awesome reputation. Macklin thereby redeems himself for his earlier lapse by refusing to kill the man who had insulted him, in part because he wishes to show his contempt for young Fiske, in part because his adversary is the brother of the woman he has worshiped from afar.

Earlier, in a conversation with Miss Fiske, who is attempting to stop the duel, Captain Macklin explains that her brother "insulted my regiment, and my general. It was that I resented, and that is why I am fighting," a simple and honorable explanation but one that the woman rejects (233). Instead, having been primed with lies by Fiske's business associates, she accuses the hero of playing a part in a conspiracy against her father, claiming that Laguerre's foreign legion "will use any means to win," including murdering her brother (236).

"What she had charged was so monstrous, so absurd that I could answer nothing in defence. My brain refused to believe that she had said it. I could not conceive that any creature so utterly lovely could be so unseeing, so bitter, and so unfair" (236). Further conversation follows, all of it merely digging a deeper hole of misunderstanding between the two. When he subsequently refuses to kill Fiske, Macklin earns the gratitude of his sister, given from a carriage in a driving rain as the family flees the capital city. For Tegucigalpa is by then under fire from Honduran soldiers once again loyal to President Alvarez, and Laguerre's new republic is doomed, a fate predictable from the start save by Laguerre and his loyal men.

Shortly after he arrived in Honduras, Macklin was informed by the American counsel, Aiken, that "almost every republic in Central America is under the thumb of a big trading firm or a banking house or a railroad. For instance, all these revolutions you read about in the papers—it's seldom they start with the people. The *puebleo* don't often elect a president or turn one

out. That's generally the work of a New York business firm that wants a concession" (74). This was a point made by Davis in *Three Gringos,* in which the
foreign firms in question were German, where in his fictionalized Honduras
it is the Isthmian Line, owned by Joseph Fiske. The American capitalist also
owns the Coban Silver Mines, whose operators, headed by a man named
Graham, have misrepresented the local situation to Fiske. They have bilked
the Honduran government of a half million dollars, inspiring the latest
revolution, while telling Fiske that Laguerre and his Honduran allies are
merely greedy malcontents.

Throughout the ensuing action Aiken, who had earlier worked as a private detective and has a dark view of the world, maintains a cynical attitude
toward Central American matters. It is he who early on is blamed by Macklin "for having so shaken my faith and poisoned my mind. . . . He had made
it all seem commercial, sordid, and underhanded" (93). But Aiken's cynicism is eventually proven correct, for at the moment of their greatest triumph, having taken the capital city, the foreign legion is fired on by men led
by one of their own officers, a German named Heinze, who has been bribed
by Graham into changing sides.

As Aiken informs them, General Garcia, the former Honduran president
they are supporting against Alvarez, has also been bought off by representatives of the Isthmian Line. Hopelessly outnumbered, the legion is defeated and Laguerre's plan for establishing a true republic is crushed. The
general, badly wounded, manages to escape the country, followed shortly
afterward followed by Macklin, who has also been shot and barely makes it
alive to Amapala, on the Pacific side of the isthmus. His education in the realities of Central American politics is now complete.

Carried in an American ship back to New York, Macklin recovers from his
wounds and under pressure by his lovely cousin, Beatrice, agrees to seek a
regular job. On a visit to the city for that purpose, he once again meets Miss
Fiske and learns that her father, having been informed of the true situation,
has fired the men who deceived him and paid back the money owed, "not to
that odious Alvarez man, but in some way, I don't quite understand how, but
so the poor people will get it" (315). Nor do we see how such an arrangement
will be managed, and this final assurance seems largely in the service of defending the character of Joseph Fiske, the representative of U.S. capitalism
in Honduras, further confusing the issues.

Davis's mixture of American business interests, a beautiful woman, and
a corrupt Central American government is familiar to readers of *Soldiers of
Fortune,* but critical differences remain. First and foremost, perhaps, Mack-

lin does not get to marry the beautiful and wealthy Miss Fiske. But equally important, the insurrection against the corrupt Alvarez is a failure, thanks to the interference in the revolution by the equally corrupt American interests, acting in the name of Joseph Fiske but without his knowledge. In all this Davis seems to be attempting to keep his cake and serve it up as well, much as in *Soldiers of Fortune* he held back the U.S. Navy until the grand finale, but here it does not work.

Instead of reinforcing the new imperialism in a positive manner, in *Captain Macklin* the U.S. Navy compounds the ethical snarl. The dilemma is given voice by a young lieutenant who is staying with the Fiske party so as to report to his captain on the revolution, a handsome and good-natured fellow named Lowell to whom Macklin is instantly attracted. Lowell is on leave from the *Raleigh,* a white-hulled gunboat stationed in the harbor at Amapala "to protect American interests," as he explains, "because the Isthmian Line demanded protection" (251).

But then, when in conversation with General Laguerre, Lowell hears that Fiske's associate Graham has threatened to have the U.S. Marines assist in putting down the revolution, he objects to the notion of having the navy take its orders from civilians. "'I hate it!' he cried, 'I hate to think that a billionaire, with a pull at Washington, can turn our Jackies into Janissaries. Protect American interests!' he exclaimed, indignantly, 'protect American sharpers! The Isthmian Line has no more right to the protection of our Navy than have the debtors in Ludlow Street Jail'" (252).

This argument, with which Davis seems entirely in sympathy, recalls the point made by Van Wyck Brooks, who added *Captain Macklin* to *Soldiers of Fortune* as expressions of Davis's "contempt for American sharpers," being "the best memorials perhaps of the days when American traders financed revolts" in the isthmian republics (107). As there are no "American sharpers" in *Soldiers of Fortune,* it would seem to be the subsequent novel to which Brooks was referring. Brooks, moreover, not knowing of Davis's reservations regarding *Captain Macklin,* saw the hero as yet another autobiographical projection, for the author himself also "loved the 'kiss and caress of danger' . . . [and] preferred a free, untrammelled knight-errant's life watching the shells bespatter the earth while he threw his leg over a saddle and slept in a blanket by a camp-fire" (105). Here again is the mythic Davis, for although the real one was certainly courageous, he much preferred the comforts of an officer's club to a blanket by a campfire.

More important, the point of *Captain Macklin* is that the bravest knight-errant can do nothing to stop the operations of American sharpers, no more than Lieutenant Lowell or his captain can disobey orders from Washington, whatever their origin. As the American consul warns, Central America is run by people in the control of U.S. business interests, and everything that happens in the course of the novel proves Aiken right. That Joseph Fiske is not aware of what his people are doing in his name is beside the point, as is his attempt to see to it that the swindled money gets into the hands of the Honduran people.

Davis's argument in 1902 seems to be that Central America will remain a Balkans of the Western Hemisphere, a permanently unstable region, thanks to the synergetic interplay of American commercial interests with the propensity for corruption of Latin American officials. Fiske may replace his agents with honest men, but the process of interference in local affairs will go on, whether by Americans or by soldiers of fortune without specific nationality, like General Laguerre and his legion of officers recruited from around the world.

: IV :

Again, very little of the material Davis gathered in *Three Gringos in Venezuela and Central America* got into *Soldiers of Fortune,* but his subsequent novel about revolution in Honduras depends greatly on that earlier work of nonfiction. Laguerre's little army by necessity follows the same rough road up through the mountains that Davis took and establishes a base in Santa Barbara before marching on the capital city. More important, a number of the opinions Davis expressed about Central American countries are carried forward to the novel, with quite a different context.

Earlier I cited from McCullough's book on the Panama Canal the episode in which John Hay used *Captain Macklin* as a coded message conveying U.S. intentions regarding the revolution that would create an "independent" Panama. I can here add that Davis's novel contained a subtext concerning the heavy presence of American commerce that the revolutionary party should perhaps have heeded. It certainly provides balance for *Soldiers of Fortune,* in which the investment of capital in Central America is given a clean-shaven and honorable face. Moreover, by sending its putative hero off to Indochina to fight for the French, the novel gave the invasive presence of the United States in the Caribbean a prophetic profile: In 1902 Davis leapfrogged the ongoing military campaign in the Philippines for Vietnam itself, suggesting that the revisionists have been reading the wrong book, that once again Davis was there before them. For *Captain Macklin* is in many respects an updated version of "The Reporter Who Made Himself King," but without the lighthearted view of imperialism.

As I said at the start, it is a confusing and confused novel, largely because Davis chose to have the hero tell his own story, with a voice that from time to time picks up the themes the author himself had broached in *Three Gringos in Venezuela and Central America.* Yet because of the ubiquitous presence of the quixotic General Laguerre, it acts to discount the validity of those imperialistic notions. Overcast by the tragic shadow of William Walker, with whom one of Laguerre's men identifies the general, the novel is heavily weighed with futility and seems to despair of ever setting things right in Central America, a message antithetical to that of *Soldiers of Fortune.*

Davis was disappointed by the reception of *Captain Macklin,* which he regarded as his most ambitious novel to date. It seems that most of his readers, like Van Wyck Brooks, himself a boy of sixteen when it was published, improperly confused the hero with the author, an easy mistake to make. But a careful reading reveals how the novel was shaped to emphasize the uselessness of any attempt to form a corruption-free republic in Central America, caught as that region was between the pervasive influence of American commerce and the propensity of its governing bodies to be manipulated for gain.

If *Soldiers of Fortune* romanced the empire, *Captain Macklin* did not. It was hardly written in the service of the new imperialism but openly attacks the presence in Latin American countries of U.S. companies, which act to increase the tendency of those republics toward corruption. Something obviously influenced Davis's thinking on that subject between 1897 and 1902, and it began to happen soon after *Soldiers of Fortune* was published. It is perhaps significant that after *Captain Macklin,* Davis would abandon warfare as a romantic subject. But then, by 1902, he had already experienced a war that seems to have fulfilled his notion of romance, as well as other wars that did not.

War takes a long time.
STEPHEN CRANE

11 : SHADOWS ON THE PLAIN

: I :

"He has seen the greatness and parades, and they remain, glitteringly stored in his swift, smooth sketches and long reports," wrote Thomas Beer of Richard Harding Davis (249). Most of the sketches and reports to which Beer referred are themselves stored in a single volume, *A Year from a Reporter's Note-Book,* published in 1898, and were written, as Davis noted, "between the months of May, 1896, and June, 1897" (v). It was surely the annus mirabilis for lovers of spectacles as well as a marvelous time for RHD, his heyday perhaps as a reporter, even though his fame as a war correspondent was yet to come.

In May 1896 Davis was in Moscow for the coronation of Czar Nicholas and Alexandra, and in June he was in Budapest for the Banderium, a millennial celebration of much pomp and circumstance. During the summer presidential campaign he enthusiastically supported William McKinley against William Jennings Bryan lest the western silver interests should destroy the nation's economy by displacing the gold standard. He also covered McKinley's inaugural in March 1897 before traveling to London later that same month for Queen Victoria's Diamond Jubilee. Though the presidential inauguration lacked the expensive display of the European ceremonies, RHD found it all the more impressive because of its democratic simplicity.

Davis foresaw that the shift of power from a Democratic to a Republican administration would have vast consequences, signaling "a great transformation which the people could not see," an invisible wave of energy that passed "over the whole of the land, and its influence penetrated to the furthermost corners of the earth" (*Year* 162). As a consequence of the election, "the lakes of Nicaragua moved as though a hand had stirred the waters, and began to flow from ocean to ocean and to cut a continent in two; stocks rose and fell; ministers of foreign affairs in all parts of the world planned new treaties and new tariffs; a newspaper correspondent in a calaboose in Cuba saw the jail doors swing open and the Spanish comandante beckon him out;

and the boy orator of the Platte, who had been given the votes of nearly seven million citizens, heard the door of the White House close in his face and shut him out forever" (163).

Davis could not have been aware of the full extent of the reverberations which the election of McKinley would cause, but he certainly understood that the man in the White House had assumed what would become an imperial presidency. Indeed, by March 1897 Davis had already written another travel book whose particulars would help turn the power of the executive branch in an expansionist direction, much as *Soldiers of Fortune* cast a romantic aura over armed intervention in Caribbean affairs.

Davis's allusion above to matters in Cuba derives from a trip he took there in January, after McKinley's election but before his inauguration. He traveled as a correspondent for William Randolph Hearst's *Journal,* with the intention of covering the ongoing insurrection against the Spanish colonial government. It was an attractive assignment both because of the large sum Hearst was willing to pay and because Davis hoped to witness the fighting between the rebels and the Spanish forces, thereby fulfilling his lifelong ambition to cover a war. He was frustrated in that ardent wish, but stories sent back by RHD from Cuba describing the terrible conditions there began to appear in the *Journal* starting in February.

They were all quite graphic in describing the suffering of the Cubans, but one of the stories appealed to his readers more than the others and was picked up from Hearst's *Journal* and circulated throughout the country by other newspapers. This was the most famous piece Davis wrote about the Cuban insurrection, preceding by a year the actual entrance of the United States into the war, following the explosion of the *Maine.* He subsequently included it not only in his full-length account of his trip in 1897, *Cuba in War Time,* published in 1898, but in *A Year from a Reporter's Note-Book,* published that same year.

Davis did not cover the sinking of the *Maine,* his famous luck failing him for once, but during his visit to Cuba in 1897 he chanced upon an otherwise minor episode that produced a searing image in the American consciousness, giving dramatic point to his exposé of the sufferings of the Cuban people under Spanish rule. The episode, unlike his arguments in *Three Gringos* and the romantic drama in *Soldiers of Fortune,* had nothing to do with the ongoing debate regarding the extent to which the Monroe Doctrine could license U.S. interference in Latin American republics. Cuba in 1897 was still very much under the control of Spain; indeed, it was the last vestige of Spanish empire in the Western Hemisphere. The question was not

whether the United States had any business directing the fortunes of an independent nation; the question was whether the United States could any
longer tolerate the activities of a tyrannical empire in waters just off its own
continental limits.

: II :

When Davis went to Cuba in 1897, he was accompanied by Frederic Remington, who had illustrated *The West from a Car Window*. As Remington's bi-
ographers have noted, it began to look as though the trip would result in a
companion volume, "Cuba from a Car Window," owing to the reluctance of
the Spanish authorities to allow contact by American reporters with the
rebel army (Samuels 248). This policy was enforced by restricting their
travel to trains and steamships, always under strict supervision of government agents. Cuba at that time was in the repressive grip of General Valeri-
ano Weyler y Nicolau, sent over from Spain to deal firmly with the insurgents, who were burning crops in the field, a strategy intended to injure the
Cuban economy.

Weyler's solution was to gather nonbelligerent rural populations into
fortified concentration camps, a policy that worked terrible hardship on the
Cuban people and led to the general's becoming known in the American
press as "Butcher" Weyler. Davis was therefore pleasantly surprised to find
Weyler a civil and cultivated gentleman, as were all his Spanish hosts, always a plus for RHD. He was less happy with the restrictions placed by
Weyler on foreigners seeking to travel about the country, which guaranteed
that Davis and Remington would not be able to establish contact with the
insurgents. In any event, the rebels were guerrilla fighters difficult to find
without help from Cubans sympathetic to their cause, who because of fear
of reprisals were reluctant to come forward.

Remington by 1897 had become a studio artist, hugely overweight and
unused to exercise. Moreover, he was a stranger to restraint, whether imposed by himself or others. He soon tired of the adventure and Davis soon
tired of him, so that when Remington departed for the United States a short
week after their arrival, he was not much missed. And yet when RHD's journalistic reactions to this first Cuban trip were gathered together as *Cuba in
War Time* later that year, they were illustrated with the usual photographs
taken by Davis but also with sketches done by Remington "from personal
observation while in Cuba." Remington's contribution suggests that the
artist not only made good use of the very brief time he was on the island but

had psychic powers as well, for a number of the sketches were of the insurgent Cubans he and Davis never found.

Despite Davis's failure to contact the rebels, he saw sufficient evidence of the hard hand of General Weyler to satisfy Hearst's endless appetite for sensational copy, and his account of the reconcentrados served to validate rumors of the sufferings experienced by the Cuban populace. According to Davis the island was an armed camp, "studded" with a number of small fortifications, the chief evidence of the Spanish presence, which was otherwise kept within "cities, towns, seaports, and along the lines of the railroad," all protected by other forts (*Cuba* 13). The rest of the country was under the "control," as he facetiously put it, of the rebels, whose presence was signaled by the devastation they wreaked on the countryside.

Davis was inside Cuba, but it was Spanish Cuba he was inside, and the Spanish were not willing to let him out: "A stranger in any city in Cuba today is virtually in a prison, and is as isolated from the rest of the world as though he were on . . . a floating ship of war" (14). Spanish soldiers also stayed inside the fortified towns as much as possible; when they did venture forth, they returned each night. Though willing to do battle with bands of insurgents they might encounter, they never pursued the enemy for fear of being ambushed. Davis compared this craven and unproductive behavior to the courage and persistence displayed by the troop of U.S. cavalry he had traveled with in Texas. As in other aspects of his account, he seems to be suggesting that any armed conflict between Spanish and American forces would be no contest.

The *pacíficos,* or nonbelligerent Cubans, were placed in camps just outside these fortified towns, their homes and crops having been destroyed by the Spanish so as to deny them to the insurgents but in effect denying them also to the pacíficos. The insurgents continued to torch the countryside, so that the beautiful island of Davis's memories was "blotted with the grim and pitiable signs of war" (24). Everywhere were ruins of buildings destroyed by burning, and smoke continued to rise from other fires (24). The waste was caused by both sides of the conflict, and Davis expressed no more sympathy with the insurgents in this particular than with the Spanish authorities. He predicted that the destructive stalemate would continue "unless the United States government interferes on account of some one of its citizens in Cuba, and war is declared with Spain" (20).

Davis accused the Spanish army of self-interest rather than patriotism in prolonging the conflict. Foreign service meant double pay, to which could be added protection money extorted from planters: "A certain class of Spanish officer has a strange sense of honor. He does not consider that robbing his government by falsifying his accounts, or by making incorrect returns of his expenses, is disloyal or unpatriotic. . . . He might be perfectly willing to die for his country, but should he be permitted to live he will not hesitate to rob her" (30). Davis praised the conscripted Spanish "Tommies," most of them farm boys, for enduring hardships stoically, including brutal hectoring by their superiors, but he depicted the officers as hopelessly corrupt and craven. Even worse for a man who equated cleanliness with civilization, the Spanish officers seldom if ever bathed.

Finally, the Spanish army in Cuba had "contributed little to the information of those who are interested in military science" and employed tactics, such as the famous British square, that were useless against attacks by bands of insurgent partisans, instead of emulating the open "skirmish line" associated with combat against American Indians in the West (30–31). And though their barricaded fortifications, called *trochas,* seemed formidable obstacles against the insurgent soldiers, there were numerous instances of their having been penetrated, and they would be more of a handicap than a protection should the island be invaded. In sum, the unstated but obvious argument suggested by Davis's report is that the Spanish army would be no match for American forces.

Cuba in War Time opens with a general introduction reviewing conditions on the island, followed by a chapter titled "The Fate of the Pacificos," with a detailed description of the sufferings of the people forced into crude and crowded shelters by the Spanish. Hundreds, even thousands, of Cubans were "herded together on the bare ground, with no food, with no knowledge of sanitation, with no covering for their heads but palm leaves, with no privacy for the women and young girls, with no thought but as to how they could live until to-morrow" (43). The conditions in these internment camps, as Davis announced, "seemed to furnish a better argument to those who think the United States should interfere in behalf of Cuba, than did the fact that men were being killed there, and that both sides were devastating the island and wrecking property worth millions of dollars" (42).

After pages of description of the crowded and disease-infested camps, Davis summed up what he had seen, testimony reinforced by his earlier experiences as a reporter and travel writer: "I saw the survivors of the Johnstown flood when the horror of that disaster was still plainly written in their eyes, but destitute as they were of home and food and clothing, they were in better plight than those fever-stricken, starving pacíficos, who have sinned in no way, who have given no aid to the rebels, and whose only crime is that they lived in the country instead of in the town. They are now to suffer because General Weyler, finding that he cannot hold the country as he can the towns, lays it waste and treats those who lived there with less consideration than the Sultan of Morocco shows to the murderers in his jail at Tangier" (50). Davis liked to wear his medals when in formal dress, and we have here a prose equivalent, which displays the author's credentials as a famous, world-traveling reporter.

In his conclusion to "The Fate of the Pacificos," Davis returned to his initial proposition, the necessity for intervention by the United States in Spanish-Cuban affairs. He gave his appeal urgency by emphasizing that while Americans debated the possibility of entering the war in Cuba, their inaction would result in still more deaths among the pacíficos, as the rainy season came on, bringing with it conditions that fostered yellow fever, in addition to the smallpox already raging in the internment camps: "Whatever may happen later, this is what is likely to happen now, and it should have some weight in helping to decide the question with those whose proper business is to determine it. . . . It will not do to put it aside by saying that 'War is war,' and that 'All war is cruel,' or to ask 'Am I my brother's keeper?'" (54–55).

As Arthur Lubow has noted, Davis's account of the miseries of the Cuban people seems to have had less effect on his readers than did the story immediately following, "The Death of Rodriguez." It described an event that not only inspired Davis himself to the heights of his powers as a writer but in turn aroused the sympathies of U.S. readers who, although relatively unconcerned over the sufferings of faceless masses, were drawn to the account of the death of one brave man. Like his otherwise quite different account of William Astor Chanler's adventures in Africa, Davis's story begins with a matter-of-fact tone: "Adolfo Rodriguez was the only son of a Cuban farmer, who lives nine miles outside of Santa Clara, beyond the hills that surround that city to the north," and goes on in a similar fashion to recount the bare details of the insurgent's trial and inevitable sentence (59).

"I witnessed his execution," Davis declares simply, "and what follows is an account of the way he went to death. The young man's friends could not be present," for obvious reasons, "and I like to think that, although Rodriguez could not know it, there was one person present when he died who felt keenly for him, and who was a sympathetic though unwilling spectator" (60). This characteristic note of sentimentality not only acts to promote a bond between Davis and the brave young Cuban, in effect making them comrades, but is calculated to draw the reader into the brotherhood of courageous men as well, much as Davis's account of Rodriguez's execution by its vividness makes the reader a witness.

Davis renders a detailed and precise description of the landscape that would be the scene of the execution, seen first in the lingering light cast by a full moon at dawn, "a plain two miles in extent broken by ridges and gullies and covered with thick, high grass and with bunches of cactus and palmetto," with the "walls of the old town" on one side of the plain, while on the other side "rose hills covered with royal palms, that showed white in the moonlight, like hundreds of marble columns" (60). As with so much of Davis's wartime reporting, this simplicity and precision looks forward to Hemingway's style, a similarity that has been noted by a number of critics interested in the sources of the younger writer's sparing way with words. We may add to this RHD's admiration for the condemned man's stoic courage, his lack of fear when confronting certain death, the sort of thing Hemingway associated with toreadors and with loyalists during the Spanish Civil War.

Davis described how the moonlight gradually faded, so that when the soldiers and civilian witnesses gathered on the plain it was still dark, but as daylight broke, "a mass of people" could be seen "hurrying from the town with two black figures leading them," the priests who had spent the night with the prisoner and who would stay with Rodriguez until his final moments. In the United States, Davis remarked, a condemned man has only a short way to walk to the place of execution, hidden behind prison walls, and even then he is often unable to make it unassisted, while Rodriguez was seen striding bravely over the plain, with the priests and the trailing crowd having to run to keep up with him: "He had a handsome, gentle face of the peasant type, a light, pointed beard, great wistful eyes and a mass of curly black hair. He was shockingly young for such a sacrifice, and . . . wore a new scapula around his neck, hanging outside his linen blouse" (65).

But it was not this token of the young man's piety that most impressed Davis, who was drawn to an object that signaled Rodriguez's coolness and courage in the face of what was certain to happen: "It seems a petty thing to have been pleased with at such a time, but I confess to have felt a thrill of satisfaction when I saw, as the Cuban passed me, that he held a cigarette between his lips, not arrogantly nor with bravado, but with the nonchalance of a man who meets his punishment fearlessly, and who will let his enemies see that they can kill but can not frighten him" (65).

His arms tied behind him, Rodriguez spat out the cigarette soon thereafter in order to kiss the cross held out by one of the priests, but it would have a very long life, not only as "a tiny ring of living fire," burning on the ground after the man had been shot, but as a standard accoutrement to death by firing squad thenceforth. It is one of those facts in RHD's account of wartime Cuba that merges with fiction, much as his description of Rodriguez's death has the tight closure of a short story.

Rodriguez was led to the place of execution by the officer in charge and was left standing alone, his back to the line of rifles, facing "the hills and the road across them which led to his father's farm," his eyes fixed "immovably on the morning light which had just begun to show above the hills. . . . He made a picture of such pathetic helplessness, but of such courage and dignity, that he reminded me on the instant of that statue of Nathan Hale, which stands in the City Hall Park, and teaches a lesson to the hurrying crowds of moneymakers who pass beneath" (65–66). This last is a definitive touch, linking Rodriguez to the heroes of the American Revolution, and it is very much au courant, as Frederick MacMonnies' statue of the young schoolteacher who had declared his regret over having only one life to give for his country had only recently been put in place.

Rodriguez's stiffly erect posture, worthy also of being cast in bronze, persisted even after a terrible blunder by the Spanish officer, who, having already given the order for his men to raise their rifles, realized that the line of fire would hit not only the condemned man but also the Spanish soldiers stationed opposite. He stepped forward and put his hand on Rodriguez's shoulder so as to reposition him, and Davis observed that "it was not pleasant to think what that shock must have been" to a man who had "steeled himself to receive a volley of bullets in his back" (68).

Yet the brave young Cuban did not even flinch but followed the order of the Spanish officer to change his position, then "straightened his back again, and once more held himself erect," a gesture worth any number of defiant last words. It was "an exhibition of self-control" that in Davis's estimation ranked "above feats of heroism performed in battle," where a man has "thousands of comrades to give inspiration," while Rodriguez "was alone, in the sight of the hills he knew, with only enemies about him, with no source to draw on for strength but that which lay within himself." After this final display of courage, the execution itself was an anticlimax, as "the men once more leveled their rifles, the sword rose, dropped, and the men fired," the impact of the bullets causing the head of the still-standing dead man to snap back before "his body fell slowly, as though some one had pushed him gently forward from behind and he had stumbled. . . . He sank on his side in the wet grass without a struggle or sound, and did not move again, . . . the blood from his breast sinking into the soil he had tried to free," as "the cigarette still burned, a tiny ring of fire" (71–73).

First published in Hearst's *Journal* on February 2, 1897, "The Death of Rodriguez" was picked up by other newspapers and contributed to the growing hostility in the United States toward the Spanish presence in Cuba. The importance of the story is suggested by the placement of an illustration by Remington as a frontispiece to *Cuba in War Time,* which showed the bound Rodriguez standing in the foreground, his back to the firing squad, with the outlines of Santa Clara silhouetted in the distance. Once again, the artist was already home in New York when the execution took place, and like a number of the illustrations he provided, Remington drew this one second-hand, as he did a much more notorious sketch that Hearst published in company with a story by Davis describing the strip search of Cuban women by Spanish detectives on an American ship, the *Olivette.* The picture showed a naked young woman in profile, surrounded by Spanish men in civilian dress, whose arrogance and callousness is revealed by their expressions.

The story and picture aroused considerable anger toward Spain in the United States, but no one was more outraged than Davis himself, for as it turned out the search had been carried out not by men but by a female detective, a detail he neglected to mention in his original dispatch and an omission that caused considerable embarrassment to the correspondent who had insisted on the accuracy of his reports on conditions in Cuba. The version of the story in *Cuba in War Time,* in the concluding chapter titled "The Right of Search of American Vessels," added the necessary information and was, naturally, unaccompanied by Remington's sensational picture: "For the benefit of people with unruly imaginations," wrote Davis in acid tones, "of whom there seem to be a larger proportion in this country than I had supposed, I will state again that the search of these women was conducted by women and not by men, as I was reported to have said, and as I did not say in my original report of the incident" (122).

By this time Davis had left Hearst's *Journal,* disgusted over distortions of the reports he filed, and the remark is in harmony with his attacks elsewhere on "hysterical head lines" and on reporters who file unsubstantiated stories from their hotel rooms in Florida. In "The Question of Atrocities," Davis states that he had been "somewhat sceptical of Spanish atrocities until I came to Cuba, chiefly because I had been kept sufficiently long in Key

Frontispiece to Cuba in War Time. *Drawn entirely from Davis's description, Remington's composition places the condemned man in the foreground, yet emphasizes his vulnerability and stoic courage.*

West to learn how large a proportion of Cuban war news is manufactured on the piazzas of the hotels of that town and of Tampa by utterly irresponsible newspaper men who accept every rumor that finds its way across the gulf, and pass these rumors on to some of the New York papers as facts coming direct from the field." Once again we are reminded of Davis's prophetic "The Reporter Who Made Himself King," but not by Davis, who was unamused by this abuse of reportorial privilege, which not only was dishonest but dishonored those brave correspondents who actually traveled to Cuba to report the facts: "If one story proves to be false, how is the reader to know that the others are not inventions also?" (104).

Though Davis himself, as he admits, was never in danger of imprisonment or execution, other correspondents were, and he ends his own narrative, based on eyewitness accounts of atrocities committed by guerrillas in the service of the Spanish, with a tribute to those brave men who took great risks that the truth be told, as opposed to the "fakirs" and "sensation-mongers" who remain in Florida (115).

> They are taking chances that no war correspondent ever took in any war in any part of the world. For this is not a war—it is a state of lawless butchery, and the rights of correspondents, of soldiers and of non-combatants are not recognized. . . . They risk capture at sea and death by the guns of a Spanish cruiser, and, escaping that, they face when they reach the island the greater danger of capture there and of being cut down by a guerrilla force and left to die in a road, or of being put in a prison and left to die of fever. . . . The fate of these . . . American correspondents has not deterred others from crossing the lines, and they are in the field now, lying in swamps by day and creeping between the forts by night, standing under fire by the side of Gomez . . . [and] going without food, without shelter, without the right to answer the attacks of the Spanish troops, climbing the mountains and crawling across the trochas, creeping to some friendly hut for a cup of coffee and to place their despatches in safe hands, and then going back again to run the gauntlet of Spanish spies and of flying columns and of the unspeakable [Spanish] guerrillas. (116–17)

Davis addressed himself to his fellow Americans, sitting "comfortably at your breakfast in New York" and reading in a newspaper "the despatches which these gentlemen write of Cuban victories and their interviews with self-important Cuban chiefs," and urged that they "remember what it cost them to supply you with that addition to your morning's budget of news. . . . The reckless bravery and the unselfishness of the correspondents in the field in Cuba to-day are beyond parallel. It is as dangerous to seek for Gomez as Stanley found it to seek for Livingston" (117).

Aside from the familiar allusion to Henry M. Stanley, the specific reference here is to Grover Flint, whose account of his experiences searching for and then interviewing and accompanying the insurgent general Máximo Gómez was published as a series of dispatches in Hearst's *Journal* in 1896 and then gathered together as *Marching with Gomez* in 1898. It was Flint's report of life on the march that promoted Gómez as the Cincinnatus of Cuba Libre, being "a farmer by birth, the son of a farmer, with an Anglo-Saxon tenacity of purpose, and a sense of honor as clean and true as the blade of his little Santo-Domingo machete" (Flint 119). In Flint's pen-and-ink illustrations the insurgent general bears a remarkable resemblance to Robert E. Lee.

A native of Santo Domingo, who had served with the Spanish army there in putting down an insurrection, Gómez had undergone a subsequent conversion and joined the Cubans in their war for independence. As American army officers were soon to learn, he was a very prickly and at times moody and uncooperative individual, not quite the Braveheart depicted by Flint and his fellow correspondents. But by then Gómez had learned that the American army was not in Cuba to help him so much as help themselves to victory over the Spanish.

: III :

Davis stresses throughout *Cuba in War Time* that he had no particular case to make for the cause of the insurgents, who were as self-interested and destructive in their way as the Spanish. What aroused Davis's outrage were the sufferings of the Cuban people in the hands of a cruel and corrupt Spanish government and the audacity of that same government in sending agents aboard American ships to search and if possible seize persons they suspected of conveying letters and dispatches unfavorable to Spain. The chivalric Davis was outraged by the indifference of the captain of the American steamer toward the treatment of the Cuban women by Spanish detectives aboard his ship, and he fumed that "there is not an unwashed, garlicky, bediamonded Spanish spy in Cuba who has not more authority on board the *Olivette* than her American captain and his subservient crew" (128). A year earlier, Davis noted, the United States had been willing to go to war with Great Britain over the Venezuelan border dispute, a minor matter in which American interests were concerned, but now the Congress, like the *Olivette's*

captain, seems unconcerned over this abuse of the "self-respect and property and freedom of Americans . . . by this fourth-rate power" (129).

It was, he admitted, perfectly legal for Spanish detectives to do so, if the
ship was still in the Havana harbor, but it was a law that needed to be
changed, "for it gives the Spanish authorities absolute control over the persons and property of Americans on American vessels," a situation reminiscent of the complaints against the British that resulted in the War of 1812. It
was a "privilege" so dangerous to Americans in Cuba that "there is no reason nor excuse for not keeping an American ship of war in the harbor of Havana" to protect U.S. citizens, including American reporters, from being
seized and imprisoned (127). Though we may doubt any immediate cause
and effect, it is notable that President McKinley soon thereafter sent the
Maine to Havana harbor, supposedly on a goodwill mission but with the intention of safeguarding Americans and their property.

Where Henry Adams and his protégé Henry Cabot Lodge argued for intervention in Cuba by citing the Monroe Doctrine, Davis's rationale for U.S.
involvement was quite different. He stressed the atrocious treatment of
both Cubans and Americans by the Spanish, an argument based on the notion of human rights that became familiar during the last half of the twentieth century but was much less so in 1897:

> Before I went to Cuba I was as much opposed to our interfering there
> as any other person equally ignorant concerning the situation could be,
> but since I have seen for myself I feel ashamed that we should have stood
> so long idle. We have been too considerate, too fearful that as a younger
> nation, we should appear to disregard the laws laid down by older na-
> tions. We have tolerated what no European power would have tolerated;
> we have been patient with men who have put back the hand of time for
> centuries, who lie to our representatives daily, who butcher innocent
> people, who gamble with the lives of their own soldiers in order to gain a
> few more stars and an extra stripe, who send American property to the
> air in flames and murder American prisoners. (129)

Davis doubted if the American people wanted war, for "if we did not go
to war with Spain when she murdered the crew of the *Virginius,* we never
will" (130). We may remember that Davis associated the fate of Robert
Clay's father with this episode, the outcome of a filibustering episode in
1873, in which the American captain and several others—not the entire
crew—were executed. The problem, as Davis saw it, was that the American
people do not yet understand the seriousness of the situation in Cuba,

which he had been laboring to render in detail, supplying "sufficient reasons" for interfering in that island's affairs (133).

Davis sought to arouse Americans "in the name of humanity," "not because we are Americans, but because we are human beings. . . . What further manifestations are needed? Is it that the American people doubt the sources from which their information comes? They are the consuls all over the island of Cuba. For what voice crying in the wilderness are they still waiting? What will convince them that the time has come?" (133–34).

RHD's appeal on behalf of the Cubans "in the name of humanity" is not a trumpet of imperialism but a rallying cry for service to a higher authority than temporal, in effect appealing to the chivalry of American men. Ironically, given Davis's political conservatism, it is not much different from the appeal to a higher law by Emerson and Thoreau during the abolition dispute, and his account of the death of Rodriguez created another John Brown. We hear nothing of the riches to be mined or harvested in Cuba, no echoes of the complaint in *Three Gringos* that the people there are inadequate to the resources they might command. What Davis demands is that justice be carried out, in the name of the Cuban and the North American people, indeed the peoples of the world. His is an argument without ideology but saturated with chivalric idealism, identified always with defending the defenseless and protecting the helpless.

Revisionists have faulted RHD and his contemporaries for appealing to the manhood of young Americans to take up arms against Spain. Given the subsequent history of the United States regarding not only the territories it acquired as a result of the Spanish-American War but also its interference in the presumably independent republics in the Caribbean rim as a whole, we cannot but sympathize with this retrospective view. That is, from the far side of the situation we can see how concern for the Cuban people served as a convenient mask for the grandiose geopolitical schemes of Captain Mahan and his eager disciples, Lodge and Theodore Roosevelt, among other jingoes of the day. But in 1897, that was hardly Davis's intention, whose outrage was sincere and who wrote without any regard to the expansion of America's sphere of influence beyond rescuing Cuba from the tyranny of Spain. Davis was always, as we have seen, comforted by the sight of great white warships sitting in Central American harbors, but as in *Cuba in War Time* that presence signaled the protection of American interests, not their expansion.

The line between protection and expansion is a difficult one to cut, admittedly, and because Davis was no clear thinker on such matters, it is easy enough to read his call for U.S. intervention in Cuba as in harmony with the jingoistic war cries of the yellow press and the brazen trumpetings of Lodge and Roosevelt. But, carefully read, *Cuba in War Time* is far more in keeping with today's American policy regarding military intervention, namely, limited engagement in international situations that are either threats to U.S. interests or matters of humanitarian relief, rather than a vast expansion of the national presence along traditionally imperial lines. Obviously, such engagements are often, if not inevitably, exploitative in character, being hallmarks of the "new," oblique colonialism as defined by Walter LaFeber, which first emerged during the McKinley administration.

We must also keep in mind that Americans can be aroused to military action not by abstract economic considerations but by arguments similar to those of RHD in 1897. Drawing on his deep well of chivalric and romantic idealism, his call for action was the sort of thing that appealed to the same people who had made Dick Davis a best-selling author. These were the readers already saturated with the chivalric literature found on the library shelves in Henry Canby's home in Wilmington, Delaware, and their response, whatever Canby's subsequent reservations regarding the Spanish-American War, was predictable.

To those revisionists who object to Davis's appeals to national honor and Christian idealism as specious masks for national expansion, the question remains, echoing that asked by Harriet Beecher Stowe in the last chapter of *Uncle Tom's Cabin:* What should we do when confronted by evidence of man's inhumanity to man? Is Milton's formulaic response, that those also serve who stand and wait, adequate for such occasions? Are national borders implicit limits to humanitarian action? Should the United States have stood by and let the suffering and dying in Cuba continue as diplomats maneuvered for a peaceful solution? It is not a question limited to the issues of 1898.

Davis may in effect have been serving the cause of jingoism, but he was not himself a jingo. Though maintaining that if "the United States is to interfere in this matter she should do so immediately," as hundreds of deaths were occurring daily, he insisted "she should only do so after she has informed herself thoroughly concerning it," acting not on "the reports of the hotel piazza correspondents" but by sending "men to Cuba on whose judgment and common sense she can rely. . . . In three weeks any member of the Senate or of Congress who wishes to inform himself on this reign of terror in Cuba can travel from one end of this island to the other and return competent to speak with absolute authority" (140).

Davis was convinced by his own experience that no man, whatever "his prejudices may be, can make this journey and not go home convinced that it is his duty to try to stop this cruel waste of life and this wanton destruction of a beautiful country." The situation in Cuba was in effect a mutually destructive stalemate, the Spanish and the insurgents alike "laying waste the land, and neither side shows any sign of giving up the struggle. . . . The matter lies at the door of Congress. . . . No European power dare interfere, and it lies with the United States and with her people to give the signal. If it is given now it will save thousands of innocent lives; if it is delayed just that many people will perish" (140–43). Davis closes on this note of urgency, and his call did not go unheeded.

In mid-March 1898, Senator Redfield Proctor of Vermont reported back to his colleagues in Washington concerning what he had seen during his visit to Cuba a few weeks earlier, a speech that is credited by Walter LaFeber and Gerald Linderman with having removed the last objections to U.S. intervention in the insurrection. The *Maine* had been sunk in Havana harbor a month earlier, but the cause of the tragedy had yet to be officially determined, and though newspapers were certain of Spanish complicity, the popular outrage needed further point. This Proctor provided in detail, and while describing in glowing terms the investment opportunities in Cuba, thereby arousing the business interests in the United States—hitherto nervous over the possibility of war with Spain—Proctor's primary stress was humanitarian, an appeal to Congress and the American people to relieve the horrors of Spanish oppression.

There were, Proctor declared, four hundred thousand innocent Cubans suffering and dying because of Weyler's inhuman strategy: "Torn from their homes, with foul earth, foul air, foul water, and foul food or none, what wonder that one-half have died and that one-quarter of the living are so diseased that they can not be saved." Children were to be seen with emaciated limbs and swollen stomachs, cases deemed hopeless by physicians; Cubans were "found dead about the markets in the morning, where they had crawled, hoping to get some stray bits of food" (Proctor 38). To this description of human misery, Proctor added "the spectacle of a million and half of people, the entire native population of Cuba, struggling for freedom and deliverance from the worst misgoverning of which I had ever had knowledge" (45–46). This struggle, to Proctor's mind, put forth a far greater appeal to the American people than did "the barbarity practiced by Weyler" or "the loss of the *Maine,* terrible as were both of these incidents" (45).

In his study of contemporary attitudes in the United States regarding the war in Cuba, Gerald Linderman gives especial emphasis to the impact of Senator Proctor's speech on the American public: "Never would Hearst's New York *Journal* match Proctor in witnessing to the profound horrors that Americans then decided were being inflicted on Cubans. There was in the practices of the Spaniard an evil to be obliterated, a sinfulness of which Americans too had to be absolved" (45). Later in his book, Linderman cites Davis's activities as a war correspondent in Cuba, but for whatever reason he ignores *Cuba in War Time* as influential on attitudes in America, even though the book (and the articles on which it was based) appeared a year before Proctor made his much cited speech, which in essence repeats Davis's evidence and argument throughout.

Indeed, it may have been Davis's call for a visit by a representative from Congress that spurred Proctor's trip, the reasons for which have never been clear. To a reporter's question at the time, Senator Proctor replied, "We are just going over there to see what's going on, to be where the excitement is" (Linderman 47). It was a motive perfectly in harmony with Davis's own impulse, as was Proctor's explanation for his visit in an interview given shortly before he died, in 1908: "The Maine had been blown up and I knew that something was very likely to follow. Boys love adventure and don't outgrow it as they become men" (54). This last observation is especially apt, given Davis's own reputed boyishness and the appeal of his writings to the perpetual boy in his male readers.

Then as now, travel abroad by members of Congress who propose to inform themselves on international situations was a questionable practice, hardly warranted by the legislative powers outlined in the Constitution; though Proctor paid for the trip out of his own pocket, there were those cynics among his contemporaries who felt it was a very good personal investment, and not only in terms of his political profile. The senator had a controlling interest in the Vermont marble industry, and it was jokingly proposed that when he urged the United States to declare war on Spanish Cuba, it was with the expectation that the demand for marble gravestones would soon rise. Linderman likewise devotes considerable space to sifting through other possible conflicts of interest, including a tentative business deal between Proctor and Russell A. Alger, McKinley's secretary of war and an outspoken war hawk, but ends by concluding that Proctor was undoubtedly sincere in his expressions of shock and outrage.

As for Richard Harding Davis, while his angry account of human suffering in Cuba was equally sincere, he too profited from the positive response to his and Proctor's call, which gave him the opportunity for which he had so long been waiting. Of the war correspondents whose reputations were made during the conflict that followed, RHD was surely the foremost. Given the emphasis by Linderman and others on Proctor's speech, the burden of which had been anticipated by Davis's coverage of the war in Cuba, it does seem as though the king of reporters had, like Kipling's volunteer monarch, helped himself to the crown.

: IV :

Though it was his coverage of the Spanish-American War that made him famous as a correspondent, it was not Davis's first experience under fire. Upon his return from Cuba in 1897, he had traveled to the Greco-Turkish border, where an invasion by Greek forces was under way, in support of the Macedonian uprising mentioned by MacWilliams in the closing pages of *Soldiers of Fortune.* The Greek action was territorial and hardly in "the name of Liberty," but it was a war, and with a pack of other reporters smelling the ink of battle from afar, Davis heeded the call that his hero Robert Clay had ignored. Among the Americans accompanying him was Stephen Crane, who would be able to report back that he had got it right in *Red Badge of Courage,* even though, as the headline to one of his news stories put it, the craven behavior of Crown Prince Constantine had made over the Greek flag into a "Blue Badge of Cowardice" (*War Dispatches* 33).

Davis did not much care for Crane on first acquaintance. On the boat they shared in crossing the Channel he snubbed Crane's mistress Cora Taylor for a frump with peroxided hair. Still, he certainly realized that the other man was a serious rival and admitted in a letter home that the author had a formidable talent. Davis chortled that he saw more of the key encounter between Greek and Turkish forces at Velestino than did Crane, who was down with a toothache, and a comparison of their finished accounts of the battle, written up from newspaper dispatches, not only reveals different styles but also suggests different purposes. Crane famously said that the Greco-Turkish War validated the battle scenes in his novel, and he seems to have been careful to describe what he saw in reminiscent terms. Because Davis had not earlier attempted to render warfare in fiction—the clash of arms in *Soldiers of Fortune* being an impromptu and short-lived affair—he had nothing to prove. His description of Velestino is thus less mannered than Crane's, though no less calculated.

Where Crane is sardonic throughout, Davis maintains the faintly jocular tone of his best travel writing. As always, he is alert for incidents that are striking because different from what might be expected, and his account of the battle begins with a description of the unlikely behavior of men who are already within the sound of artillery. The countryside around, as at Prevesa, under fire from Greek warships, was beautiful, so much so it seemed a stage set "for a pastoral play—perhaps a comic opera. . . . Against the glaring blue sky are the snow-topped mountains, and below the snow-line green pasturelands glowing with great blocks of purple furze and yellow butter-cups and waving wheat, that changes when the wind blows, and is swayed about like waves of smoke" (*Year* 210–11). Even as the bombardment of the city continued, in the countryside "the world went on much as it had be-fore—the sheep-bells tinkled from every hill-side, the soldiers picnicked under the shade of the trees" (212).

Adding to this unwarlike scene was the lack of discipline among the Greek soldiers, who, being perfect democrats, did not hesitate to argue with their officers over any order that displeased them. As Stephen Crane re-marked, tersely, "a certain part of the Greek nature, or rather the nature of certain Greeks, can in action make it clear to the Anglo-Saxon that he has another way of doing things" (*War Dispatches* 64). But Davis, for whom Anglo-Saxon attitudes were second nature, was perhaps more charmed than alarmed by the informal spirit that characterized the Greek army.

He told of riding out one day to the Greek camp on the ancient battle-ground of Actium, where he found an artillery regiment, two officers, and, in a solitary stone hut, a cable-operator:

> A merry sergeant explained that a correspondent had come all the way from America to describe their victories; and the regiment gathered out-side the stone hut and made comments and interrupted their officers and contradicted them, and the officers regarded the men kindly and with the most perfect good feeling. It was not the sort of discipline that obtains in other Continental armies, but it was probably attributable to the scenery—no colonel could be a martinet under such a sky. The cable-operator played for us on a guitar, and the major sang second in a rich bass voice, and the colonel opened tinned cans of caviare and Danish but-ter, and the army watched us eat with serious and hospitable satisfac-tion. . . . It reminded one of a camp of volunteers off for a week of sham-battles in the country." (213–14)

Again, this was hardly the high heroism of Greek epics, being more suited to Gilbert and Sullivan. Even on the march into hostile Turkish territory, "the soldiers carried themselves like boys off on a holiday, and, like boys, enjoyed it all the more because they were trespassing on forbidden ground" (215).

En route to what was supposed to be a great battle that day, Davis and the 10th Regiment of Infantry instead encountered refugees fleeing what had already been a Turkish victory. Soon after "we came in sight of long lines of men crawling into the valley from all sides, and looking no larger than tin soldiers against the high walls of the mountain" (218). It was a slow retreat and not a rout, but the road to Arta soon became a crowded mass of soldiers and civilians, mostly peasants who had brought their animals with them. This mob "jostled the soldiers for the right of way, which they shared with little donkeys, carrying rolls of tents and bedding, and women, who in this country come next after four-legged beasts of burden, staggering under great iron pots and iron-bound boxes. . . . And so for many hours the two armies of peasants and of soldiers panted and pushed and struggled towards the high narrow bridge that guards the way to Arta" (200–201).

The steep bottleneck at the bridge provided a scene that seemed to Davis symbolic of the entire conduct of the war, a tumultuous disorder that guaranteed the Greek army's defeat:

> It is such a bridge as Horatius with two others might have held against an army; it rises like a rainbow in the air, a great stone arch as steep as an inverted V. It is made of white stone, with high parapets. Into this narrow gorge cannon and ammunition wagons, goats and sheep, little girls carrying other little girls, mules loaded with muskets, mules hidden under packs of green fodder, officers struggling with terrified horses that threatened to leap with them over the parapet into the river below, peasants tugging at long strings of ponies, women bent to the earth, under pans and kettles, and company after company of weary and sweating soldiers pushed and struggled for hours together, while far out on either side hordes of the weaker brothers, who, leaving it to others to demonstrate the survival of the fittest, had dropped by the way-side, spread out like a great fan, but still from time to time feeding the bridge, until it stretched above the river like a human chain of men and beasts linked together in inextricable confusion. (221–22)

Beyond such tangled particulars demonstrating the inefficiency and waste of the Greek campaign, the overall conduct of the two armies, as Davis saw it, "was but little more complicated than two football teams when they are lined up for a scrimmage. When the game began, the Greeks had possession of the ball, and they rushed it into Turkish territory, where they lost it almost immediately on a fumble, and after that the Turks drove them rapidly down the field, going around their ends and breaking through their

centre very much as they pleased" (193). Davis may not have been trained in
military science, but he knew a one-sided match when he saw it.

The Greeks not only had the disadvantage of being outnumbered three
to one, but their lack of discipline further increased the odds in a contest
whose end was foreordained: "If an eleven from Princeton played three
elevens from Yale at the same time, one can see that the game would hardly
be interesting; and to carry out the simile still further, and then to drop it, it
was as though this Princeton eleven was untrained, and had no knowledge
of tricks nor of team-play, and absolutely no regard for its captain as a captain" (194). These figures of speech repeat the dominant metaphor in *Soldiers of Fortune,* suggesting once again the notion then prevalent in America
that warfare was the ultimate sport.

"From a distance it was like a game," wrote Stephen Crane, describing
the particulars of the battle at Velestino, which viewed from afar was a
bloodless, expressionless action, with "no horror to be seen" (30). Close up,
of course, in the Greek trenches, the gamelike quality disappeared, and
Crane was quite graphic in his descriptions of sudden death and grotesque
wounds. In his dispatch from the front, he described how amid a pitched
battle a "member of the Foreign [i.e., the Philhellenic] Legion came from
the left, wounded in the head. He was bandaged with magnificent clumsi-
ness with about nine yards of linen. I noticed a little silk English flag em-
broidered on his sleeve. He was very sad and said the battle was over. Most
wounded men conclude that the battle is over" (31). I don't mean to spend
much time comparing Crane's account of the war with Davis's, but the way
in which Crane later expanded his original account of the wounded soldier
is worth considering:

> On the lonely road from Velestino there appeared the figure of a man.
> He came slowly and with a certain patient steadiness. A great piece of
> white linen was wound under his jaw, and finally tied at the top of his
> head in a great knot like the one grandma ties when she remedies her
> boy's toothache. The man had a staff in his hand, and he used it during
> his slow walk. He was in the uniform of the Greek infantry, and his
> clothes were very dusty—so dusty that the little regimental number on
> his shoulder could hardly be seen. Under other circumstances one could
> have sworn that the man had great smears of red paint on his face. It was
> blood. It had to be blood; but then it was weirdly not like blood. It was
> dry, but it had dried crimson and brilliant. In fact, this hue upon his face
> was so unexpected in its luridness that one first had to gaze at this poor

fellow in astonishment. . . . Behind him was the noise of the battle, the
roar and rumble of an enormous factory. This was the product, not so
well finished as some, but sufficient to express the plan of the machine.
This wounded soldier explained the distant roar. He defined it. This—
this and worse—was what was going on. This explained the meaning of
all that racket. Gazing at this soldier with his awful face, one felt a new
respect for the din. (61–62)

I have omitted about half of Crane's lengthy description of the bloody
man, which bears comparison to the description of the wounded Jim
Conklin in *Red Badge* and seems a novelistic enlargement and revision of
the much simpler and terse description in his original dispatch. The extended version appears at the start of his account of the battle of Velestino
and places the encounter on the road between the battle and the port city of
Volo, toward which the wounded man is heading, a grim introduction to the
scenes that follow. It is certainly a stark contrast to the comic opera Davis encountered on the road he took from Prevesa to Arta, a lighthearted scene that
ended with the soldiers getting friendly with drink, "greeting old friends like
lost brothers, and unconscious of the shadow of war that hung over them,
and of the fact that the Turks were already far advancing on Greek soil, and
were threatening Pharsala, Velestinos, and Volo" (*Year* 223–24).

Where Crane approached the battle of Velestino along the road from
Volo, Davis places himself immediately in the trenches, with the Greek soldiers who are "panting and breathing heavily" in the terrific heat that followed after a hail storm, as "the heat-waves danced and quivered about
them, making the plain below flicker like a picture in a cinematograph"
(228).

Down in the plain below there was apparently nothing at which they
could shoot except the great shadows of clouds drifting across the vast
checker-board of green and yellow fields, and disappearing finally between the mountain-passes beyond. In some places there were square
dark patches that might have been bushes, and nearer to us than these
were long lines of fresh earth, from which steam seemed to be escaping
in little wisps. What impressed us most of what we could see of the battle
then was the remarkable number of cartridges the Greek soldiers wasted
in firing into space, and the fact that they had begun to fire at such long
range. . . . The cartridges reminded one of corn-cobs jumping out of a
corn-sheller, and it was interesting when the bolts were shot back to see
a hundred of them pop into the air at the same time, flashing in the sun

as though they were glad to have done their work and to get out again. They rolled by the dozens underfoot, and twinkled in the grass, and when one shifted his position in the narrow trench, or stretched his cramped legs, they tinkled musically. It was like wading in a gutter filled with thimbles. (229–30)

Aside from the contrast between Crane's surreal description of the wounded soldier as a product of a machine and Davis's interest in the army as a coordinated and wasteful process rather than a gathering of specific individuals, there is a common use of images with domestic implication, Crane's bandage recalling a boy with mumps, Davis's cartridges compared to corncobs and thimbles. Each man is governed by his own sense of style, but they share certain devices in common, used to promote contrasts for the sake of effect.

Likewise, for Davis the battle suddenly came alive when out of a house located below the Greek trenches there suddenly burst "a man in a fez . . . followed by many more."

The first man was waving a sword, and a peasant in petticoats ran to his side and pointed up with his hand at our trench. Until that moment the battle had lacked all human interest; we might have been watching a fight against the stars or the man in the moon, and in spite of the noise and clatter of the Greek rifles, and the ghostlike whispers and the rushing sounds in the air, there was nothing to remind us of any other battle of which we had heard or read. But we had seen pictures of officers waving swords, and we knew that the fez was the sign of the Turk—of the enemy— . . . who were at the moment planning to come up a steep hill on which we happened to be sitting and attack the people on top of it. And the spectacle at once became comprehensible, and took on the human interest it had lacked. (235–36)

It is typical of Davis to define what he is seeing in terms of art, of conventional depictions of sword-waving officers, much as the plain below flickers "like a picture in a cinematograph," in 1897 surely a novel figure in contrast to the chromos he seems to have in mind in describing the man with the sword.

As the battle continued, the wounded began the long trek back to Volo, another scene that did not bear out the heroic tradition of warfare. These were men who "did not wear their wounds with either pride or braggadocio, but regarded the wet sleeves and shapeless arms in a sort of wondering surprise. There was much more of surprise than of pain in their faces, and they seemed to be puzzling as to what they had done in the past to deserve such a punishment" (239–40). Davis saw other men being carried up from the trench and set down on the high grass, who lay there still and "utterly oblivious of the roar and rattle and the anxious energy around them that one grew rather afraid of them and of their superiority to their surroundings. . . . The dead gave dignity to what the other men were doing, and made it noble, and, from another point of view, quite senseless. For their dying had proved nothing" (240–41).

It was not only that their cause was worthless, cheapened by the perceived cowardice of their crown prince, but also that the determination of who died and who lived was nothing more than a matter of "mere dumb chance. There was no selection of the unfittest; it seemed to be ruled by unreasoning luck," a view of death in battle that comes as a shock to a reader habituated to Davis's chivalric attitudes:

> If a man happened to be standing in the line of a bullet he was killed and passed into eternity, leaving a wife and children, perhaps, to mourn him. "Father died," these children will say, "doing his duty." As a matter of fact, father died because he happened to stand up at the wrong moment, or because he turned to ask the man on his right for a match, instead of leaning towards the left, and he projected his bulk of two hundred pounds where a bullet, fired by a man who did not know him and who had not aimed at him, happened to want the right of way. One of the two had to give it, and as the bullet would not, the soldier had his heart torn out. The man who sat next to me happened to move to fill his cartridge box just as the bullet that wanted the space he had occupied passed over his bent shoulder; and so he was not killed, but will live for sixty years, perhaps, and will do much good or much evil. (242)

Perhaps because of the futility of the Greco-Turkish War, the outcome of which was predictable given the great odds, Davis here seems to be revising his attitude toward warfare. Now that he has actually encountered men in battle, he sees it less as a melodramatic conflict between forces representing good and evil—though certainly to his mind the Greeks were good and the Turks were evil—than as a game of chance: "Leaving out the fact that God ordered it all, the fortunes of the game of war seemed as capricious as matching pennies, and as impersonal as the wheel at Monte Carlo. In it the brave man did not win because he was brave, but because he was lucky" (243). There is certainly no vestige of romantic idealism here but rather something very close to Crane's own view of war, evincing the nihilism expressed by naturalist writers, for whom nobility and courage are empty words when held up against the bright glare of event.

The day of battle ended with a final ferocious attack by the Turks on the exhausted Greek soldiers, a cataclysmic explosion of rifle and artillery fire that provided Davis yet another opportunity to present the stupifying reality of modern warfare, which left no room for individual displays of courage, the sort of thing identified with the chivalric tradition.

> The Turks were so close on us that the first trench could do little to help itself, and the men huddled against it while their comrades on the surrounding hills fought for them, their volleys passing close above our heads, and meeting the rush of the Turkish bullets on the way, so that there was now one continuous whistling shriek, like the roar of the wind through the rigging of a ship in a storm. If a man had raised his arm above his head his hand would have been torn off. It had come up so suddenly that it was like two dogs springing at each others' [*sic*] throats, and in a greater degree it had something of the sound of two wild animals struggling for life. Volley answered volley as though with personal hate—one crashing in upon the roll of the other, or beating it out of recognition with the bursting roar of heavy cannon. At the same instant all of the Turkish batteries opened with great, ponderous, booming explosions, and the little mountain-guns barked and snarled and shrieked back at them, and the rifle volleys cracked and shot out blistering flames, while the air was filled with invisible express trains that shook and jarred it and crashed into one another bursting and shrieking and groaning. It seemed as though you were lying in a burning forest, with giant tree trunks that had withstood the storms of centuries crashing and falling around your ears, and sending up great showers of sparks and flame. This lasted for five minutes or less, and then the death-grip seemed to relax, the volleys came brokenly, like a man panting for breath, the bullets ceased to sound with the hiss of escaping steam, and rustled aimlessly by, and from hill-top to hill-top the officer's whistles sounded as though a sportsman were calling off his dogs. The Turks withdrew into the coming night, and the Greeks lay back, panting and sweating, and stared open-eyed at one another, like men who had looked for a moment into hell, and had come back to the world again. (253–55)

Whatever their differences in style and point of view, it can be said that both Stephen Crane and Richard Harding Davis found what they came looking for in the Greco-Turkish War, the first man seeking verification of the battle scenes in *The Red Badge of Courage,* the other a simpler errand, to see war firsthand. What Davis had expected to find he does not tell us, but what he found he renders in detail, and it was a phenomenon that was difficult to reconcile to the romantic worldview that distinguishes his fiction and not all that easy to accept on its own terms. The photographs he took at Velestino are necessarily limited to the battle seen from the trenches, the bent backs of soldiers firing down on the advancing lines of Turks, hardly a heroic posture.

Where in *Soldiers of Fortune* a certain confusion reigns during the pitched battle in Valencia, it is only momentary, and the forces of right soon gain the ascendancy, with Robert Clay emerging as the victorious hero and the corrupt General Mendez meeting an appropriate fate. But here, no heroic postures are possible, no champion emerges. The whole battle is a meaningless clash of faceless soldiers fighting in a chaotic mass of purposeless sound and fury. The disputed territory was, from a historical perspective, classic ground, but warfare was no longer a marble affair.

Although for once Davis did not say so, it was something similar to the Johnstown Flood, only here the raging forces were not expressions of nature out of control, they were expressions of regimented men and their machines of destruction on a vast and awesome scale. War, certainly, was like nothing to be found at the Chicago World's Fair, with its covert but elegant expressions of imperialism, never mind the playing fields of Yale or Princeton. For whatever it was that Dick Davis witnessed in Velestino, despite his initial allusion to the traditional game between Yale and Princeton, it was not football. He had yet to find his war, one that would validate *Soldiers of Fortune,* whereas Crane found in Turkey sufficient evidence that he had indeed got it right in *The Red Badge of Courage.*

There's glory!
LEWIS CARROLL

12 : THE LOOKING-GLASS WAR

: I :

After returning to the United States from Central America in 1895, Davis had read in the newspapers "that three British ships of war were anchored in the harbor of Corinto, with their guns loaded with ultimatums and no one knows what else besides, and that they meant to levy on the customs dues of that sunny little village" (*Three Gringos* 161). This gunboat diplomacy, known as the Hatch incident, was the result of the British demand for reparations in reaction to General Zelaya's having deported the British vice-proconsul. I have already noted that the Nicaraguan president, in anticipation of trouble with the British, gave a friendly interview to three young men he assumed might persuade the United States to cite the Monroe Doctrine on his behalf.

Apparently unaware of Zelaya's problems with the British at the time, Davis in recounting the news story ignored its relevance to the Nicaraguan president's generous views toward the United States. Instead, RHD emphasized the contrast between the warships and the placid and empty harbor he remembered, the news being "as much of a shock to me as it would be to the inhabitants of Sleepy Hollow were they told that the particular spot was wanted as a site for a World's Fair" (*Three Gringos* 161). Then, perhaps remembering the plot of his story about the reporter who had made himself king and thereby guaranteed the destruction of a Pacific island, Davis went on to imagine that "a whole comic opera could be written on the difficulties of a Nicaraguan acting as an English and American consul, with three British men-of-war in the harbor levying on the customs dues of his native land, and an American squadron hastening from Panama to see that their English cousins did not gather in a few islands by mistake" (166).

Davis at the time was writing *Soldiers of Fortune,* which though derived from his experience in Central America was not a comic opera. Nor did the complexities of the Nicaraguan situation lend themselves to a romance, the plots of which are best served by melodramatic oppositions, as in the confrontation between the stern but just American engineer and the corrupt Olanchoan general. It would be in *Captain Macklin* that Davis would come close to rendering the situation in Nicaragua in fiction, for as he explained in connection with the Hatch incident, such problems arise because of the financial entanglements between Central American governments and consular agents, who are of nationalities different from the countries they are supposed to represent, indeed chiefly look after the commercial interests of foreign firms.

Still, there is nothing comic about the situation in *Captain Macklin* either. Paradoxically, the comic-opera war Davis imagined late in 1895 was the one declared between the United States and Spain in 1898, though Davis, along with the other journalists covering the Spanish-American War and most of the American people, took the war very seriously, as did the soldiers who enlisted to fight the Spanish. Still, there were aspects of the conflict that Finley Peter Dunne made over into high comedy, especially Teddy Roosevelt's account of his contribution, and as time went on the ridiculousness of the war increasingly loomed large.

In 1931 the war's comic-opera aspect was amply displayed by Walter Millis, and although *The Martial Spirit* has been criticized by subsequent historians for sacrificing fact to satiric effect, it may be ranked with Henry Adams's history of the Jefferson administration as a more truthful account than mere facts would allow. Millis expressed the debunking spirit of his age by treating the American side of the war as an exercise in vainglorious bungling—in effect the opéra bouffe that Davis anticipated breaking out in Nicaragua—elements of which resembled the comedy of "The Reporter Who Made Himself King."

At the start the Cuban conflict was a war by cable, fomented by the Yellow Kid press, to which Richard Harding Davis made a definitive contribution with his stories about the victims of Spanish tyranny. At a higher level, expansionists on the order of Clarence King and Henry Cabot Lodge fired off learned broadsides in literary periodicals. Business interests, remembering what Cleveland's message about Venezuela did to the stock market, were nervous about declaring war until they realized the kinds of advantages listed by Senator Proctor in his argument for interference in Cuba. Even the American humor magazines *Life* and *Judge* began banging pots and pans in ferocious fashion.

As these pressures mounted, President McKinley declared a war for which his country was certainly prepared in terms of popular opinion but not at all ready where adequate supplies and experienced soldiers were concerned. The result was a tangle of logistical ineptitude and the release of untrained, poorly equipped troops into terrain for which they were un-prepared. The war would have been a national tragedy had not the Spanish army been worn down by years of futile fighting with Cuban guerrillas and its navy reduced to a sad lot of obsolete hulks thanks to a depleted Spanish treasury. If it turned out to be a splendid little war, nothing was owed to the McKinley administration.

Caught up in the enthusiasm, Davis early on wangled an army captain's commission, using his connection with Roosevelt, then assistant secretary of war. He soon resigned it, fearing that his assigned duties might keep him far from the action, where as a reporter he would be free to place himself in the front lines. Although no jingo, he was still a war lover, seeing a purpose in this conflict that had been lacking in the Greek invasion of Turkey. Be-cause he had from the start championed the U.S. presence in Cuba, he did not see the essential humor of the situation—that is, he did not get the joke as defined by Finley Peter Dunne's Mr. Dooley. Perhaps he realized that he was part of the problem, having done his part to hasten the war, but most likely he did not. As his most recent biographer, Arthur Lubow, has correctly stated, Davis is a classic case of the unexamined self. But then, unlike Dunne, Davis was not in Chicago but in Cuba and lacked the perspective available to those who were not in the midst of things.

At the start of the Cuban campaign Davis wrote no dispatches critical of the conduct of the war and censured other correspondents as unpatriotic for having done so. But as matters grew worse because of what he and oth-ers ascribed to government inaction, he described the problems hampering the U.S. forces, whether he was on a gunboat positioned off Cuba or sitting on a hotel porch in Tampa waiting for nothing to happen. Moreover, once the actual invasion was well under way, he shared the consternation of Theodore Roosevelt regarding the unhealthy conditions in the army hospi-tals and camps in Cuba. Later, as matters grew worse owing to what he re-garded as stupid and uninformed actions at the highest levels, he became increasingly angry about the situation and used his vantage point as a re-porter in the front lines to express his outrage.

Because he was where he wanted most to be, RHD's account of the war, published as *The Cuban and Porto Rican Campaigns,* saw matters almost lit-erally through the eyes of the invading army, meaning the officers and men who did the fighting at the front. His war stories do not lack humor, but it is the sardonic, acid-edged kind. If the suffering of the Cubans prior to the in-vasion was a result of an inhuman policy administered by General Weyler,

the terrible losses experienced by the American army after the invasion began were attributed to General William Shafter, who was in charge of the
operation. As for Theodore Roosevelt, portrayed by Dunne as a modern
miles gloriosus, Davis celebrated the young colonel as the true hero of the
war; indeed RHD was largely responsible for TR's subsequent and enduring
fame as the officer who led the charge at San Juan.

Davis's account of the invasion conveys the vast confusion that is any war
for persons too close to appreciate the broad view of strategists, precisely
the point of view that lent verisimilitude to *The Red Badge of Courage.* Thus,
as confusion resolved itself into blunder after blunder, like any soldier he
began to blame it on the general in charge of the operation, when in truth
the problem was lack of preparation because of the ill-considered hurry in
which the United States entered the war. Much as he had contributed to the
haste by the articles sent off to Hearst's *Journal* in 1897, so he contributed to
the confusion because of his reluctance to report the hard facts during the
early stages of the war. He then made matters only worse by generalizing in
print about the course of the war based on his very limited experience.

The result is an approximate fiction, to which his own presence was central. We can start with the coincidence that brought him along with the invading army to the harbor at Daiquirí that he had visited twelve years before
and had recently used as the setting for *Soldiers of Fortune.* Then too,
whereas Davis fills the traditional role of disinterested witness in so much of
his other reporting, as a war correspondent he often served as a participant
in the events he was covering. At last his image as a reporter merged with
that of Henry Stanley, who created the events about which he wrote and
who was the hero of the unfolding action as he described it. Because of his
novelistic impulse, Davis had a tendency to impose a romantic order on the
essential disorder of warfare.

In sum, it is difficult in RHD's account of the Spanish-American War to
distinguish between fact and fiction. Though it justified Davis's reputation
as a great correspondent, it brought together the realism of his reporting
and travel writing and the romantic discourse found in his fiction. Those
younger writers who gaped in admiration as Dick Davis strode out of the
jungle and into the Waldorf Astoria were no less confused on this point than
was Davis himself. What we have in RHD's account of the war, then, is a
work of literature that is virtually without genre, although it would serve as
the model for much subsequent war reporting, which whether by Ernie Pyle
or John Steinbeck sacrifices overview for anecdotal, "literary" episodes.

The best of Davis's Cuban reportage, like "The Death of Rodriguez," not only reads like fiction but borders on fiction as well, thanks to his skill at creating atmosphere and eliminating details detracting from the effect he hoped to achieve. We may assume that Davis was sincere in what he wrote but that he served, first, as a propagandist for the entry of the United States into the Cuban War and, second, as a celebrant of the American soldiers whose courage and daring he witnessed, likewise cannot be disputed.

It is important to insist on the facts, which has been ably done by any number of historians of the war, but it is equally important to insist on the fictions, which I am attempting to do. Again, it took a while for Davis to grasp the full implication of what was happening in Cuba, and the final published account of his experience, worked up from dispatches sent back to the United States from the front, is a progressive narrative of encounter. It is therefore best to follow Davis as he moved through the war, for although there were many other reporters in the field, who saw things from other and much different perspectives, of primary concern here is Davis's account of his own experience, the high point of which came when Colonel Roosevelt led the charge of the Rough Riders at San Juan.

: II :

Davis's writings, whether journalism or fiction, demonstrate both an abiding sense of the ridiculous and a strict moral purpose that together explain his repeated references to the works of Lewis Carroll. Likewise, RHD's account of the battles he witnessed during the Spanish-American War appears at times an artful Dodgson-like performance that mingles an awareness of the ineptitude of the American generals with a deep respect for the men who displayed such courage in carrying out orders that seemed at the time (and thereafter) as counterparts to the commands of the pack of cards that rule in Alice's Wonderland.

From the first days that Davis spent strolling the decks of the flagship *New York,* lying off the coast of Cuba, the war had an unreal and even absurd quality: "a peaceful blockade does not lend itself to [the] illusion . . . that we were really at war." The land of the enemy presented such "a peaceful panorama of mountain ranges and yellow villages, royal palms and tiny forts," that when the first prisoner of war was brought on board, he "was almost as much of a surprise to the ship as the ship was to him" (19).

Here at last was the face of the enemy, hitherto "hidden away somewhere along the smiling line of the coast." Seen up close, the man did not resemble the caricatures "in the comic papers," being "real and human" (20). The captive Spanish officer was very obliging, moreover, responding to all questions put to him. But when the prisoner discovered that the man interrogating him in his own language was Sylvester Scovel, a newspaper reporter so hated in Havana that there was a large reward on his head, the episode ended with one of those ironic reversals that are the stock-in-trade of the professional novelist: "It must be bewildering to find that you have been overwhelmed with courtesies by the man whose death, had he been your prisoner and you had killed him, would have brought you a reward . . . and a vote of thanks from your Government" (23).

Twists of plot aside, the episode is given meaning by the contrast between Captain Chadwick of the *New York* and reporter Scovel, for it was over the objections of the naval officer that the correspondent continued to question the Spaniard, who then proceeded "to give him the information which the blockading squadron desired"(21). The lessons at the start of *The Cuban and Porto Rican Campaigns* held pretty much throughout, that reality often takes the form of fictional formulas and that war correspondents often know more about the business at hand than do the senior officers in charge.

The brief war proved to be, as Stephen Crane observed of the battle of Velestino, "a good tight little fight," but by Davis's reckoning, derived from his experiences at the front, it could have been much better and a great deal tighter had the commanding general executed his responsibilities more capably (Crane 71). Again, whatever may have been General William Shafter's personal faults, and they were several, his conduct of the war was severely hampered by problems not of his creation. Here too Davis's penchant for romancing the war played a defining part, the general filling the role demanded by melodrama, if not the villain precisely, certainly the blustering ignoramus who hampers the hero.

Davis's hostility toward General William Shafter was at the time notorious, exacerbated by a heated argument between the reporter and the general at the start of the invasion. Davis objected in person to Shafter's order keeping reporters out of the boats filled with soldiers heading for the beach at Daiquirí, and when Shafter remained obdurate, Davis persisted, claiming that he was a cut above other journalists, being a historian, not a mere reporter. Such obstreperous questioning of orders is not the sort of thing an army general is used to, and Shafter abruptly dismissed Davis, declaring that he frankly didn't "care a damn what you are" (Lubow 172).

General Shafter, in short, was not as impressed by Davis's fame as was Davis, who, being as capable of arrogance and imperiousness as the other man, would return the insult in spades. Moreover, as Arthur Lubow emphasizes, Davis's antipathy was also a matter of aesthetics: Shafter had grown old in the service of his country and by 1898 was grossly overweight; he was clearly unsuited for active command, which was assigned him on the basis of political influence, not military qualifications. He was, however, superbly fitted for the part to which Davis assigned him, being a very model of a Gilbert and Sullivan modern major general.

Shafter was not Davis's idea of a general who could be taken seriously— that is, he was not Nelson A. Miles, the commander in chief of the entire operation, already famous for having put down the Sioux uprising at Wounded Knee and the Pullman strike in Chicago. Perhaps more to the point, Shafter was not Theodore Roosevelt: lean, youthful, dynamic, coura- geous, at home in the saddle, and at ease with his men. In effect, Roosevelt perfectly filled the role already prepared for him in Davis's fiction, especially the hero of *Soldiers of Fortune,* whose western background and ability to seize the moment he shared.

Roosevelt did not return the favor. In his brief posthumous tribute to RHD in 1916, Roosevelt noted that his only "intimate association" with Davis was "while he was with my regiment in Cuba": "He was indomitably cheer- ful under hardships and difficulties and entirely indifferent to his own per- sonal safety or comfort. He so won the esteem and regard of the regiment that he was one of the three men we made honorary members of the regi- ment's association. We gave him the same medal worn by our own mem- bers" (*R.H.D.* 55–56). Roosevelt's tribute reads more like a letter of recom- mendation than a funeral obsequy, not grudging, perhaps, but not eloquent either.

During their few social encounters previous to the Spanish-American War, Roosevelt had not been much impressed by Davis's "breeding," and in the private letter I referred to earlier, he once dismissed the reporter as "a cad" (Lubow 166–67). RHD's display of courage in Cuba and his Roosevelt- friendly account of the invasion may have somewhat tempered Teddy's low opinion, but a certain reservation seems still to have applied. Certainly, Davis was not subsequently honored by being admitted to Roosevelt's social circle, and when they parted after the attack on San Juan there were no op- portunities for a reunion, even though a decade later they both believed that the United States should come to France's aid in the First World War.

Davis's emphasis on Roosevelt's role in the invasion was not perhaps as great as readers like Finley Peter Dunne seemed to have thought at the time. Nonetheless, Davis's account of Roosevelt and his Rough Riders was enthu- siastic, and he gives it a central and climactic place in his book on the war in Cuba. But it gains much of its effect there from the contexts in which it is placed, for Davis followed a chronological account of his own adventures during the invasion. And since he accompanied the Rough Riders throughout, the sequence led up to the battle for San Juan, which he necessarily regarded as definitive in determining the American victory. Here, again, we have a tidiness of event approximating fiction.

Likewise, RHD's experience aboard the *New York* was informed by his initial encounter with the face of war, for the peaceful (and boring) prelude was followed by the bombardment of Matanzas, a relatively brief engagement but one famous in the newspapers. Davis declared that he found the quarter-hour cannonade from the *New York* "far more trying than all the Turkish shells had been at Velestinos, when they raced continuously overhead for the better part of two long, hot days . . . because the guns of your own side beat you about and deafened and blinded and shook you" (*Cuban . . . Campaigns* 34). While reminding his readers that he was now a seasoned war correspondent, Davis drew on his earlier experience to drive home the sudden shock that the bombardment produced on his sensibilities after so long a wait for action to commence.

Perhaps the most important point to be derived from RHD's brief tour aboard the *New York* was that the conduct of the U.S. Navy aroused in him the same admiration he had felt for the British army on Gibraltar: "The discipline of the New York was rigid, intelligent, and unremitting, and each of the five hundred men on this floating monastery moved in his little groove with the perfect mechanism of one of the eight-inch guns. A modern warship is the perfection of organization" (16). What he later encountered was by contrast a shambles of disorganization approximating anarchy, thanks to the ineptitude and ill-informed arbitrariness of General William Rufus Shafter. Again, Davis's reaction to the war, as in so much of his travel writing, was a matter of aesthetics: the rage for orderliness is essential to the imperial élan, but it has a literary coefficient as well.

Although he does not mention it in his book, Davis pulled strings to gain access to the decks of the *New York,* but that rare privilege was soon contested by correspondents who were denied it, with the result that he and other reporters were put ashore from the flagship by Admiral William Sampson to wait out the invasion in Tampa. The admiral's was a power that General Shafter came to wish he also had, especially after correspondents, Davis chief among them, sent home from Cuba regular dispatches critical of his command. If, as historians have observed, the Spanish-American War was the last U.S. operation in which correspondents were allowed to roam unimpeded about the battlefields, it was undoubtedly because of the negative stories that resulted. Such freedom was essential to Davis's desire to be where the action was, a desire intimate with his romantic nature; it may not have been in the best interests of the war effort, but it contributed to the vividness of his account of the war.

Although he held back his pen regarding the poorly organized and frequently stalled invasion preparations that he witnessed in Tampa, Davis mockingly called this boring interval "The Rocking-Chair Period," from the chairs placed along the great porch to the Tampa Bay Hotel, where reporters and army officers alike sat waiting for the long-delayed invasion to start. On May 1 Admiral George Dewey had sunk the Spanish fleet in Manilla Harbor, earning instant fame and even a brief political future, and Admiral William Sampson and Commodore Winfield Scott Schley were searching for the phantom squadron that had been sent to Cuba from Spain. But nothing was happening in Tampa to write about except that nothing was happening in Tampa, a situation reminiscent of what Davis had encountered in the no-longer-wild West.

It is a modern axiom that service in the army is a matter of hurrying up to wait, and the corps of reporters and officers had plenty of experience in that service. The hotel they were put up in was a suitable setting for the absurd situation, being the only considerable building in the very small village that made up the Port of Tampa. It was one of those grandiose structures associated with a world's fair under construction or a real estate boom that has collapsed, "a giant affair of ornamental brick and silver minarets in a city chiefly composed of derelict wooden houses drifting in an ocean of sand" (46). The hotel was "larger than the palaces which Ismail Pasha built overnight at Cairo, and outwardly not unlike them in appearance, and so enormous that the walk from the rotunda to the dining-room helps one to an appetite," and when they were not rocking, talking, and drinking iced tea, Davis and his friends did a lot of walking (49).

At first the prolonged wait had its good moments, providing the opportunity for reunions by army officers who had not seen each other since they were together at West Point, "men who had fought together and against each other in the last war." They had been scattered ever since in isolated garrisons over the wide spaces of the Far West but were now "gathered together apparently for an instant onslaught on a common enemy, and were left to dangle and dawdle under electric lights and silver minarets" (50). Davis did not make much of the geopolitical implications of this gathering, heralded elsewhere as having reunited Confederate and Union veterans by facing them with a "common enemy" in Cuba, a theme several times repeated in Theodore Roosevelt's meditations on the war in *The Strenuous Life*.

But then Davis's interests were seldom those of the man he helped make famous, his admiration being limited to the young colonel's boundless energy and courage. Whereas Roosevelt was invariably ideology in motion, Davis's notion of heroism was idealism in action and had little to do with realpolitik. This does not deny the other his measure of gallantry, but Roosevelt's display of manhood in Cuba was thoroughly in syncronization with Mahan's worldview, while Davis admired it as a selfless exhibition of personal courage.

Gradually life in Tampa took on the air of a summer holiday, given interest by the stories told by young reporters and officers who had been gathered "from every part of the country and from every part of the world." They were the kinds of tales that Davis equated with explorers such as William Chanler and reporters like Stephen Bonsal, both of whom were in Tampa. Chanler had earlier seen service running guns to the insurgents (not mentioned by Davis) and to get into the fight had obtained a commission in Gómez's army. When Davis met him, "Willie" was "in the uniform of a Cuban colonel, from which rank he was later promoted to that of captain in our own Volunteer Army" (a "promotion" worth pondering) (53).

As for Bonsal, Davis's ideal correspondent was "just back from Siam" and "discoursed on sacred elephants and white ants." Also present and accounted for was "Lieutenant Rowan, just back from six weeks with Garcia," Rowan being the young naval officer who would be celebrated by Elbert Hubbard for having carried a message from President McKinley to that Cuban general. Among the other journalists was "Grover Flint, who had been 'marching with Gomez'" and who, like Rowan, had stories to tell of life in insurgent camps (53).

Along with this group of courageous young men who had already earned a measure of fame by their activities in wartime Cuba, there was a roster of visiting civilians that reads like a gathering at Jay Gatsby's mansion, which the Tampa hotel resembled: "There were also General O. O. Howard and Ira Sankey, who busied about in the heat, preaching and singing to the soldiers; Miss Clara Barton, of her own unofficial Red Cross Army; Mr. George Kennan and Mr. Poultney Bigelow, who had views to exchange on Russia and why they left it, and General Fitzhugh Lee, looking like a genial Santa Claus, with a glad smile and glad greeting for everyone, even at his risk of becoming Vice-President in consequence" (55).

Of literary as well as sectional interest, "there was also General 'Joe'

Wheeler, the best type of courteous Southern gentleman, the sort of whom [Thomas Nelson] Page tells us in his novels, on whom politics had left no mark, who was courteous because he could not help being so, who stood up when a second lieutenant was introduced to him, and who ran as lightly as a boy to help a woman move a chair, or to assist her to step from a carriage" (55–56). General Joseph "Fighting Joe" Wheeler was probably the most senior and famous of the Confederate officer veterans who were reunited with their former Union opponents in Tampa. He had been paired by Robert E. Lee with J. E. B. Stuart as his two most effective leaders of cavalry.

As a congressman after the Civil War, Wheeler had devoted himself to low tariffs and reconciliation between the North and the South, and though President McKinley disagreed with Wheeler on the tariff question, he certainly chose a suitable commanding officer if the impending conflict was to bind the wounds (as the phrase went) of a nation. In 1898 Wheeler was in his early sixties but because of his white hair and beard appeared older, and because of illness he did not serve an active part during the attack on San Juan. Although RHD accorded General Wheeler respect as a type and symbol of the Old South, once the warriors left the hotel piazza, he was less laudatory, and "Fighting Joe" did not emerge from Davis's account of the war as a modern equivalent of Hawthorne's Grey Champion.

Given the direction Davis's narrative would take, of note is his first description of Colonel Roosevelt, who, with his "energy and brains and enthusiasm enough to inspire a whole regiment," was more at home on a horse than in a rocking chair, though there were those who at the time thought a rocking horse was the most likely mount (56). Davis also gave Frederic Remington a polite nod, as one of "the two men of greatest interest to the army of the rocking-chairs," because of his fame as a painter and illustrator, but he gave most of his attention to the other of the two, "Great Britain's representative with our army, Captain Arthur H. Lee." Remington was, as Davis noted, "an old story," but Lee was not, being both "the new friend and the actual sign of the new alliance" between Great Britain and the United States (56). He was also type and symbol of that side of the British character Davis most admired, the side that carried a sword.

The recent rapprochement between the old rivals was a diplomatic maneuver designed to forestall entry into the war by the Great Powers on the side of Spain. It was therefore a much more important reunion for champions of an expanded American empire than was that between the North and the South, but Davis was chiefly interested in the personality of the man who was in Cuba as a representative of British empire: "There was no one, from the generals to the enlisted men, who did not like Lee. I know many Englishmen, but I know very few who could have won the peaceful victory this young captain of artillery won; who would have known so well just what to see and to praise—and when to keep his eyes and mouth shut. No other Englishmen certainly could have told American stories as well as he did and not have missed the point" (56–57). It is always amusing to view Davis confronting a representative of the English nation under favorable circumstances, as it permits the full exercise of his Anglophilia, with the usual mild humor at the Englishman's expense. But we may take him at his word that there was no one who didn't like Arthur Lee.

Still, Davis's admiration extended itself wide and generously over the group of adventurers and correspondents gathered at the hotel, men who knew the amours of every consul along the coasts of both the Malay Peninsula and East Africa, who had "been chased by elephants and had shot rinoceri," and who had been fired upon themselves "in Corea . . . in Egypt . . . in Cuba, and . . . in Thessaly. One of them had taken six hundred men straight across Africa, from coast to coast; another had explored it for a year and a half without meeting a white man. . . . There was one who had been to school with an emperor, and another who had seen an empress beheaded" (58). Davis reckoned that their stories, had they been permitted to continue, would have amounted to a new *Thousand and One Nights,* but the war was what these men had come to Tampa for, and when the invasion began, the stories stopped or were augmented by ensuing events.

Although Davis's impatience for the action to begin was as great as anyone's, his excitement over finding himself in such company made waiting much easier. After all, these men with whom he sat rocking and drinking iced tea filled the heroic roles which RHD had been celebrating in his fiction and which he sought to emulate in his own life. They were equivalents to those fearless gentlemen to whom Kipling had paid tribute in the dedicatory poem to *Barrack Room Ballads,* only they were gathered together in Tampa not for eternity but for one marvelous moment. They made up an impromptu version of those private clubs which always appealed to Davis's social sensibilities, an aggregate and therefore intense example of the "interesting," his invariable ideal for companionship.

Even though he modestly presented himself as merely an admiring auditor of the stories being told on the hotel porch, Davis was nonetheless included in that company, and most of his readers would recognize the kinship. For had RHD not covered the Johnstown Flood, the coronation of the czar, and the pursuit of a Mexican renegade in Texas; stood in the thundering trenches at Velestino; and interviewed presidents and potentates in Central and South America? Did he not have stories of his own to tell? And did he not borrow further glory from that band of adventurers, gilt as it were by association?

Although RHD was attracted to this elite gathering, as a reporter he had sense enough to pay some attention to the enlisted troops bivouacked four miles beyond the hotel. The army was made up of volunteers and regulars, and of the two Davis found the former the most "interesting" because as "amateurs" they reacted to everything they saw with amazement and wonder. The regulars regarded departure from home as routine, but for the volunteers it was new and meant the pain of farewell to loved ones and the agony of a prolonged separation. But when it came to the serious business of military spirit and discipline, Davis gave the laurels to the regular army, "as fine looking a body of soldiers as can be seen in any of the Continental regiments" (79).

These qualities were best displayed during cavalry maneuvers, for American troopers are as home in the saddle "as a cowboy, or a cockswain in a racing-shell," a split analogy that needs to be kept in mind, given the makeup of the celebrated Rough Riders. For the benefit of his readers, Davis rendered an account of one such maneuver, displaying not only the troopers' skill at horsemanship but also his own skill at describing it:

It was a wonderful sight to see two thousand of these men advancing through the palmettoes, the red and white guidons fluttering at the fore, and the horses sweeping onward in a succession of waves, as though they were being driven forward by the wind. It will always puzzle me to know what the American people found to occupy them that was of such importance as to keep them from coming to see their own army, no matter how small it was, while it was rehearsing and drilling among the pines and palms of Florida. There will be few such chances again to see a brigade of cavalry advancing through a forest of palms in a line two miles long, and breaking up into skirmishes and Cossack outposts, with one troop at a trot and another at a walk, and others tearing, cheering through the undergrowth, their steel swords flashing over their heads and the steel horse-shoes flashing underfoot. It was a fine spectacle, and it was due to such occasional spectacles in and around the camps that the rocking-chair life was rendered bearable. (83)

Whatever Davis's intention—it seems to me that his second sentence delivers the punch—this paragraph contains an underlying and unintended irony. His description of cavalry maneuvers is graphic but essentially irrelevant to the campaign in Cuba, for not only was there insufficient room on the transports for the army's horses, but as Davis and the rest discovered, the terrain they were to move through on the trail to Santiago allowed no room for cavalry maneuvers. The only mounted cavalryman in the famous rush to gain the heights at San Juan was Colonel Roosevelt, who was privileged to bring his own two horses with him.

Thus, the most meaningful charge during the layover in Tampa was that of the officers and correspondents when the arrival of the "commander in chief," General Nelson Miles, signaled the departure of the invading army for Cuba, a scramble that, unlike the cavalry demonstration, was without order or plan. As Davis noted, though everyone was in a "desperate hurry" to depart, "we had no idea where we were going, nor for how long. No secret, be it said to the credit of the censor and the staff officers, was ever better kept; but we knew, at last, that we were going, and that was the joy, and the tears and rage of those who were to be left behind was a fine thing to see" (84). Instead of information, the invasion party had rumors, based on overheard conversations between staff officers, which served to cancel one another out, so that "no one knew up to the hour when we were ordered on board" where the invasion would take place (85).

This was not, as Davis and the others involved would soon learn, the first time that communications would be imperfect between those who were supposed to give the orders and those who were charged with the responsibility for carrying them out. Even the departure, after the initial hurried abandonment of the hotel, was a disappointment in terms of high drama, the actual sailing of the transports having been announced and then delayed so often that when the fleet finally left the harbor, the "popular interest" in its departure was represented by "three colored women and a pathetic group of perspiring stevedores" on the dock.

: III :

For a correspondent seeking copy, the invasion fleet itself was another disappointment, for though the number of transports and escorting warships might have suggested "the Spanish Armada . . . a great flotilla, grim, sinister, and menacing, fighting its way through the waves on its errand of vengeance and conquest," the reality was quite different: "as a matter of fact the expedition bore a most distinct air of the commonplace" (89). As I have suggested, Davis was skilled at making a story out of the lack of a story, and his account of the invasion as seen through a porthole makes much of nothing much, noting that the fleet moved unimpeded by adverse weather or the enemy: "a sea as smooth as a lake, undisturbed by Spanish cruisers or by shells from Spanish forts" (59).

Though leisurely, the progress of the fleet was hardly enjoyable, and Davis's desire to arrive in Cuba was further frustrated by the frequent halts made by the flotilla, owing in part to "the fact that two of the steamers were each towing a great scow or lighter, on which the troops were to be conveyed to shore" (90). The transports drifted apart and moved in careless and unmilitary disorder, so that their naval escort served as a kind of shepherd dog, officers barking commands through megaphones as they attempted to round up strays. Once again, the navy put on the sort of display that Davis admired, the gunboats being "so workmanlike and clean, and the men . . . so smart in their white duck" (91).

Davis and the other correspondents were assigned to the headquarters vessel, like all the transports a passenger steamship that had been stripped of its comforts and supplied with water that "smelled like a frog-pond or a stable-yard" (94). The food provided for the officers and correspondents by the profiteering steamship line was equally bad, far inferior to the "good beans, corned beef, and coffee" given the enlisted troops by the government (96). Strung out to the horizon and beyond, the ships of the flotilla kept all their lights burning at night and made the observer "think he was entering a harbor, or leaving one," but it was the lights that finally warranted a comparison to the Spanish Armada, for when after three days the ships reached the Cuban coast, they discovered that the lighthouses had been put out at night, which not only meant that the invasion squadron had been sighted but also showed "that the lesson of the Armada has not been lost on the Spaniard" (96).

And yet, though forewarned, the Spanish did not send out even a single torpedo boat, which could with ease have sunk several ships as they lumbered along. The luck of the U.S. Army in this matter, reckoned Davis, surely outranked that of its British counterpart, of which "Mr. Kipling boasts," and though the fleet at night was illuminated as brightly "as Brooklyn or New York, with the lights of the Bridge included," the Spanish chose to let slide this advantage, otherwise they could have "given us a loss to remember even greater than that of the *Maine*." The fleet's slow, halting, irregular, and well-lit progress was accompanied by "bands banging out rag-time music," a final measure of ridiculousness that gave a music-hall dimension to the operation (98).

Davis put the best face possible on the invasion as "a most happy-go-lucky expedition, run with real American optimism and readiness to take big chances, and with the spirit of a people who recklessly trust that it will come out all right in the end, and that the barely possible may not happen, that the joker may not turn up to spoil the hand, who risk grade crossings and all that they imply, who race transatlantic steamers through a fog for the sake of a record" (98–100). And yet he could not help but think that though it was entirely in keeping with the boisterous and optimistic American character, "our army's greatest invasion of a foreign land was completely successful . . . chiefly . . . because the Lord looks after his own."

Once the Cuban shore had been reached, there was not one but two "first" landings of the army of invasion, both preceded by another when the marines had seized Guantánamo Bay and raised an American flag over the island. This triplication approximated the three places "where Columbus is said to have landed," with a similar confusion as to the spot "where the American troops first landed when they came to drive the Spaniard across the sea and to establish the republic of Cuba" (100). Aside from the humor derived from the untidiness of the operation, it is this last emphasis that gives the necessary point to what was happening. Six years after the anniversary of the arrival of Columbus, the U.S. forces were about to relieve Cuba of the oppressive Spanish presence, not in the name of conquest and annexation but with the aim of creating a free republic. Thus, among the first party ashore were not only General Shafter and Admiral Sampson and their subordinates, along with the attachés of foreign countries and the correspondents there to record the event, but "General Castillo, of the Cuban Army" (103).

The landing provided Davis and his fellow correspondents their first opportunity to encounter "the Cuban revolutionists in the field," which he had sought in vain in 1897. What "impressed us most favorably was the appearance of the officers. They were fine-looking, young gentlemen, well, and even smartly uniformed, and with the bearing and assurance of officers and of men accustomed to command." Admittedly, "their soldiers were ragged and half-starved, and inadequately armed, but they obeyed the few commands we heard given them correctly, and showed a rudimentary grasp of company drill and discipline. They spent the time given to the conference in studying the new-comers with cheerful curiosity, but their officers went on about their duties without wasting their time on men who did not for the moment concern them" (111–12).

Despite this initial reaction, Davis would soon share the disappointment of the officers and men in the invading army concerning the value of the Cuban insurgents to their operation. In contrast to the stories they had read in the Yellow Kid press about the courage and initiative of the Cuban fighters, the Americans encountered what they regarded as a tatterdemalion bunch of undisciplined partisans, unequal to the highly organized warfare the situation demanded. Davis himself, during his account of the fighting that followed, has very little to say about the Cuban army, which may be ascribed to courtesy but which in effect makes the insurgents as invisible as the frustrated American officers found them, which means they seldom found them when they were most needed.

Though RHD does not emphasize the Americans' disillusionment, it was very real and was the result of misunderstandings that arose in part from the leading role previously played by the Cuban rebels and that subordinate place which the U.S. forces expected they would willingly assume. Recent studies of the war have argued that the relatively easy victory of the Americans was largely due to the long struggle waged by the Cuban rebels, which had demoralized the Spanish army, where Davis credits it to the sudden departure of Cervera's fleet from Santiago, which removed the city's chief means of defense. We may allow both contributions to the victory over Spain, but Davis's observations, which gave no credit to the Cubans, reflected the attitude of the American army at the time.

Davis's portrait of General Calixto García, who met with General Shafter and Admiral Sampson soon after the "powers" landed, is nonetheless moving and worth repeating, if only to balance his subsequent account of the Cuban officers he met in the field: García was dressed "in a slouch hat and linen uniform, with high military boots," and Davis found him "a handsome man, with a white mustache and goatee. . . . In his forehead, between the snow-white eyebrows, is a deep bullet wound, which shows where he tried to kill himself when, ten years ago, he was a prisoner in the hands of the Spaniards. It had been a long, hard, and desperate struggle for the white-haired old soldier, and as he sat at last in his own camp, with the Admiral of the Atlantic Squadron on his right and the American General on his left, he must have thought that at last his reward had come" (107–8). Davis's arrangement is certainly symbolic, and the Cuban hero would soon discover that the powerful men sitting next to him were not so much his supporters as his supplanters, that in subsequent pictures of the "powers," as

Davis called them, the central figure in the trinity would become wholly a ghost.

During the conference, "while the great men talked under the palm-trees, the Americans and the Cubans made each other's acquaintance, and the blue-jackets mixed with the barefooted soldiers, and the two attachés made snap-shot photographs for the education of the British and German armies. Their presence with the invading army filled the officers of the Cuban Army with an idea that their struggle for liberty was stirring the nations of the world" (108–11). Davis himself seems to have carried along his usual camera, for the book is filled with photographic illustrations and with line drawings taken from photos credited to him, and we are given a picture of García standing next to General Shafter, with a shadowy group of Cuban soldiers in white linen uniforms and sombreros in the background.

Behind them a stand of trees is visible, and for all intents and purposes it would be back into those trees that General García and his barefoot soldiers would fade until entirely absorbed by the landscape, described by Davis as "painted in high lights" and with "no shading," being "all brilliant, gorgeous, and glaring" (108). Because for future generations of Americans General Calixto García would be famous not for his acts of courage in bringing freedom to the Cuban people but as an equivalent Livingstone, buried in the "mountain fastnesses of Cuba," where the indomitable Lieutenant Andrew Rowan would find him. Rowan, through the agency of Elbert Hubbard, became the type and symbol of American get-up-and-go, disappearing into the jungle on one side of the island and not reappearing on the other side until McKinley's message to the furtive general had been delivered, while García remained in the Cuban mountains forever.

For Elbert Hubbard and the millions of readers his booklet reached over the long years ahead, "in all this Cuban business there is one man who stands out on the horizon of my memory like Mars at perihelion. . . . Civilization is one long anxious search for just such individuals. Anything such a man asks shall be granted. His kind is so rare that no employer can afford to let him go. He is wanted in every city, town and village—in every office, shop, store and factory. The world cries out for such; he is needed, and needed badly—the man who can carry a message to Garcia" (Hubbard 254–58).

Hubbard's essay was published in 1899, a year after Davis's book on the Cuban war appeared. But aside from Hubbard's Rotarian notion of valor, his recipe for American initiative, with its debased Emersonian formula, does not differ much from the general outlines of the man who emerged from

In Davis's photograph Shafter's bulk looms large next to the Cuban general, who bears the scar of his self-inflicted gunshot wound, a deep indentation between the eyes. From The Cuban and Porto Rican Campaigns.

Davis's account of the war as the hero of the Cuban campaign. For if there was one man who for Davis stood out in full relief on the horizon of the "Cuban business," it was not Lieutenant Rowan but the young colonel on horseback who led the charge at San Juan.

But before Roosevelt could have his defining moment, the troops had to debark from the transports and be organized for the march to Santiago. This all took place at Daiquirí, where Davis had come ashore twelve years earlier on his visit with William Thurston, at a point in U.S. military history where amphibious operations were as yet infrequent, awkward, and dangerous even without facing enemy fire. The familiar Higgins landing craft of World War II were a half century in the future, and in Cuba in 1898 and other hot spots in the Caribbean thereafter, American soldiers and marines were put ashore from deep-draft longboats, into which they "tumbled from the gang-way ladder" and from which they had to leap overboard and then wade through the surf to the shore.

At Daiquirí there was a pier constructed to provide mooring for Thurston's iron ore ships. Designed for that function, it stood well out of the water, so that it could only be used to land troops at high tide, and then by having the men leap up as the boat rose on a wave and clamber onto what remained loose planks for the duration of the landing. During this maneu-ver the "heaving boats . . . dropped from beneath them like a descending elevator or rose suddenly and threw them on their knees. It was much more dangerous than anyone imagined, for later in the day when two men . . . were upset at the pier, the weight of the heavy cartridge-belt and haversack and blanket-roll carried them to the bottom" (116). These hazards, along with the probability of Spanish resistance to the landing, were what Gen-eral Shafter had in mind when he forbade Davis and other reporters from accompanying the boats ashore, but RHD found no room in his account of the landing for that skirmish of egos.

His point of view, however, was clearly limited to what he could see aboard the *Segurança,* which was Shafter's floating command post: The blue water was dotted with "rows of white boats filled with men bound about with white blanket-rolls and with muskets at all angles, and as they rose and fell on the water and the newspaper yachts and transports crept in closer and closer, the scene was strangely suggestive of a boat-race, and one almost waited for the starting gun" (116). The yachts hired by the American press certainly added the proper sporting note, so often for Davis the defin-ing image, but the seriousness of the scene was emphasized when the gun-boats opened fire on the shore.

Once again, there was no response from the Spanish forces, so that the landing, though a confused and noisy matter, was unopposed save for the difficulties imposed by circumstances, which in no way dampened the fighting spirit of the soldiers. No sooner had the first boats "driven through the surf to the beach itself, and the men tumbled out and scrambled to their feet upon the shore of Cuba," than the men on the transports (including Davis) heard a faint cheer rising from the shore, which was picked up by the sailors on the warships. "It was caught up by every ship in the transport fleet, and was carried for miles over the ocean," so that "the combined cheering seemed as though it must surely reach to the walls of Santiago and tell them the enemy that the end was near" (118–19).

An even louder shout went up at a later moment when, "outlined against the sky, we saw four tiny figures scaling the sheer face of the mountain up the narrow trail to the highest block-house." The fort was empty of Spanish soldiers but was significant nonetheless, when "thousands of feet above the shore the American flag was thrown out against the sky, and the sailors on the men-of-war, the Cubans, and our own soldiers in the village, the soldiers in the long-boats, and those still hanging to the sides and ratlines of the troop-ships, shouted and cheered again, and every steam-whistle on the ocean for miles about shrieked and tooted and roared in a pandemonium of delight and pride and triumph" (119). In reading about this exploit, the modern reader of a certain age is unavoidably reminded of the moment, less than fifty years later, when an equivalent group of American soldiers scaled Mount Suribachi on Iwo Jima and planted a flag on the height. That accomplishment also served to rouse the spirits of the invading forces, but in 1898 as in 1945, the contest was a long way from being won.

In 1898 two deadly land battles lay ahead, for if the blockhouse on the shore had been abandoned, it was because of a tactical withdrawal by Spanish forces, who sought to defend Santiago as the obvious target of the invading army. As Davis noted wryly, that city had been chosen because it was there Admiral Cervera lay with his fleet, unwilling to venture forth and do battle with Admiral Sampson, nor was Sampson willing to enter the harbor, which had been mined in anticipation of his arrival. Lieutenant Richmond Hobson had been sent with a skeleton crew aboard the collier *Merrimac* into the narrow neck of the harbor, where he sank his brief command with the intention of bottling up Cervera's fleet. But the effort, though widely heralded as an example of American courage, was only partly successful, the hulk having sunk at a sideways angle and not completely across the channel. Eventually celebrated as a hero, for the time being Lieutenant Hobson, along with his men, languished in a Spanish dungeon.

In the meantime a stalemate arose between General Shafter and Admiral Sampson, both unwilling to sacrifice their men in an operation the burden of which each thought the other should carry. In the end, it was the value of the new battleships that had been built for just such an occasion that determined the course of the war, and over his objections Shafter's army was sent unsupported by Sampson's guns against Santiago de Cuba. As Davis noted, "the reason for sending an army to Santiago was a somewhat peculiar one," for where warships traditionally prepare the way for an invading army, "this is probably the only instance when a fleet has called upon an army to capture another fleet" (121). But before this action could be fully carried out, indeed at the moment the American troops seemed to be fading under withering Spanish fire, the ships in Cervera's creaking flotilla obligingly sailed out of the harbor, one by one, providing an equivalent shooting gallery for the American warships. But this great naval victory was still weeks away and took place long after the invading army had reached the heights over Santiago.

From the start, things took longer than the conventional notion of heroic warfare allowed. Having come ashore at Daiquirí, the American soldiers did not immediately march off to meet the foe but had to wait for a subsequent landing at Siboney, which took place at night, the darkness illuminated by a full moon and searchlights from the fleet, that lit up the beach like "a ballroom" (136). The soldiers at Daiquirí were marched to the Siboney beachhead, and all through the night the troops behaved in a manner reminiscent of the Greek soldiers as they entered Turkey:

It was one of the most weird and remarkable scenes of the war, probably of any war. An army was being landed on an enemy's coast at the dead of night, but with somewhat more of cheers and shrieks of laughter than rise from the bathers in the surf at Coney Island on a hot Sunday. It was a pandemonium of noises. The men still to be landed from . . . the transports, were singing in chorus, the men already on shore were dancing naked around the camp-fires on the beach, or shouting with delight as they plunged into the first bath that had offered in seven days, and those in the launches as they were pitched head-first at the soil of Cuba, signalized their arrival by howls of triumph. On either side rose black overhanging ridges, in the lowland between were white tents and burning fires, and from the ocean came the blazing, dazzling eyes of the search-lights shaming the quiet moonlight. (137–38)

In the midst of this the Rough Riders "were cooking their coffee and bacon," diverted by the constant passage through their camp of the Cuban officers, whose headquarters lay beyond, their "half-starved ponies scattering the ashes of the camp-fires, and galloping over the tired bodies of the men with that courtly grace and consideration for Americans which invariably marks the Cuban gentleman" (136–37). This revision by Davis of his initial estimate of the insurgent army will be on ongoing process, in keeping with the changing attitude of the U.S. forces.

Once Davis managed to get ashore, he sought out Roosevelt, perhaps because of their previous acquaintance but also because the colorful young colonel stood out from the other officers while in Tampa. Davis knew good copy when he saw it. The Rough Riders were the first to leave the camp, at five in the morning, after only several hours of sleep, but save for a few officers, mounted riders they were not, although the road ahead was certainly rough. Little more than a trail, it cut through impenetrable brush, which rose up so high on both sides as to block the view in all directions for men on foot, forcing the soldiers to march in single file, preceded by two Cubans serving as scouts.

As Arthur Lubow has explained, Davis was experiencing frequent attacks of sciatica, which would plague him throughout the Cuban campaign, and had been given a horse, which put in him on a par with Colonel Roosevelt. The added height allowed for an expanded perspective: "It was not unlike a hunting excursion in the West; the scenery was beautiful and the view down the valley one of luxuriant peace." As a man familiar with the Cuban flora and fauna, Davis served as an informal guide to Roosevelt, who observed that "it looked like a good deer country," whereas for Davis it seemed more like "the trail across Honduras." Despite their contrasting because limited view, the mood of the dismounted Rough Riders remained cheerful, and all agreed "it was impossible to appreciate that we were really at war—that we were in the enemy's country" (140). Soon enough, however, the Americans were confronted by the grim reality of their situation.

The men were halted in about an hour by Colonel Leonard Wood, to whom Roosevelt had surrendered command of the Rough Riders because of the other man's military training. While they rested, Wood and another officer disappeared down the trail to verify a report by the Cuban scouts that the Spaniards were waiting for them at a place called La Guásimas. Returning, Wood deployed his troops in a skirmish line, just as the entrenched Spanish opened fire, but any attempt to spread out in response to the attack was futile: "It was like forcing the walls of a maze" (143).

The Rough Riders were both pinned down and boxed in, and the Spanish not only had the tactical advantage of occupying a height but used smokeless powder, which rendered them invisible: "It was an exceedingly hot corner. The whole troop was gathered in the little open place blocked by the network of grape-vines and tangled bushes before it" (145). Men began to fall, wounded and killed, and efforts by Colonel Wood to deploy his troops in more effective positions were hampered by the terrain: "The men were at times wholly hidden from each other, and from him; probably at no one time did he see more than two of his troops together. It as only by the firing that he could tell where his men lay, and that they were always steadily advancing" (149).

The advance was halting, "made in quick, desperate rushes," and Davis again used the inevitable sports analogy: "Sometimes the ground gained was no more than a man covers in sliding for a base." But the discipline held, and those "prophets of evil" who in the comfort of the Tampa Bay Hotel had predicted that Roosevelt's cowboys "would shoot as they chose, and . . . act independently of their officers" were proven wrong: "As it turned out, the cowboys were the very men who waited most patiently for the officers to give the word of command" (149).

Davis also noted that the cowboys demonstrated the advantages of having "hunted big game in the West," for where the college boys on given the order to advance did so in a rush, "like men trying to get out of the rain, and fell panting on their faces . . . the Western trappers and hunters slipped and wriggled through the grass like Indians; dodging from tree-trunk to tree-trunk, and from one bush to another. They always fell into line at the same time with the others, but they had not exposed themselves once while doing so" (165). But Davis seems to have identified himself with the athletes in the ranks, for he continued to define the advance in terms of college sports: "At all times the movement was without rest, breathless and fierce, like a cane-rush," and in the savage heat the men "had stripped as though for a wrestling-match" (150).

At a later point RHD met a "tall, gaunt young man with a cross on his arm," striding back toward the beach with "a wounded man much heavier than himself across the shoulders," and recognized "the young doctor with the blood bathing his breeches as 'Bob' Church, of Princeton," a well-known football player: "Some of the comic paragraphers who wrote of . . . the college swells of the Rough Riders organization, and of their imaginary valets and golf clubs, ought, in decency, since the fight at Guasimas to go out and hang themselves with remorse. For the same spirit that once sent these men down a white-washed field against their opponents' rush-line was the spirit that sent Church, Channing, Devereux, Ronalds, Wrenn, Cash, Bull, Larned, Goodrich, Greenway, Dudley Dean, and a dozen others through the hot grass at Guasimas, not shouting, as their friends the cowboys did, but each with his mouth tightly shut, with his eyes on the ball, and moving in obedience to the captain's signals" (151–53).

It is in passages like this, as in similar metaphors used in his description of the Greco-Turkish War, that we can trace a line back to Davis's early years as the editor of *Harper's Weekly* and his regular coverage of college football games and celebrations of the game's heroes, who occasionally were indeed heroes. It is a line that intersects with *Soldiers of Fortune* during the equivalent attack by Robert Clay and his little army against the entrenched forces of evil in the governor's palace in Valencia, the town modeled after Santiago de Cuba, toward which the Rough Riders were making their painful and often fatal way. By the 1890s it was a commonplace that the victory at Waterloo was prepared for by the games played at Eton, but for RHD and his generation it was a truth reinforced by their own experience in Cuba.

From the pep rally on the beach at Siboney, with boys dancing around campfires, and singing what well might have been college songs, to the desperate headlong rushes at Guásimas, the correspondences cannot be denied. Moreover, where Davis's analogies to football in his account of the war in Turkey seem startlingly out of place, given his description of the battle at Velestino, here they seem exactly right. Not only was the invasion staged in a series of advances, rather than being waged from fixed positions, but Davis witnessed the war in the field, not from behind but actually in the line of battle.

Moreover, as Davis saw it, the invasion was a matter of gallant individuals, not a faceless army, rushing headlong against the enemy. It was thus easily accommodated to his love of football, much as the sports-loving Colonel Roosevelt served as an equivalent Robert Clay, leading his volunteer troop of cowboys and college athletes against the foe. This metaphorical consistency is one of the factors that makes an equivalent fiction out of Davis's factual, eyewitness account of the Cuban invasion. Another is his insistence on reporting only what he himself witnessed, which necessarily focused Davis's account of the war on only a few aspects of the battles at which he was present, in effect promoting a linear and simplified advance approximating a plot. We need only turn to the account of the Santiago campaign by Stephen Bonsal, RHD's ideal war correspondent, to understand both the limitations and the advantages of Davis's point of view.

In Bonsal's *The Fight for Santiago*, the reporter interjects considerable personal commentary and occasionally digresses in anecdotal fashion, but he nonetheless attempts to cover all aspects of the campaign. As a consequence, he stresses that the battle for El Caney was vital to the taking of Santiago, a fight hardly mentioned by Davis, who did not witness it. Likewise, in Bonsal's version of the Cuban campaign, Theodore Roosevelt's contribution, famously celebrated by Davis, becomes a relatively minor part of the whole.

Indeed, although Bonsal portrays the storming of San Juan as a strategic victory, he virtually ignores Roosevelt's charge up Kettle Hill. Equally significant, Bonsal took special care to defend General Shafter from RHD's savage attacks, justly putting the blame for the faulty campaign on the overall unpreparedness of the U.S. invading force, which originated in the undue haste of politicians and bureaucrats to rush the troops to Cuba. Ironically, Davis's letters home from Tampa are filled with an urgency regarding the need to get the American army into battle as soon as possible, suggesting that he was once again part of the problem (cf. *Adventures* 231).

Moreover, Bonsal's argument removes a vital part of Davis's carefully constructed strategy, by means of which a bungling, adipose, and ailing old general provides dramatic contrast to the courageous, able-bodied, and charismatic young colonel who took matters into his own hands and, by leading a charge up Kettle Hill, in effect turned the tide of battle. Bonsal also backed Stephen Crane's definition of the fight at La Guásimas as an "ambush" by the Spanish, which Roosevelt in his own account of the Rough Riders in Cuba angrily denounced. Davis for his own part simply ignored the dispute, even while blaming the bungling strategy of General Shafter for the many American deaths.

Stephen Bonsal's book about the taking of Santiago certainly warrants RHD's praise of his colleague's journalistic skills, while Davis himself renders a highly selective, even subjective version. Despite the several points of resemblance between the initial invasion of Cuba and the early stages of the Greco-Turkish War, which in both cases was a youthful idyll followed by terrible destruction and loss of life, Davis nowhere gives expression to the cynicism inspired by the first war he covered. We hear no reference to the defining role played by luck, fortune, or chance in determining which soldiers died and which survived. His is throughout a heroic chronicle that imbues the Cuban campaign with an aura of chivalry, a crusade, as it were, without a cross going before but with the American flag and various regimental banners and pennants fluttering in the breeze. Ahead of the entire procession rides Colonel Roosevelt on his thoroughbred mount, a proper knight for the occasion.

I rushed down a steep hill and when we fought again I defeated them
and rushed up to another position and again encountered and beat them.
They were now forced to receive me as an honored soldier.

THEODORE ROOSEVELT (age 12)

13 : A GENTLEMAN UNAFRAID

: I :

Even in death, rendered particularly grotesque by the activities of vultures and repulsive carrion-eating land crabs, a measure of nobility was bestowed on the Rough Riders by Davis. As he walked back along the trail to assist the wounded while the battle at La Guásimas was raging behind him, he found himself passing through "one of the most grewsome [*sic*] and saddest pictures of the war. . . . [T]he rocks on either side were spattered with blood and the rank grass was matted with it. Blanket-rolls, haversacks, carbines, and canteens had been abandoned all along its length." It looked like a path left by an army in retreat instead of one advancing, and except for the "clatter of the land-crabs . . . and the whistling of the bullets in the trees, the place was as silent as a grave. For the wounded lying along its length were as still as the dead beside them" (153–54).

As he continued back up the trail, Davis discovered the body of the first soldier who had fallen in the battle, heroic even in death, and a monumental statue of sorts:

After death the bodies of some men seem to shrink almost instantly within themselves; they become limp and shapeless, and their uniforms hang upon them strangely. But this man, who was a giant in life, remained a giant in death—his very attitude was one of attack; his fists were clinched, his jaw set, and his eyes, which were still human, seemed fixed with resolve. He was dead, but he was not defeated. And so Sergeant Fish died as he had lived—defiantly, running into the very face of the enemy, standing squarely upright on his legs instead of crouching, as the others called to him to do, until he fell like a column across the trail. "God gives," was the motto on the watch I took from his blouse, and God could not have given him a nobler end; to die, in the forefront of the first fight of the war, quickly, painlessly, with a bullet through the heart, with his regiment behind him, and facing the enemies of his country. (159–60)

The dead sergeant was Hamilton Fish, grandson and namesake of Lincoln's secretary of war and a prominent member of New York society; his columnar presence across the trail, like his early sacrifice in the war, was a token to Davis and hence to his readers that knighthood in its modern guise is not difficult to detect. One of the qualifications is still a highborn place of origin, certified by the heraldic motto engraved on Sergeant Fish's watch.

Still, Davis did not ignore the courage of enlisted men: There were no reserves held back to support the Rough Riders, so that none could be spared to help carry the wounded to the rear, and many soldiers, having been slightly injured, would rejoin the fight, even against orders, like "Rowland, of Deming," New Mexico. Having been shot through the ribs, he was three times ordered back to the dressing station by Roosevelt and each time returned, explaining "sheepishly" when asked the reason, "I didn't seem to be doing any good there." Rowland was finally permitted to remain "and went into the fight of the San Juan hills with the hole still through his ribs" (167).

In his account of the battle at La Guásimas, Davis alluded to the attack led by General Samuel B. M. Young "on our right, which was equally desperate, and owing to the courage of the colored troops of the Tenth in storming a ridge, equally worthy of praise." The neglect of the bravery of African American soldiers in accounts of the fighting in Cuba is notorious, but Davis's rationale for this passing mention is derived from his conviction that it seemed to him "better not to try and tell of anything I did not see, but to limit myself to the work of the Rough Riders, to whom, after all, the victory was due" (171). Once the circumstances of the battle for San Juan brought "colored" soldiers of the Ninth Cavalry into the arbitrary frame imposed on his narrative, Davis made up for his neglect.

As I have suggested, Davis's restricted view of the action promotes the fictional aspect of his account of the Cuban campaign, in that the war as he saw it was indeed "won" by the Rough Riders, a viewpoint not shared by other correspondents. Moreover, as Davis explains, it was the flanking charge led by the Rough Riders under Colonel Leonard Wood that permitted the advance of Generals Young and Wheeler, "their own stubborn attack in front having failed to dislodge the enemy from the rifle-pits" (171). Both senior officers were veterans of the Civil War as well as of the protracted struggle with Indians along the western frontier, whereas Colonels Wood and Roosevelt were untried military leaders but were, as Arthur Lubow has noted, young men who demonstrated the virtues RHD had celebrated as editor, reporter, fiction writer, and correspondent. He was, in his view, one of them, and whatever Roosevelt's personal reservations may have been at the start of the invasion, the colonel was willing to certify the bond by making the reporter an honorary member of the Rough Riders at war's end.

In Davis's account, Roosevelt emerges as the central figure of the war. Wood's strategy may have won the battle at La Guásimas, but it was Roosevelt who, having "picked up a carbine" so as to direct the fire of his men, "determined upon a charge," the kind of action that typified the raw courage of the Rough Riders:

> Wood, at the other end of the line, decided at the same time upon the same manoeuvre. It was called "Wood's bluff" afterward, for he had nothing to back it with; while to the enemy it looked as though his whole force was but the skirmish-line in advance of a regiment. The Spaniards naturally could not believe that this thin line which suddenly broke out of the bushes and from behind trees . . . cheering and filling the hot air with wild cowboy yells . . . was the entire fighting force behind it. They supposed the regiment was coming close on its heels, and as they hate being rushed as a cat hates water, they fired a few parting volleys and broke and ran. (169–70)

Throughout, the Rough Riders had overridden all the conventional rules of war, advancing after firing each volley, which unnerved the Spanish soldiers, so that, "when . . . the Rough Riders rushed at them, the dismayed enemy retreated upon Santiago, where he announced he had been attacked by the entire American Army" (170).

Having beaten back the Spanish at La Guásimas, the Rough Riders advanced to where the road crossed two streams, with the hill at El Poso just beyond, and there encamped for nearly a week, waiting for the rest of the army to catch up to them in preparation for the attack on San Juan. Supplies reached them by mule-train and wagon, a slow process because of the narrowness of the trail, which became a sluice of mud when it rained. Food was at all times inadequate, thanks to the intransigency of the captains aboard the transports, who persisted in taking their ships out to sea at a whim, being the employees of the owners of the vessels and not in their own opinion subject to the control of the armed forces.

What was needed, as RHD saw it, was "a strong man in command of the expedition," a leader who would not only order the transports to remain in place but also have them firmly anchored bow and stern in the harbor. But no strong man was in charge; what they had was General Shafter, who because of age and debility remained confined, apparently indifferent to the condition of his men at the front. As a direct result, according to Davis, the

TR and RHD on location in Cuba, as depicted in Davis's Cuban and Porto Rican Campaigns. *Courtesy Culver Pictures.*

supply ships were allowed to roam about at will. In truth, because the supply vessels were not directly under the command of the military, it is doubtful if any senior officer could have influenced their actions.

With their typically high spirits, the Rough Riders managed to keep busy, scavenging for coconuts and mangoes or just resting in the shade, while their officers "reconnoitred the hills above them," yet for whatever reasons no one was ordered to make any reconnaissance of the approach to San Juan. "The temper of the young officers was keen for just such an adventure . . . to make actual surveys of the trails leading to Santiago, to discover the best cover and the open places, where the fords crossed the streams, and the trails which flanked the Spanish trenches. But their services were not required." Only one senior officer "acquainted himself with that mile and a half of unknown country into which, on the 1st of July, the men were driven as cattle are chased into the chutes of the Chicago cattle-pen" (178).

By June 27 it was clear that the fortifications below San Juan were being improved, as "a long yellow pit opened in the hillside . . . and in it we could see straw sombreros rising and bobbing up and down, and under the shade of the block-house, blue-coated Spaniards strolling leisurely about" (180). And yet despite these obvious signs, no artillery was sent up the line to interrupt the bobbing sombreros or disturb the tranquillity of the Spanish garrison. Instead, "for four days before the American soldiers captured the same rifle-pits at El Caney and San Juan, with a loss of two thousand men, they watched these men diligently preparing for their coming, and wondered why there was no order to embarrass or to end these preparations" (180).

The chief blame, as always, lay with General Shafter, for if he had assigned the responsibility for determining tactics to younger commanders in the field familiar with the lay of the land, he would have saved many lives, but he refused to do so: "General Shafter saw the field of battle only once before the fight took place. That was on June 29th, when he rode out to El Poso hill and surveyed the plain below. He was about the last officer in his army corps to climb that hill and make that survey and he did not again go even that far to the front until the night after the battle, and he did not see the trenches for days after the battle had taken place." Shafter's headquarters lay only three miles from El Poso, but the trip had been "apparently too much for his strength, and the heat during the ride prostrated him so greatly that he was forced to take to his cot, where he spent the greater part of his stay in Cuba before the surrender" (183).

Unlike Shafter's officers, who in their anger blamed the general for "allowing his personal safety to stand in the way of his duty," RHD saw the
problem as a matter of Shafter's physical inability to carry out his duties
(184). But he was outraged that the commanding general had not resisted
"the temptation to accept responsibilities his political friends thrust upon
him, responsibilities he knows he cannot bear," that he held on to this
command to the end, because of his supreme "self-confidence": "His self-
complacency was so great that in spite of blunder after blunder, folly upon
folly, and mistake upon mistake, he still believed himself infallible, still bul-
lied his inferior officers, and still cursed from his cot" (185).

Again, Davis had his personal reasons for despising Shafter, and yet he
was hardly alone in criticizing the ailing, gouty general for his stubborn in-
flexibility and inability to delegate authority. Perhaps, as Bonsal insisted,
the extremes of this portrait are unfair, but the obese invalid blustering and
cursing while sweating on his cot is an apt literary symbol if not entirely factual. But even if Shafter was not solely to blame, he and the other generals
in command of the army should not have heeded the politicians who
pushed them into action long before their troops were ready. The losses
would have been far worse had the Spanish themselves been better prepared; the American victory was much more a matter of good fortune than
of either strategy or readiness.

But for Davis, who saw chance dealing the cards at Velestino, in Cuba the
war was a morality play in which General William Rufus Shafter, a caricature of self-interestedness and incompetence, serves as a foil for Theodore
Roosevelt, who was none of those things. In the minds of even his friendliest
critics, Teddy had sufficient faults of his own, of which vaingloriousness
was the chief, but Davis was not one of those critics, most of whom stayed
at home. In RHD's account of the war it was Roosevelt who would save the
day, redeeming the honor of the army and his country. Even the advance on
San Juan mirrored the ill-informed strategy conceived by the sick general
left behind on his cot, for as any number of commentators have remarked,
it was the passage of men inadequately prepared down a narrow trail that
acted in the manner of a trap. It was a virtual funnel through which the
Rough Riders were forced to pass under heavy fire from the Spanish soldiers
occupying the San Juan height.

We are once again in Lewis Carroll country, violently conceived, and the
infamous observation balloon bobbling above the advancing column and
drawing heavy fire from the rifle pits as it moved forward is the defining
touch. As Davis noted, "A balloon on the advance line, and only fifty feet

above the tops of the trees, was merely an invitation to the enemy to kill everything beneath it" (212). When the balloon itself was finally shot down, the observer was able to report the significant information that he had seen "men up on those hills" and that "they are firing at our troops" (213).

Of equal stupidity in Davis's opinion was the position of the minimal artillery brought forward to support the attack. The field cannons had opened fire from the height at El Poso on the Spanish blockhouse atop San Juan, and having been supplied with black powder, the artillerymen were hampered by smoke each time they fired, making them a target for the opposing artillery. To make matters worse, the guns had been placed in front of a farmhouse sheltering "Cuban soldiers and other non-combatants" (a significant grouping), as well as Rough Riders "who had been ordered to halt in the yard." Moreover, the location of the artillery endangered the First and Tenth Cavalry, who were "encamped a hundred yards from the battery along the ridge" (196). "I took pains," Davis declared, "to find out by whose order these troops were placed within such close proximity to a battery, and was informed, by the general in command of the division, that his men had been put in that exact position by the order of the Commanding General" — that is, Shafter (198–99).

The American artillery got off twenty shots before the enemy replied, and it took only three shells before the Spanish guns found their range, the third falling "among the Cubans in the [farm]-house and among the Rough Riders and the men of the First and Tenth Cavalry, killing some and wounding many" (199). This incredible stupidity aside, the artillery, as Davis reported, played almost no part in the American victory, being of insufficient numbers and size to count: "Military experts say that the sixty guns left behind in Tampa would have been few enough for the work they had to do," and in setting out with "only sixteen three-inch guns" with which to besiege a city, the attacking army was like a fire company "going to a fire with a hook and ladder company and leaving the hose and the steam-engines in the engine-house" (199).

The advance of the American army toward San Juan began in the afternoon of June 30, leaving the veteran generals Young and Wheeler behind, who had "relinquished their commands" because of illness. The order having been given to all the regiments at once, they "stepped down into the trail together. It was as though fifteen regiments were encamped along the sidewalks of Fifth Avenue and were all ordered at the same moment to move into it and march down town. If Fifth Avenue were ten feet wide, one can imagine the confusion," and the march did approximate what has become famous as Macy's Parade, thanks to the observation balloon floating ahead of the line (188).

There were no bystanders as such, but the troops were joined in their advance by sundry observers, including military attachés, "in strange uniforms, self-important Cuban generals, officers from the flagship New York, and an army of photographers," to say nothing of the journalists, which Davis did not: "Twelve thousand men, with their eyes fixed on a balloon, and treading on each other's heels in three inches of mud, move slowly, and after three hours, it seemed as though every man in the United States was under arms and stumbling down that trail. The lines passed until the moon rose. They seemed endless, interminable; there were cavalry mounted and dismounted, artillery with cracking whips and cursing drivers, Rough Riders in brown, and regulars, both black and white, in blue. Midnight came, and they were still slipping forward" (190).

This absurd procession, moreover, was marching through a country "as yet utterly undiscovered," save, of course, by the defending army, which knew it very well. "Three miles away, across the basin of mist, we could see the streetlamps of Santiago shining over the San Juan hills. Above us, the tropical moon hung white and clear in the dark purple sky, pierced with millions of white stars. As we turned in, there was just a little something in the air, which made saying 'good-night' a gentle farce, for no one went to sleep immediately, but lay looking up at the stars, and after a long silence, and much restless turning on the blanket which we shared together, the second lieutenant said: 'So, if anything happens to me, tomorrow, you'll see she gets them, won't you?'" The young officer's uneasiness was an anticipation of the grim business ahead, which was not unwarranted: "Before the moon rose again, every sixth man who had slept in the mist that night was either killed or wounded" (193–94). As for Davis's nervous blanket-mate, the next day ended with him "sitting on the edge of a Spanish rifle-pit, dirty, sweaty, and weak for food, but victorious, and the unknown she did not get them" (194).

The victory, however, resulted in the death of many American soldiers, for the Spaniards not only knew the difficulties of the terrain ahead but how to capitalize on them: "On the following morning [the army] was to attack San Juan on the two flanks, under cover of artillery. The objection to this plan, which did not apparently suggest itself to General Shafter, was that . . . the whole basin was covered by the fire from the rifle-pits. The army could not remain in the woods even by daylight when it was possible to seek some slight shelter, but according to the plan it was expected to bivouac for the night in those woods, and in the morning to manoeuvre and deploy and march through them out to the two flanks of San Juan. How the enemy was to be hypnotized while this was going forward it is difficult to explain" (194–95).

With the artillery that was supposed to be supporting them drawing deadly fire and the balloon overhead assisting the Spanish in identifying their progress, the first division of men marched out of the inadequate cover of the underbrush into heavy fire, being in full view from the rifle pits on San Juan. But when General Samuel Sumner, to whom the ailing Wheeler had relinquished his command, asked for instructions, he was told by one of Shafter's aides "to await further orders," which was, as Davis wryly remarked, "probably the last order General Sumner received from General Shafter, until the troops of his division had taken the San Juan hills" (200–203). Because the trail behind them was packed with advancing troops, no word could be sent to or received from headquarters, and because of the order to wait, the division was forced to halt in the open beside a shallow stream dignified as the San Juan River.

> The enemy saw the advance and began firing with pitiless accuracy into the jammed and crowded trail, and along the whole border of the woods. There was not a single yard of ground for a mile to the rear which was not inside the zone of fire. Our men were ordered not to return the fire but to lie still and wait for further orders. Some of them could see the rifle-pits of the enemy quite clearly and the men in them but many saw nothing but the bushes under which they lay, and the high grass which seemed to burn when they pressed against it. It was during this period of waiting that the greater number of our men were killed. For one hour they lay on their rifles staring at the waving green stuff around them, while the bullets drove past incessantly, with savage insistence, cutting the grass again and again in hundreds of fresh places. (204)

Back along the trail, Spanish sharpshooters fired on American troops from hiding places in the trees, so that bullets came "from every side."

> Their invisible smoke helped to keep their hiding places secret, and in the incessant shriek of shrapnel and the spit of the Mausers, it was difficult to locate the reports of their rifles. They spared neither the wounded nor recognized the Red Cross. . . . For a time it seemed as though every second man was either killed or wounded, one came upon them lying behind the bush, under which they had crawled with some strange idea

that it would protect them, or crouching under the bank of the stream, lapping up the water with the eagerness of thirsty dogs. As to their suffering, the wounded were magnificently silent, they neither complained nor groaned, nor cursed. . . . White men and colored men, veterans and recruits and volunteers, each lay waiting for the battle to begin or to end so that he might be carried away to safety . . . but neither questioned or complained. (209)

During the fight Davis did what he could to help with the wounded, and in doing so he "came across Lieutenant Roberts, of the Tenth Cavalry, lying under the roots of a tree beside the stream with three of his colored troopers stretched around him":

He was shot through the intestines, and each of the three men with him was shot in the arm or leg. They had been overlooked or forgotten, and we stumbled upon them only by the accident of losing our way. They had no knowledge as to how the battle was going or where their comrades were, or where the enemy was. At any moment, for all they knew, the Spaniards might break through the bushes about them. It was a most lonely picture, the young lieutenant, half naked, and wet with his own blood, sitting upright beside the empty stream, and his three followers crouching at his feet like three faithful watch-dogs, each wearing his red badge of courage, with his black skin tanned to a haggard gray, and with his eyes fixed patiently on the white lips of his officer. When the white soldiers with me offered to carry him back to the dressing-station, the negroes resented it stiffly. "If the Lieutenant had been able to move, we would have carried him away long ago," said the sergeant, quite overlooking the fact that his arm was shattered.

"Oh, don't bother the surgeons about me," Roberts added, cheerfully. "They must be very busy. I can wait." (211)

Revisionists searching for evidence of racism in accounts of the Spanish-American War have fastened with triumph upon this scene, the brave young lieutenant surrounded by his devoted, doglike black soldiers providing a virtual chromo that illustrates their thesis.

And yet, while a modern sensibility surely is offended by the postures into which this group is placed, there can be little doubt that Davis is crediting the black soldiers with heroism as well as devotion, for each bears the "red badge" that in Stephen Crane's novel is a stigmata of courage, not shame. It is a composition that, like the fallen hero Hamilton Fish, substantiates RHD's chivalric reading of the war, a tableau in which the black soldiers, like the white officer, have their place, a role that may be subordinate but not contemptible, quite the reverse. It is the overweight, older white general on his sodden cot who personifies the contemptible, while these black men, along with all the other wounded, line the paths of glory that led to San Juan Hill.

: II :

At the time, those paths seemed to converge at the place the poet Thomas Gray proposed, well short of the heights where the Spanish were entrenched. The troops in the front line were pinned down by enemy fire, and "the situation was desperate," for the Americans "could not retreat, as the trail for two miles behind them was wedged with men. They could not remain where they were for they were being shot to pieces. There was only one thing they could do—go forward and take the San Juan hills by assault" (214). But the solution was "as desperate as the situation itself," being as impossible a tactic as the famed charge at Balaklava and potentially as fatal:

> To charge earthworks held by men with modern rifles, and using modern artillery, until after the earthworks have been shaken by artillery, and to attack them in advance and not in the flanks, are both impossible military propositions. But this campaign had not been conducted according to military rules, and a series of military blunders had brought seven thousand American soldiers into a chute of death, from which there was no escape except by taking the enemy who held it by the throat, and driving him out and beating him down. So the generals of divisions and brigades stepped back and relinquished their command to the regimental officers and the enlisted men.
> "We can do nothing more," they virtually said. "There is the enemy." (214)

As at La Guásimas, it was Colonel Roosevelt who seized control of the situation, and breaking "from the woods behind the line of the Ninth, and finding its men lying in his way, shouted: 'If you don't wish to go forward, let my men pass, please.'" But instead of standing aside, "the junior officers of the Ninth, with their negroes, instantly sprang into line with the Rough Riders, and charged at the blue block-house on the right":

> I speak of Roosevelt first, because, with General Hawkins, who led Kent's Division, notably the Sixth and Sixteenth Regulars, he was,

without doubt, the most conspicuous figure in the charge. General Hawkins, with hair as white as snow, and yet far in advance of men thirty years his junior, was so noble a sight that you felt inclined to pray for his safety; on the other hand, Roosevelt, mounted high on horseback, and charging the rifle-pits at a gallop and quite alone, made you feel that you would like to cheer. He wore on his sombrero a blue polka-dot handkerchief . . . which, as he advanced, floated out straight behind his head, like a guidon. Afterward, the men of his regiment who followed this flag, adopted a polka-dot handkerchief as the badge of the Rough Riders. (217)

Here again we find Davis being drawn to men his own age, and thus it was Roosevelt who dominates his account, despite the picturesqueness of the white-haired Hawkins. It was the older man who actually took San Juan Hill, whereas the Rough Riders seized the lesser height they themselves called Kettle (inspired by a large iron sugaring pot they found there), but these details were soon expunged from the legend. In Frederic Remington's celebrated painting *The Charge of the Rough Riders at San Juan Hill*, it is Roosevelt and his men who dominate the composition. Remington, however, did not place the colonel in the foreground, which is taken up by charging troops, but in the background, with a resulting emphasis on the courageous soldiers. As Davis noted in his own description of the charge, "No one can claim that any two men, or any one man, was more brave or more daring, or showed greater courage in that slow, stubborn advance than did any of the others" (217).

Remington was close by, trapped with the soldiers in the perilous passage through the woods, but he did not witness the charge led by Roosevelt, and the artist's depiction (as his sole emphasis on the khaki-clad Rough Riders suggests) was a product of his imagination. But within limits it was accurate, especially when compared with the popular prints that depicted the event, as Davis noted:

I have seen many illustrations and pictures of this charge on the San Juan hills, but none of them seem to show it just as I remember it. In the picture-papers the men are running up hill swiftly and gallantly, in regular formation, rank after rank, with flags flying, their eyes aflame, and their hair streaming, their bayonets fixed, in long, brilliant lines, an invincible, overpowering weight of numbers. Instead of which I think the thing which impressed one the most, when our men started from cover, was that they were so few. It seemed as if someone had made an awful

Remington's Charge of the Rough Riders at San Juan Hill, *1898. (Oil on canvas. Courtesy Frederic Remington Art Museum, Ogdensburg, New York.) Roosevelt, the only man on a horse, is placed in the background but in such a way as to draw attention to his figure. Careful scrutiny will reveal a single black soldier, bareheaded, with his regulation blues obscured by the cluster of Rough Riders around him. He is placed virtually at the center of the composition but is almost invisible because of the surrounding men.*

and terrible mistake. One's instinct was to call to them to come back. You felt that someone had blundered and that these few men were blindly following some madman's mad order. It was not heroic then, it seemed merely terribly pathetic. The pity of it, the folly of such a sacrifice was what held you.

They had no glittering bayonets, they were not massed in regular array. There were a few men in advance, bunched together, and creeping up a steep, sunny hill, the tops of which roared and flashed with flame. The men held their guns pressed across their breasts, and stepped heavily as they climbed. Behind these first few, spreading out like a fan, were single lines of men, slipping and scrambling in the smooth grass, moving forward with difficulty, as though they were wading waist high through water, moving slowly, carefully, with strenuous effort. It was much more wonderful than any swinging charge could have been. They walked to greet death at every step, many of them, as they advanced, sinking suddenly or pitching forward and disappearing in the high grass, but the others waded on, stubbornly, forming a thin blue line that kept creeping higher and higher up the hill. It was as inevitable as the rising tide. It was a miracle of self-sacrifice, a triumph of bull-dog courage, which one watched breathless with wonder. The fire of the Spanish riflemen, who still stuck bravely to their posts, doubled and trebled in fierceness, the crests of the hills crackled and burst in amazed roars, and rippled with waves of tiny flame. But the blue line crept steadily up and on, and then, near the top, the broken fragments gathered together with a sudden burst of speed, the Spaniards appeared for a moment outlined against the sky and poised for instant flight, fired a last volley and fled before the swift-moving wave that leaped and sprang after them.

The men of the Ninth and the Rough Riders rushed to the block-house together, the men of the Sixth, of the Third, of the Tenth Cavalry, of the Sixth and Sixteenth Infantry, fell on their faces along the crest of the hills beyond, and opened upon the vanishing enemy. They drove the yellow silk flags of the cavalry and the Stars and Stripes of their country into the soft earth of the trenches, and then sank down and looked back at the road they had climbed and swung their hats in the air. And from far overhead, from these few figures perched on the Spanish rifle-pits, with their flags planted among the empty cartridges of the enemy, and overlooking the walls of Santiago, came, faintly, the sound of a tired, broken cheer. (218–23)

In Remington's painting the charge up San Juan Hill was made on the run, but it is being made by that ragged line described by Davis, an advance approximating the sketch Remington had done for *Harper's Weekly* seven years earlier of a scrimmage line of football players racing down the field. The artist's version may be a sacrifice of fact for visual drama, which Davis is able to supply without bending the truth, prose description having resources denied the graphic arts. As I have observed, Remington likewise limits the attacking soldiers to the Rough Riders, white men wearing dark shirts and khaki trousers. Notably, he represents soldiers of the Ninth by a single black man, dressed in regulation blue, but barely discernible in the midst of the charging line.

Davis, while emphasizing the Rough Riders, opens up the ranks to include "men of the Ninth" in blue, warranting his "thin blue line" in emulation of Sir William Howard Russell's "thin red line" of British troops in the Crimea, though Davis's use of the image is most likely indebted to Kipling,

Remington's A Run behind Interference, *published in* Harper's Weekly,
*December 2, 1893. (Courtesy Frederic Remington Art Museum, Ogdensburg,
New York.) Reflecting the new emphasis of the magazine on college sports, a result
of RHD's editorship, the picture also recalls Remington's brief career as a player
at Yale under the legendary Walter Camp. Most important, it bears comparison
for its imagery of young men in violent action with the artist's famous
depiction of the charge at San Juan Hill, painted five years later.*

who used it in his popular poem "Tommy," a celebration of the British common soldier. Otherwise, Davis's account is color-blind, for he had already acknowledged that the men of the Ninth were black and were one with the
white men who made up the Rough Riders (a fact virtually ignored by Remington). In effect it was a faceless hence raceless wave of men advancing on
the Spanish rifle pits. Even the Spaniards are given a measure of courage,
standing their ground until overwhelmed not by numbers but by the kinetic
force of the charging soldiers in blue.

Davis was credited by his contemporaries with having made Roosevelt the
hero of the day, a process that began with Finley Peter Dunne's Mr. Dooley,
who not only poked fun at the colonel's account of his "Cubian" adventure
but called RHD "Tiddy's . . . brave an' fluent bodyguard" (Dunne 105). And
yet anyone carefully reading Davis's description of the famous charge must
concede that although Roosevelt made the initial move, it was the soldiers

inspired by his example who won the hill. Moreover, having taken the heights above Santiago, they were put in yet another precarious position, "painfully suggestive," as Davis put it, "of Humpty-Dumpty on the wall."

: III :

Though the Americans had taken possession of "several block-houses and rows and rows of abandoned rifle-pits," there lay below them, "in the valley that stretched between the city of Santiago and the hills on which they crouched, thousands of Spanish rifles . . . spluttering furiously and shriek-ing with rage and disappointment, making the crest of hills behind which our men lay absolutely untenable" (224–27). Their situation, Davis reck-oned, was "like that of a man clinging to a church steeple and unable, with-out breaking his neck, to slip down on any side; but who still proclaimed to the air about him, 'See how I hold this steeple.'" He was also reminded of "the words of Stephen Crane's trooper, who sank upon the crest of the hill, panting, bleeding, and sweating, and cried: 'Well, hell, here we are!'" (227).

As the reference to Crane suggests, it was during RHD's account of the dangerous position in which the troops who had occupied San Juan Hill found themselves that he rendered a delayed tribute to the correspondents who were courageous enough to share "whatever danger there was with the soldiers." For "while the hills were still swept with the enemy's fire Stephen Crane and John Hare . . . came up . . . and later John Fox . . . and James Whigham, the golf champion, who was acting as the correspondent of the Chicago *Tribune,* and Sir Bryan Leighton . . . of the New York *Jour-nal.* These were the only correspondents I saw that far up on that day," among whom, of course, was Davis himself, though his presence is tacit in this catalogue (235).

A moment later he notes that his constant companion during that day, Floyd Campbell, the artist for the *New York Herald,* felt compelled to "take a photograph of Santiago from the crest of the hill, and I had to go where he did," taking a fleeting look at the city that was "only long enough to enable me to say truthfully that I had seen it, but not long enough to enable me to recognize it if I saw it again" (235–36). This self-deflating manner is charac-teristic of RHD's correspondent persona and requires comparison with the facts of his behavior as recounted in his letters home, which included pick-ing up a carbine during the battle at La Guásimas and firing at the enemy, violating his noncombatant status but certifying his own physical courage (*Adventures* 250–51).

Likewise, after the charge up Kettle Hill, Davis wrote home that he had "got excited and took a carbine and charged the sugar house, which was what is called the key to the position. If the men had been regulars I would have sat in the rear . . . but I knew every other one of them, had played football, and all that sort of thing, with them, so I thought as an American I ought to help." Afterward, he told his parents, Roosevelt made a speech in his honor, offered him a captaincy in the regiment, and "told the Associated Press man that there was no officer in his regiment who had 'been of more help or shown more courage' than your humble servant, so that's all right" (255). In his posthumous tribute, Roosevelt also acknowledged Davis's contribution to the victory in Cuba, for the correspondent "was not merely present at but took part in the fighting" (*R.H.D.* 55). But what Davis boasted of in his letters home, he was silent about in his account of the war, omitting his own active role while bestowing praise on officers and men and the correspondents who shared the risk.

By contrast, RHD's account of the war in Cuba is highly critical of the contributions, such as they were, of the senior officers. It is a dark background against which the courage and sacrifices of the junior officers and their men becomes even brighter. We will remember Davis's picture of General Wheeler as he sat on the piazza of the Tampa Bay Hotel, a very model of southern chivalry, and while chivalry was very important to Richard Harding Davis, so was fairness. He noted that "Fighting Joe" Wheeler had spent his time during the charge up San Juan Hill in the temporary hospital set up behind the lines, "seated at the foot of a great tree" (*Cuban . . . Campaigns* 228).

Only after the hill had been taken was Wheeler able to come up to the front; he was thereby given the advantage of the actions of other men, including General Sumner, under whose leadership if not initiative the charge had been made: "I mention this because in General Shafter's general order congratulating the troops on the victory of San Juan, he gave the entire credit for the work of the cavalry division to General Wheeler, speaking of him as leading the dismounted cavalry at the front. He did not mention General Sumner at all. As a matter of history, General Sumner bore the heat and brunt of the day, and was in command of the cavalry division long after the hills were taken, until about four o'clock, when General Wheeler reassumed command. General Wheeler has won so many laurels in the Civil War, and again in this last war, that he does not need honors which belong to another" (229).

When RHD asserts himself forthrightly, as here, it is invariably to set the account straight, whether criticizing the incompetence of General Shafter, correcting the record regarding General Wheeler, or speaking out on equally important matters. Early on, while still in Tampa, Davis had opined that the volunteer troops were more "interesting" than the regulars, but after his experience during the attack on San Juan, he came down strongly against the use of volunteer regiments, citing the Seventy-first New York, whose behavior during the battle was shameful, largely because of the cowardice of some of its officers, and yet the regiment had been praised by New York newspapers for reasons of local pride.

There were exceptions among the New York soldiers, a number of whom joined in the attack, but only after hanging back at first. Such timidity was understandable given that it was the first time these men had been under fire, but it argued against "the use of amateurs in time of war" (241). Davis fulminated against "that national menace called the National Guard," which he saw as a creation of politicians, and declared that the "country needs to know . . . that in actual warfare the volunteer is a nuisance, that it always takes one regular to offset his mistakes, to help him cook his rations, and to teach him to shelter himself and to keep himself clean." If Colonel Roosevelt had boasted that the Rough Riders were "five times as good as any other regiment of volunteers, he was in my opinion far too modest," but at the same time, "any regiment of regulars is many times better than any regiment of volunteers" (238).

What held for regulars included the black men in their ranks, and Davis noted that the soldiers of the Tenth were the first to return from San Juan Hill to get more ammunition. "The web belts of most of them were empty, and in no one belt were there more than a half-a-dozen or ten of the one hundred and fifty cartridges with which the men had begun the day. The negro soldiers established themselves as fighting men that morning," and though they, like their fellow regulars, were hungry and thirsty, they were "overjoyed at the fact that the wagons held cartridges and not, as some supposed, rations" (244). They were apparently willing to do without food or water, "so long as they had ammunition." Here again, Davis is willing to give credit where it is due, and his categorization may be racist, encouraged by the army's segregation of black troops into their own companies, but his praise is balanced. By contrast, as Richard Slotkin demonstrates, Roosevelt's own account of the fight for San Juan downplayed the courage of African American soldiers by insisting on their dependency on white officers for direction (Slotkin 105).

The battle continued into the night, and the situation of the American troops on the hill became increasingly untenable by morning, the men having had little sleep, no food, and, most critical, no tobacco, "which is much more necessary to the nerve than is food to the stomach" (249). The white-haired and barely recovered General Wheeler had taken up a position in the hills, where he remained until Santiago fell, improving the American situation by having further trenches dug, but of the commander in chief nothing was seen. Shafter had been carried as far as El Poso, and lying on a door salvaged from the remnants of the farmhouse destroyed by Spanish guns, he conferred with his generals, but with no positive conclusions. To men and officers sitting cramped in the rifle pits to keep from being killed, the delay was intolerable, and "the Generals of division and of brigade were unanimous in declaring that the situation was most desperate, and that the Commanding-General must show himself at the front or ask to be relieved of his command" (250).

In the long interval, negotiations with the Spaniards were carried on under flags of truce, much to the outrage of the men dug in on the hills, who in defiance had placed their regimental banners along the line of their trenches. And "though they afforded the enemy a perfect target and fixed our position as clearly as buoys mark out a race-course, the men wanted the flags there, and felt better at seeing them there, and so there they remained. The trenches formed a horseshoe curve five miles in length, and the entire line was defiantly decorated with our flags. When they fluttered in the wind at full length, and the sun kissed their colors, they made one of the most inspiring and beautiful pictures of the war" (255–56). It is in aesthetic touches like this that Davis emphasizes the essential chivalry of the Cuban campaign, the fluttering banners and pennants being equivalents to those displayed by knights in both tournaments and battle array.

Another dramatic tableau was provided by the return of Lieutenant Richmond Hobson, the naval officer who had sunk the *Merrimac* at the entrance to the Santiago harbor and who had been held in a Spanish prison for six weeks. From his cell he could watch the U.S. Army growing closer each day, "winning the ground between him and themselves by the sweat of their brows." Finally released in a prisoner exchange, Hobson was able to join the ranks he had been watching. Because his arrival had long been anticipated, officers and men gathered on the banks of the trenches waiting for him, "broiling in the sun and crowded together as closely as men on the bleaching-boards of a baseball field" (265).

When Hobson finally arrived, he was received as a sports hero. Still dressed in his naval uniform and pale from his prison confinement, he passed in a wagon through a triumphal arch of palm branches with the sun sinking behind him: "For a moment he sat motionless, and then the waiting band struck up 'The Star-Spangled Banner,'" as every soldier "rose to his feet slowly, took off hat slowly, and stood so, looking up at Hobson in absolute silence. It was one of the most impressive things one could imagine. No noise, nor blare, nor shouted tribute could have touched the meaning or the depths of feeling there was in that silence" (265–66).

But then one soldier gave the call "Three cheers for Hobson," and the stillness was broken with a roar, as the "mob rushed at him . . . with a wild welcome of friendly cheers. Few men, certainly very few young men, have ever tasted such a triumph" (266). By contrast, Stephen Crane, despite his own love of sports, rendered a sour account of Hobson's reception, his early enthusiasm fading when sudden fame apparently went to the navy lieutenant's head. But Crane's reporting of events in Cuba was a minor aspect of his work, lost in the files of the Yellow Kid press for half a century, while Davis, like Hobson, was made famous by the war.

: IV :

Davis described at length the miserable life in the rifle pits as the hard-bitten, ragged, and sunburned men waited out the Spanish surrender, paying tribute not only to the Rough Riders but also to brave soldiers from other regiments who gave their lives in the war. But here I want to hurry on to his conclusion, not set in Santiago de Cuba but in Puerto Rico, for Davis calculatingly missed the ceremony of surrender so that he could accompany General Nelson Miles in his invasion of that other island. In RHD's estimation Miles was everything that Shafter was not, the tough old Indian fighter measuring up to his notion of conventional military bearing and behavior. The general certainly was aptly named, although there was an element of "gloriosus" in his makeup that Davis failed to detect, and like Remington before him he rendered a favorable portrait that Miles undoubtedly thought would further his presidential ambitions.

If, Davis posited, the campaign in Puerto Rico seemed to people at home like "a successful military picnic, a sort of comic-opera war, a magnified field-day," he credited it to General Miles's superior leadership (296). Still, the officials and citizens of the cities through which Davis passed did seem overeager at times to surrender, which considerably diminished the glory factor. More than one town surrendered more than once, and even Davis

himself was surrendered to and found himself "for twenty minutes . . .
mayor and military governor and chief of police of Coamo" (348).

The town of Ponce "surrendered officially and unofficially on four separate occasions. It was possessed of the surrender habit in a most aggravated
form. Indeed, for anyone in uniform it was most unsafe to enter the town at
any time, unless he came prepared to accept its unconditional surrender"
(309). Despite Davis's protests, the situation was a running joke even by his
own account, the war being "nipped by peace almost before it could show its
strength," and yet he persists in calling it a great victory, even while admit-
ting that the regiments who fought in Puerto Rico, "with but three exceptions, were composed of volunteers" (303). It was largely a comic exercise
and as such compensated for the horrors of "the bungling at Santiago, and
the scandal and shame after the war of the treatment of our sick soldiers on
the transports and in the fever camps" (326).

The invasion of Puerto Rico worked like a well-oiled, finely adjusted machine, compared with the creaking and cumbersome operation in Cuba, the
Americans establishing law and order in each town as it was captured, going "about the task of setting up the new empire of the United States as
though our army had always been employed in seizing islands and raising
the flag over captured cities. They played the conquerors with tact, with
power, and like gentlemen. They recognized the rights of others and they
forced others to recognize their rights" (329).

It was, though RHD does not suggest it, empire on the British plan. It also
resembled a change of administration in Washington as Davis had described it in his account of McKinley's inauguration, a peaceful turning out
of one government and the arrival of another, nonetheless a change with
enormous consequences:

> It was the new step on the floor and the new face at the door. The son
> and heir was coming fast, blue-shirted, sunburned, girded with glisten-
> ing cartridges. He was sweeping before him the last traces of a fallen Em-
> pire; the sons of the young Republic were tearing down the royal crowns
> and the double castles over the city halls, opening the iron doors of the
> city jails and raising the flag of the new Empire over the land of the sugar-
> cane and the palm. . . .
>
> Peace came with Porto Rico occupied by our troops and with the Porto
> Ricans blessing our flags, which must never leave the island. It is a beau-
> tiful island, smiling with plenty and content. It will bring us nothing but

what is for good, and it came to us willingly with open arms. But had it been otherwise, it would have come to us. The course of empire to-day takes its way to all points of the compass—not only to the West. If it move always as smoothly, as honorably, and as victoriously as it did in Porto Rico, our army and our people need ask for no higher measure of success. (353, 360)

From the start of the war, Puerto Rico was to become a U.S. possession, while Cuba, because of Senator Henry Teller's amendment, was to become an independent republic after a suitable interval of acculturation under the supervision of American authorities. As Captain Mahan had insisted, the United States needed a deep-water port in the Caribbean if it was to protect the new shipping lanes that the completion of the canal through the Isthmus of Panama would mandate. There were those who wanted to annex Cuba as well, but they were blocked by congressional fiat, nor as Mr. Dooley observed were American farmers who had invested heavily in sugar beets much interested in competing with cane produced on that island.

It is this difference that drives a defining wedge between Davis's early declaration about creating a new republic in Cuba as opposed to his jingoistic paean here to the blessings of the flag raised over Puerto Rico. He was simply reflecting the inevitable, and the easy victory over the remnant Spanish forces in Puerto Rico, combined with the warm welcome given to the American troops by its people, did make the ownership of the island by the United States seem foreordained. It was a version of Manifest Destiny, that imperial ideology which had been associated with the western frontier and which would transform the Monroe Doctrine into an expansionist rationale, and in 1898 Richard Harding Davis was its champion.

But RHD's final chapter on the Puerto Rico campaign, whatever its potential comedy, comes as a letdown after the intensity of the battles in Cuba. The victory may have seemed godsent, but it was too easy with too few acts of courage and self-sacrifice to drape it with flags. There was some fighting, but only some, and Davis even delivered a eulogy of sorts to the brave Spanish officers who died defending their country's doomed empire, for "with all the rumors of peace that there were in the air, it seemed a pity that they should have died at all." Though "the lives of a few Spanish officers would not have counted to the American people . . . they probably counted for a great deal to someone somewhere in Spain" (352). This is a gallant note, a show of good sportsmanship at the end of a game well won.

But no one can read the last pages of *The Cuban and Porto Rican Campaigns* without understanding where Dick Davis's heart lay, which was along the trail from Siboney to San Juan, with all the American boys who had given their lives not for the sake of an expanded empire but to rid Cuba of Spanish control. That was the meaning of Lieutenant Hobson's ride in triumph through the American lines, as a stand-in for a country long held prisoner by a cruel and oppressive Spain but now free at last. It is a moment that defines the difference between the Greco-Turkish War and the campaign in Cuba: the first was a muddled mess from the beginning, in which brave men died for a craven prince, but the second was a brave if unnecessarily bloody battle for the sake of a cause that endowed the invasion with a romantic aura. It was the same sort of transcendent righteousness that gave Robert Clay such heroic stature in *Soldiers of Fortune*.

If the war in Cuba was for empire, then it was imperialism on a new plan, fueled by idealism, animated by courage, stiffened by moral convictions regarding right and wrong. It was, in sum, a new version of chivalry embarked on a new crusade, an element associated with the romances of Sir Walter Scott but missing from Walter LaFeber's definition of "new empire"—which was purely a commercial concern. If looking back we can see how mistaken Davis was, how shortsighted, how naïve his notion of international affairs, which saw things always as across a football gridiron, we must also give him and the Americans for whom he spoke some measure of credit for what were the noblest of intentions. Davis would go on, covering the Boer War and traveling up the Congo in quest of the atrocities associated with King Leopold's cruelly oppressive rule, and in every instance he would praise the right and condemn the wrong, even if it meant changing his mind in the middle of his argument, even if it meant losing the admiration of the English elites he so much admired.

Davis was not proud of the activities of the U.S. Army in the Philippines, of which he was reminded by the actions of the British army in South Africa, noting that "in our newspapers we give our war a short quarter of a column of space a day, partly because we are rightly ashamed of it," while the British beat the drum and rattled the tambourine in celebrating their "victories" over the hapless Boers: "It is not what we have learned in the past to expect from our English cousins" (*With Both Armies* 125). Here he expresses what was a considerable consensus in the United States, given heft by protests from such popular authors as Davis's famous mother, who by 1901 had widened the focus of her social concerns, joining a number of conscientious citizens protesting "the methods resorted to by the English leaders in South Africa to put an end to the war" (*Rebecca Harding Davis Reader* 436).

By that time, the son of Rebecca Harding Davis had come to think that "war is all sad, and it is all wrong. It is a hideous relic of the age of stone. It is outrageous and indecent. But as it must obtain we should lend to it every semblance of dignity." In the British South African campaign "everything seems to have been done to degrade war, to make it even more brutal than it is; to callous the mind toward it; to rob it of all of its possible heroism and terrible magnificence. . . . These incidents make warfare worse than brutal. It becomes vulgar," perhaps the most abusive term in Dick Davis's vocabulary. Not even the British officers acted like the gentlemen their rank supposedly guaranteed and boasted of "sticking" the Boer soldiers with lances like "pigs" (*With Both Armies* 131).

Perhaps even more monstrous was the invading British army seen at a distance, for "twenty-five thousand men advancing in full view across a great plain appeals to you as something entirely lacking in the human element. . . . You would as soon attribute human qualities to a plague, a tidal wave, or a slowly slipping landslide" (203). It was war practiced on a huge scale, as in Turkey, and as in Turkey it was a dehumanized spectacle, "not," as RHD wrote his mother, "the kind of war I care to report" (*Adventures* 277). Nor, we must assume given Davis's demonstrated lack of interest, was the ongoing conflict in the Philippines the "kind of war" he wished to cover.

In July 1899 Rebecca Harding Davis wrote a powerful anti-imperialist article "The Mean Face of War," drawing on her horrifying experiences as a girl living in Wheeling during the Civil War but pointing as well to the recent conflict in Cuba: "Our campaign last summer . . . loomed before us in June a glorious outburst of high chivalric purpose and individual courage. But when we looked back at it in September war had come to mean polluted camps, incompetent officers appointed by corrupt politicians, decayed meat and thousands of victims of disease and neglect" (430).

Few accounts of the Cuban invasion had put out more flags than those written by RHD, but his attacks on General Shafter and his reports on the unhealthy conditions in army camps were honest also to the closer view of "the god of war" emphasized by his mother. On the other hand, there is no evidence that RHD ever changed his mind regarding the destruction of the Spanish presence in the Caribbean.

If in 1899 Rebecca refused to share her son's high-minded view of the war in Cuba, she was outspokenly critical of the ongoing war in the Philippines, which the United States was pursuing with the intention of placing "the

crown of Imperialism on its brows, to gird a sword on its thighs and drive another nation into civilization and Christianity—at the point of a bayonet"
(*Reader* 430). With a view of increasing the U.S. presence in the Philippines
to a standing army, certain "interested politicians" were calling on young
American men to make a career of the military life: "The talk of glory and
heroism and the service of the country is very tempting [to] these gallant
immature boys. What is really intended, of course, is the establishment
of a uniformed guard to police the Philippine islands in the interests of certain trusts. But our brave young fellow sees only the waving of the flag"
(430, 433).

This was an argument similar to Mark Twain's objections to the American
presence in the Pacific, but Rebecca's son remained silent regarding the
nature and purpose of defeating the Filipino insurrectionist army. On the
other hand, by 1900 Davis seems to have felt that the Spanish-American had
been the last good war, which is to say a literally civil war, from the courteous message sent by Admiral Cervera to Commodore Schley, assuring him
"of the safety of Hobson and his crew after they had attempted to bottle up
the Spanish fleet, and to congratulate him on their courage," to Captain
Phillips calling "to his men when they had sunk the Spanish battleship,
'Don't cheer! those men are drowning!'" (*With Both Armies* 131 32).

In comparison with the little that was accomplished by so many experienced British generals during the war in South Africa, Davis held up the example of "Theodore Roosevelt, who never saw a battle until he went to
Cuba" but who because of his great intelligence would make "a better general to-day than any of these gentlemen." And Roosevelt was but one of the
many who emerged transformed from "the crucible of our little war," including Admiral Dewey and Colonel Wood, "who is now Governor General
of the whole island of Cuba. All these men did something; they sank a fleet
or took a fort: they showed intelligent executive ability. . . . Dewey was not
an accident" (136).

Davis's account of the war in South Africa closes with the surrender of
Pretoria and the departure of "these long-bearded, strong-eyed Boers with
their drooping cavalier's hats, their bristling bands of cartridges, their upright seat in the saddle, and with the rifle rising above them like the lance of
the crusader. They are the last of the crusaders" (236–37). But these troopers were but an afterimage of the Rough Riders, who would remain for
Davis the enduring pattern for chivalric soldiers ("crusaders") enlisted in a
righteous cause, a point of high-minded, courageous reference against
which all other wars would be measured.

: V :

After *Captain Macklin,* which gave closure to his romantic view of war in fiction, Davis turned to conventional romance, love stories that would become increasingly weak and hurried, turned out to earn the money that would maintain the life he identified with the privileged people with whom he wanted to be associated, in the popular mind if not in actuality. He wrote plays, highly successful in their day; he helped turn *Soldiers of Fortune* into a movie; he did what he could to maximize the earnings from what he had already written. Richard Harding Davis remained a celebrity, indeed holds a certain priority in that regard, as the testimony of all those younger writers validates. In effect, he had become that about which he had written, although it became increasingly difficult to keep up to the mark he himself had set.

Along with Theodore Roosevelt, Davis would urge the United States to enter World War I, and at fifty, a relatively advanced age for a correspondent, he visited the battle lines in France and Belgium and reported back what he saw, in terms hardly complimentary to the German forces, for Dick Davis never loved a German. Courageous to the point of foolhardiness, he was captured for a spy and nearly executed, thanks to the military style of the outfit he had designed as suitable for a war correspondent. He famously described the entrance of the German army into Brussels as a vast operation of anonymous gray.

In effect, that faceless invading British army in South Africa was extended into a procession marching for two days and a night through the Belgian capital, a machinelike demonstration of what war had become. As RHD would have discovered had he lived, the notion of chivalric endeavor meant little after 1916 save for the helmeted and scarved young men in their spindly, fragile airplanes, new cavaliers for a new age, "gallant boys," as Teddy Roosevelt called them in a memorial apostrophe to his son Quentin, who, "on the golden crest of life, gladly face death for the sake of an ideal" (Hagedorn 413).

Though he wrote what for a time was a famous short story about the war, "The Deserter," RHD necessarily left the American experience in that conflict for younger men to frame in fiction, like Hemingway and Faulkner, whose Spengler-like sense of doom was never his. If Davis did not survive to witness the entrance of the United States into the war, his early death in 1916 was hurried by his wartime experiences, and he died like those young Spanish officers in Puerto Rico, defending a world that was soon to disappear.

In 1910 he had served as one of O. Henry's pallbearers, presumably at the other man's request, not such a strange association for anyone familiar with their short stories, though few any longer are. Both men were celebrants of chivalry in different forms, whether disguised by the top hat and evening dress of Cortlandt Van Bibber or the burglar's cap and mask of Jimmy Valentine. Chivalry as a concept and a creed is now long out of fashion, regarded by revisionist historians as a glorification of white, male, Anglo-Saxon superiority. And so it was.

For myself, in reading the works of Richard Harding Davis I have come to admire the writer if not the man, who was described succinctly in 1940 by Hemingway as "a great snob, but a first rate war correspondent" (775). He was both, surely, but it is with the writing that I have been chiefly concerned here, and I think he was first-rate there as well, less in fiction than in his reporting, but worth more than the passing, dismissive glance he has so often been accorded. Moreover, as I have worked to suggest throughout, RHD remains important to us for a quality similar to that "second value" identified by Thomas Beer. Beer predicted that Davis would in time be celebrated for having recorded the important events of his day, but what RHD wrote about the passing scene is perhaps less valuable as a record than as a gauge allowing us to take the moral measure of Americans at the end of the nineteenth century. Like Davis, they prized virtues we still hold in high esteem, if in somewhat different forms, and were willing on occasion to die for them, a road that is seldom if ever taken today. Paths of glory now have little allure, not because they invariably lead to the grave but because glory, as in the movie based on Humphrey Cobb's novel of that title, is no longer a word that has a positive meaning.

As in 1898, Theodore Roosevelt in 1915 sought approval to organize a troop of volunteers he would lead into combat in France, but his request was denied by President Wilson. Roosevelt was outraged, but in truth his was a gesture in harmony with the mistaken idealism of those chivalric young men who earlier sailed gallantly from England to die horribly in the fields at Flanders, a repetition of the folly described by Rebecca Harding Davis in "The Mean Face of War." Surely the First World War proved to have a very mean face, and it would seem that even in the timing of his death, Richard Harding Davis's famous luck still held. He died a year short of America's entry into a war which may have been waged to make the world safe for democracy but which laid knight-errantry to rest. Whatever we may make of the war in Cuba that we associate with RHD's most famous experience as a correspondent, it gave a meaningful point to the marvelous year of "greatness and parades" with which Thomas Beer associated Davis's career.

Moreover, the year ended fittingly in the company of Teddy Roosevelt, Beer's "burly figure of earth with its blue neckerchief" standing "in a prodigy of sunlight below the hills outside Santiago de Cuba." It is there, I think, that we should place Richard Harding Davis, in a surrounding glory shed by a tropic noon. For he had at last found his war, his West, his warrior-hero, and, to a very great extent, himself, or at least the role he had been seeking to fill for the previous ten years. That convergence brought together the chivalric sensibility of Davis and the imperial sense of Roosevelt, with consequences that have not yet run their course for the United States.

There's the river up an' brimmin', an'
there's 'arf a squadron swimmin'
'Cross the ford o' Kabul river in the dark.
RUDYARD KIPLING

ENVOY

In 1906, Davis returned to Cuba, accompanied by Cecil, his expenses paid by *Colliers,* and found few vestiges of the battles of the war in which he had taken part. In "The Passing of San Juan Hill," the essay that resulted from the trip, he described the changed landscape in detail, opening with a telling remark: "When I was a boy I thought battles were fought in waste places selected for the purpose. I argued from the fact that when our school nine wished to play ball it was forced into the suburbs to search for a vacant lot. I thought opposing armies also marched out of town until they reached some desolate spot" (*Notes of a War Correspondent* 113).

The actual experience of war taught him otherwise, but "even later, when I saw battles fought among villages, artillery galloping through a corn-field, garden walls breached for rifle fire, and farm-houses in flames, it al-ways seemed as though the generals had elected to fight in such surround-ings through an inexcusable striving after theatrical effect—as though they wished to furnish the war correspondents with a chance for descriptive writing" (113). Though written in retrospect, and somewhat with tongue in cheek, the combination here of figures drawn from sports and the theater put a definitive frame around Davis's account of the Spanish-American War.

San Juan Hill, when the American army first saw it, had been cleared of undergrowth and fortified with a blockhouse and trenches by the Spanish, in preparation for the fight that was sure to come. It had therefore become a proper battlefield, unlike the present-day site, now once again returned to a peaceful landscape, "a sunny, smiling farm land, the trenches planted with vegetables, the roofs of the bomb-proofs fallen in and buried beneath creeping vines, and the barbed-wire entanglements holding in check only the browsing cattle" (116). It was only with difficulty that Davis was able to identify places still vivid in his memory but virtually erased from the land-scape. Little by way of a monument had been erected, and that was already falling into ruin. A park had been set aside on San Juan Hill, but the govern-ment official in residence spoke only Spanish and the guides employed by the hotel, "like most Cubans," were "not inclined to give much credit for what they did in Cuba to the Americans" (132).

They insisted that the Americans had arrived "just as the Cubans themselves were about to conquer the Spaniards, and by a lucky chance received the surrender and then claimed all the credit." Davis was doubtful about this claim but let it rest, for it was part and parcel of the Cuban landscape itself, which had erased the evidences of the American presence. Moreover, he admitted that when matched against the famous battles of the Civil War, the affair at San Juan had been not much more than a skirmish.

The American victory had its intended result, Davis noted, having made Cuba a republic, but for RHD that was not the important thing about the war: What would keep the memory of San Juan alive, despite the lack of stone or bronze memorials, was its "human interest. . . . The men who fought there came from every State in our country and from every class of our social life. We sent there the best of our regular army, and with them, cowboys, clerks, bricklayers, foot-ball players, three future commanders of the greater army that followed that war, the future Governor of Cuba, future commanders of the Philippines, the commander of our forces in China, a future president of the United States" (129).

All those soldiers, now returned home and once again "clerks and millionaires and dentists," would recall fondly "the days they lay huddled together in the trenches on that hot and glaring sky-line" (129). We may here once again recall that brief essay Davis wrote for *Harper's Weekly,* describing the intensity of regret felt by older men standing on the sidelines who were now "out of the game" but still sustained by memories of having once played as a team. Davis recognized that his values were sentimental as much as historical, and along with those figures of speech drawn from sports and the theater, they provide a retrospective key to his career as a war correspondent, indeed signify his signal influence on several generations of reporters who would, as it were, follow RHD into battle, from Ernest Hemingway to John Steinbeck to Ernie Pyle.

We have recently seen the stunning success of a book entitled *The Greatest Generation,* which in many ways casts a retrospective look at the Second World War in ways that bring it in line with RHD's attitude toward the Spanish-American War, despite the difference in duration, extent, and complexity. Like "The Passing of San Juan Hill," that book carries an *ubi sunt* motif, suggesting that such wars, with their intense human interest and drama, given meaning by a virtuous cause, are a thing of the past. I have early on drawn parallels between the reasons for the entry of the United

States into the Cuban insurrection and the rationale for sending American troops to Kosovo, points forming a centennial continuity with a chivalric basis. As I write these lines late in 2001, we are engaged in another war, quite different in nature from any previous conflict in our history, against an enemy that is virtually invisible and flies no flags.

From our present perspective, there is no nobility detectable in this war, no chivalry, no pretext that we are fighting to preserve the freedom of a country under the threat of totalitarian rule. Only late on has the harsh repressiveness of the Taliban regime been cited as an excuse for the war, yet had that government cooperated with U.S. demands for the surrender of terrorists, it would have been allowed to continue in place unimpeded. From other perspectives, *we* represent the threat of totalitarianism, and our motives combine a desire for vengeance with the hope of ridding ourselves of a menace threatening our national stability. Ironically, we are back in the place where chivalry began, fighting an enemy from whom the crusaders absorbed the very ideals that sustained British imperialism for so long. We might wonder, what if Richard Harding Davis were alive today, but of course he is not.

In 1910, when Davis gathered "The Passing of San Juan Hill" into a collection of his war reporting, he noted wryly that the Spanish-American War was important in part because it "enriched or impoverished us with colonies," in effect changing the United States from a republic into "something like an empire." That transition was completed in 1902, with the successful end of the campaign by U.S. troops against native insurrectionists in the Philippines. We are now passing through the centennial of that victory, if victory it was, having long since determined as a nation that the colonies we acquired because of the Spanish-American War—the acquisition of which was never the stated purpose of the conflict—did not enrich but impoverished us, as Davis hinted they might. And as for the expense of becoming an empire, not a republic, the cost is still rising, much as our national emblem is now a bird come home to roost.

ACKNOWLEDGMENTS

Beyond the formal indebtednesses registered in the bibliography
of secondary texts that follows, I owe a great deal to my friend William
Spengemann, Avalon Professor of American Literature at Dartmouth
College, who gave the manuscript of this book a critical reading at two
stages of its composition and whose suggestions have been incorporated
into the text throughout.

BIBLIOGRAPHY

PRIMARY TEXTS

WORKS BY RICHARD HARDING DAVIS

The textual history of Richard Harding Davis's works is a mess, there having been a number of collected sets of his fiction but only one set that includes his nonfiction, and a number of his later nonfiction books were never given a unified format. What follows is a list of the specific texts consulted for this study. There is, fortunately, an excellent bibliography of Davis's works compiled by Henry Cole Quinby (and published by E. P. Dutton in 1924), which is very useful in tracking down the writer's early and never reprinted journalistic writings. Davis's contributions to *Harper's Weekly* and *Harper's Monthly (Magazine)* are identified in the text and are not duplicated here.

Where dates are given in brackets, the reference (as elsewhere in the bibliography) is to the copyright page, and the text used is from the first collected edition of Davis's works, which was issued in 1898 by Harper and Brothers without volume numbers as a premium for magazine subscriptions (see Quinby, p. 95).

About Paris. New York: Harper and Brothers, [1895].
Adventures and Letters. Edited by Charles Belmont Davis. New York: Charles
  Scribner's Sons, 1917.
Captain Macklin: His Memoirs. New York: Charles Scribner's Sons, 1916.
The Congo and the Coasts of Africa. New York: Charles Scribner's Sons, 1907.
Cuba in War Time. New York: R. H. Russell, 1897.
The Cuban and Porto Rican Campaigns. New York: Charles Scribner's Sons, 1898.
The Exiles and Other Stories. New York: Harper and Brothers, [1894].
Gallegher and Other Stories. New York: Charles Scribner's Sons, 1907.
Notes of a War Correspondent. New York: Charles Scribner's Sons, 1912.
Our English Cousins. New York: Harper and Brothers, [1894].
Real Soldiers of Fortune. New York: Charles Scribner's Sons, 1912.
"The Reporter Who Made Himself King." In *Stories for Boys.*
The Rulers of the Mediterranean. New York: Harper and Brothers, [1893].
Soldiers of Fortune. New York: Charles Scribner's Sons, 1916.
Soldiers of Fortune. Play-Goer's Edition. New York: Charles Scribner's Sons, 1902.
Stories for Boys. New York: Charles Scribner's Sons, 1916.
Three Gringos in Venezuela and Central America. New York: Harper and Brothers,
  [1896].

"An Unfinished Story." In *Van Bibber and Others.*
Van Bibber and Others. New York: Harper and Brothers, [1892].
The West from a Car Window. New York: Harper and Brothers, [1892].
With Both Armies in South Africa. New York: Charles Scribner's Sons, 1900.
With the Allies. New York: Charles Scribner's Sons, 1914.
With the French in France and Salonika. New York: Charles Scribner's Sons, 1916.
A Year from a Reporter's Note-Book. New York: Harper and Brothers, [1897].

WORKS BY OTHER AUTHORS

Adams, Henry. *The Education of Henry Adams.* Edited by Ernest Samuels. Boston:
    Houghton Mifflin, 1974.
Bonsal, Stephen. *The Fight for Santiago.* New York: Doubleday and McClure, 1899.
Choate, Joseph H. *Speeches and Addresses.* Edited by Frederick C. Hicks. St. Paul:
    West Publishing, 1926.
Clemens, Samuel L. *Mark Twain's Speeches.* Vol. 28 of *Writings.* Stormfield ed.
    New York: Harper and Brothers, 1929.
Crane, Stephen. *The War Dispatches of Stephen Crane.* Edited by R. W. Stallman and
    E. R. Hagemann. New York: New York University Press, 1964.
Custer, Elizabeth B. *Tenting on the Plains.* New York: C. L. Webster, 1887.
Davis, Charles Belmont. See *Adventures and Letters,* under R. H. Davis, above.
Davis, Rebecca Harding. *A Rebecca Harding Davis Reader.* Edited by Jean Pfaelzer.
    Pittsburgh: University of Pittsburgh Press, 1995.
Depew, Chauncey. Introductory remarks to "Through the Great Forest," by Sir
    Henry Morton Stanley. In *Modern Eloquence.* Edited by Ashley H. Thorndike.
    Vol. 13. New York: Lincoln Scholarship Fund, 1929.
———. *Mottoes, Aphorisms, and Nuggets from the Speeches of Hon. Chauncey M.
    Depew.* Compiled by Edward Sundell. New York: James Kempster Printing, n.d.
Dunne, Finley Peter. *Mr. Dooley on Ivrything and Ivrybody.* Selected by Robert
    Hutchinson. New York: Dover Publications, 1963.
Emerson, Ralph Waldo. *The Complete Writings.* 2 vols. New York: Wm. H. Wise,
    1929.
Flint, Grover. *Marching with Gomez.* With an introduction by John Fiske. Boston:
    Lamson, Wolffe, 1898.
Hawkins, Anthony Hope. *Memories and Notes.* Garden City, N.Y.: Doubleday,
    Doran, 1928.
Hemingway, Ernest. *Selected Letters, 1917–1961.* Edited by Carlos Baker. New York:
    Charles Scribner's Sons, 1981.
Hubbard, Elbert. "A Message to Garcia." In *Selected Writings.* Vol. 1. New York:
    Wm. H. Wise, [1928].
Kipling, Rudyard. "The Bridge Builders." In *The Day's Work.* London: Macmillan,
    1964.
———. *The Light That Failed.* London: Macmillan, 1951.
———. *Rudyard Kipling's Verse.* Garden City, N.Y.: Doubleday, [1940].
———. *Soldiers Three.* London: Macmillan, 1965.

Lang, Andrew. "Rudyard Kipling." In *Harper's Weekly* 34 (August 30, 1890): 688.

Lodge, Henry Cabot. *Speeches and Addresses: 1884–1909*. Boston: Houghton Mifflin, 1909.

Mahan, Albert Thayer. *The Influence of Sea Power upon History, 1660–1783*. 1st English ed. London: Sampson Low, Marston, 1892.

———. *Lessons of the War with Spain and Other Articles*. Boston: Little, Brown, 1899.

Proctor, Redfield. "Cuba: Its Condition at the Beginning of 1898." Introduction to *An Illustrated History of Our War with Spain. . .* , by Henry B. Russell. Hartford, Conn.: A. D. Worthington, 1898.

Ralph, Julian. *Harper's Chicago and the World's Fair. . . .* New York: Harper and Brothers, 1893.

Reid, Whitelaw. Introductory remarks to "Through the Dark Continent," by Henry Morton Stanley. In *Modern Eloquence*. Edited by Ashley H. Thorndike. Vol. 3. New York: Lincoln Scholarship Fund, 1929.

Remington, Frederic. *Selected Writings*. Introduction by Peggy Samuels and Harold Samuels. Secaucus: Castle, 1981.

Roosevelt, Theodore. *Ranch Life and the Hunting Trail*. Vol. 1 of *The Works of Theodore Roosevelt*. National ed. New York: Charles Scribner's Sons, 1926.

———. *The Rough Riders*. Vol. 11 of *The Works of Theodore Roosevelt*. National ed. New York: Charles Scribner's Sons, 1926.

———. *The Strenuous Life*. Vol. 13 of *The Works of Theodore Roosevelt*. National ed. New York: Charles Scribner's Sons, 1926.

Scott, Sir Walter. *Essays on Chivalry, Romance, and the Drama*. Vol. 6 of *The Prose Works*. Edinburgh: Robert Cadell, 1834.

Stanley, Sir Henry Morton. *The Autobiography*. Edited by Dorothy Stanley. Boston: Houghton Mifflin, [1909].

Stevenson, Robert Louis. "Records of a Family of Engineers." In *Letters and Miscellanies*. Vol. 38 of [*Works*]. New York: Charles Scribner's Sons, 1908.

Waugh, Alec. *Hot Countries*. New York: Farrar and Rinehart, 1930.

Wister, Owen. *My Dear Wister—the Frederic Remington-Owen Wister Letters*. Edited by Ben Merchant Vorpahl. Palo Alto: American West Publishing, 1972.

———. *Owen Wister Out West: His Journals and Letters*. Edited by Fanny Kemble Wister. Chicago: University of Chicago Press, 1958.

———. *The Virginian*. In *The Writings*. New York: Macmillan, 1928.

SECONDARY SOURCES

Anstruther, Ian. *Dr. Livingstone, I Presume*. New York: E. P. Dutton, [1956].

Beer, Thomas. *The Mauve Decade*. New York: Alfred A. Knopf, 1926.

Brooks, Van Wyck. *The Confident Years: 1885–1915*. New York: E. P. Dutton, 1952.

Brown, Charles H. *The Correspondents' War: Journalists in the Spanish American War*. New York: Charles Scribner's Sons, [1967].

Burlingame, Roger. Introduction to *From "Gallegher" to "The Deserter": The Best Stories of Richard Harding Davis.* New York: Charles Scribner's Sons, [1927].

Burton, Richard. *Literary Likings.* Boston: Copeland and Day, 1898.

Canby, Henry Seidel. *The Age of Confidence: Life in the Nineties* (1934). In *American Memoir.* Boston: Houghton Mifflin, 1947.

Cawelti, John G. *Adventure, Mystery, and Romance.* Chicago: University of Chicago Press, 1976.

Dobson, John M. *America's Ascent: The United States Becomes a Great Power, 1880–1914.* DeKalb: Northern Illinois University Press, [1978].

Downey, Fairfax. *Portrait of an Era as Drawn by C. D. Gibson.* New York: Charles Scribner's Sons, 1936.

———. *Richard Harding Davis and His Day.* New York: Charles Scribner's Sons, 1933.

Friedel, Frank. *The Splendid Little War.* Boston: Little, Brown, [1958]. [1960].

Garraty, John A. *Henry Cabot Lodge. A Biography.* New York: Alfred A. Knopf, 1953.

Girouard, Mark. *The Return to Camelot: Chivalry and the English Gentleman.* New Haven: Yale University Press, 1981.

Hagedorn, Hermann. *The Roosevelt Family of Sagamore Hill.* New York: Macmillan, 1954.

Harris, Sharon M. *Rebecca Harding Davis and American Realism.* Philadelphia: University of Pennsylvania Press, 1991.

Hoganson, Kristin. *Fighting for American Manhood: The Gender Politics behind the Spanish-American War.* New Haven: Yale University Press, 1998.

Kaplan, Amy. "Black and Blue on San Juan Hill." In *Cultures of United States Imperialism,* ed. Amy Kaplan and Donald E. Pease. Durham: Duke University Press, 1993.

———. "Romancing the Empire: The Embodiment of American Masculinity in the Popular Historical Novel of the 1890s." *American Literary History* 2 (Winter 1990): 659–90.

Kazin, Alfred. *On Native Grounds.* New York: Reynal and Hitchcock, [1942].

Knight, Grant C. *The Critical Period in American Literature.* Chapel Hill: University of North Carolina Press, [1951].

———. "The 'Pastry' Period in American Literature." *Saturday Review of Literature,* December 16, 1944, 5–7, 22–23.

———. *The Strenuous Age in American Literature: 1900–1910.* Chapel Hill: University of North Carolina Press, [1954].

LaFeber, Walter. *The New Empire: An Interpretation of American Expansion, 1860–1898.* Ithaca: Cornell University Press, [1998].

Lande, Nathaniel. *Dispatches from the Front: A History of the American War Correspondent.* New York: Oxford University Press, [1998].

Langford, Gerald. *Alias O. Henry: A Biography of William Sidney Porter.* New York: Macmillan, 1957.

———. *The Richard Harding Davis Years.* New York: Holt, Rinehart and Winston, 1961.

Leech, Margaret. *In the Days of McKinley.* New York: Harper and Brothers, [1959].

Linderman, Gerald F. *The Mirror of War: American Society and the Spanish-American War.* Ann Arbor: University of Michigan Press, [1974].

Lubow, Arthur. *The Reporter Who Would Be King: A Biography of Richard Harding Davis.* New York: Charles Scribner's Sons, [1992].

McCullough, David. *The Path between the Seas: The Creation of the Panama Canal, 1870–1914.* New York: Simon and Schuster, [1977].

Millis, Walter. *The Martial Spirit: A Study of Our War with Spain.* Boston: Houghton Mifflin, 1931.

Milton, Joyce. *The Yellow Kids: Foreign Correspondents in the Heyday of Yellow Journalism.* New York: Harper and Row, [1989].

Musicant, Ivan. *Empire by Default: The Spanish-American War and the Dawn of the American Century.* New York: Henry Holt, [1998].

O'Toole, G. J. A. *The Spanish War, an American Epic—1898.* New York: W. W. Norton, [1984].

Payne, Darwin. *Owen Wister: Chronicler of the West, Gentleman of the East.* Dallas: Southern Methodist University Press, 1985.

Pérez, Louis A., Jr. *The War of 1898: The United States and Cuba in History and Historiography.* Chapel Hill: University of North Carolina Press, [1998].

Puleston, W. D. *Mahan: The Life and Work of Captain Alfred Thayer Mahan, U.S.N.* New Haven: Yale University Press, 1939.

Quinby, Henry Cole. *Richard Harding Davis: A Bibliography.* New York: E. P. Dutton, [1924].

R.H.D.: Appreciations of Richard Harding Davis. New York: Charles Scribner's Sons, 1917. Essays originally published as introductions to the twelve volumes of *The Novels and Stories of Richard Harding Davis.*

Rickover, H. G. *How the Battleship Maine Was Destroyed.* Annapolis: Naval Institute Press, [1995]. Facsimile of the 1976 edition, published by the Naval History Division, Department of the Navy.

Rosenberg, Emily S. *Spreading the American Dream: American Economic and Cultural Expansion, 1890–1945.* American Century Series. New York: Hill and Wang, [1982].

Rydell, Robert W. *All the World's a Fair: Visions of Empire at American International Expositions, 1876–1916.* Chicago: University of Chicago Press, [1984].

Samuels, Peggy, and Harold Samuels. *Frederic Remington.* Austin: University of Texas Press, 1982.

Shapiro, Michael Edward, and Peter H. Hassrick. *Frederic Remington: The Masterworks.* New York: Harry N. Abrams, 1988. *Charge of the Rough Riders on San Juan Hill* is on p. 106. *A Run behind Interference* is on p. 241.

Slotkin, Richard. *Gunfighter Nation: The Myth of the Frontier in Twentieth-Century America.* New York: HarperCollins, 1992.

Spengemann, William. *The Adventurous Muse.* New Haven: Yale University Press, 1977.

Sullivan, Zohreh T. *Narratives of Empire: The Fictions of Rudyard Kipling.* Cambridge: Cambridge University Press, [1993].

Thomas, Lately. *A Pride of Lions: The Astor Orphans; the Chanler Chronicle*. New York: William Morrow, 1971.

Tichi, Cecelia. *Shifting Gears: Technology, Literature, Culture in Modernist America*. Chapel Hill: University of North Carolina Press, [1987].

Trachtenberg, Alan. *Brooklyn Bridge: Fact and Symbol*. New York: Oxford University Press, 1965.

———. *The Incorporation of America: Culture and Society in the Gilded Age*. New York: Hill and Wang, 1982.

Traxel, David. *1898: The Birth of the American Century*. New York: Alfred A. Knopf, 1998.

Vorpahl, Ben Merchant. *Frederic Remington and the West: With the Eye of the Mind*. Austin: University of Texas Press, 1978.

Walter, Dave, comp. *Today Then: America's Best Minds Look 100 Years into the Future on the Occasion of the 1893 World's Columbian Exposition*. Helena, Mont.: American and World Geographic Publishing, 1992.

Wassermann, Jacob. *Bula Matari: Stanley, Conqueror of a Continent*. New York: Liveright, [1933].

The West as America: Reinterpreting Images of the Frontier, 1820–1920. Edited by William H. Truettner. Washington: Smithsonian Institution Press, 1991.

White, G. Edward. *The Eastern Establishment and the Western Experience: The West of Frederic Remington, Theodore Roosevelt, and Owen Wister*. New Haven: Yale University Press, 1968.

Wiebe, Robert H. *The Search for Order: 1877–1920*. New York: Hill and Wang, [1967].

Ziff, Larzer. *The American 1890s: Life and Times of a Lost Generation*. New York: Viking, [1966].

INDEX

John Seelye is a native of Connecticut. He received his B.A. from Wesleyan University and his Ph.D. from the Claremont Graduate School. His numerous publications include *Melville: The Ironic Diagram* (Northwestern University Press, 1970), *The True Adventures of Huckleberry Finn* (Northwestern University Press, 1970), *The Kid* (Viking, 1972), *Prophetic Waters: The River in Early American Life and Literature* (Oxford University Press, 1990), *Beautiful Machine: Rivers and the Republican Plan, 1755–1825* (Oxford University Press, 1991), and *Memory's Nation: The Place of Plymouth Rock* (University of North Carolina Press, 1998). He has received a Guggenheim Fellowship and two National Endowment for the Humanities (NEH) Fellowships. During 1985–86 he was in residence at the American Antiquarian Society as an NEH Fellow. Professor Seelye has been a Phi Beta Kappa Visiting Professor and has served since 1979 as the general editor of the Penguin American Library. He has been Distinguished Alumni Service Professor at the University of North Carolina, Chapel Hill, and has also taught at the University of Connecticut and the University of California, Berkeley. He is Graduate Research Professor of American Literature at the University of Florida in Gainesville. He lives in Hawthorne, Florida, and Eastport, Maine, with his wife, Alice.